PUBLIC LIVES

New Zealand's Premiers and Prime Ministers
1856 – 2003

PUBLIC LIVES

New Zealand's Premiers and Prime Ministers
1856 – 2003

Ian F. Grant

The New Zealand Cartoon Archive, founded in 1992, and situated in the
Alexander Turnbull Library, Wellington is the national collection of cartoons
and caricatures. Copies of cartoons from the collection can be viewed in Turnbull
Library Pictures on the ground floor of the National Library in Wellington.
The cartoons are indexed on the National Library's TAPUHI catalogue
http://tapuhi.natlib.govt.nz and many of the images can be viewed on
http://timeframes.natlib.govt.nz The Cartoon Archive's website is:
http://www.cartoons.org.nz
The New Zealand Cartoon Archive sponsors are: APN New Zealand Ltd,
Fairfax NZ Ltd, Gault Mitchell Lawyers, Grant Thornton, KPMG,
Newspaper Publishers' Association of New Zealand (Inc),
Norske Skog Tasman Ltd and Profile Publishing.

First published by the New Zealand Cartoon Archive,
Alexander Turnbull Library, P O Box 12349, Wellington,
New Zealand, October 2003
Second Printing, November 2003

ISBN: 0-9582320-2-4

Publishing Consultant: Fraser Books,
Chamberlain Road, RD8, Masterton.
Formatting: Graham Kerrisk, Printcraft, Masterton
Distribution: Nationwide Book Distributors, P O Box 4176,
Christchurch
Printed by Publishing Press Limited, 31 William Pickering Drive,
Albany, Auckland

CONTENTS

ACKNOWLEDGEMENTS

Although this topic had been of personal interest to me for many years, it was the NPA's Hilary Souter who actually suggested the project, longer ago than I care to remember.

I am very grateful for the financial and other support from the Newspaper Publishers' Association, the book's principal sponsor, and particularly thank Lincoln Gould and Hilary Souter.

I would like to thank those people who willingly subjected themselves to lengthy interviews. I spoke to all living ex-prime ministers in person or by other means – David Lange, Geoffrey Palmer, Mike Moore, Jim Bolger and Jenny Shipley. I also greatly benefited from the insights of Michael Bassett, John Henderson, Gerald Hensley, Jonathan Hunt, and Colin James.

Margaret Clark and Nigel Roberts provided additional information and Phillip O'Shea, director of the Honours Secretariat and NZ Herald of Arms, helped greatly with the compilation of a list of all the premiers, prime ministers and their ministries.

The New Zealand Cartoon Archive appreciates the willingness with which the country's cartoonists, whose work appears in this book, or their representatives, have given permission for their cartoons to appear. The same applies to the publications where the cartoons first appeared and I particularly want to record my thanks to the *New Zealand Herald* for the use of the Minhinnick and Klarc cartoons.

Every effort has been made to trace copyright holders, and advice about any omissions would be appreciated.

Not for the first time, Mark Winter (Chicane) gave freely of his time to draw caricatures, from scanty available photographs, of five 19th century premiers – Sewell, Domett, Weld, Waterhouse and Pollen – who seem to have escaped the attention of early cartoonists.

The Cartoon Archive's Rachel Macfarlane and Cerridwyn Young have been diligent and inventive in their search of the 160 plus cartoons and caricatures in the book. As always, Margaret Calder, chief librarian, Alexander Turnbull Library, has been fully supportive and I greatly appreciate the assistance and expertise from staff in a number of National Library and Turnbull Library departments.

Diane, my wife, best friend and editor, has made her usual crucial contribution.

IFG

INTRODUCTION

"The issues have changed, but the basic prime ministerial qualities remain the same"

New Zealand has had 37 premiers and prime ministers. They are as varied a collection of men – and two women – as one might imagine, as a raw colonial frontier and its institutions have changed and matured.

There was an early expectation among the well-educated and politically aware settlers prominent in the New Zealand Company settlements, in Auckland, and later in Otago and Canterbury, that the new colony would become self-governing. The Colonial Office in London concurred but it was not until 1852 – 12 years after William Hobson declared British sovereignty – that the Constitution Act established a General Assembly. This consisted of a House of Representatives with between 24-42 members elected for five year terms by all males over 21 years of age owning a minimal amount of property, and a Legislative Council with members appointed for life. The country was also divided into six provinces, each with a superintendent and Provincial Council elected every four years.

The General Assembly had legislative control of the currency, customs duties, post services and the court system; the provincial councils had the authority to regulate its use and sell land, make local development decisions, and adopt education, roading, hospital, and immigration policies. The governor retained control of native policy and the British government had no intention of letting the settlers dabble in any foreign policy making.

New Zealand's first premiers and early parliamentarians were strikingly similar, despite their personal differences. A few were the younger sons of 'good' county families; most were solidly middle-class – professionals, merchants or with substantial farming interests.

With few exceptions the early premiers had come to New Zealand in search of fortune, and possibly adventure, rather than fame. Most had sufficient resources to invest in the opening up of the country. Although it might not have been their intention, the early premiers gravitated to politics out of a sense of duty, sometimes garnished with self-interest. Keith Sinclair wrote: "As a group, the founders of New Zealand parliamentary life were good, honest gentlemen, who thought politics was an unpleasant duty." [1] Jeanine Graham, Frederick Weld's biographer, added a twist when she wrote: " …a sense of duty was not enough to sustain those who did not have enthusiasm for political chicanery." [2]

Clearly some of the early premiers enjoyed the political life, or were personally ambitious, despite their claims to the contrary. Certainly they made considerable sacrifices in terms of time, loss of income, family life and personal comfort to participate. Travel to and from meetings of the General Assembly in Auckland, and then Wellington, were major and sometimes dangerous enterprises. In late June 1862, for example, the *White Swan*, carrying William Fox, most of his cabinet and other parliamentarians to a 'trial' General Assembly session in Wellington, was wrecked on the wild and scantily populated Wairarapa coast, miraculously without loss of life. [3]

Nearly half a century before political parties in New Zealand there were, broadly speaking, two factions in early parliaments. The 'centralists', though, were not hell-bent on abolishing provincial governments and very few 'provincialists' supported separatism. As Raewyn Dalziel wrote: "A politician might be a centralist at one time and a provincialist at another; centralists and provincialists could and did serve in the same governments." [4] Or as Sinclair put it: " …. 'centralism' was merely an alternative method of satisfying provincial aspirations, one which survived long after the abolition of the provinces." [5] Other issues waxed and waned in importance, but this division, however ambiguous, was more meaningful than the British 'Whig', 'Conservative', 'Liberal' and 'Radical' labels that did not usefully survive the long sea voyage to the bottom of the world. The pragmatic, day-by-day decisions that needed to be made were not greatly helped by the principles of 'liberalism' or 'conservatism'.

But it was more complicated than that. Dalziel again: "Ministries were formed not as a result of the voting at the polls nor usually because of their political programmes but as the result of parliamentarians coming together behind one leader on the basis of personal friendship, family or business relationship, national origins or religious affiliation, regional or local ties, or shared views on particular issues." [6]

Not surprisingly, given their essential fragility, most early ministries were short-lived. According to Keith Jackson: "Between 1856 and 1891 (inclusive), New Zealand was governed by no less than 25 separate ministries, each of which remained in office less than 18 months on average." [7]

David Hamer wrote: "In a sense 'the government' had had a continuous existence from 1856 until at least 1884." [8] There was a parliamentary parlour game of musical chairs involving a small, rotating group of ministers. There might have been 25 ministries during the first 35 years but there was only half that number of premiers and probably less than half of the administrations were significantly different in their composition.

During the early decades, with only a limited number of people having the time, skills and inclination to be politicians, the potential pool of ministerial talent was very proscribed. For example, Henry Sewell, early in the period, and Frederick Whitaker, later, were many premiers' first choice as attorney general and colonial treasurer respectively. Similarly, Donald McLean had a reputation as the only man able to handle Maori affairs. Cabinets were small – with rarely more than eight to 10 members – and with the public service in its infancy, it was important to include one or more able administrators.

The issues that most exercised the generally cultivated minds of early parliamentarians were the provinces and their powers, revenue distribution, where the capital should be, and relations with Maori. As a rough rule of thumb the politicians from weak provinces like Taranaki saw more advantages in a strong central government than those from Otago and Canterbury who favoured more provincial autonomy and less involvement with the north's land problems.

During these years, Parliament grew as the franchise widened. In 1861 the number of seats in the House was increased to 53 and then, in 1866, to 72. Parliament moved to Wellington in 1865. In 1868, Maori seats were introduced – as a temporary measure. The secret ballot dates from 1870. After 1879 the parliamentary term was reduced to three years which slowed the, until then, rapid turnover of

members of parliament (MHRs). From 1879 a residential qualification was the only prerequisite to voting – for males. Plural voting – by those owning land in more than one electorate – was abolished in 1889.

'War policy' dominated parliamentary debate in the early 1860s, with heated argument about who should command the troops and pay for the Taranaki land war. Sir George Grey, now governor for a second time, and no enthusiast for power sharing, had his orders that settler administrations must accept political and financial responsibility for the war. Dalziel wrote: "A series of ministries foundered on the handling of the war and the question of responsibility. Fox, Alfred Domett, and Whitaker went in and out of office arguing with Grey and Parliament over responsibility for native affairs." [9] In late 1864, Weld effectively ended the bickering with his 'self reliance' policy.

A stagnant economy gave impetus to, and support for, Julius Vogel's ambitious plans and the 1870s became the 'development decade', with £10 million of mainly borrowed money poured into assisted immigration and infrastructure – roads, railways, telegraph cables. It was a massive 'Think Big' exercise that Vogel controlled, but only periodically from the premier's chair. The provinces had been sidelined and they were replaced with a profusion of local bodies.

The preoccupation of legislators was now whether the rush of development was fast enough or needed to be slowed during periods of economic difficulty. Vogelism, with the increasing domination of central government, foreshadowed the Liberal era of the 1890s. It has been claimed Liberalism had its beginnings in the Stout-Vogel government of 1884-87, but that administration owed its existence more to the safeguarding of personal business interests, not uncommon in the late 1870s and through the 1880s as politics provided businessmen and speculators with opportunities to consolidate or salvage their financial gains.

John Ballance's election as 'opposition' leader in 1889 helped set the scene for party politics, the defining difference of the second parliamentary era in New Zealand. As Hamer wrote: "The election of Ballance was of considerable significance because it was done by an Opposition 'caucus' comprising members from many parts of the country." [10]

By 1890 a more democratic electorate, unimpressed with the sterility of the old 'oligarchy's' views, and a lack of money for regional public works, was beginning to replace the 'pork barrel' with talk of political philosophies and manifestos. At that year's election, opposition candidates had an agreed policy of labour and land reform, the overwhelming support of the urban working class, and a degree of union co-operation. Dalziel wrote: "The days of informality, of the 'floating' politician, of bargaining for the support of the uncommitted members were over. ....economic change, population growth, urbanisation, and the increasing interest of labour in politics introduced new issues that could not be resolved within the old structure of politics." [11]

For the next 106 years, until the first MMP election in 1996, the political party winning a majority of seats at each general election formed the government, its leader also the country's prime minister. The Liberal administrations of Ballance, Richard John Seddon and Joseph Ward established the new ground rules. As Hamer has written: "They have been widely regarded as establishing the foundations of many important features of modern New Zealand – party government, a major role in the system for a strong Prime Minister with a populist style and appeal, control of most aspects of New Zealand life by regulations implemented by a centralised bureaucracy, the industrial conciliation and arbitration system, the welfare state, State housing, State provision of cheap credit." [12]

At the end of the 19th century, when he had been premier for about seven years, Seddon began, on occasion, to call himself 'prime minister'. "The *New Zealand Gazette* of June 11, 1906 announcing R J Seddon's death refers to him as 'Prime Minister' but was issued from the 'Premier's Office'." [13] William Hall-Jones was the first to be officially appointed prime minister at the beginning of his fleeting tenure in June 1906. But Seddon was, of course, the prototype of the modern prime minister as he dominated his party and barnstormed his way to election-winning popularity around the country. Premiers, on the other hand, had always been far more dependent on the opinions of their parliamentary peers than the confidence of electors who had no influence on the rise or fall of ministries.

The 20th century brought with it a new breed of political leader. Sinclair wrote: "Rarely since that time [pre-1891], has any member of the former oligarchy held influential political office; rarely have prime ministers been either wealthy or well-educated, though a few have been well-read." [14]

In the modern era, parties, and some prime ministers, have been in office for much longer periods. The Liberals were in power from 1891 until 1912, a record of 21 unbroken years that has never been beaten, partly because opposition groupings had difficulty in thinking and acting in 'party' terms. The Reform Party was continuously in office from 1912 until 1928 (including a wartime coalition with the

Liberals), Labour occupied the government benches from 1935 to 1949 and National's hold on power lasted 35 years between 1949 to 1984, with just two three-year interruptions. Subsequently, Labour and National have had two and three term treasury bench stints respectively. In contrast to New Zealand's parliamentary beginnings, in the last 35 years there have been only 11 prime ministers (with three of those in one 13 month period).

What can be said, en masse, about the 19th century premiers and what comparisons can be made with the later prime ministers?

The early premiers were well educated. Of the first 13 premiers, up to 1891, five qualified as lawyers (Sewell, Fox, Domett, Whitaker, Robert Stout), one was a doctor (Daniel Pollen), two attended university (Edward Stafford, Weld), one was an army officer (Grey) and the remaining four went to secondary school for varying periods (George Waterhouse, Vogel, Harry Atkinson, John Hall). Overall, educational standards in the House of Representatives were higher in the first 30 years than they were to be again for the next century and longer. Apart from Francis Dillon Bell, playing a caretaker role for a fortnight, there were no university-educated premiers or prime ministers in the 81 years from 1891 to 1972.

Of those first 13, nine had English forebears, three Irish and one Scottish. One of the premiers, Vogel, was Jewish and Weld was a devout Roman Catholic.

Today, there is a perception that our prime ministers are getting younger. This is true, but only marginally so. The average age of the last five, when they became prime minister, was 48 years compared with the five before, going back to John Marshall, who averaged 50 years. On the other hand, the average age of the first five premiers, Sewell to Whitaker, was 46. The age at which incumbents took up the role has see-sawed over the decades. Walter Nash was the oldest at 75, closely followed by Bell. The youngest, just 37, was Stafford, but Vogel (38), Stout (40), Weld and Mike Moore (41) were not far behind. Among the 36 ex-premiers and prime ministers the average 'starting' age was 52.

The stresses and strains of the job have not appreciably affected longevity. While some like Seddon literally wore themselves out, the average age at which premiers and prime ministers died was 74 years. Grey, Stout and Nash all lived to 86, with Hall-Jones and Bell just a year behind. The youngest to die were Norman Kirk (51) and Ballance (54); these two plus Seddon, William Massey and M J Savage were the only ones to die in office. Ward had very grudgingly given up the prime ministership before he died, but was still a minister.

Four of the first five premiers were lawyers, although not always practicing ones. Since 1856 the predominant occupations of premiers and prime ministers have been runholding/farming (10) the law (9) and business (7). Other occupations have ranged from stationary engine driver (Kirk) to colonial administration (Grey).

Several of the early premiers led a number of ministries over lengthy periods of time: Fox headed four, only one of them of any duration, over a 17 year period; Stafford led three, two of them substantial, over 16 years; and Atkinson was premier four times, once for three years, during a 15 year period.

Only Stafford had terms – twice – of longer than three years. Hall, Stout and Atkinson headed ministries approaching three years in length. Cumulatively, Stafford was premier for nearly nine years and Atkinson and Fox for a little over five and four years respectively.

There was nothing like this turnover in the 20th century, except for the 13 month period in 1989-1990 when there were three Labour prime ministers – David Lange, Geoffrey Palmer and Moore.

The shortest ministries were during a turbulent period in 1884, with Stout's first government surviving just 12 days and the following Atkinson administration half that time! The first two ministries in 1856 – headed by Sewell and Fox – both lasted 13 days. Stafford and Fox also headed governments lasting barely a month.

The shortest serving prime ministers were Thomas Mackenzie in 1912 (43 days), Keith Holyoake in 1957 (52 days) and Moore in 1990 (59 days).

The longest continuously serving premier or prime minister was Seddon at just over 13 years. Massey was only a few months less, but four of those years were at the head of a national wartime government. Next longest in order were Holyoake (11 years), Peter Fraser (9), Robert Muldoon (8), Sidney Holland (8) and Jim Bolger (7).

In some cases the position was more illusory than real. Although named premier, it was not really possible for Waterhouse (1872-73) or Pollen (1875-76), isolated in the Legislative Council, to have any effective control over their administrations, with Vogel and Atkinson respectively controlling the purse strings in the House of Representatives. Like it or not, they were 'front men'. Two caretaker ministries – Hall-Jones in 1906, waiting for Ward to return to New Zealand, and Bell in 1925, awaiting the outcome of Reform's election of a new leader – lasted 46 and 16 days respectively.

Seven of the first 11 premiers went 'home' to Britain when they retired; since then all have remained in New Zealand. Tom Brooking, writing about Weld, said: "He always thought of himself as an Englishman and never regarded his time in New Zealand as anything other than a temporary experience. He was, therefore, a colonist rather than a colonial." [15]

The first New Zealand-born prime minister, in 1925 after 69 years of responsible government, was Bell, whose father, a minister in several early administrations, had come to the country as a New Zealand Company agent in 1843. The first Labour prime ministers, Savage, Fraser and Nash, were born overseas, but apart from them all prime ministers since Bell were born in New Zealand.

The Legislative Council, particularly when appointment was for life, provided a congenial retirement occupation, sometimes for years for some former premiers. Pollen served as a minister for the last time in 1877 but sat in the Legislative Council until he died 19 years later in 1896, five years after the terms of members (MLCs) had been reduced to

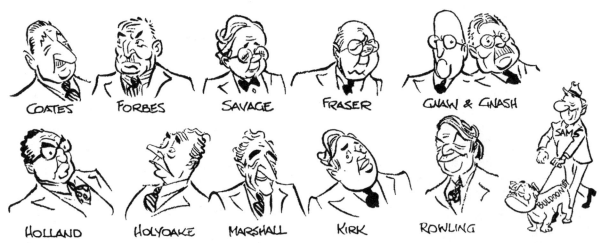

Minhinnick studied and drew a half century of prime ministers and was knighted for his efforts. Gordon Minhinnick, New Zealand Herald, January 31, 1976. (ATL ref: H-725-002-1)

seven years. In recent times, some prime ministers, like Muldoon and Lange, have continued as back-benchers. Others, young enough for new careers, have made a quick exit. Shipley was 51 when she left politics, Palmer 48 years old and Moore only 47.

"There's nothing worse than a 'dead' politician," says Jenny Shipley. "I wanted to demonstrate to the public that New Zealand politicians can move on, and use their skills effectively in the private sector." [16]

Several have had distinguished careers before and after becoming premier or prime minister. Weld went on to be governor of Tasmania and the Straits Settlements and Grey had been governor of South Australia, the Cape Colony and New Zealand (twice) before becoming premier. Waterhouse was premier of South Australia before moving to New Zealand. Holyoake has been the only prime minister appointed, controversially, to the country's non-political governor generalship. More recently, Moore went on to become director general of the World Trade Organisation (WTO).

There have sometimes been 'glittering prizes' for former premiers and prime ministers. Vogel and Mackenzie were appointed agent general in London; Stafford expected to be and was disappointed. Hall-Jones also went to London, the title now changed to high commissioner. Bassett wrote: " …. The Agent-Generalship was one of the most prized offices in the Government's gift. It carried a generous salary, with likelihood of a pension upon retirement, and

was a position believed, in Wellington, to be of some consequence in London. Not surprisingly, it dazzled colonial politicians." [17]

Two ex-prime ministers, Bill Rowling and Bolger, served as ambassador in Washington, a post pioneered by Nash in 1942 while he remained a member of the New Zealand war cabinet.

In a country abounding with sporting and military myths, very few premiers or prime ministers have shone in either field. Grey trained as an army officer in England but the closest he came to action was some frontline direction of skirmishes during the land wars in New Zealand. Atkinson rose to the rank of major during the Taranaki war and Ballance was a corporal in the Wanganui militia during the same period. Gordon Coates, Holland, Marshall and Muldoon served with New Zealand forces overseas; Coates was awarded the Military Cross for bravery during the First World War. There were no rugby players of great distinction, although George Forbes did represent Canterbury. Stafford had the more unusual distinction of being a champion jockey as well as a prominent racehorse breeder.

As befitting Victorian gentlemen, the pre-1891 premiers were cultured, with wide-ranging interests. Fox and Weld were capable watercolourists, Domett a published poet, Sewell a perceptive diarist, Vogel wrote a novel and Grey was a writer, botanist, linguist and book collector. He, Fox and Weld were notable explorers as well.

Arbor Day. *Up to 1890, Legislative Council appointees had amended or rejected legislation passed by the House of Representatives; it lost any relevance as later governments were 'packed' with members beholden to the government. Gordon Minhinnick*, New Zealand Herald, *August 10 1950. (ATL ref: H-723-008)*

Very few of the 19th century premiers were professional politicians in today's terms, although Sewell and Whitaker served in their attorney general and treasurer roles in a number of different ministries. William Pember Reeves wrote: "One serviceably industrious lawyer, Mr Henry Sewell, was something or other in nine different Ministries between 1854 and 1872. The Premier of one year might be a subordinate Minister the next; or some subtle and persistent nature, like that of Sir Frederick Whitaker, might manage chiefs whom he appeared to follow, and be the guiding mind of parties which he did not profess to direct." [18]

Fox invariably led the opposition when not in government and, later in life, spent several years investigating and settling Taranaki land disputes for subsequent administrations. While he was premier for nearly nine years, Stafford was unusual in not serving in anyone else's ministry. Probably the closest to a professional politician was Atkinson. Judith Bassett wrote: "Unlike most of his contemporaries who took a turn of duty in Wellington for a few years, and for whom their private affairs were paramount, Atkinson made politics his chief occupation for 20 years." [19]

There have been professional politicians in New Zealand since the beginning of the 20th century. But, for some years, they tended to come to the House after careers as farmers, trade unionists, teachers or businessmen. Politics was not exactly a retirement job, but it was not the primary career it has been for the last 20 years. Michael Bassett wrote: "These days, if politics is an urge to be indulged, it has to be satisfied at a relatively early age; outside careers are usually in their infancy when the modern parliamentarian enters the House. The First Labour Cabinet in 1935 had an average age of 56. The Prime Minister, M J Savage, was 63. The average age of the Fourth Labour Cabinet in 1984 was slightly less than 45, and David Lange was not yet 42." [20]

Politics in the modern era, particularly for prime ministers, has become an all-consuming occupation. There have been no noted painters, poets, explorers or linguists among them. The premiers, with the limited exception of Sewell, did not write about their political lives,

although Vogel and Ballance were newspaper owners and editors and uninhibited about using the press to political advantage. By comparison, several prime ministers – Marshall, Muldoon, Lange, Moore and Bolger – have penned political memoirs of variable interest and quality. Palmer has combined political practice with academic training to write about constitutional matters.

⁂

The responsibilities of the office have always been broadly the same, whether for the 19th century premier or the 21st century prime minister. There is, though, a much greater preoccupation with the media today and party politics has given extra weight to the leader's election-time role, but the coalition-building gymnastics of recent prime ministers has its parallels in the cobbling together of ministries in the pre-1891 period.

If most people know what a prime minister is, very few can define in any detail his or her actual role. "The flexibility of the Westminster system of government is such that every leader and every cabinet conducts things differently," says Palmer. "The role is too diffuse to accurately capture academically." [21]

As the New Zealand cabinet office manual – an important and comparatively recent guide – says: "There is no statutory provision that establishes the

Muldoon on Muldoon, chapter one, tape one.

– In the beginning I created heaven and earth....

Political autobiography was one way of influencing the historical record. Tom Scott, NZ Listener, November 26 1977. (ATL ref: H-725-003)

office of Prime Minister or defines its role." On the other hand, a number of functions and powers have evolved over time and are now established conventions.

Clearly, the prime minister is the head of the government. Constitutionally, the prime minister has the sole right to advise the governor general on the appointment, resignation or dismissal of ministers, and to dissolve Parliament and hold a general election. As head of executive government, the prime minister forms and maintains his or her administration – determining the scope and allocation of portfolios and ministerial rankings, and then overseeing and co-ordinating the government's general policy direction.

Cabinet member selection differs between parties. As John Henderson explains: "The Labour caucus elects ministers to cabinet, but leaves it to the prime minister to choose those outside cabinet, and to allocate portfolios. National leaders make their own cabinet selections. In the process of forming a coalition government discussions will take place over the allocation of portfolios." [22]

As chair of cabinet, the prime minister sets the agenda and runs the meetings, and usually chairs key cabinet committees as well. It is customary for the prime minister to take charge of the country's intelligence services. And, of course, the prime minister is also the leader of his or her parliamentary caucus and the wider party.

The expression 'first among equals' is still accurate in the sense that under the cabinet system of government a prime minister cannot make decisions unilaterally. "Cabinet government is a collective system and the prime minister is only one part of it," says Palmer. "But at times the media gives the impression it's the only part." [23] It is often said, with the media's prime ministerial preoccupation, that the system is becoming more 'presidential'. "It is not a presidential system in fact, law or constitutional practice," says Palmer," although it might seem to be in the conduct of election campaigns." [24] The need for parties to 'sell' themselves in simple television-ese terms and the media's obsession with personality and preference for entertainment over analysis have converged to make leaders actual or hopeful political pin-ups. Undoubtedly they are, as Richard Mulgan puts it, "the guardian of the party's electoral chances". [25]

In tandem with the growth and influence of mass media, the prime minister has become more clearly differentiated as the chief spokesperson for the government. As John Henderson says: "The Prime Minister's statements are taken by the media to be the authoritative view of government." [26] Televised post-cabinet press conferences were a feature, and sometimes a dramatic one, of the Muldoon and Lange administrations. Bolger and Shipley stopped them as they attempted a greater stage-management of press relations. Helen Clark has reinstated the practice and also has a 'stand up' press conference before Tuesday morning caucus meetings.

Under the Mixed Member Proportional Representation (MMP) system, the prime minister's co-ordination role is more important than ever, although staffers manage coalition issues on a daily basis. Palmer says: "The prime minister has always been the minister for co-ordination but today, when policy issues get sticky, she can be involved in negotiations with any of seven other parties." [27] Bolger says: "You now share part of the leadership role in the process of reaching agreement with the leaders of smaller parties." [28] And, as political scientists Boston, Levine, McLeay and Roberts add: " …. the Prime Minister's role as a mediator, conciliator, and final arbiter of inter-party and intra-party disputes will doubtless be more important." [29]

Today, the prime ministership is more complex and challenging than ever. Colin James says: "Compared with 30 years ago, there are now wave after wave of complex, difficult issues that have to be dealt

David Fletcher, 'The Politician', Dominion, September 13 2002. (ATL ref: DX-005-380)

with in the fishbowl of television and the Official Information Act, which make our governmental processes the most open in the world." [30]

Women prime ministers have had an additional burden. "There were many issues with the way we acted and looked," says Jenny Shipley. "I've certainly never heard male colleagues analysed or criticised to the extent the present PM or I were: our haircuts, ear-rings, necklines, and trousers v. skirts." [31]

Early premiers were very much on their own, sometimes without even a private secretary to assist.

In 1919 the Department of External Affairs was set up to administer New Zealand's island territories, co-inciding with acceptance of the League of Nations mandate to administer Samoa. In 1926 Coates announced an embryonic prime minister's and external affairs department, headed by Carl Berendsen, principally concerned with prime ministerial correspondence and speech writing, but also to assist with the country's international dealings, to that point largely with Britain, Empire countries and the League of Nations.

The 1926 Balfour Report defined the 'dominions' as de facto independent states. This was enshrined in the 1931 Statute of Westminster, not adopted by the New Zealand Parliament until 1947. Despite an apparent unwillingness to cut the symbolic apron strings, New Zealand had declared war in 1939 as a sovereign nation and Bell was the first minister of external affairs as early as 1925. Over the next 65 years the prime minister generally held the external/ foreign affairs portfolio. During the Second World War, with additional overseas posts and a more independent foreign policy stance to be fashioned, Peter Fraser established a new department of external affairs. From the end of the war, and for the next three decades, one person headed both this and the Prime Minister's Department, which consisted of the PM's private office with secretaries and press officers and the cabinet office, headed by the secretary of cabinet. They, and their diplomatic colleagues, all crowded into the rabbit warren of offices and corridors on the third floor of Parliament Buildings and in the linked wooden extensions built during the war.

By the early 1970s, and as political life grew in complexity, it was of increasing concern that policy advice to prime ministers was narrowly based, and largely from senior foreign affairs and treasury officials. Norman Kirk's frustration with the situation led to his informal and controversial economic 'think tank' in 1974.

Robert Muldoon, the incoming prime minister, acted promptly after the 1975 election, the most important innovation an 'advisory group'. Jonathan Boston wrote: " ….. it has provided the Prime Minister, for the first time, with a continuous source of advice on a wide range of policy issues separate from the existing bureaucratic network." [32] The group tapped into the business community as well as the bureaucracy and undertook a liaison role with sector leaders, interest groups and government departments.

The two departments were then separated: the Ministry of Foreign Affairs moved to The Terrace several hundred metres away and, in 1977, the Prime Minister's Department moved into the top floors of the Beehive.

The Prime Minister's Department now had five sections: the PM's private office, with its secretaries; the semi-autonomous cabinet office; the press office; the External Intelligence Bureau (EIB); and the advisory group. The structure was practically unchanged until 1987.

Advisory group members, high flyers in their 30s 'on loan' from both the public and private sectors, worked in their specialist areas for about two years, not long enough, as Gerald Hensley says, "to put down roots in the bureaucracy". [33] Hensley became permanent head of the department in 1980, replacing Bernard Galvin. One of his main tasks was recruiting and running the advisory group. "Muldoon wanted to know what was going on, preferably before his ministers, but the advisory group was also used as a log-jam breaker, facilitating or chairing inter-departmental committees when needed," he says. [34] Muldoon's Friday afternoon meeting with the group was sacrosanct. Afterwards, Hensley and the group members retired to his 8th floor office to look for any fishhooks in the next Monday's cabinet papers.

At the root of the 1987 replacement of the Prime Minister's Department with two autonomous offices – the prime minister's office and the cabinet office – was David Lange's suspicion of the advisory group, largely inherited from the Muldoon era. In the new set-up, John Henderson, an academic who had previously run Labour's research unit, and had become director of the advisory group in mid-1985, was in also in charge of the private and press offices. Meetings moved from Friday afternoons to Monday morning prior to cabinet.

Following Lange's resignation, Palmer instituted a review of the structure he had inherited. "'I was concerned about the blurring of the lines between impartial and partisan advice," says Palmer. "And having worked in the much larger and more potent PM's department in Canberra, I felt we needed to beef up the amount and quality of advice we were getting." [35] The resulting report's recommendations, particularly relating to two distinct streams of advice to the prime minister, were accepted. A new Department of the Prime Minister and Cabinet – which came into existence on January 1 1990 – was to provide impartial, high quality advice and support to the PM and cabinet. Other groups within the department, all operating with a high degree of independence, included an enlarged policy advisory group, a communications unit, domestic and external security secretariat, external assessments bureau, and cabinet office. The quite separate prime minister's private office provided the incumbent with personal support, media services and party political advice.

During the last decade the department has grown considerably bigger, and predictably more bureaucratic. It has also spread from the Beehive to the Reserve Bank building nearby and the prime minister's regular, personal advisory group briefings are a thing of the past.

Henderson has written: "Bolger and Shipley kept the assistance of about fifteen policy advisers. However the Department itself grew much larger, as it sought to play a key role in coordinating overall government activities. Additional staff were employed to undertake special tasks in major policy areas, such as health, crime, and employment. Clark has preferred to rely heavily on the support of her principal advisor, Heather Simpson, who plays a key role in both political and policy advice, as well as overall coordination." [36]

Was the premiership in the pre-1891 era suited to the gifted amateurs who took up and put down the reins so regularly? How does the degree of difficulty compare to the tasks faced by the more hardened professionals who followed them?

Initially, the job was not particularly demanding or complex. As Hensley says: "You could go away for months and communicate by occasional letter; not a long one discussing endless policy but usually a rather chatty one looking at the problems in the coming session of the General Assembly." [37] The population was small, the issues as basic as funding the beginnings of development and establishing an embryonic infrastructure, and responsibility was shared.

Hensley again: "There was no foreign relations, very little economic activity apart from the government's own budget, no welfare, education and the other more practical things that were in the hands of provincial governments of varying quality and energy." [38]

On the other hand, largely inexperienced men were starting from scratch, the model of their intentions 12,000 miles and many sea months away. There was only a skeleton of a parliamentary and administrative structure from the pre-1856 period and few useful local precedents to fall back on. The civil service was small and poorly organised.

Undoubtedly, the complexity of government increased as the country's population mushroomed, massive loans were negotiated in London, relations with Maori passed to the politicians, along with the fighting and funding of military campaigns and, with the passing of the provinces, premiers and their ministries took charge of public works schemes and immigration campaigns. In the mid 1860s fewer than 2,000 public servants were scattered among a few government departments; a decade later the numbers had more than trebled. And with the expansion of central government's role, the power and authority of the premier increased.

It is difficult at this distance to gauge the power of the early premiers. In theory it was considerable. As Bassett says: "In the beginning there was so little bureaucracy and so few conventions to be gone through before decisions were made." [39]

Cabinets were small and premiers often worked closely with one or two confidantes. The General Assembly met infrequently; early on, only every two years. Parliament was in session for relatively short periods when it did meet. There were no 'control' departments, as known today, advising on policies drafted by other departments. 'Pork-barrel' politics

'Boy!!' *The growth of the Prime Minister's Department has been even more rapid in recent years. Sid Scales,* Otago Daily Times*, September 16 1953. (ATL ref: H-723-006)*

9

was a fact of life particularly in the public works era when money was short and used, without embarrassment, to shore up a premier's parliamentary support or with an eye to the next election. Bassett, Ward's biographer, recounts how Sir Joseph would make expenditure decisions on the spot while talking to constituents. "There was a time," says Bassett, "when a word from the premier was something you could bank like a cheque." [40] Seddon was a master in dispensing patronage. Alan Henderson wrote: "Many were the citizens who felt a personal obligation to the Premier – whether for an appointment to a board or position, a liberal retirement allowance, a transfer, or a salary increase." [41]

But in practical terms premier power was limited in a number of ways. For a start, during the early years responsibility was shared with the provincial councils (education, health, roading), the governor (relations with Maori) and the British government (defence and negotiations with other countries).

Welfare simply did not concern the government and it was not until the 1870s that its economic role began to expand, even modestly. The insecurity of early premiers also proscribed their power severely. They had no party or caucus support behind them; they survived by accommodating the agendas of sufficient colleagues to maintain a majority. Cabinets sometimes consisted of the leaders of various parliamentary factions and the convention of collective responsibility was often honoured more in the breach. An unpopular decision or legislative miscalculation could, and did, bring a ministry to an abrupt end, there being no guarantee of a fixed term in government.

Seddon ushered in the modern political era in a number of ways. He was a professional politician, or "vulgar populist" to the old school conservatives. Decades before mass media developed he became a national personality. As Hamer wrote: "His fight to establish himself became a fight to establish the dominance of the Premier in the system." [42] Prime ministers were possibly at their most powerful during the first half of the 20th century. Forceful leaders – Seddon, Ward, Massey and Fraser – dominated stable party caucuses and ran cabinet in their own idiosyncratic ways. As late as the 1940s there were no proper cabinet agendas, proposals were only sometimes backed by documentation and Treasury reports the exception not the rule, although the population and the economy were much larger. The welfare state hugely expanded the bureaucracy and the role of government in people's lives. Yet in the 1940s the House of Representatives was unlikely to be in session as many as 90 days in a year.

Today, as chair of cabinet, the prime minister not only decides what will be discussed but, because of the convention of rarely taking votes, his or her summing up of a discussion inevitably influences, unintentionally or quite deliberately, the wording of the subsequent 'cabinet minute'. Recent prime ministers have treated cabinet very differently: Shipley reduced their frequency to once a fortnight; Lange raced through them, weakening his own position by allowing previously unseen papers to be tabled at meetings; Bolger's cabinets lasted most of the day.

"The power's been there, but some prime ministers have not been very good at grasping or exercising it," says Bassett. [43] The choice of portfolios has been one defining factor. Until 1990, prime ministers were often minister for external affairs/foreign affairs – for 40 out of the 65 years since the first minister was named in 1925 – as well as responsible for the Security Intelligence Service.

With the growing complexity of managing coalition or minority governments in the MMP era, it is unlikely that prime ministers will again hold major portfolios. They will, though, play a major foreign affairs role on overseas trips and as they host visits from foreign leaders. "Foreign affairs and trade is now a never-ending 12 months of the year job," says Bolger.[44] The detailed day-to-day workload in foreign affairs and trade now requires the dedicated attention of senior ministers.

Shipley was minister of women's affairs, and Clark holds the arts and culture portfolio, largely for symbolic reasons. Before them, Lange took on education at the beginning of his second term to hurry up change and Palmer had a particular interest in the environment.

Prime ministers like Holyoake and Lange were, in varying degrees, chairmen of the board; Muldoon was the ultra-activist opposite. It is unlikely any prime minister had exercised so much personal power previously, and certain that none will again. As prime minister, Muldoon dominated cabinet with his grasp of the business at hand and impatience with those who could not keep up; as minister of finance he controlled the most influential government department and the nation's purse-strings. (In the modern era the only other prime ministers to also hold the finance portfolio were Ward for 18 months at the end of the 1920s, then Forbes, immediately afterwards, for a little over a year and Holland from 1949-54.)

With his intellect, periodic ruthlessness and abrasive manner, few colleagues or bureaucrats stood up to Muldoon. On key issues his will prevailed regardless of the opposition or arguments arrayed against him. Jon Johansson wrote: "Ultimately Muldoon became a prisoner to his own worldview, trapped into a nostaglic view of a New Zealand that was no more." [45] As well, he was the first prime minister to benefit from the systematic stream of targeted information and alternative advice from the advisory group established in his office at the end of 1975. It was no exaggeration to say he often knew more about critical issues involving portfolios than the relevant ministers. John Henderson wrote: "Muldoon liked to describe his advisers as an extension of his 'eyes and ears', and they certainly helped to consolidate the domination Muldoon held over his ministers." [46]

The personal power of New Zealand prime ministers has diminished since the late 1970s. There are at least three reasons for this: *Fitzgerald v. Muldoon*, the parliamentary reforms of the fourth Labour government and MMP.

Following the 1975 election, Muldoon scrapped the NZ Superannuation Scheme by press statement. When his deductions to the scheme were stopped, Mr Fitzgerald, a clerk in the Education Department, brought an action against the prime minister, arguing that he had acted illegally under the Bill of Rights 1688, an important English constitutional document in force in New Zealand. It was his contention that the scheme remained in force until such time as Parliament repealed it. Fitzgerald won the case. "It was a salutary reminder that Parliament is the supreme rule maker and that the prime minister is not above the law," says Palmer. [47] More significantly the decision led to a comprehensive rewriting and enlargement of the cabinet office manual, which now sets out constitutional conventions more authoritatively than any other source. "It sets out the do's and don'ts of cabinet government for everyone concerned with the process," says Palmer. "And these checks in the system mean you can't always do what you might have decided in cabinet to do." [48]

Until the mid-1980s the conduct of Parliament provided few checks to the exercise of prime ministerial power. Palmer wrote: "There had been a habit of having Parliament meet only about half the year, something convenient to an executive wanting to avoid parliamentary scrutiny." [49] Further, 'urgency'

was used to ram through legislation in all-night sittings not conducive to sensible law-making. And select committees were severely restricted in what they could consider. Changes by the Labour government following the 1985 Standing Orders review means Parliament now meets during 10 months of the year, there is a virtual ban on all-night sittings and select committees have the authority to examine every aspect of government policy, administration and finance.

The MMP system, in operation since the 1996 election, has substantially weakened the power of cabinet and, consequently, the prime minister. For a start, the increase in the number of MPs from 99 to 120 means that cabinet is unlikely again to have effective control of Parliament via its 'block-voting' majority in caucus.

It is also highly unlikely that New Zealand will again see majority single party governments. By definition a minority government in coalition with one or more other parties has to compromise. The post-1996 Bolger and Shipley cabinets included several members from minority parties, as was the case with the 1999-2002 Clark government. This meant decisions had to be negotiated within, rather than simply agreed by, cabinet.

As Jonathan Hunt, Speaker of the House of Representatives and MP since 1966, says: "No longer can a PM come to cabinet and force something through on Monday, force it through caucus on a Tuesday and make it law by Friday." [50]

Also, as Mulgan wrote: "The prime minister has no control over ministerial appointments from other parties. Matters of portfolio allocations need to be negotiated with the leaders of other parties belonging to the coalition. Conversely, Cabinet ministers, particularly those who are not from the prime minister's party, will have fewer reasons to avoid incurring the prime minister's displeasure." [51]

In the current Clark administration there is only one non-Labour minister, but a range of legislative initiatives depend on the support of one or more other parties represented in the House. Among the more profound changes resulting from MMP has been the

Jenny Shipley favoured fortnightly cabinet meetings, quite common in other countries. David Fletcher, 'The Politician', Dominion, March 17 1999. (ATL ref: H-725-019)

modification of the convention of collective responsibility so that junior partners in a government can signal their disagreement with a cabinet decision.

Shrewdly, Clark has gone about her prime ministerial business for all the world like the leader of a majority government; consequently the significance of the power shift has not been well-appreciated. There is nothing transparent about the backroom politicking involved but, needless to say, the government will not introduce legislation if it lacks the numbers; bills will be buried or disappear from the order paper. As Palmer says: "Parliament is now functioning more in a classical 19th century manner. There are certainly parties now rather than more informal groupings, but some of those parties are in constantly shifting coalitions depending on the issue at hand. For example, it has not been unusual in 1993 for the Greens to vote for and against the government in the same week." [52]

Ultimately, a prime minister's position, and authority, depends on the judgment of his or her colleagues. A prime minister wins and maintains support in a number of ways. Possibly the hike to the top – forming friendships and alliances and showing a high level of competence in key areas – is easier than keeping one's balance on the exposed summit.

Prime ministerial longevity depends on performance in the House. "Doing well in the House takes your people with you," says Hunt. "Holyoake was very comfortable in the House, Muldoon was a master but absolutely ruthless, Lange was considerable and finally bested Muldoon, Kirk was a superb orator at his best, and Clark is a very able performer." [53]

It depends on effectiveness at press conferences and on the hustings. It depends on cabinet selections and portfolio allocations. It depends on the ability to win elections. Election losses are not fatal – Massey, Holland, Nash, Kirk and Clark all lost twice before winning – so long as the future looks rosier. The Labour caucus signaled it was time for Lange to go in 1989 when Roger Douglas was re-elected to cabinet against the prime minister's express wishes. In the MMP era survival also depends, as Bolger discovered, on how successfully colleagues believe the relationship with the junior coalition partner or partners is being managed.

Fear can quell opposition in the short-term but is eventually highly corrosive.

At the same time, a little well placed patronage still counts. List MPs, without electorate muscle behind them, may now be more beholden to a prime minister, and the Department of the Prime Minister and Cabinet administers the honours system and approves a large number of government appointments.

Much has been written about the qualities needed for political leadership. In the New Zealand context, possibly the most authoriative contribution has come from Michael Bassett who combines the skills of an historian and the experience of a well-blooded politician. He wrote: "The need for robust health, high energy levels, a good temperament, intelligence, a willingness to take the right, as opposed to a political decision, and a modicum of luck, have been constants throughout the century." [54]

These attributes were also important in the pre-1891 period. Bassett says: "The issues have changed from infrastructure to quality of life, and to that extent some skills will be more important at different times, but the basic prime ministerial qualities remain the same." [55]

Good health has always been important, and has undoubtedly become increasingly so. Some 19th century premiers continued in office when seriously ill, but this was less of an issue then because pressures were not so intense and there were lengthy periods when rest and recuperation could at least be attempted. Up to the Second World War, and a decade beyond, prime ministerial expeditions abroad were by ship with the built-in guarantee of several weeks of relative quiet and time for reflection.

The modern world does not provide this luxury. Today's prime minister is rarely 'off duty', even on holiday. The complexity of government and truckloads of paper to study, the month in month out routine of Parliament, cabinet and caucus, 'instant' communications and the pressure to be accessible, the overseas trips crammed into a few days, and society's 'constant change' mentality all combine to make rude health and high energy levels prime ministerial prerequisites.

Of course, some of this activity is unnecessary – possibly flattering to the prime ministerial ego or a device to avoid sustained contemplation. There is also an expectation in New Zealand that prime ministers will open everything from bridges to bridge clubs. An exasperated David Lange once spoke of the "intolerable need for having to go here, there and elsewhere …. off down to the West Coast where the planes are smaller than I am …" [56] At the best of times, prime ministership is a sedentary occupation with long hours and snatched meals, and has been particularly hard on some of the 'larger-than-life' incumbents. Few prime ministers have been sufficiently organised, or had the good sense, to take the sort of regular, vigorous holidays Helen Clark enjoys.

Richard Seddon had extraordinary energy for a man of his size, and chronic heart failure did nothing to slow a frenetic schedule during his last 18 months. Norman Kirk had several heart turns – well kept secrets – before he became prime minister and, sadly, tried to hide his final, fatal illness from his colleagues, fearing they might try to remove him from office. Similarly, dying prime ministers like Michael Savage and Joseph Ward were loath to resign.

Bill Rowling once commented that David Lange would never become party leader, let alone prime minister, because he had to take the lift to his first floor office in Parliament Buildings. A stomach-stapling operation later, Lange was to achieve both but his prime ministerial term adversely affected his health.

Hensley believes political analysts give insufficient emphasis to the rigours of the job. "There's a creeping tiredness, if not exhaustion, that overcomes prime ministers and governments after a certain period of time." [57] He believes this contributed to Muldoon's uncharacteristically illogical behaviour in 1984 after nine years in power as prime minister and minister of finance.

"The working day is outrageously long," says Bolger. "I'd arrive at the office by 8.30 in the morning at the latest and rarely leave before midnight at the earliest, and most weekends were spent attending functions around the country." [58]

The lack of opportunity to think is, he says, a major concern. "It's important not to get bogged down with the endless, immediate process issues, but to find the time to read with sufficient breadth to know what others are thinking and to relate this to the big issues the country will face in the future." [59]

It is unlikely that anyone with the wrong temperament would become prime minister in the modern era, although doubts have been expressed about Lange, who did not serve the usual lengthy political apprenticeship. Lange came to Parliament, via a by-election, in 1977; be became deputy Labour leader in 1979, the party leader in early 1983 and prime minister in 1984. "When I became prime minister I'd never even seen the cabinet room," he remembers. "One minute I was an opposition MP and lapsed lawyer with a bunch of nice ideas and the next I'm being briefed by people I'd never heard of in my life." [60] Hensley, who observed Lange at close quarters, says: "There's no such thing as a prime ministerial personality, but they generally have some things in common. Lange had charm, great intelligence, and a way with words, but in other ways he was not at all in the pattern. He was not at all authoritarian and you have to be a tough boss to herd the load of cats any average caucus is." [61]

Political decisions, sometimes tantamount to

ELLISON

Post cabinet press conferences, a feature of the New Zealand political landscape, are not the norm elsewhere. Anthony Ellison, Sunday Star, *May 30 1993. (ATL ref: H-123-005)*

election bribes, often pay a short-term dividend. But a cynical stratagem like the 1981 Springbok rugby tour can, as it did with Muldoon, begin the erosion of confidence in leadership. Peter Fraser's decision to keep New Zealand troops in the Middle East when Japan entered the Second World War – unlike the Australian forces which were brought back to the Pacific – caused considerable consternation at the time, but he was thinking and acting strategically not politically.

Intelligence has always rated highly as a key leadership trait, and some of the most plodding prime ministerial examples, like George Forbes, have been the least successful in the job. Some of the most intelligent and perceptive prime ministers like Fraser, Nash and Kirk had limited formal education but were voracious and wide-ranging readers.

Political commentator Colin James believes intellect has become more vital. "Despite appearing to retreat, government is actually much more ambitious than even 15 years ago," he says. "Policies are more complex with a number of whole-of-government, cross-portfolio issues requiring intellectual depth rather than just native intelligence on the part of prime ministers." [62]

Some premiers and prime ministers have definitely been luckier than others. Few, Bassett believes, were luckier than Forbes. "When Sir Joseph Ward's second premiership came to an end in May 1930, Forbes was elected leader of the United Party with as few as 15 votes out of the 28 or 29 then constituting its pitifully small caucus." [63] Holyoake

might have been unlucky to have had less than three months as prime minister in 1957, but lucky that he faced the country's oldest ever prime minister, and leader of the 'Black Budget' government, in 1960. Muldoon benefited greatly from Kirk's unexpected death in 1974. Bolger was probably lucky he did not succeed Muldoon in late 1984; similarly Clark's position was helped by not leading Labour into the 'no-win' 1990 election.

Marshall was doubly unlucky: to have so short a time to show his mettle in 1972 and then to lose the party leadership to Muldoon shortly before Kirk's death. Rowling was unlucky to have been sandwiched between two of the 20th century's larger-than-life prime ministers – Kirk and Muldoon. Coates' considerable ability was fettered by depression, coalitions and a world war.

Luck, or lack of it, is quite random as things will inevitably happen that a prime minister can't anticipate or control. But some make their own luck better than others, or minimise the fallout from problems. As Hensley says: "The stronger the personality, the quicker the intelligence and the greater the energy, it's more likely that even bad events can be survived." [64]

"Timing is everything in politics," says Mike Moore. "And I suspect a sense of humour and proportion are necessary attributes as well. Also a consistency of vision and direction builds trust and enables change to be accepted more easily." [65]

Another quality might be added to Bassett's list: the kind of persona that inspires confidence, trust,

THE EVOLUTION OF A LABOUR PRIME MINISTER

Labour had three prime ministers in !3 months. Chicane (Mark Winter) Southland Times, ca 1990.
(ATL ref: H-723-011)

even respect – and looks confident and trustworthy on television. And a sub-set of this is the ability to make and maintain close, harmonious personal and political relationships. Then there is the ability to win elections – but this is probably a reflection of how many of the necessary qualities a leader demonstrates.

Personality, or force of personality, has always been important. For the pre-1891 premiers it was their ability to enthuse or convince their colleagues that they could broker a credible administration. Early premiers also had to deal with Machiavellian governors like Grey and pompous, self-important ones like Sir George Bowen. Later, prime ministers needed the strength of personality to win and hold the support of their caucuses. This has meant the willingness to be 'clubbable', to mix and drink with parliamentary peers. During his rise to power, Muldoon 'worked' the rooms of National Party colleagues after Parliament rose for the evening; it was something that sat less comfortably with Marshall, Jim McLay and Lange.

The ability of a premier or prime minister to communicate effectively has always been important, but it has become crucial since the television era began in New Zealand in the early 1960s. Within a decade politicians were having to adapt techniques used in rambling press interviews and rousing platform performances to the merciless electronic eye of a medium beamed into practically every living room in the nation. It was imperative to be succinct, clear, simple and preferably memorable. Television magnified mannerisms and uncertainty into shiftiness and incompetence. As Bassett noted: "The new medium played into the hands of the young, the smart and the telegenic." [66] Today, the public has much more appetite for personalities than issues and politicians have been forced to play the game.

Television, according to James, is not so much about projecting personality as convincing viewers that you are someone they want to bother with; that you have the substance people are looking for. [67]

Political scientists Stephen Levine and Nigel Roberts have assessed the 11 prime ministers in the TV era – between 1961-2003 – in terms of their ability to communicate via, and their attitude towards, the news media, Their top five news media communicators were Lange, Muldoon, Clark, Kirk and Moore. [68]

The top five, in terms of their responsiveness to the media, were Clark, Lange, Moore, Marshall and Bolger.

Levine and Roberts note of Muldoon, " …. at his best, his mastery of the media was his ultimate weapon." [69] It was very different for his political mentor Keith Holyoake. He was never at ease on

television during the 1960s, looking pompous and sounding plummy. If he had become prime minister a decade later his time at the top might have been much shorter.

It is unlikely many of the earlier prime ministers and premiers would have been effective on television. Seddon, for example, had too 'big' a presence and personality. The strengths that let him dominate the public platform would have overwhelmed on the small screen to the point of parody. In contrast, Muldoon, a small man, looked much bigger and more powerful on television.

In studies of prime ministers the importance of close political and personal relationships is often overlooked.

The relationship between a prime minister and his or her deputy is vital, but an unusual one in the world of politics, calling as it does for a high degree of trust and compatibility. As Palmer puts it: "A prime requirement of the Deputy's job is loyalty to the Prime Minister. The Deputy Prime Minister is in a position to undermine the Prime Minister more effectively than anyone else in caucus." [70]

Holyoake was the first officially designated deputy PM following the 1954 election and since then there have been 14 more, only four of whom were subsequently prime minister. There was a period between 1972-84 when there was a succession of deputies who did not become prime minister – Hugh Watt, Bob Tizard, Brian Talboys and Duncan MacIntyre.

Some deputies served long apprenticeships in the No. 2 spot – Marshall 11 years, Nash nine, Holyoake eight, Talboys six, and Palmer five years. MMP has complicated matters; Don McKinnon was Bolger's deputy PM from 1990-96, giving up the position to Winston Peters in the subsequent coalition government while remaining, for a period, deputy leader of the National Party. Several prime ministers – Kirk, Rowling, Lange, Moore, Bolger, and Jenny Shipley – were never deputy.

Palmer again: "There does need to be clear agreement and understanding …. between the Prime Minister and the Deputy as to the respective roles of each. No two administrations ever work the same way due to differences in temperament, aptitudes and interests." [71] Some of the most effective partnerships – Fraser and Nash, Holyoake and Marshall, Muldoon and Brian Talboys, Lange and Palmer, Clark and Michael Cullen – have involved very different people bringing complementary skills to the relationship.

Colin James says: "The Clark-Cullen working relationship is the most effective I've seen in over 30 years. There are very few chinks in their armour and if one opens up they're usually quick to close it again." [72]

Loyalty and ambition make uncomfortable bedfellows. In most cases there is an expectation that the deputy will, one day, move up to the top job. A lack of agreement about the timing for this, or fudging of the issue, can be a cause of frustration, resentment or worse. Holland had to be persuaded to resign, giving Holyoake less than three months in the job before the 1957 election; he, in turn, stayed on until 10 months before the 1972 election, allowing his long-time deputy Marshall insufficient time to build a prime ministerial reputation.

Since 1954 two Labour prime ministers have been replaced, one by his deputy; two National prime ministers were 'persuaded' to resign and another counted heads in caucus and bowed out. Talboys might have become prime minister in 1981 had he actively contested the leadership; even so it required a desperate, no-holds-barred campaign by Muldoon to save his political skin. Muldoon then turned on his deputy who resigned the position and then left politics at that year's election.

A number of deputy prime ministers have made significant contributions: Holyoake as minister of agriculture in the 1950s, Marshall and Talboys as trade ministers in the 1960s and 1970s and Palmer as 'manager' of Labour's frenetically busy 1984-87 government. Before the title existed, Nash was the very influential minister of finance between 1940-49 and, earlier still, Sir James Allen, Massey's deputy, was acting prime minister for 23 months during 1916-19 while the National ministry's Massey and Ward were in Europe.

In New Zealand, but hardly anywhere else, a deputy becomes acting prime minister when the leader is out of the country. It is a convention that continues even though the reason for it – prime ministers being out of the country and contact for long periods – no longer applies.

On the personal relationship issue, Bassett wrote: "Settled and supportive domestic lives are also important to prime ministerial success. As Jim Bolger once said to me, it's hard to expect people to believe you if your personal life is a lie." [73] Prime ministers' wives rarely get the credit they deserve, particularly those whose husbands had long political careers and lengthy spells in office.

The five premiers and prime ministers whose first wives died all remarried and, remarkably, only one prime ministerial marriage has ended in divorce. There has been the recent novelty, with accompanying media interest, of the country's first two prime ministerial husbands.

The wives of several prime ministers – notably Janet Fraser and Christina Massey – had considerable community involvements quite separately from their husbands. Five were honoured with damehoods for a variety of reasons and Christina Massey was the first New Zealand woman to become a Dame Grand Cross (GBE) rather than the more usual Dame Commander (DBE) of the Order of the British Empire. DBEs were subsequently awarded to Ruth Kirk and Thea Muldoon, and Norma Holyoake became a Dame Commander of the Order of St Michael and St George.

❧

It could hardly be said that premiers and prime ministers have been motivated by money or status. The first premiers, in 1856, were paid a salary of £700, roughly equating to $70,000 in today's terms. Until 1862, when the figure had increased to £1,000, premiers and ministers were paid the same amount. Subsequently, the premier earned more. By 1873 the premier's annual salary was £1,750, with a house provided, but it was cut back sharply to £1,000 at the time of the 1887 depression. There were similar reductions during difficult economic conditions in the early 1920s and again in the 1930s. The £2,000 paid to Massey in 1920 (about $96,000 in today's money) was more than any subsequent prime ministers received until 1951 when the amount was increased to £3,000 and allowances were formalised. The MPs themselves set parliamentary salaries until 1951. Then, until 1973, a series of royal commissions did the job and, since then, the Higher Salaries Commission has had the responsibility. By 1981 the prime minister was receiving $79,717 plus $14,000 in allowances. Today, Helen Clark, managing director of New Zealand Inc, is paid about 10 percent of the salaries, bonuses and share preferences earned by the CEOs of the country's larger companies.

At times premiers did not take their salary. In his biography of Stafford, Edmund Bohan wrote: "He had spent much of his own money during the past four years and had drawn no official salary for the whole of 1859." [74] After Labour won the 1935 election Savage proposed, and his colleagues agreed, that the salaries of the prime minister, ministers and MPs be pooled in a trust account and divided equally among caucus members – and in the process his salary dropped from £1,800 to £600. [75]

Julius Vogel had been a vocal advocate of General Assembly members being paid a salary rather than a small daily honorarium. He said, in 1871: " 'If there were not payment of members the government of the colony would be thrown almost exclusively into the hands of one class, and even that class had not so large a number of idle and wealthy representatives as to give the people a very large choice'." [76]

In 1873, when Vogel became premier, his salary and travelling allowances were he "maintained 'not sufficient to go a long way in maintaining a comfortable style of living; and that unless a person in the position I occupy have private means such a position would be a very intolerable one'." [77] In the event, Vogel's salary was increased significantly, with one member pointing out that it was a preposterous salary when most households were lucky to have between £200-300 a year to live on.

New Zealand premiers and prime ministers have not lived splendidly either. Most have been ambivalent, largely to appear 'egalitarian' in a small country, about a local version of the 'White House' or '10 Downing Street'.

The closest New Zealand equivalent is Premier House in Tinakori Road in Wellington. The house has had a chequered history. It grew out of an 1843 cottage and was purchased as a ministerial home when the capital moved south in 1865. Stafford was the first premier to live there, in 1867-69, and there was some unseemly scrapping when he refused, on his defeat, to vacate the house in favour of Fox until the end of the parliamentary session. Characteristically, it was Vogel who had grander plans that, with some architectural assistance and no little cost, resulted in an elegant two-storeyed residence with a sprung floor ballroom and the country's first lift. The latter was more necessity than indulgence because by 1872, when the Vogels began the first of their two stints at Premier House, he was increasingly incapacitated by gout. Dalziel wrote: "While they inhabited the Premier's residence in Tinakori Road, Wellington came to have a social season comparable to that of other capitals around the world. Balls, receptions, drawing-rooms, and banquets as well as the less formal at-homes became frequent events." [78] Other premiers to live there, for varying lengths of time, included Pollen, Whitaker, Atkinson, and Ballance.

Ward and his family lived there for 12 years, christening it 'Awarua House'. The house was vacant when Ward moved to Wellington permanently in 1900, the spacious reception rooms suiting his pretensions and the three acres of gardens comfortably accommodating the Ward children's love of ponies, dogs and other animals. Again, the house was at the centre of Wellington's social scene. There were regular garden parties including one for

Katherine Beauchamp (Mansfield) when she left New Zealand for the last time in 1908. Premier Seddon lived at Oriental Bay, but was a regular visitor. Michael Bassett wrote: "Seddon, particularly when he was trying to reduce weight by regular horse-riding, would come by on his way home from the office." [79]

The Massey family lived there during his lengthy prime ministership, followed by Coates and Forbes. Michael Joseph Savage, Labour's first prime minister and a bachelor, considered the house much too ostentatious for his simple tastes. For years he had lived in boarding houses, his belongings in a suitcase. Later he rented a room in the Auckland home of friends, who then moved to Wellington when he became prime minister. The same arrangements continued, although Savage owned the house they lived in together.

With health care now a major government priority, Premier House became a children's dental clinic for 39 years from 1937. To several generations of Wellington children 260 Tinakori Road gained a new name – the 'Murder House'.

It then had a variety of uses from 1977 until 1989 when Michael Bassett, historian and minister of internal affairs, made Premier House's refurbishment a 1990 project, marking the country's 150th anniversary. The house was strengthened, rooms were restored and a small prime minister's flat fashioned from the maze of

Joe Ward as the angel of light. *Ward's first knighthood was in recognition of his introduction of universal penny postage. William Blomfield,* New Zealand Observer & Free Lance, *September 22 1900. (ATL ref: A-312-1-004)*

upstairs rooms. Since then prime ministers Palmer, Bolger and Shipley have lived in Premier House. Clark camps there, as she puts it, during her Wellington week.

John Ballance died in Premier House. He had been unwell for some time before bowel cancer was finally diagnosed; a makeshift operating theatre was set up in the house, but he did not survive operations on successive days.

Another impressive home, Vogel House in Lower Hutt, has also been a prime ministerial residence. It was bequeathed to the government by Jocelyn Vogel in 1965; 32 years before it had been a wedding present to her and husband James Vogel, Sir Julius's grandson. The house, with its large garden, was extended and altered before Rowling and then Muldoon lived there during their prime ministerships. David Lange lived there for a few months in 1985. Subsequently it has been occupied by senior ministers.

A number of prime ministers have lived in family homes or ministerial houses of no particular distinction. Holland and Holyoake both lived at 41 Pipitea Street. Holyoake, who also insisted on a phone book listing, liked the comfortable, unostentatious two-storey family home, in part because it was a short walk to and from Parliament. Nash lived in a suburban Lower Hutt street very close to Vogel House. Kirk lived in Seatoun and Fraser in Northland.

The one consistent concession to status and vanity by premiers and prime ministers has been the acceptance of honours. Twenty of the 35 male premiers and prime ministers accepted knighthoods. Nearly all (17) were either KCMGs or GCMGs. Sir George Grey, who had been awarded his KCB at the precocious age of 36, liked, in his waspish way, to disparage the Order of St Michael and St George, "an order … [he] had denounced as created to keep colonials out of the great orders of knighthood". [80] Several – including Seddon, Massey, Fraser, Lange, and Bolger – declined knighthoods and others accepted lesser honours. Since its introduction in 1987, three prime ministers – Lange, Moore and Bolger – have received the country's highest award, the Order of New Zealand (ONZ), restricted to 20 living recipients. Shipley's DCNZM is the equivalent of a damehood.

In recent years political scientists and historians have delved deeper than biographical details and parliamentary and party structures in search of a better understanding of the motivation and actions of our political leaders.

John Henderson's work on the psychology and leadership styles of New Zealand prime ministers has been based on a framework developed by political psychologist James David Barber in the 1970s to analyse the behaviour of US presidents. Henderson noted: "…. The study of the actions and inactions of

Fraser and Holland – two leaders who dominated nearly two decades of political life from 1940 – limber up for the 1949 elections which ended Labour's long run. Neville Colvin, Evening Post, *November 26 1949. (ATL ref: C-132-877)*

individuals and groups will explain much more about the political process than the traditional political science focus on structures." [81]

Barber identified three core 'role demands' which determine leadership styles: the rhetorical function (the ability to communicate persuasively), interpersonal relations (working effectively with colleagues, staff and others) and the management function (coping with the pressures of paperwork and decision-making).

Henderson says: "Recent New Zealand prime ministers and party leaders have been characterised by one of these three styles." [82]

According to Henderson, the political success of Muldoon and Lange owed a great deal to their ability to perform on television and on the public platform. Bolger's and Moore's success had much more to do with their interpersonal relations skills. Palmer, Shipley and Clark concentrated on the management aspect of the prime ministerial role. Palmer, Bolger, Shipley and Clark all struggled with their public performances but, significantly, Clark has transformed herself into an effective public communicator.

While 'personality', increasingly synonymous with how a leader 'comes across' on television, is important to political success, it is different from 'character', the deep-seated traits that define a person.

A prime minister's performance will be conditioned by character traits as well as his or her leadership style.

Put simply, the Barber analysis also asks two questions: how much energy does the leader expend on the job and is the work enjoyable and fulfilling or something to be endured? From this a matrix is constructed with four character types: active-positive; active-negative; passive-positive; and passive-negative. Henderson sees Palmer, Bolger, Shipley and Clark as examples of the 'active-positive' type, energetic prime ministers who enjoyed the job. He says: "They take an essentially rational view of politics, and what can and cannot be achieved. They are prepared to move on from politics when they feel they have contributed all they can." [83]

'Active-negative' leaders, like Muldoon and Moore, work hard with little personal satisfaction. Power is the principal motivating force. Henderson wrote: "They seek to dominate their parties and administrations …. and, having achieved high office, are most reluctant to relinquish it." [84]

Given the nature of politics there are fewer passive types. 'Passive-negative' leaders are in politics from a sense of duty and do not seek a leadership role. Henderson again: "Labour leader Bill Rowling, who took over as prime minister following Kirk's death, is an example of a leader who did not push himself forward, but was prepared to be drafted for the job by his colleagues." [85] 'Passive-positive' types, and Lange

is the best recent example, "are attracted to the group and social context of politics, which is a people orientated profession," says Henderson. "They seek to feed on the affection of their followers, but avoid the conflict that is also an inevitable part of politics." [86]

Logically, the MMP environment will require rather different prime ministerial skills. In terms of style, the ability to manage and work with others will become more important. With a minority government since 1998, it is necessary to assemble a coalition for every legislative measure. An ideologically driven or idealistic leader is likely to be less acceptable than a flexible, pragmatic one. Currently, Clark's assertive, 'active-positive' leadership refutes the theory that a more conciliatory approach works best under MMP. Regardless of political systems, 'active-positive' leaders have the clear advantage, as Henderson puts it, "of being able to separate their political goals from personal ego needs". [87]

Another political scientist, Jon Johansson, has used a framework devised by political psychologist Stanley Renshon to ponder why Muldoon blocked change in New Zealand for so long and so stubbornly. The Renshon approach suggests three components underpin character – ambition, character integrity and relatedness. Using this framework, Johansson has written insightfully about one of the country's most complex prime ministers: "Muldoon's greatest attributes – his impressive cognitive faculties, his genuine concern for ordinary New Zealanders, his superior parliamentary skills and his rhetorical prowess – were all ultimately swamped by the fatal disjunction that occurred between Muldoon's character limitations and a turbulent epoch that required a more questioning and open-minded leadership than he was able to provide." [88]

It has been a popular pursuit of the business press during the 1990s to examine business leadership and find it wanting, both locally and internationally. Two often used words in the business leadership literature are 'visionary' and 'inspirational'. While few business leaders may actually earn these epithets, they are words rarely used in the political world at all.

James McGregor Burns's pioneering book, *Leadership*, has been responsible for much of the business world's thinking on the subject since he made the distinction between 'moral' leaders, who inspire change, and 'transactional leaders,' who manage the here and now. It has been argued that the poverty of business world leadership can be addressed by 'visionary' and 'inspirational' leadership which raises or redefines the aspirations of the people working for or with companies.

Most New Zealand premiers and prime ministers – battling to break in the country and then guarantee a standard of living – have been transactional leaders.

Muldoon might have been pilloried for saying he wanted to leave the country no worse than he found it, but it might just as easily have been the catch-cry of many of his predecessors.

The list of visionary or inspirational leaders is a short one: Vogel with his development dream; Seddon and his South Pacific 'empire'; Massey's goal of becoming Britain's outlying farm; Savage, Fraser and Nash with their big government solution to transforming lives. Kirk and Lange inspired the public with their hopes for New Zealand society but, for more practical reasons, they failed to inspire their colleagues to the same degree. Bolger was interested in ideas like 'social capital', but did not present them in a way that engaged his fellow New Zealanders.

Mike Moore was the ideas politician personified. "I was told that I wrote too many books and didn't focus enough on the short term," he recalls. "Perhaps they were right." [89]

Paradoxically, although New Zealanders might respond to a degree of visionary leadership they also want leaders' feet firmly planted on the ground. Colin James says: "One-of-us-ness is a very important quality for New Zealand prime ministers, but they have to be 'above' us as well." [90]

It is the way of the media to occasionally want to know who the best prime minister was – or the worst – and to rank the top five or 10. It is a political party game that academics, pundits and bureaucrats have all played on occasion.

Commentators are generally loath to nominate the best among the 19th century premiers. Apart from the distance they have receded into, governments were so constructed that the 'strong men' – like Vogel and Whitaker – were not always premier. While the attributes of good leadership were not markedly different, the lack of parties and caucuses, the comparative smallness of government, particularly during the provincial council era, and the slowly evolving responsibility for Maori affairs and foreign relations make a comparison between the centuries virtually impossible. But in the 19th century context, three men, Seddon aside, particularly stand out for their contributions: Stafford, the longest serving premier, for establishing constitutional government and an effective civil service; Vogel for opening up the country with his bold immigration and public works schemes; and Weld, whose promotion of 'self-reliance' was an important stepping stone on New Zealand's path to independence.

Using the leadership qualities outlined above, Bassett ranks Fraser first, with Seddon, Massey, Savage and Holyoake also on the list of best 20th century prime ministers. He wrote: " …. For the weight of his achievements on so many fronts, for the sheer magnitude of the problems he handled with skill during the war, and for his canny ability to manage the rapidly changing world environment at mid-century, I'd give

This Other Eden. *Several prime ministers had long waits in the deputy role. Neville Colvin,* Evening Post, *ca 1953-56. (ATL: H-705-014)*

the prize for New Zealand's greatest twentieth-century prime minister to Peter Fraser." [91]

Hunt says: "From my observation, the most successful prime ministers have been slightly to the left of their caucus if they're National and slightly to the right if they are Labour." This has given them a wider electorate appeal and he cites Holyoake's insistence on sending only volunteers to Vietnam, Muldoon's left-leaning economic views and Clark's ability to get alongside big business and the RSA." [92]

Political scientist Simon Sheppard surveyed a small number of academics, politicians, journalists, and public servants in 1998. [93] The questionnaire covered leadership qualities, parliamentary skills, party and crisis management, and legislative achievements. Respondents were also asked to qualitatively rank the 30 premiers and prime ministers surveyed in 'overall terms'. The results suggest that little was known about some of the early premiers. All its flaws aside, the survey ranked the 'Top 10' as: Seddon, Fraser, Savage, Ballance, Holyoake, Kirk, Massey, Vogel, Muldoon, and Stafford. The bottom five were Whitaker, Hall, Fox, Weld and Moore. Interestingly, the top five just in terms of leadership qualities were Seddon, Savage, Kirk, Fraser, and Lange.

David Hamer has written: "Seddon has never been rivalled in: (a) his ability to win elections – five in a row (although Holyoake came close and against stronger party opposition than Seddon ever had to face) (b) his mastery of parliamentary business (c) his handling of crises – of which many buffeted his regime'." [94] After a four decade career as a political scientist, Keith Jackson rated Keith Holyoake most highly among the country's prime ministers. The two others to make the greatest impression were Kirk for his commitment to the idea of New Zealand as a South Pacfic nation and Muldoon for his 'Napoleonic' approach to winning politically. [95]

Gustafson has written: " …. in my opinion and taking into account the length of time and the extent to which they personally dominated the political agenda, there are eight great political figures in New Zealand history over the past hundred years: Seddon, Massey, Savage, Fraser, Sidney Holland, Holyoake, Muldoon and Roger Douglas." [96] (In addition to Douglas, other highly influential ministers in the modern era have included Arnold Nordmeyer and Bill Birch.)

In their study of the 11 prime ministers in the TV era, Levine and Roberts looked at their media effectiveness and their willingness to submit to its demands. Because they are of critical importance, they also factored in political skills, based on patterns of performance during their time in office, to their analysis, and in doing so came up with very different prime ministerial rankings. Interestingly, Clark, at only the midway mark of her second term, heads the list, followed by Kirk/Muldoon, Moore/Bolger, Holyoake, and Lange. [97]

Although Carl Berendsen, an outstanding civil servant and diplomat, personally abhorred Labour's domestic policies, he was a Savage admirer. Gustafson wrote: "In later years Berendsen recorded that of all the Prime Ministers with whom he had worked closely – Coates, Ward, Forbes, Savage, Fraser, Sidney Holland and Nash – Savage was, in his opinion, the best, the most considerate and easy to work for, a very competent administrator, a transparently good man, the nearest person to a true Christian that Berendsen ever met, and a man he 'admired, respected and loved'". [98] Gerald Hensley, a more recent senior public servant of similar standing, who worked to a greater or lesser degree for 10 prime ministers, is reticent about picking out the country's most outstanding prime minister. "Our history, with long periods of 'steady as she goes' and short fairly frenetic bursts of reform – in the 1890s, 1935-38 and 1984-87 – after which we sink back into tranquility, doesn't provide a lot of scope for greatness." [99] He would, though, include Fraser, Seddon, Holyoake, and possibly Vogel and Weld, in a top five selection.

Hunt has observed a parade of prime ministers over the last 37 years. In overall terms he considers the top five have been Holyoake, Lange, Muldoon, Clark and Bolger.

If success means the firmest hold on the levers of power, John Henderson, political scientist and prime ministerial advisor, would rate Seddon, Muldoon and Clark most highly. "The ones who changed things most were probably Seddon, Savage and Lange," he says. "They mightn't have been his ideas, but Lange didn't compromise on nuclear policy when some of his colleagues would have." [100]

Political cartoons capture the essence of personality and policies. "Cartoons have freshness and spontaneity; they catch the mood, anxieties, passions of the moment." [101] Certainly, cartoonists of any era are often the most astute interpreters of public opinion, "reflecting the anger, dismay or grief their fellow citizens are feeling". [102]

Sir John Marshall put it well: "A good cartoon can convey, at a glance, a wealth of information; it can epitomise an idea better than a thousand words; it is remembered when words are forgotten; it is instant enlightenment." [103]

It is obvious from even a cursory glance at the popular weeklies in the 1890s and the first years of the 20th century that Seddon completely dominated the public arena. Pouter-pigeon chested in ceremonial garb, 'King Dick' was shown lording it over Wellington, the

South Pacific and even the British Empire. Seddon was premier for 13 years, longer than anyone else before or since in New Zealand, but the cartoons and caricatures by William Blomfield ('Blo'), EF Hiscocks and others were generally affectionate.

Subsequently, cartoonists have had fun with the foibles of Ward, Massey, Savage, Peter Fraser, Holyoake and Kirk. But it was the dimple-cheeked, stumpy and spectacularly belligerent Robert Muldoon who launched the second great era of political cartooning in New Zealand.

Despite his constant barnstorming tours around the country, it was the cartoons of Seddon in *The Observer*, *NZ Graphic* and *Free Lance* that did the most to mould his larger than life image. With Muldoon, the first politician in New Zealand to master television, cartoons worked away at exposing the cracks and contradictions in the public persona he created for himself.

Cartoonists and politicians have always needed each other. As Sir Gordon Minhinnick wrote: "It has sometimes been remarked that, for its size, New Zealand has produced a surprising number of cartoonists. It has also produced an even more surprising number of politicians, and since cartoonists thrive on the activities of politicians and the volume of politicians shows no sign of decreasing, the ecological balance is probably maintained by a symbiotic arrangement whereby the organisms depend for their existence on nourishment derived from each other." [104]

To the eternal astonishment of cartoonists, many politicians rush to purchase cartoons so unflattering that, had the ideas or inferences appeared in type, they would have been seeking legal advice just as quickly.

Certainly, politicians benefit from the attention of cartoonists as they scramble up the 'greasy pole'. It is a very rare cabinet minister's office that is not decorated with cartoon originals. Backbenchers' walls are decorated differently only because they have yet to arrive or catch the attention of cartoonists, which is often the very same thing. Famously, savage British caricaturist Gerald Scarfe – who drew Margaret Thatcher as an axe beheading the unemployed and Harold Wilson as a toad – has said: "Most politicians would rather be caricatured as a glob of phlegm dripping off a barbed wire fence than not be drawn at all." [105]

Cartoonists greatly regret the passing of prime ministers, particularly those more distinctive in terms of appearance as well as policy. When Minhinnick heard that Muldoon was leaving politics he said: "I felt a spasm; I just had to do one." [106]

Cartoons have caught and preserved the essence of many New Zealand premiers and prime ministers. Early New Zealand cartoonists dressed Seddon with a PC (Privy Councillor) fob prominently on his ample chest as they had him stalking, swaggering and strutting the political stage. As R M Burdon wrote about Massey: "Cartoonists turned to good account the Premier's bulky figure, round red choleric face and white moustache. He not only played but looked the part of a farmer turned politician, and, as leader of a party largely representative of agrarian interests, his bucolic appearance was a decided asset." [107] Joseph Ward's biographer, Michael Bassett wrote: ".... The cartoonist David Low said that Ward

ABOUT 1969 –70

HOW MULDOON CHANGED IN MY CARTOONS THROUGH THE YEARS

← 1993

Eric Heath, Dominion, *1969-1993 (ATL ref: DX-015-001)*

'always dressed as though he had a lunch engagement at Downing Street'." [108]

Former PM Marshall wrote: "Cartoonists delight to exaggerate peculiarities and idiosyncrasies, and always complained that I was difficult to cartoon because I looked too ordinary, but that did not stop them trying to make the best of a bad job." [109]

Cartoonists of the Muldoon era were more than happy to concentrate on his distinctive physiognomy – the chin, large head and dimpled cheek. Muldoon, despite the tough, aggressive public image, was sensitive about his appearance and size and, increasingly, he did not handle pointed criticism well. Tom Scott, one-time *Listener* political columnist as well as cartoonist, said: "I quickly realised I could give more offence with the cartoons. Muldoon was not happy when I drew him with fingers barely out of his sleeve, a little trolley on wheels." [110] Peter Bromhead's cartoons about Muldoon's smearing of Labour MP Colin Moyle's reputation were far more direct and to the point than any newspaper editorial would have dared to go.

From the time Thomas Nast's relentless political cartoon campaign in *Harper's Weekly* in the 1870s ended the career of the infamous New York politician William Marcy Tweed to the present day, cartoons have always been able to make a political point much more robustly than the printed word. New Zealand politicians, and Muldoon was no exception, have regularly sued the print and electronic media for aspersions supposedly cast.

Sir Geoffrey Palmer, speaking at the Cartoonists' Convention at the National Library in Wellington in June 2001, said: "History suggests that cartoonists – who often deal savagely with politicians and others – are relatively safe. The Press Council receives a number of complaints about cartoons, but that's usually as far as it goes. A cartoon is, after all, an analogy and cartoonists are generally on safe ground as long as they express genuine opinions." [111] (A 1992 law change had replaced the 'fair comment' with the stronger 'honest opinion' defence.)

There is only one New Zealand instance of a court case involving a political cartoon. In 1911, William Massey, then leader of the opposition, sued the *NZ Times* over a cartoon he claimed portrayed him as a liar and responsible for mean and despicable acts. The jury concurred that the cartoon did indeed depict Massey in the way alleged but, being political comment, was not libellous.

A study of Muldoon's treatment by cartoonists over the nine years he held the top two political posts is an interesting indicator of hardening public attitudes. As Karl du Fresne wrote in a catalogue introduction to a 1994 exhibition of Eric Heath's

There is nothing a cartoonist likes less than a bland and regularly featured prime minister. Peter Bromhead, Auckland Star, November 27 1981. (ATL ref: A-330-091)

Dominion cartoons: "On a savagery scale of one to ten he probably rates a two, at best (or worst, depending on one's perspective)." [112] Yet Heath found, as he recorded in a personal scrapbook, that the way he drew Muldoon changed over the years – the caricature becoming markedly more savage.

Today, political cartoons are particularly instructive and insightful because they 'cut to the chase', stripping away both the wordy humbug of politicians and the fabrications of the armies of spin doctors they now employ.

Ian F Grant
September 2003

1

HENRY SEWELL
1807-1879

"His mind had breadth, but it was slippery, and unable to grasp great principles"

In recent times there has been amused, even scornful, comment on the length of the Palmer and Moore ministries after David Lange resigned in 1989, but they had lengthy tenures compared to the country's first two ministries in 1856.

While some, including Guy Scholefield, editor of the first *Dictionary of New Zealand Biography*, have viewed James Edward FitzGerald as the country's first premier, this is partly semantics, partly disagreement about the constitutional conditions necessary for a genuine premiership. It is now generally accepted that the honour belonged, however briefly, to Henry Sewell.

Henry Sewell was 45 years old when he first arrived in New Zealand. He was not held here by a passion for colonising a new land; as a man of literary and cultural

Chicane (Mark Winter), 2003.
(ATL ref: A-230-041)

interests, his enthusiasm for the rough and sometimes acrimonious colonial society was decidedly muted. He spent only 17 years in New Zealand, including two lengthy return visits to England. If anything it was his interest in land transfer systems, his journeyman competence as a politician and some success in land dealings that kept him in New Zealand.

While several of his brothers had distinguished academic careers and his sister Elizabeth was well known for her novels and devotional books, Henry Sewell remained firmly in the shadow of his father, steward of the Isle of Wight. After qualifying as a

solicitor he spent two decades in estate management and court work in his father's firm. It was only when Lucy, his first wife and mother of his six children, died that Sewell went to London and through some minor personal and family connections became involved in the embryonic Canterbury Association. He saw the new colony as an opportunity to give life to his theories about registering land titles under the supervision of legally-qualified registrars.

By 1850 the Canterbury Association faced a number of financial and political problems, not the least the winding up of the New Zealand Company which had acted as its agent in reserving land in the colony, so the Association's leaders decided to appoint a salaried deputy-chairman who could deal effectively with the Colonial Office.

Edward Gibbon Wakefield's approach to Sewell marked the beginning of a long, often difficult relationship. For the next two years Sewell was the Association's energetic chief executive officer in London while John Robert Godley continued as its agent in New Zealand.

Sewell, now married again, changed his mind several times about whether or not to visit New Zealand. What finally decided the issue was the passing, in June 1852, of the New Zealand Constitution Act, which would lead to the province of Canterbury, and the need for some suitably qualified person to negotiate the transfer of the

Association's assets and powers to the new province. In October, the Sewells sailed to New Zealand in the company of Edward Gibbon Wakefield, who was finally visiting one of the six Australasian colonies he had played a crucial role in establishing.

The *Minerva* slipped into Lyttelton harbour on the second day of February 1853. His first impressions, recorded in his diary, were typical of his basically unsympathetic attitude to pioneer life in a new colony; it was less than two years since the first settlers had arrived, but Sewell was not impressed with what he saw: "Was much struck with the laziness and stagnation of the place. Nobody stirring at half-past seven .... I can hardly tell what my first impressions were. I think the main idea was of newness and unfinishedness. Streets laid out without pavements – Roads unmacadamised. Small low Sheds serving for Shops and dwellings – Gardens only half cultivated – rough palings – Little white wooden buildings dotted here and there on the spurs of the hills apparently without method or order – Everything in short appearing as if done yesterday in a great hurry...." [1]

He was also taken aback by the brash egalitarianism he encountered. "Colonial manners are mightily republican. The fashion of Servants is to speak of their fellow Servants and labourers as Mr and Mrs, but of gentlefolks by their surnames only." [2]

As his confidence grew along with his grasp of the legal issues facing the young colony, his fundamental indecisiveness and lack of any strong personal conviction were less noticeable. Charles Bowen, the inspector of police in Canterbury, was however a shrewd judge of character. In a letter to Godley, now returned to England, Bowen gave his impressions of Sewell: "He is an example of what an honest man may come to by being a solicitor. Besides all this he is always in a diluted state.... I should recommend him to take tonics, eschew long letter writing, and to fight a man of his own weight every morning before breakfast just to give him a little decision ...." [3]

Nevertheless, during the next three years, despite distrustful colonists, sometimes hostile clergy and an unhelpful Governor George Grey, Sewell managed to wind up the affairs of the Association to the relative satisfaction of the Canterbury Provincial Council, the clergy (forced to modify their ambitious church and school hopes), the government in Auckland, and those back in England who had loaned sizeable sums of money. One outcome of the ecclesiastical settlement was the establishment of Christ's College.

Scholefield wrote: "Sewell had intended to return to England in 1855 but, being invited by the inhabitants of Canterbury, he was not able to resist the temptation to participate in provincial politics." [4] He was not popular but his dogged determination was quickly recognised and, later in 1853, he was comfortably elected as the member for Christchurch in the first election for the new General Assembly.

Since 1840 an executive council of appointed members, chaired by the governor, had run the country but in 1853 about 30,000 voters elected the first members to provincial councils and then, later in the year, to the General Assembly. There were 37 members in the new House of Representatives, with 18 of them elected unopposed. Meeting for the first time in Auckland in May 1854, and with only one vote in opposition, the General Assembly demanded responsible as well as representative government, or control over who served on the executive ministry appointed by the governor and what they did.

The administrator since Governor George Grey left New Zealand on leave at the end of 1853, Colonel Robert Wynyard, was a soldier uncomfortably out of his depth, trying to grapple with both constitutional issues and the quicksilver minds and quick tempers of some of the leading parliamentarians. In an attempted compromise, he appointed a mixed ministry of officials and three elected politicians in June 1854. Headed by FitzGerald, who had arrived in Lyttelton on the *Charlotte Jane* in late 1850 and became editor of the *Lyttelton Times* and then Canterbury superintendent, the three politicians were given desks in the government survey office in Auckland. ".... We three sat down together to make a government," [5] Sewell, a tireless diarist, wrote. The third politician was Frederick Weld, who was also to be premier subsequently. However, after six unsatisfactory weeks the trio was in no doubt that the real power remained with the officials and they resigned.

Another politician, the scarcely remembered Auckland draper Thomas Forsaith, was then prodded, with two other colleagues, into leading another mixed ministry that lasted three days without any claimant to the premiership. For the next year, in the absence of FitzGerald, who had angina problems, Sewell took charge in the House of Representatives when it was in session. During that year, at the end of March 1855, a dispatch from England contained the welcome, but expected, news that Her Majesty's Government had "no objection whatever" to responsible government.

In September 1855 Governor Gore Browne arrived in New Zealand. Before the end of the year he called the first election under the system that has remained substantially unchanged ever since and in May 1856 Henry Sewell formed the first, short-lived responsible ministry.

As Sewell made the lengthy, tedious voyage to

Auckland via Wellington, Nelson and New Plymouth for the General Assembly, he gave sustained thought to the future of responsible government, now imminent, and particularly the financial relationship between the centre and the provinces. Within a day of arriving in mid-April 1856, Sewell was asked by Gore Browne to form the first responsible ministry as FitzGerald remained in poor health. Sewell demurred then, in the absence of anyone better qualified, agreed. He announced the members of his ministry on May 7 – and resigned on May 20, after factions in the House had refused acceptance of parts of his Address in Reply that dealt with the relationship between the provinces and what was called the 'general government'. His strong belief that, while they would be delegated powers in many areas and would control land policy, the provinces must be ultimately subordinate to the centre, but his cogent expression of these views did not convince a narrow majority of committed 'provincialists'.

During a fortnight of attempted deals and brief, unlikely alliances that made the first attempts at MMP coalition-making in 1996 look very tame, Sewell continued, as a temporary colonial secretary, to conduct government business. When William Fox, a leading 'provincialist', became New Zealand's second premier, in practice his policies differed very little from those proposed by Sewell. His first ministry was to be equally short lived.

William Gisborne, perceptive colonial official and politician observed of Sewell: "He was a man of culture and of considerable ability; and his conversation sparkled with cleverness and wit .... He was remarkably quick in seeing the points of a complicated subject, though in treating it he used too much the arts of the advocate. His speeches, though occasionally eloquent and effective, often had the flavour of forensic insincerity.... His nature was supple and pliant; it was not robust enough to stand alone, but clung to natures of stronger fibre and a firmer growth. His mind had breadth, but it was slippery, and unable to grasp great principles; its strength was dissipated on small things .... The political stage was to him what the warren is to the rabbit: he was ever dodging in and out of holes .... He was fond of office; and he was not exclusive in his political associations." [6]

Henry Sewell was not premier again, but he sat in the General Assembly for a total of 11 years – four in the House of Representatives and a further seven in the nominated upper house, the Legislative Council. His durability and usefulness were remarkable.

Aside from his own brief ministry, he served in other 'responsible' ministries headed by Edward Stafford, William Fox, Alfred Domett and Frederick Weld, usually as attorney general, before finally leaving politics in 1873.

As Scholefield commented: "Sewell always faced the rising sun. Each new premier as he took office seemed to him to be the only possible premier, and Sewell himself the only possible attorney-general." [7]

He remained a 'centralist' at heart but, with the need to make a living more pressing than personal political beliefs, he served in the ministries of the most determined 'provincialists' with seeming equanimity. He also pioneered loan and shipping negotiations in Australia and England in 1857-58 and in fulfillment of his arcane passion for land title systems, became the country's first registrar general of lands in 1860.

Henry and Elizabeth Sewell left New Zealand in 1876, and he died in England three years later.

W P Morrell wrote: "He was a good man of business .... and he had already shown in 1854 that besides his talent for administration he possessed unusual talent for debate. But there was something lacking in him too. It was found that, though fond of office, he had no fixity of purpose. A little too conscious, perhaps, of his abilities, he was yet not robust enough for leadership, and never really won the confidence either of the House or of the country." [8]

David McIntyre has observed that Sewell was lonely, pessimistic and snobbish. He also wrote: ".... he was a tireless correspondent, negotiator and committee man, a great drafter of bills and resolutions. He was the chief 'man of business' in the first New Zealand Parliament." [9]

2

SIR WILLIAM FOX
1812-1893

"In his public life he was a complex and often contradictory personality"

In many ways, New Zealand's first and second premiers could hardly have been more different. Sewell was a middle-aged, accidental and unenthusiastic colonist; William Fox young and passionately committed when he sailed for New Zealand. Sewell believed central government should be accorded primacy; Fox was a devoted provincialist.

It was this critical political difference that led to the collapse of Sewell's ministry and the next equally short-lived one headed by William Fox. In May 1856, Sewell's mild and sensible plan to shore up central authority in key areas was defeated in the House of Representatives following motions proposed by Fox. After Edward Stafford failed to rally sufficient like-minded members, William Fox became premier on May 20. He was not so much defeated, just a fortnight later, by a regrouping of the centralists than by small cabals and individuals with a multiplicity of agendas.

See the great teetotaller, William—
See the lawyer, politician,
Full of rage and spleen and bitters,
In the throes of composition!

William Blomfield, The Observer & Free Lance, *May 23 1891. (ATL ref: H-722-086-1)*

Henry Sewell was premier only once, William Fox, an ardent provincialist for most of his political career, was to hold office a total of four times over a span of 17 years.

The third son of George Townshend Fox, deputy-lieutenant of Durham, and Ann Stote Crofton, William Fox had a comfortable county childhood. He was educated locally and then at Oxford before reading for the Bar at the Inner Temple and making a close study of colonisation. After marrying Sarah Halcomb in 1842, he immediately bought passages for New Zealand, at the same time publishing a short booklet setting out his reasons for leaving for the bottom of the world.

When he and his wife arrived in Wellington in November 1842, William Fox, now 30 years old, expected to practice the law. However, the expectation was short lived as Fox considered the chief justice's requirement that he should swear an oath disclaiming any previous wrong doings an insult to his profession and to him as a gentleman. Instead, he became editor of *The New Zealand Gazette and Wellington Spectator*, championing the rights of New Zealand Company settlers in their disputes with the embryonic Auckland-based central government.

In 1843 he joined a party of gentlemen explorers searching for farming land in the Wairarapa and exploration of his adopted land remained a passion after he replaced the murdered Captain Arthur Wakefield as the New Zealand Company's resident agent in Nelson. After restoring calm he pioneered, early in 1845, a route between Nelson and the Wairau plains. In 1846 he explored the region extensively in the company of Thomas Brunner and Charles Heaphy.

Temperance was already of consuming interest. Keith Sinclair wrote: "In 1847 William Fox, a Wellingtonian, was appalled to learn that in Auckland there was one conviction for drunkeness for every eight persons."[1] His views were to remain consistent, unlike his flip-flopping approaches to central government and Maori land ownership.

The next year, following Colonel William Wakefield's death, Fox was appointed the New Zealand

Company's principal agent. After a bid to buy land in the Wairarapa failed, he travelled to the South Island in search of a site for the Canterbury Association. He also bought 5,000 acres for himself in the Rangitikei district north west of Wellington. Half he divided into small farms, making them available on deferred payment to poor settlers.

In 1851 the New Zealand Company gave up its charter and William Fox returned to England with the winding up documents. While there he advised the Colonial Office on the drafting of the New Zealand Constitution Bill. He published another book, *The Six Colonies of New Zealand*, in which he "set out in admirably clear prose the constitutional aims of the southern associations for British politicians and public to read, uncluttered by Sir George Grey's denigrating and self-justifying commentaries."[2]

He returned to the Southern Hemisphere via Canada and the United States where his interest in republicanism, the temperance movement and the secret ballot were further stimulated.

Back in New Zealand he joined the Wellington Provincial Council in 1854, his service until 1862 underlining his commitment to the region where he had settled. He was particularly persuasive in stopping outer districts attempting to become separate provinces. Fox's devotion to Wellington nettled Henry Sewell: "Fox might be the most important man in New Zealand, but as far as one can judge, he declines it."[3]

An accomplished explorer on foot, Fox might have been excused a lack of enthusiasm for the tedious, lengthy and sometimes dangerous sea voyages to the early parliamentary sessions in Auckland. Sewell himself describes, in a long, colourful diary entry, the 12 day odyssey from Canterbury to the first General Assembly session in 1854 via Wellington, Nelson and New Plymouth.

Fox was elected to the General Assembly for the first time in November 1855, as member for Wanganui, and was premier less than six months later. His first ministry was out of power before anything could be achieved and he would have willingly retired permanently to his farm except for his anger at the way Taranaki and Waikato Maori were being treated.

As the Taranaki situation worsened he led the parliamentary opposition to the Stafford government's policies that resulted in war in the province, beginning with the shelling of Wiremu Kingi's pa in March 1860.

When Stafford was defeated on a confidence motion by one vote in mid-July 1861 Fox was in charge again. Shortly afterwards Governor Gore Browne's six year term ended and his successor was also his predecessor – Sir George Grey. Fox and Grey had had an uneasy relationship previously but now their shared concern for the Maori drew them closer and they agreed in principle that the government should take full responsibility for 'native affairs'. Yet, in July 1862, when Fox sought to re-affirm this long-held view in the House, opposition members managed, with the help of the speaker's casting vote, to defeat him, arguing that it would stop the governor from acting decisively.

James FitzGerald declined to form a ministry, deferring to Alfred Domett, who was not known for his Maori sympathies. Domett lasted an ineffectual year before being replaced by Frederick Whitaker, a member of the Legislative Council, in October 1863. It has been said that Whitaker defined as a rebel any Maori whose land he wished to confiscate. His long-time law partner Thomas Russell, a land speculator of similar views, was defence minister.

Inexplicably, Fox, who had intended to travel overseas, was persuaded by Governor Grey to join this ministry as leader of the House, colonial secretary and native minister. Guy Scholefield wrote: "With too great deference to his comrades Fox was led into a native policy which seemed in direct opposition to all that he had stood for."[4]

In explanation it has been argued that, while he believed

The Modern Don Quixote. *After Fox lost his parliamentary seat in 1881, he concentrated his energies on social concerns. William Hutchison,* The Wellington Advertiser Supplement, *December 24 1881. (ATL ref: A-095-012)*

Taranaki Maori to have been unjustly treated, the uprising in the Waikato was nothing short of rebellion. Certainly he used his journalistic skills to defend the ministry's policy, including land confiscation, against English criticism.

At the time, Crosbie Ward, newspaper owner, politician and former supporter, said of Fox that he was "one of those enlightened men who despise consistency as a sign of a weak, if not imbecile mind". [5] It is unlikely that Fox had many regrets when the Whitaker ministry fell in October 1864. He resigned his seat early in 1865 and then spent three years in England and the United States where, in the state of Maine, he took particular interest in liquor control experiments.

During Fox's absence Frederick Weld's short ministry championed a 'self-reliant policy', Stafford began his second ministry in October 1865 and there were strong separatist movements in Auckland and Otago and constant demand for greater provincial autonomy. Stafford, in 1867, created four Maori electorates, to provide "a voice in the administration of the Colony", balanced by four additional European seats for miners of no permanent abode.

When William Fox returned to New Zealand in 1868, he was in no haste to resume his parliamentary career. It was not long, however, before a member resigned to facilitate his return to the House and, invigorated by his absence and travels, he was soon energetically leading the opposition, promoting a welter of motions of no-confidence. As Raewyn Dalziel wrote: "Fox had two lines of attack on the Government. He could criticise them for failing to keep the peace and he could accuse them of war on the provinces. He took full advantage of both opportunities." [6]

In June 1869 Fox was premier for the third time, heading a generally pro-Maori ministry including Donald McLean, long-time government land purchase officer and Julius Vogel, a 35 year old ambitious to govern more expansively. McLean, who spoke the language and knew all the prominent Maori leaders, played a major part in extinguishing the lingering embers of the Waikato War and Fox, now nearly 60, had the satisfaction of seeing his long-wanted secret ballot introduced for the European seats at the 1870 House of Representatives election. He retained the leadership after the election but, increasingly, Vogel was the ministry's dominant personality. As Scholefield wrote, unkindly but with some truth: "Anybody might call himself premier so long as they would dance to Vogel's tune and let him leave the Colony whenever he felt inclined." [7] Perhaps more accurately, "Fox became a follower, accepting Vogel's idea of borrowing overseas to develop the colony." [8]

William Fox's enthusiasm for politics had been waning for some time but, amenable as ever, he

Old Reynard's Last Transformation. 'He congregations sought of fowls'. *Cartoonists liked to draw the four times premier as a wily old fox. J H Wallis,* New Zealand Punch, *(Wellington),January 21 1880. (ATL ref: H-693-020)*

provided a more acceptable public face for ministries in which Julius Vogel, conscious that his Jewish race and brashness were unpopular, began to implement his policies and consolidate his power.

The ministry, now only nominally led by Fox, was defeated in September 1872. Edward Stafford was again briefly premier before Fox, not wanting office again, recommended George Waterhouse and he became titular head of the second ministry dominated by Vogel, who controlled the purse-strings as treasurer. Their working relationship broke down barely three months later, and Fox served a fourth term, just a month long, as a stopgap measure while Vogel returned from abroad.

However, he was in the House of Representatives when it became obvious that the provinces he had supported so vigorously would be abolished, telling his colleagues "he was 'content … to be one of the pall-bearers of provincialism'." [9] He was overseas when the legislation passed in late 1876.

If Fox's knighthood (KCMG) in 1879 was acknowledgement of decades of public service, he was still to make a significant contribution in the early 1880s, first as one of the two West Coast commissioners investigating disputed land claims in Taranaki and then ensuring their recommendations were carried out, including the return of a significant acreage to Maori ownership.

Although he was in and out of Parliament until 1881, by now Fox had directed his considerable energy and intelligence to social issues, most particularly prohibition. In 1886 he was one of the founders of the New Zealand Alliance, modelled on a similar organisation in England, and remained its president until he died in June 1893, a year after his wife Sarah.

The couple had no children, but their adoption of a young Maori boy, Ngatau Omahura, captured in the Taranaki bush in 1868, perplexed fellow colonists at the time, and was the subject of a book – *The Fox Boy* – over 130 years later.

William Fox's political career has received mixed reviews. As Jill Trevelyan wrote: " … in his public life he was a complex and often contradictory personality. As New Zealand Company agent, he was completely unsympathetic to Maori aspirations, yet later, as native minister and premier, he became deeply involved in Maori issues and seems to have been sincere in his attempts to resolve grievances." [10]

William Gisborne wrote: "Sir Edward Stafford distinguished himself as the leader of the Government, while Sir William Fox was eminent as the leader of the Opposition.…. Aggressiveness was the law of his nature ….Impetuous, vehement, unrivalled in sarcasm and in force of invective, and always eager for the fray, he had at his command eloquence, humour, political knowledge, debating power, and all the artillery of attack. He was the very man to be placed in the forefront of a party fight, when, as in the case of the Opposition, there is comparatively small responsibility, and great room for brilliant execution." [11]

W P Morrell agreed that he made a formidable opponent for any premier: "On the other hand, his impulsiveness, his lack of discretion, and his tendency to run to extremes made him far less successful when in office himself. He was hardly capable of himself initiating and carrying through a great stroke of policy." [12]

His reputation as an artist is much more positive. It was not so unusual for someone of Fox's class and culture to have some artistic pretensions; but it was unusual that this very physical colonist (he climbed Mt Egmont in his 80th year) and acerbic politician should be such an accomplished watercolourist, his work better known and appreciated today than during his lifetime. As Trevelyan wrote, Fox's commitment to the business of colonisation was evident in his art. "This fascination is plain in his watercolours, with their meticulous rendering of the signs of settlement: houses, churches, enclosures, ships, livestock, crops, and jaunty colonists. But at their best, his serene and beautiful watercolurs are more than a mere description of the colonising process. Fox's art represents the private vision of a complex 19th century man, whose image of an ideal New Zealand sustained him through a long and turbulent career in the colony." [13]

Raewyn Dalziel and Keith Sinclair have the measure of the man. "He knew what he did not like, but had little positive vision of what he did want. Consequently, more determined men, who did know what they wanted, could dominate him. He was not a great leader … but few New Zealand leaders have made a mark in so many areas – constitutional development, politics, social reform, painting and exploration." [14]

Act 2. *Fox, the ardent prohibitionist, spent much of the 1880s jousting with brewing interests. William Blomfield,* The Observer & Free Lance, *February 23 1889. (ATL ref: H-722-028)*

3

SIR EDWARD WILLIAM STAFFORD
1819-1901

"Cautious without timidity, bold without rashness, self-confident without jealousy of others"

Edward Stafford was, unlike nearly all his contemporaries, much more comfortable as premier than as a duty-bound parliamentarian. He never served in any other than his own ministries and then for nearly nine years, in total longer than the eight ministries led by William Fox and Harry Atkinson. At a time when politics was very much a constantly changing kaleidoscope of temporary coalitions forming around individuals and cabals sharing similar if hazily defined views, Stafford was very much his own man. He might have been considered arrogant, but he was also the most accomplished politician of his era. His particular brand of "pragmatic moderation", as his biographer Edmund Bohan puts it, was the cement that kept his ministries from crumbling as nearly all others did during the period.

Detail from 'The Dismissal', cartoonist unknown, Auckland Punch, *April 3 1869. (ATL ref: H-686-012-1)*

He became as devoted to the premiership as he had, initially a little begrudgingly, to playing a leading role in the political and social life of the communities he lived in. He was not a passionate New Zealander and his strong interest in constitutional history and government would probably have led to the same contribution to public life if chance and circumstances had resulted in him settling in Australia or, perhaps, Canada.

Stafford was born in Edinburgh in 1819, the eldest son of Berkeley Buckingham Stafford, an Irish squire, and Anne Tytler. His then prosperous Irish Protestant antecedents had long been established in County Louth, but he was to become equally familiar with the land of his Scottish mother, a member of the intellectually formidable Tytler family. His passion for riding and hunting may have been a reason why, despite his intelligence and undoubted ability, he was to leave Trinity College, Dublin without a degree. As it turned out, his skills as a jockey and ability to judge and breed bloodstock were to be of more durable value in New Zealand than his flair for Greek composition.

He came to New Zealand in 1843, rather more by accident than design. He had travelled to Australia with young cousins and then, after a period, on to Nelson, where he found a congenial group of young 'gentlemen' of moderate means but unbounded enthusiasm for exploring and profiting in this picturesque yet challenging corner of Empire.

Barely six months later Stafford was sufficiently involved in politics to move Nelson's vote of no confidence in Governor FitzRoy's response to the killing of Captain Arthur Wakefield and 20 settlers at Wairau.

When his father died in 1847, Stafford, as the eldest son, accepted responsibility for considerable estate debts in Ireland and the support of spinster aunts and sisters. This gave added urgency to the profitable growth of his sheep-farming and horse-breeding activities.

Although not a supporter of provincial government Stafford became Nelson's first superintendent in 1853. In that role he was arguably the most successful in the country. There was derision when Stafford appeared at the Provincial Council's opening session resplendent in formal coat and cocked hat; there was to be envy in other parts of New Zealand as he skillfully managed Nelson's affairs, pioneering a free, secular and compulsory education system, building roads and running a public works programme without recourse to loans. Ironically, given his centralist leanings, the cocked hat incident was never entirely forgotten. As Edmund Bohan wrote: "That cocked hat was to remain the symbol of the follies of a system by which small local councils – or fishing villages as Stafford himself was later to describe them – appropriated to themselves the style and trappings of full-blown parliaments." [1]

New Zealand's passage from 'representative' to 'responsible' government between 1854-56 was a messy business. Stafford's stated reason for not being a candidate for the first General Assembly in Auckland in 1854 was his belief that it was wrong to hold colonial and provincial office at the same time. However, this principle did not inhibit him in late 1855 from becoming the member for Nelson Town in the first settler-controlled parliament. Stafford coolly resisted efforts to involve him in the first two brief and floundering ministries led by Henry Sewell and William Fox. With his principal rivals shown wanting, Stafford was in a much stronger position when he become the country's third premier on June 2 1856.

Alfred Saunders wrote: "Mr Stafford had few – if any – warm personal friends in the House, he was not a prime favourite even with the Governor, and no House would long consent that the strongest half of his Ministry should be taken from the Legislative Council. But Mr Stafford was not an infant to be frightened from his post by the crack of a whip. He knew that he had been sent for, not because he was loved, but because he was needed." [2]

Bohan concurred: "He had convinced riven and partisan Auckland that he was less dangerous than Fox, and provincialist Wellington that he was less menacing than Sewell; significantly he had given his rivals their chances to fail. In this first parliamentary era, with its confusion of personalities, interests and shifting cabals, Stafford was in his element." [3]

From the beginning his vision was national rather than parochial and his 1856 'Compact' took a clear-headed view of the highly-charged issue of the financial relationship between the central and provincial governments, and cleared away the long-festering problem of the New Zealand Company's debt.

Stafford began cabinet government in New Zealand, he and his ministers meeting privately without the governor. He also favoured ministers participating in a rough and tumble House of Representatives rather than remaining aloof and unchallenged as Executive Council appointees.

Bohan wrote: "His wide knowledge of constitutional history and contemporary government gave him an unmatched awareness of how the new parliamentary

THE NEW ZEALAND BISMARCK.—RE-ARRANGING THE MAP OF THE COLONY.
[After the manner of the PRUSSIAN BISMARCK.]

There was strong separatist sentiment in Otago when Stafford began his second ministry in 1866. Cartoonist unknown, Otago Punch, *September 8 1866. (ATL ref: H-686-004)*

system ought to develop, and of the need to pass a body of specifically New Zealand law. In 1856 a total of 36 acts were passed and in the following session, in 1858, a further 86." [4]

In those days, with travel between the country's isolated settlements lengthy and uncomfortable, the General Assembly met every two years. Life was much more measured and there was no media industry, insatiable for 'instant' news. It may seem extraordinary now, but it was not considered unusual for a premier to absent himself from the country for considerable periods, as Stafford did in 1858-59.

Although he had appointed the country's first immigration agent while in London, Stafford did not favour confiscation to appease land-hungry settlers. But it was during this absence that Governor Gore Browne, who had retained control of Maori affairs, forced the sale of land on the Waitara Plains, with minimal opposition from Stafford's ministerial colleagues. This and other short-sighted decisions precipitated a costly, divisive war, but Stafford resisted the temptation to resign, showing more of a concern for the concept of ministerial responsibility than some of his successors. Stafford's administration limped on until mid-1861 when Fox defeated him, capitalising on recession, resentment at legislation that weakened the influence of the original provinces and doubts about Stafford's commitment to fighting the Maori.

Raewyn Dalziel wrote: "A sound administrator, cautious and prudent in finance, Stafford had been the only man who could contain the friction caused by provincial and personal rivalries, but he lacked the political acumen and flair to remain in power in war-time." [5]

Stafford had married for the second time in 1859. His first wife, Emily Charlotte, the daughter of Colonel William Wakefield, was only 18 when they married in Wellington in 1846. It had been a love match and Stafford was privately distraught but publicly stoical when she died in 1857. Bohan wrote: "For all his constant political, sporting and business endeavour, for all his public skills in dealing with men and women, he had grown in his maturity into an essentially solitary and private soul driven by the urges to make his fortune and to be politically dominant." [6] Two years later he married Mary, the politically astute daughter of Thomas Bartley, Auckland barrister and Legislative Council speaker. They were to have six children.

The old pattern of short-lived ministries returned until late 1865 when Stafford shrewdly judged his fellow politicians and the public were ready again for a period of stable, sensible administration. He accepted the premiership but, having few political friends left, quickly called for a dissolution. Until Governor Grey granted it he virtually ran the administration single-

Nolens Volens. Sir G-e B-n: 'What can I possibly say to all these petitions?'
Mr St-ff-d: 'Say, Your Excellency? Say that here I am and here I mean to stop.'
After more than three years in power, Stafford's support was wavering. Cartoonist unknown, Auckland Punch, *January 30 1869. (ATL ref: H-686-010)*

handedly as colonial secretary, treasurer and postmaster general; he also personally supervised the embryonic civil service.

Scholefield wrote: "He began without a single minister who had cabinet experience, and he knew he was only there because the country needed him, not because Parliament wanted him …. Since he was the only Premier who had ever held office long enough to learn the work, he had to flog himself harder than ever to care for the key portfolios." [7]

While this might have been further evidence of his immense self-confidence, voters at the 1866 election could not ignore his political and economic acumen. Securely in power, he now appointed able ministers, mostly leading provincialists. This effectively weakened opposition to his centralist policies.

The land wars, that he had feared and opposed, continued to be a financial strain, but Stafford managed to cut military expenditure while building up the colonial forces and militia and weathering the threats represented by Te Kooti in Poverty Bay and Titokowaru's initially successful campaigns in Taranaki and Wanganui.

In mid-June 1869 Stafford was defeated in the General Assembly, this time the Governor refusing him a dissolution and opportunity to rally his now tattered support.

Stafford's 1866-69 ministry has been assessed less favourably than it deserved. Bohan wrote: "Its positive achievements in finance with the consolidation of loans and reforms in Treasury have been down-played or overlooked, its administrative ability has been ignored and its Maori policy and defence management have been undervalued or misunderstood." [8]

In the unaccustomed position of opposition leader, Stafford then attacked the administration, if not the principles, of Vogel's public works and immigration schemes. Vogel, premier in fact if not yet in name, gradually lost support as Stafford displayed his superior skills in debating and grasp of administrative detail. But he, in turn, was unable to hold together his third and final ministry, in September-October 1872, for more than a month.

Stafford was a small, wiry man with an abundance of nervous energy and, in spite of the mental and physical rigours of nine years as premier, applied the same intensity to a wide range of other interests on the increasingly rare occasions when there was time to do so. Scholefield wrote: "The trainer Edward Cutts is said to have considered Stafford an unequalled judge of horseflesh and the best jockey in New Zealand." [9] Edward Wakefield, a long-time family friend, noted: "He was 'never happier than when laying out a garden, or among his cattle, or giving free scope to his singular aptitude for forestry; and as fond of society as he well could be; it was no trifling self-denial on his part to abjure all these things'." [10]

The two long ministries Stafford energetically led largely set up and then consolidated responsible government in New Zealand, enacting much of the foundation legislation that the country was subsequently built on and nurturing the beginnings of a civil service that was to grow enormously in size and power.

In 1866, as Bohan wrote, the civil service was over-staffed, poorly organised and without clear career paths. "Stafford's reforms hit the civil service hard and many officials became redundant as departments were ruthlessly trimmed to reduce spending. Government agents felt the cold blast too as Commissariat funds, hitherto easy pickings for the unscrupulous, were at last brought under control." [11] Stafford stayed on in Parliament for another five years. Refusing offers to lead or be in several mooted ministries, his principal preoccupation was a concerted campaign aimed at the abolition of the provinces. He had hoped to return to Britain as New Zealand's agent-general in London, but Vogel took the plum job himself.

This, together with his dislike of George Grey, now premier, was enough for Edward Stafford to move permanently to England in 1878 and devote the rest of his life to business and family affairs. On arrival there he was awarded the KCMG but, weary of public life, turned down the governorships of Madras and Queensland. Edward Stafford died in London in February 1901, little over a year after his wife Mary.

Two men who worked closely with Stafford – William Gisborne, who assisted with the reform of the civil service and Edward Wakefield, who was the country's first cabinet secretary – wrote perceptively about their one-time boss.

Gisborne wrote: "Sir Edward Stafford has a well-balanced mind, characterized by what is called the 'golden mean', that rare and valuable statesmanlike quality. Cautious without timidity, bold without rashness, self-confident without jealousy of others, and not unwilling to take good advice, fond of personal power, but careful to use it legitimately, he has good judgment, a tenacious memory, a broad grasp of politics, and a fair knowledge of men." [12]

When Stafford left New Zealand for the last time, Wakefield wrote: " ' .... His judgement of the ultimate issue of any political operation never was seriously at fault; even though the emergencies of the hour might compel him, perhaps, to deal with surrounding conditions as if counting on a different result. This is the vital quality of statesmanship and this Mr Stafford alone has displayed of all those in New Zealand's first political generation.'" [13]

Rather a poser. Friendly native: 'Will the great Chief tell me how it is, whilst we go to the front, the Queen's fighting men remain within the towns?' His Excellency: 'Well, you see – that is – ahem – they are retained here at present more for ornament than use.' *Stafford cut military spending by making more use of colonial forces. Cartoonist unknown,* Auckland Punch, *1868. (ATL ref: H-705-016)*

4
ALFRED DOMETT
1811-1887

"He conceived great ideas, but loved to brood over them in poetic solitude"

Alfred Domett was a poet who became a politician, but was a more effective public servant than parliamentarian.

William Gisborne, that shrewd, if sometimes prejudiced observer of the early New Zealand political scene, wrote: "…. in the case of Mr Domett, when I say he was more a poet than a politician, I do not mean to convey the idea that his poetic qualities incapacitated him as a public man; far from it. He abounded in imaginative and creative power, in tender sensibility, in fine taste, in great aims, and in affluence of expression…. What Mr Domett failed in was as a politician in the parliamentary sense, namely as a party man and as a Minister under responsible government. He was a hero-worshiper, and admired splendid autocracy. The seamy side of political life, as seen in the parliamentary system, was not congenial to his taste, and he was not fitted to work out what he regarded as a lower level of public service."[1]

Chicane (Mark Winter), 2003. (ATL ref: A-230-042)

Gisborne also wrote: "….Mr Domett, able as he was, never was a leader of men. He conceived great ideas, but loved to brood over them in poetic solitude, until his mind bodied them forth and launched them living into the world, but he had not the faculty of equally inspiring other men. He was in, but not of, the world of politics."[2]

Domett was born in 1811 in Surrey, England into what would now be called a comfortably middle-class family, his father a ship owner who had been in both the navy and merchant marine. Alfred attended a private school and then Cambridge, publishing a book of poetry and then travelling in North America and the West Indies rather than finishing his degree. Back in England, he studied law with less enthusiasm than he penned sufficient verse for a second volume, and was called to the Bar in 1841.

By now 30 years old, and still restless, he bought land being sold by the New Zealand Company in London, and sailed in the *Sir Charles Forbes* to join his cousin William Curling Young in Nelson. His arrival could not have been more unpromising: his cousin had drowned and the settlers were being frustrated in their attempts to expand beyond the cramped settlement. Yet he quickly found congenial company among the young, educated advent-urers in the community and they found, in him, the ability to effectively articulate and communicate their concerns. He was, in effect, a ready-made 19th century PR practitioner.

He quickly made his reputation, attacking the colony's administrators in Auckland for the Wairau affray, both in person during a deputation sent north by the Nelson settlers and in the pages of the *Nelson Examiner*. Domett became editor of the newspaper for a period, its pages carrying, in late 1845, his blistering attack on Governor FitzRoy, his administration and Colonial Office policy.

This caught the eye of the new governor George Grey who sensibly decided Domett's talents could be more usefully employed working for rather than agin the government. In 1846 he accepted nomination to the Legislative Council, remaining a member through the final years of the crown colony period. More importantly, his long civil service career was launched with his appointment, from 1848 to 1853, as colonial secretary of New Munster province (the southern portion of the North Island and all of the South Island) and then, in November 1851, civil secretary to the general government. He demonstrated his administrative skills by sorting and cataloguing the mass of ordinances passed during the Legislative Council's first 10 sessions, and his generally liberal social views with a pioneering report calling for free, secular and compulsory elementary education.

As Guy Scholefield wrote: "His correspondence with the new settlements at Otago and Canterbury delighted Grey. He wrote a flowing, clerkly hand and with all his dreaminess he showed a sort of methodical habit which was quite useful in the administrative posts to which he succeeded, one after another." [3]

Even in the mid-1850s it was useful to have a specialisation. Domett became an expert on land practices and policies during his colonial secretary years. Jeanine Graham wrote: "Although he was not averse to accumulating a fair degree of property himself, mostly in the Nelson region, Domett deprecated the system whereby wealthy men could choose large tracts of land for speculative rather than productive purposes." [4]

When the crown colony period ended, Domett was promptly gazetted, in early 1854, commissioner of crown lands in Hawke's Bay. While he managed to name a number of Napier streets after poets he admired, the appointment was short-lived. Domett was too far away from the centre of colonial affairs and unaccustomed to being answerable to a higher placed official.

Fortunately Nelson had not forgotten one of its favourite adopted sons, and they elected him to the House of Representatives in 1855. The next year he married Mary George, a widowed Wellington school teacher with children. They had one son. Also in 1856, in what was to be a familiar pattern for Domett, he became the area's commissioner of crown lands. From 1857 to 1863 he served on the Nelson Provincial Council and was provincial secretary. He was re-elected as the member for Nelson city in 1860, holding the seat until he was appointed to the Legislative Council in 1866.

It was during this period that, as a result of power plays among more prominent colleagues and to everyone's surprise, Domett became premier, surviving in the position for a little over a year.

Jane Maria Atkinson, a member of the Richmond-Atkinson clan, wrote in April 1863: "Unfortunately Mr Domett in spite of his fine intellect seems quite unfit to be helmsman in times of difficulty like these. He is letting Mr Bell be the head of the ministry, a man immensely his inferior and not trusted by Mr Domett's supporters. But a limp will, love of ease and a quiet life quite overbalances Mr D's other fine qualities and his Ministry will fall to pieces when the House meets." [5]

It was a time, in 1862-63, when responsibility for 'native' affairs had created a crisis in the relations between the British and colonial authorities. Domett's hard-line on punitive land confiscation seems to have been influenced by his practical and emotional involvement with the consequences of the Wairau affray. Scholefield comments in *Notable New Zealand Statesmen* that even his friend Thomas Arnold "admitted that the gentle poet looked upon the Maori people with Roman rather than Christian eyes". [6] It was his recommendation, in October 1863, that all Taranaki and Waikato tribal land suitable for European occupation should be confiscated, that brought down his shaky ministry.

Keith Sinclair is harsh in his judgment of Domett: "He was not a very good poet; but he was a worse politician. As Premier, he was a mere figure of speech, a rhetorical flourish. Effective power in this ministry ....lay in the hands of two able, efficient sharp Auckland lawyers, Frederick Whitaker and Thomas Russell." [7]

Alfred Domett was uncomfortable with the cut and thrust of parliamentary debate. Clearly he would have failed dismally in the image-obsessed TV era. Gisborne wrote: "His are not the qualities which at once attract admiration and fascinate attention. He does not put his best wares in his shop windows. Only those who penetrate the inner chambers of his mind can see its great powers, its wealth of information, and find themselves in the presence of genius. Fluent in writing, he is embarrassed in speech, and his inability to give full utterance to what he strongly feels leads to the impression that he is somewhat dictatorial and irritable, though in fact, beneath the surface there is depth of gentleness and good nature." [8]

While there was far from universal admiration for his political views on land policy, there was widespread regard for his administration of crown lands. So much so, in fact, that the position of secretary of crown lands, which he held during his premiership, was subsequently moved across to the civil service with Domett continuing in the role. He subsequently became land claims commissioner and then registrar general of lands.

The seeming conflict of interest was not an issue when he joined the Legislative Council in 1866. By 1870 Domett's Crown Lands Office was charged with implementing nearly all of central government's land policies, including confiscated areas. The same year the Disqualification Act put a stop to any politician also being a civil servant, but the legislation specifically exempted Alfred Domett, the consummate administrator, from the new regime.

However, able bureaucrat though he was, he did not quite abandon the artistic persona. On meeting him Charlotte Godley reported that he dressed like a poet: " .... with a round hat that would be considered shabby on any decently dressed scarecrow". [9]

The Dometts returned to England in 1872. He now had the time and means to devote to the literary enthusiasms that, at least publicly, had been largely sublimated during his 30 years in New Zealand where his most enduring cultural contribution was a close involvement in the setting up and initial operation of the General Assembly Library.

It became apparent, though, with the publication of his epic poem *Ranolf and Amohia* shortly after he arrived back in London that he had not forsaken his muse or it him. Gisborne noted: "As a poem, it is not only a comprehensive and accurate record of natural history, of scenery, and of Aboriginal life in New Zealand, but it abounds with beautiful imagery, graphic description, argumentative disquisition, all clothed in facile verse." [10] The work, sub-titled *A south-sea day-dream*, drew appreciative comments from such literary icons as Alfred Lord Tennyson, Henry Longfellow and old friend Robert Browning. Their enthusiasm for the very long and equally repetitive epic is difficult to understand more than a century later. Yet their admiration was clearly genuine. Browning wrote: " …I am sure it is a great and astonishing performance, of very varied beauty and power ….the poem is worth the thirty years' work and experience, and even absence from home …" [11] Tennyson was equally effusive, but there was more than a hint of the indigestibility that has discouraged later readers: "Intellectual subtlety; great power of delineating delicious scenery, imaginative fire – all these are there. Nevertheless I find in it an *embarras de richesses* which makes it a little difficult to read – to me at least." [12]

Domett published another book of verse in 1877 and then in 1883, four years before his death, a revised edition of *Ranolf and Amohia*. His CMG, awarded in 1880, was a lesser honour than bestowed on many of the other premiers during the early, revolving doors period of New Zealand politics.

Dame Partington and her mop. Whitaker (loq.): 'I don't think you can manage it.' Atkinson: 'I can mop up the water as well as you've mopped up the land.' *Whitaker, an unabashed land speculator, pulled the strings in Domett's ministry. William Hutchison,* Wellington Advertiser Supplement, *July 8 1882. (ATL ref: A-095-042)*

5

SIR FREDERICK WHITAKER
1812-1891

"A power in office and out of office, both before the throne and behind the throne"

Frederick Whitaker was a man of interesting contradictions.

Many of New Zealand's earliest settlers sailed to the other end of the world to 'better themselves' or to carve out careers that would have been impossible at home. Yet Whitaker was born into a world of privilege at Manor House in Oxfordshire, his father a respected magistrate and attorney and there could have been little doubt that when Whitaker was admitted to practise as a solicitor in 1839 a successful legal career stretched ahead of him in England.

Cartoonist unknown, The Observer Supplement, *Observer Cartoons No 5, January 28 1882. (ATL ref: H-722-007)*

Clearly, though, he wanted something more. Perhaps it was the feeling that anything – rather than the strict prescriptions of the law – was possible in the raw, unformed, unexploited colonies. He sailed for New South Wales before the end of 1839 but almost immediately decided to carry on to New Zealand. Perhaps, again, because in the previous 50 years some of the biggest, brightest entrepreneurial opportunities in the

Australian colonies had already been snapped up.

Whitaker quickly established himself in the Bay of Islands, practising law in tandem with seeking out rich-quick schemes, particularly in the fertile if controversial field of land speculation.

This was to be the pattern for the rest of his life and provides the most intriguing of several contradictions. Frederick Whitaker was a particularly able lawyer, an impressive courtroom barrister as well as a meticulous legal draftsman. It was the latter skill that made him invaluable to government during the crown colony period and in numerous later administrations. Whitaker had a rare, common sense approach to the law and, according to William Gisborne: " [he] excelled in drafting bills; all the clauses were admirably arranged, and their language was simple, comprehensive, and precise". [1] Yet the same man was attracted to some of the wildest and risky of business ventures, ranging from mining manganese on Kawau Island to the buying of gold mines in Thames.

Frederick Whitaker moved to Auckland in 1841; it was the new seat of government and where the action was. He was promptly appointed a country judge, beginning a wide-ranging governmental career that ran in fits and starts for the next half century.

In 1845 Governor FitzRoy appointed Whitaker to the Legislative Council and it was there, in tandem with William Swainson, the attorney general, and William Martin, the chief justice, that he framed a new code of statutes that established his reputation for law drafting mastery.

In 1843, Whitaker married Jane Griffith, stepdaughter of Alexander Shepherd, the colonial treasurer, and they were to have eight children. In 1846 he and his wife returned to England for two years. No doubt he was 'reviewing his options', but it seems the pull of a burgeoning political career and the promise of more profitable speculations drew him back to New Zealand.

By 1855, when he tried unsuccessfully – twice –

to become Auckland superintendent he was seen more as a colonial than a provincial politician, although his ties and commitment to Auckland were to remain strong.

During his political career – sometimes as an elected member and sometimes in the Legislative Council – he was attorney general in seven cabinets.

Through the first years of responsible government he was to become attorney general three times, on the last occasion from 1856-61. Mostly these administrations were subtly shifting alliances of conservative politicians, with differences marked more by personalities, particular policy issues or geographical imperatives than by any great philosophical differences. Today, in the unfolding MMP environment, it is easier to get a flavour of the politics of that time, than during the last 50 years with its rigid two-party system.

In these cabinets, Whitaker was invariably the hard-working, clear-thinking, far-sighted administrator who kept the business of government moving despite the basically unstable nature of the fluid political coalitions. William Gisborne noted: "He has often held office, colonial and provincial, but he has never been prominent, in the popular sense, even when he was Premier, though in reality always a power in office and out of office, both before the throne and behind the throne." [2]

Whitaker was a key member of New Zealand's first ministries – headed by Sewell, Fox and Stafford – but he did not have the same appetite for the premiership that he did for land, timber and mining speculation.

He was, all the same, conscious of the power he exerted. Downie Stewart told this story about Whitaker: "On one occasion he took the Attorney-Generalship with precedence over the Prime Minister, whereupon a political wag declared that Whitaker declined the premiership, but insisted on being served soup at Government House before the Prime Minister!" [3]

Since 1861 Whitaker had been in partnership with a much younger Auckland lawyer, Thomas Russell, who was a more successful financial manipulator and, possibly because of it, viewed with considerable suspicion. Russell also dabbled in politics; he was in Domett's ministry.

Whitaker became premier in October 1863, but only when the Domett ministry in which he had again been attorney general collapsed in disarray.

Frederick Whitaker was premier for barely a year, with Russell as his minister of colonial defence, but it was long enough to permanently tarnish his political reputation. As premier, he was an early 'Maori-basher'. George Grey, governor for the second time,

Paradise and the Peri – the Rejected of Eden. 'One morn Freddy at the gate of Eden stood disconsolate.' *In fact, Whitaker was once again attorney general, this time in Hall's cabinet. Arthur Palethorpe, New Zealand Punch, (Wellington), September 20 1879. (ATL ref: H-693-003)*

favoured limited punishment of Maori 'rebels' by taking some of their land, but the politicians had more ambitious plans for the Waikato. " …. Frederick Whitaker and Thomas Russell seized upon Grey's proposals and inflated them into massive confiscation on an economic rather than a punitive basis." [4] Auckland land speculators would benefit greatly while, the theory went, military setttlements kept the peace.

Governor Grey was personally affronted by both the uncompromisingly tough nature of Whitaker's Maori policy and the company he kept. With some prodding from Grey, a financial crisis ended Whitaker's first, and shorter, occupancy of the premiership in November 1864. Whitaker was subsequently attorney general in Harry Atkinson's second and third ministries in 1876-77 and in John Hall's cabinet from 1879 to April 1882.

During Hall's ministry he was the government's leader in the Legislative Council and exerted considerable authority over both cabinet and the Council. "[He] was seldom effective in addressing a multitude, or the House of Representatives of which he was occasionally a member," writes Gisborne. "He succeeded better in the Legislative Council, where debate more resembles mild conversation in a quiet room." [5]

Hall relied heavily on his advice. "The premier privately called him 'the wise old man of the North', travelling to Auckland to see him when Whitaker could not spare the time to sail to Wellington." [6]

With no great enthusiasm, Whitaker picked up the premier's reins from Hall in April 1882 and continued until September 1883, when he resigned from Parliament. "He detested living in Wellington and had found the Premiership tiresome." [7] He returned to Auckland and a succession of business worries, believing his political life to be over. The KCMG awarded him in 1884 suggested others thought so as well, but he had one final and lengthy stint as attorney general in Harry Atkinson's 1887-91 ministry, 31 years after first holding the position.

Over the years, when not in government, Whitaker practised law, sometimes sat in Parliament, and continued, seemingly with unfettered enthusiasm, his up and down business career.

Whitaker was strongly opposed to the country's capital moving to Wellington in 1865. Out of politics at the time, he responded by winning elections to become Auckland's superintendent and MP for Parnell. Back in Parliament he led a short-lived separatist movement, demanding that Auckland be administered by a lieutenant governor and provincial assembly.

The few business successes – like his early and long involvement with the Auckland Gas Company – were swamped, sometimes literally, by ambitious schemes like the plan to drain the Piako area.

Despite the honours and years of steady achievement his declining years were not happy ones. His eldest son,

Frederick, who inherited his business acumen as well as his name, committed suicide in 1887 following land speculation losses. Sir Frederick was in poor shape financially when he died in 1891 some months after leaving government for the last time. The Waikato Land Association, in which he was a major shareholder, had continued to drain his resources more quickly than it had the Piako swamp, the restored land now unsaleable in the depression that gripped the country.

R C J Stone has taken a balanced view of Whitaker: "He was cynical, yet optimistic and cheerful. He was an unabashed speculator, yet served the colony well as a pioneer of industry, mining and swamp reclamation. That he was a superb practitioner within the legal profession is beyond dispute." [8]

Gisborne, mixing personal observation with some hindsight, has summarised Sir Frederick Whitaker's contribution to New Zealand public life in more uncompromising and unflattering terms: "It is dangerous to divide responsibility and action; good influence is lessened, and intrigue, insincerity, and imprudence are endangered by that division. The public soon ceases to place trust in policy and conduct liable to be controlled by those sinister conditions. This want of trust has been felt in relation to Sir Frederick Whitaker. He has been too much the shadow of a statesman." [9]

The Phoenix - The Hon. F. Whitaker rising out of his (h)ashes. *In April 1882, Whitaker replaced Hall as premier. William Hutchison,* Wellington Advertiser Supplement, *April 29 1882. (ATL ref: A-095-030)*

6

SIR FREDERICK ALOYSIUS WELD
1825-1891

"He was the soul of honour, and he had a chivalrous sense of duty"

Frederick Aloysius Weld was an unlikely colonist, and an even unlikelier premier of New Zealand.

He was one of that extraordinary breed of Victorian gentlemen adventurers who used the many and varied red spots and splashes on the world map as their particular stamping ground. But he was unlike many of them as well.

Frederick Weld was the third son of Humphrey Weld and Maria Christina Clifford. His was an old titled English family, one that was proud and assertive about its Catholic heritage. His grandfather had welcomed monks fleeing the French Revolution and taken Charles X, the deposed French king, into his home, Lulworth Castle. From his own pocket, he founded Stonyhurst College where his grandson was educated.

Young Weld, who also studied languages at Friburg University in Switzerland, dreamed of a military career but when this proved elusive he decided to set out after a clutch of cousins – Clifford, Petre and Vavasour – all of whom were to earn walk-on parts in New Zealand history books. He purchased 100 acres and a town lot from the New Zealand Company and sailed on the *Theresa* in late 1843.

His first years in the brand-new colony belied both his 'delicate health' and penchant for music, painting and literature. His main preoccupation was sheep farming and when he returned to England in 1851, he even wrote a pamphlet on the subject, that ran to four printings. With his cousin Charles Clifford, Weld in 1844 established one of the country's earliest sheep stations, 'Wharekaka', in south Wairarapa where he

Chicane (Mark Winter), 2003. (ATL ref: A-230-043)

spent some months shepherding the pioneer flock of Australian sheep.

Then only 20 years old, he lived in a makeshift whare; contact with other Europeans was rare, food was often in short supply, he learnt sheep farming by trial and error, and relations with local Maori were uncertain. But, as Jeanine Williams writes: "Weld showed an astonishing degree of initiative and adaptability for one of his sheltered restricted background. Such pastimes as hunting, fishing, and shooting which in England had been pursued for leisure and enjoyment now became a necessary mode of behaviour and Weld responded with alacrity." [1]

Climatic difficulties at Wharekaka were the spur for Weld to explore the top of the South Island. There, again in partnership with Clifford, he established the 'Flaxbourne' station near Cape Campbell in Marlborough. Weld was closely involved in developing the station from 1847, building a homestead (and Roman Catholic chapel) and planting the English trees that soon softened an alien landscape. His nearest neighbour was 40 miles away but, a keen yachtsman, he regularly sailed back and forth to Wellington, a six-hour voyage when the sea and wind were accommodating.

In the 1850s squatting was a profitable business. Weld and Clifford were granted pastoral licences at a rent of a penny a sheep per year; with the discovery of gold in Australia breeding ewes sold from between 10/- to £1 a head.

There was time, too, for politics. Weld had been

offered a seat on Governor George Grey's Legislative Council, but he declined, believing its aim was to stall progress towards self-government. Weld 'discovered' a third Clifford-Weld property, 'Stonyhurst', in Canterbury in 1850, the same year the partnership had received the country's highest price – £20 – for their rams. Weld enjoyed the challenge of breaking in new country, but the administration of it was another matter. He wrote, in 1855: "Colonizing, exciting enough in its early struggles becomes very milk & waterish when it resolves itself into merely going certain rounds to visit sheep stations and staying a week in this settlement & a week in that." [2]

Weld took the first of a number of trips back to England in 1851; now a member of the Settlers' Constitutional Society he spent time there, with Sewell, Fox and Wakefield, debating the best constitutional arrangements for New Zealand. He returned in time to be elected the member for Wairau in the first House of Representatives, foreshadowed in the new constitution, and proclaimed in January 1853, before Governor Grey left for another colonial posting.

Weld was a member of the first brief administration, headed by FitzGerald, that resigned when it was clear that Administrator Wynyard was not prepared to allow full responsible government.

Two more journeys to England followed. On the second he married Filumena de Lisle Phillipps in March 1859, her mother a distant Clifford cousin. On their return to New Zealand in 1860 a family home was established at 'Brackenfield', a 500 acre property to the north of Christchurch and Weld, the absentee member for Wairau, was immediately asked to join Stafford's cabinet. Following the Waitara incident in Taranaki, an intractable land-sales stalemate that signaled the beginning of protracted land wars, Weld was influential in the passing of a new militia act and, as minister of native affairs, he juggled the often contradictory objectives of firmness toward and justice for Maori. Justice was not a factor, though, if Maori interests clashed with settler interests.

Between the end of the Stafford ministry in July 1861 and now-returned Governor Grey's request that he form a government in late 1864, Weld had come to the conclusion, as had the intervening Whitaker-Fox ministry, that it was time the colony took full responsibility for native affairs, including the funding and fighting of the land wars.

Jeanine Williams wrote: "The 'self-reliance' defence policy was not born out of economic necessity: it had its origins in the Wairarapa when settlers felt forced to take the initiative themselves

Paying for Promises. Customs official: 'These goods yours, sir, and very much needed? Glad to hear it, for I want the contribution you promised to the Maori war, and you can't have them until you pay.'
Weld's 'self-reliance' policy increased local militia costs, to the great dissatisfaction of southern settlers in particular. Cartoonist unknown, Punch in Canterbury, *July 8 1865. (ATL ref: H-705-015)*

in providing for their defence rather than rely on government action or inaction as the case may be." [3] He also believed colonists would not have control of internal affairs until the imperial troops left.

Frederick Weld's sole ministry, from November 1864 to October 1865, was notable for a number of significant, far-reaching decisions, some positive and others deeply resented. His 'self-reliance' policy replaced British troops with a local militia and volunteers; military posts were established between Wanganui and New Plymouth; a massive 1.2 million acres of Maori land in the Waikato were confiscated; there was an amnesty for Maori who had previously fought the government; tentative steps were taken to give Maori parliamentary representation. Also, Weld promptly removed the country's capital from Auckland to Wellington. It was, perhaps, surprising the Weld government survived the eleven months it did!

Weld retired from politics at the beginning of 1866 and the family sailed again for England in May 1867.

In another, more image-conscious era, Weld might have become something of a political pin-up. In 1848, Thomas Arnold wrote of him: "Frederick Weld, with his clear blue eyes, curly light brown hair, lithe well-knit figure, and honest, resolute expression of face, was a fine sample of the best type of Catholic aristocrat." [4]

And as Guy Scholefield wrote: " ...his religion commanded all his devotion and his Englishness all his loyalty." [5] They certainly guided his beliefs and actions during his years in New Zealand. He was a determined opponent of anti-Catholic feeling in a predominantly Protestant country. And, as he said, when he spoke for the last time in the New Zealand Parliament, "God made me an Englishman heart and soul". [6]

In 1869, his health largely recovered from another in a recurring series of debilitating illnesses, his abilities were rewarded with the governorship of the colony of West Australia. During his tenure he concentrated on the development of communications in the continent's remotest and least developed colony. He also remained consistent in his concern about the treatment of native races, famously insisting on the prosecution of a prominent settler who had murdered an Aborigine.

Frederick Weld returned to New Zealand briefly one last time in 1874 to settle partnership matters with Clifford before becoming Governor of Tasmania, where he was an early advocate of the federation of the Australian colonies. In 1880 he became Governor of the Straits Settlements, his natural sympathies crucial to the improvement of relations with the native states. His colonial career

ended in 1887, by then the prestigious GCMG jostling with a chestful of earlier honours. Sir Frederick Weld died, as he was born, at 'Chideock Manor' in Dorset in 1891 and his wife two years later at Saint Scholastica, a priory largely financed by the Welds. They had 13 children – 12 surviving infancy – their birthplaces benchmarks in a brilliant colonial career.

Frederick Weld spent 23 years in New Zealand – and another 18 as a colonial governor. His contribution to New Zealand was considerable, as a pioneering sheep farmer, a principled politician, an energetic explorer, and a talented watercolourist.

Graham, Weld's biographer, has written: "Weld's whole approach to politics was moralistic. Compromise to him implied deceit. Distinctions between a personal and a political code of behaviour were unthinkable .... Perhaps the most remarkable aspect of Weld's Premiership was the fact that a collection of fairly hard-headed colonial representatives were prepared to accept his leadership." [7]

William Gisborne's conclusion: "He was the soul of honour, and he had a chivalrous sense of duty. His political views, on the whole, were moderate, and his administrative capacity was considerable. His failings as a statesman were that he was apt to be over-hasty in his conclusions, was wanting in tact, and did not sufficiently discriminate when it was best, in view of his ultimate object, to be firm and when to give way. No statesman in a representative country can hope to go direct to his object as the crow flies; statesmen who wish for success must learn that it is often wiser to go round an obstacle than to try to go through it." [8]

7

GEORGE MARSDEN WATERHOUSE
1824-1906

"All that he demonstrably lacked was the art of ingratiating himself with the people"

George Waterhouse had the singular distinction of being premier of two colonies approximately two thousand miles apart. But the second time he was premier, in New Zealand, there was more shadow than substance to the position.

George Marsden Waterhouse was born into impeccable missionary stock in Cornwall in 1824. Educated at the Wesleyan College near Bristol, he travelled with his father, the Rev John Waterhouse, to Tasmania in 1839. While his father went on to run Wesleyan missions in Australia and throughout Polynesia, George Waterhouse settled in Adelaide, went into business and had made enough money to retire by the age of 27. He had married Lydia Giles in 1848; there were no children and he did not remarry when his wife died.

The same year, a candidate for South Australia's first partially representative assembly pulled out, and it was the accidental beginning of half a century's public service when Waterhouse's name was put forward in his place.

Liberal in his views, he served in the Legislative Council for three years before poor health, worsened by Adelaide's heat, led to his resignation and an extended world trip. In the United States his advocacy of reciprocal trade was unusual at a time when Britain was the overwhelmingly preferred market for Australasian produce.

Chicane (Mark Winter), 2003. (ATL ref: A-230-045)

Back in Adelaide, he was elected, in 1856, to the House of Assembly in the first 'responsible' government elections. Again, he resigned in poor health a year later. The cycle repeated itself once more when he was elected to the Legislative Council in 1860 and promptly named chief secretary in the administration. Another bout of ill-health and the downfall of the Reynolds ministry coincided, and agreement to head a brief, interim government blossomed into a fully fledged ministry, with Waterhouse chief secretary or premier for nearly two years.

George Waterhouse had visited New Zealand briefly with his father in 1842; his arrival in search of a more equable climate over a quarter century later attracted far more attention. R M Burdon wrote: "He came to New Zealand in 1869, when the prestige of his former experience combined with a faint resemblance to Abraham Lincoln brought him at once to prominence ..." [1]

He bought the 20,000 acre Huangarua station in south Wairarapa, part of the run originally settled by Charles Clifford and Frederick Weld and subsequently farmed by the more unlikely partnership of irascible newspaper editor Samuel Revans and William Mein Smith, Wellington's surveyor. With 18,000 sheep and rabbit and scab problems, politics could not have been further from Waterhouse's mind.

He set to work, in his persevering, clear-sighted

way, to make a success of his farming enterprise. Not content with half-measures he sailed to England to collect the grass seed, fencing material and implements he wanted. As a precaution he also invested in a boiling down plant. This was soon put to use when he returned to find scab endemic among his flock.

But the political life could not be avoided indefinitely. In about equal proportions, Waterhouse continued to have a passion for politics and distaste for the way it was usually conducted. He also had his local champions: within the year Sam Revans had plans for him to occupy the Wairarapa seat in the House of Representatives; William Fox, who had met him in South Australia, was quicker off the mark and arranged a seat in the Legislative Council in 1870, a more congenial setting for a man of Waterhouse's temperament. Moreover, he agreed to lead the Council until the end of the session.

Guy Scholefield wrote: "A sagacious adviser, a clear thinker of moderate views, a champion of democratic rights and a stickler for the purity of Parliament, Waterhouse came on the scene just when such a man was needed." [2]

Waterhouse quickly took a leading part in improving the Legislative Council's spotty reputation. As Gisborne wrote: "He has great reverence for forms and precedents and for the ancient ways and constitutional principles." [3] His sense of propriety was finely tuned; that same year he refused to be associated with a petition for a Wairarapa railway line because of 'conflict of interest', even though the proposed route was miles from his property. William Fox was now premier for the third time, but the powerhouse in his ministry was Julius Vogel, who was content to begin the implementation of his hugely ambitious immigration and public works schemes from the background. Vogel noted the arrival of George Waterhouse on the New Zealand parliamentary scene with considerable, and calculating, interest.

In turn, Waterhouse was impressed with the national scope and promise of Vogel's vision, shared his enthusiasm for international trade and favoured abolition of the provinces. He was no parochial provincialist and had said: "I detest the idea of being an inhabitant of a parish, with all the narrow views of those who never look beyond the borders of a parish. Let us look at matters from a colonial and not from a narrow provincial point of view." [4] Accordingly, he joined Fox's cabinet and steered the necessary legislation through a doubting Council.

Nevertheless, Waterhouse resigned from the executive at the end of the session, troubled by the way government business was conducted and to spend more time managing his farming interests. He promoted a system of salting meat for export as a director of the Wairarapa Meat Preserving Co, imported more stud sheep, particularly the Lincoln breed, and exhibited at Masterton's first agricultural show in 1871.

In September 1872 the Fox ministry collapsed and Stafford's replacement administration was spectacularly short-lived, even by the standards of the day. At this point Julius Vogel appealed to Waterhouse to lend his name and standing to a new ministry. As R M Burdon wrote: "Vogel found all the respectability he required incarnate in the person of George Marsden Waterhouse." [5]

To everyone's surprise – and undoubtedly to Waterhouse himself – New Zealand had a new premier who had been in the country barely three years, in Parliament for two years as an upper house appointee, who had no portfolio and, as a matter of principle, refused a salary.

Waterhouse put great store on his 'independence' but, as Raewyn Dalziel notes, " ….he must have been the only person who thought he could control Vogel". [6]

While Waterhouse, speaking in the Council, was committing himself to the premiership and offering his colleagues assistance with their departments, Vogel was making it unmistakably clear in the House that he had formed the government. Dalziel wrote: "Tensions between Vogel and Waterhouse had become apparent within days of their taking office together. In the House Vogel had rather touchily insisted on his role in forming the Ministry even though Waterhouse was Premier. Waterhouse soon discovered that he was no match for Vogel's 'much stronger mind' and that 'he had no chance of carrying any proposition he had to make in Cabinet'." [7]

Scholefield described Waterhouse's invidious position: "Even before the end of the session the inconvenience and the sham of his position were abundantly evident. He held the shadow of power; Vogel the substance." [8]

Waterhouse welcomed an opportunity to extricate himself when, in February 1873, John Hall resigned as colonial secretary. Although Vogel was overseas, Waterhouse resigned as well. Governor Bowen, about to leave the country, did not want to accept the resignation and asked Fox to mediate. Waterhouse's response was that if Vogel had formed the ministry, then Vogel could find another colonial secretary. Bowen procrasinated, but had to back down, calling on Fox to form a new ministry, when Waterhouse forbade the government steamer carrying the Governor to leave port. Fox agreed unwillingly, saying he would resign when Vogel returned to the country. It was thought this incident cost Waterhouse a knighthood.

In a letter to Vogel, Waterhouse wrote: "I have felt throughout that you have regarded yourself as the actual and me as the nominal Premier; and the strength of your will and the advantage arising from your having formed the ministry have given you an influence in the ministry which is fatal to my exerting the influence attached to my office as Premier. We have been cast in different moulds, and can not with mutual satisfaction run in harness together." [9]

In retrospect, it is puzzling that Waterhouse, suspicious as he had been of the flamboyant treasurer's willingness to agree to major financial contracts without parliamentary consultation, ever agreed to Vogel's overtures. Burdon commented: "Had he and Vogel been better acquainted, had they fully realised what each one expected of the other, it is unlikely that they would have entered into so incompatible an alliance." [10]

There was little public surprise at the latest twist in the political saga of Julius Vogel, but the press took the opportunity, as it does today, to stir up a little trans-Tasman feeling. "The *Herald* claimed Waterhouse should never have had the job being a 'fair average specimen statesman for South Australia, but he can hardly find a suitable place in New Zealand politics'." [11]

George Waterhouse, his reputation sullied to some extent, continued in Parliament as a private member for another 14 years. He played an active part in a number of community organisations and bought and sold property. At times he had employed over 100 men on the Huangarua station, which he sold to Hon John Martin in 1878, doubling his initial outlay; a portion of the property was later laid out as Martinborough. Waterhouse made regular visits to England and, like many wealthy colonists of the period, finally left New Zealand in 1888 to spend his last years in the country of his birth. He died in Devon in 1906.

Waterhouse never stood for election in New Zealand, but he contributed positively to the dignity and decorum of the political system. He was also one of the first premiers to express independent views on foreign affairs and to suggest closer links with the United States. Scholefield wrote a fitting epitaph: "Surely such a man, footloose purely on account of his health, was the very requisite of a colonial democracy, a man who wanted nothing for himself and would relinquish office more willingly than he accepted it. All that he demonstrably lacked was the art of ingratiating himself with the people – the popularity of the hustings." [12]

Effective control of Waterhouse's ministry was in Vogel's hands; here he is still Otago's provincial treasurer the year before he moved north. A P G. Dunedin Punch, February 29 1868. (ATL ref: H-695-003)

8

SIR JULIUS VOGEL
1835-1899

"The heroics of finance roused him to genuine emotional heights"

Julius Vogel was one of New Zealand's most colourful premiers and prime ministers, as much for the range of imaginative ideas that tumbled from his nimble mind as for his slightly exotic appearance and the singular way he conducted his political life.

He was born in London in February 1835, the son of Albert Leopold Vogel and Phoebe Isaac. His mother came from a prosperous Jewish merchant family; his father was of Dutch and Christian origins. Vogel's parents separated when he was six and he lived, together with his mother and sister, in his grandparents' south London house, leaving school at 15 to work in the family business.

When his mother died he turned his back on the career that had been charted for him; after more training he was to be sent to South America to open a new branch of the business. Far more beguiling was the news that gold had been discovered in Australia. Vogel studied part-time at the newly opened Government School of Mines in London, gaining a certificate of proficiency in chemistry and metallurgy, and set out for Australia in 1852. Melbourne was still largely a canvas town but the assaying business Vogel set up with A S Grant, who had sailed with him, was more successful than importing ventures. In 1854 they moved to Maryborough, a new goldfields town, and survived by peddling patent medicines to miners. Two years later Grant had had enough, but there was no going back for Vogel.

Fortuitously, about this time Vogel discovered he

Walter Leslie, Parliamentary Portraits, *ca 1887-1890. (ATL ref: H-697-006)*

had a way with words, as well as an inexhaustible supply of ideas and opinions. Others recognised his talent and he was soon editing the *Maryborough and Dunolly Advertiser*, attacking the Victorian squattocracy with vigour and calling for parliamentary reform. In the 1861 recession Vogel lost his job, and when he also lost his first election campaign, for a seat in the state general assembly, it was time to move on.

When Vogel left Australia in early October 1861 for the Otago goldfields he now had another string – journalism – to his bow. In Dunedin, he was immediately hired by the weekly *Otago Colonist* and only weeks later went into partnership with William Cutten, editor of the opposition *Otago Witness*, with the ambitious intention of launching a daily newspaper. By mid-November the *Otago Daily Times*, the country's first daily, was selling on Dunedin's streets.

Raewyn Dalziel, Vogel's most recent biographer, wrote: "At twenty-six he was a rather portly young man, his dark hair divided in the middle and on the long side, a full moustache flowing into long mutton chops on either side of his face." [1]

Vogel used the newspaper to promote his ideas and the beginnings of his public career. He was not inhibited by his Jewish background, but cautiously aware that anti-semitism was not far below the surface in any community. In Europe Jews were only just beginning to play a role in public life after centuries of exclusion but the niceties of religion were of far less concern in the raw, young colonies where a man was judged by more immediate and practical qualities.

The foundations of Vogel's political career were built on ardent provincialism – he even wanted the South Island to separate from the north – but a few short years later he took the lead in abolishing the provinces. It was his campaign to set up a separate Middle Island colony, largely to escape growing land war costs, that in 1868 lost him the editorship of the *Otago Daily Times*, now owned by a company.

In early 1863 he lost two elections for places in the House of Representatives but was finally successful in September. In the interim he won a provincial council seat. Vogel quickly became a leading figure in the Provincial Council where his zeal for investing in all forms of communications soon became apparent. Nationally, his views were at first conditioned by strong Otago associations, but the schemes he was brewing could not be constrained by provincial boundaries.

During his next six years in Otago he kept winning and losing electorates on both the provincial and national stages. These regular changes were to become one of the constants of his political career.

He made an immediate, if not entirely favourable, impact in Wellington: ".... Julius Vogel, the young editor of the *Otago Daily Times*, whose deafness had already given Speaker Monro some annoyance as had his taking the oath on the Old Testament while wearing a hat." [2]

Julius Vogel's marriage, in 1867 to Mary, daughter of W H Clayton, later colonial architect, produced four children and essential stability to his life, often plagued with ill-health and financial worries as investment schemes failed.

In 1869 Vogel left Dunedin for Auckland where, early the next year, he bought the *Southern Cross* newspaper.

Between 1865-69, with Fox out of the country, Julius Vogel was effectively opposition leader in the House of Representatives. He harried premier Stafford on provincial rights and native affairs. When Fox returned to New Zealand and formed his third ministry, Vogel became treasurer. From this powerful position he unveiled his hugely ambitious plan to open up the country, and end the fighting more effectively than extended military campaigns had managed, by building an infrastructure that would

The Provincial Treasurer's Dream. *Vogel's Otago period was nearly over; he had bigger dreams. Cartoonist unknown,* Punch, or the New Zealand Charivari *(Dunedin), May 2 1868. (ATL ref: H-695-005)*

reduce distances and diminish differences. The grand scheme would need a great deal of money and a great many more people.

As colonial treasurer – and he was to hold this powerful position for a total of 10 years – Vogel's perspective changed radically. "As strident Otago advocate he had demanded freedom for the wealthiest province to move forward at its own pace. Now, as colonial politician, he used New Zealand's collective credit to promote the whole colony's progress – and his own career. A mercurial businessman turned politician, Julius Vogel remained essentially the Victorian goldfield speculator of his youth." [3]

In June 1870 Vogel unveiled the details. It was a 'Think Big' scheme that dwarfed the early 1980s version in both scope and daring. He wanted to borrow £10 million over a decade to build roads, railways and telegraphs and to bring in thousands of immigrants, who would get land as new districts were opened up. As security for the loans, it was Vogel's intention to set aside a public estate of 6 million acres alongside the new railway lines and roads.

"Vogel .... realised that the great need of an undeveloped country was capital to develop communications and bring more land into production. Moreover, he saw loans and government expenditure as an antidote to depression, and it has been suggested that Vogel envisaged a flow of money for development creating a perpetual artificial gold rush." [4]

The Vogel theory was that the massive government expenditure would trigger greater private demand and, consequently, additional private investment. In the event, double the intended amount was borrowed through the 1870s at higher than expected rates of interest. More borrowing to stimulate an increasingly debt burdened economy, further pressured by poor export prices, simply dug a deeper financial hole.

Like most visionaries, Vogel and his grand scheme aroused more suspicion than enthusiasm. At first an apprehensive central government, with some support from Britain, nibbled away at the edges of the great enterprise. The provinces squabbled over who would get what railway or which road first, hardening Vogel against a now outdated system.

Having launched his massive development plan, and always willing, even eager, to leave the details and administrative intricacies to his colleagues, Vogel left on an extended overseas trip to advance this and other schemes. In the United States he negotiated a San Francisco-New Zealand mail service; in Britain he raised loans of more than £1 million, tried to interest the British government in annexing Samoa, and signed an agreement with an engineering company to make a start on the railway system.

The Political Pedlar. V-g-l to Cr-ght-n: 'Vot have you got there, my tear? Is it for sale? I'll buy it, I will, s'elp me.' *Cartoonists emphasised Vogel's 'Jewishness'. Cartoonist unknown,* Auckland Punch, *April 17 1869. (ATL ref: H-686-013)*

R M Burdon, Vogel's first biographer, wrote: "He was no cynical cozener of fools. The heroics of finance roused him to genuine emotional heights, and the call of a large loan on the London money market stirred his spirit as profoundly as the call to arms might rouse the soul of a warrior." [5]

Back in New Zealand, and having lost the confidence of Dunedin electors, Vogel now represented an Auckland electorate. Neither did he have the full support of Parliament for the agreements he had reached overseas; Fox and other colleagues were uneasy and the opposition antagonistic.

The Fox ministry crumbled in September 1872 and, with Stafford unable to form a lasting administration, Vogel was called to do so. However, he was not yet prepared to take a centre stage role and persuaded the gentleman-politician George Waterhouse to accept the premiership.

Dalziel, wrote: "His overt ambition and ruthless behaviour repelled some contemporaries but his openness, his powerful and magnetic personalty attracted others. He became a master at winning men over to his side by promises and patronage." [6]

Vogel intended to run the ministry as treasurer, but this was an affront to Waterhouse's principled ideas about parliamentary process and procedure. Before relations soured beyond repair, Vogel was off again, this time to discuss a trans-Tasman submarine cable with the Australian colonies. Waterhouse resigned and an obliging Fox held the fort until Vogel returned. This time, having run out of possible surrogates, he accepted the premiership in May 1873.

With new railway lines sprouting and a

spectacular leap in immigration figures, Vogel turned his attention, in 1874, to the abolition of the provinces, not that he intended to deliver the coup de grâce personally. Typically, he was out of the country again in 1875, on another financial expedition to London, when his lieutenant Harry Atkinson carried the abolition legislation.

Vogel's health had been poor since the late 1860s, but it did not dim his political and business ambitions. "Even when crippled by painful illness, he is able to concentrate his mental faculties on the most difficult questions with as much apparent ease as if he were in the enjoyment of perfect health." [7]

During this period – and it would not be acceptable for a practising politician today – Vogel sold out of the *Southern Cross* and bought an interest in the *New Zealand Times* which, in 1874, incorporated the venerable *Wellington Independent*.

When it became obvious that he would not be back in the country for the 1875 parliamentary session, Vogel suggested another leader be appointed. Daniel Pollen was named premier, but Vogel, on the other side of the world, continued to hold two portfolios and control of the real levers of power.

Sir Julius Vogel KCMG – the knighthood was conferred in England in May 1875 – was back in the country early in 1876; abandoning his Auckland seat, he had been elected, in his absence, to represent Wanganui. Pollen prompted resigned and Vogel resumed the premiership he had given up in name only.

Nevertheless, scandals involving his ministry, and the availability of a job he coveted, were reasons enough to leave parliamentary life in September.

However, as Judith Bassett has noted, "Vogel could not appoint himself Agent-General, and he needed to find a successor who would do so." After some casting around, he persuaded Harry Atkinson. [8]

Vogel was appointed agent general in London, replacing the late Dr Isaac Featherston. There, his attempts to secure his shaky financial situation with various schemes raised eyebrows and concerns in Wellington. He resigned his post in 1880, made an abortive and expensive attempt to win a House of Commons seat as a Conservative Party candidate, and promoted a string of companies involved with railways, telephones, cables, and electricity. None gave him the financial security he craved.

With his options severely reduced, Vogel visited New Zealand in 1882 and again the next year. He saw a depression that successive administrations had failed to end as an opportunity for a final political fling and there were offers of electorates from Gisborne to Ashburton. He finally stood in Christchurch North and was back in Parliament leading the majority grouping in August 1883. An initial ministry, with Robert Stout as premier, did not survive the address-in-reply debate. Harry Atkinson fared no better, and then, with a reshuffling of the faces, a Stout-Vogel administration ran until October 1887, although the treasurer failed to conjure up any economic miracles. Faring badly at the general election, the government resigned.

Keith Sinclair commented on the muddied motives of many leading politicians in the 1870s and 1880s: "By twentieth century standards there were quite unacceptably close links between business and politics. In a basic sense, politics was about land values." [9]

Leaps and bounds. *By 1887 it was clear Vogel had no solution to the depression. 'W H R',* Evening Press Supplement, *May 18 1887. (ATL ref: C-034-007)*

Vogel, his health failing, sat through the session before returning to England, with Lady Vogel, in early 1888 for the last time. There he tried to make a living from writing, publishing a novel in 1889. In the late 1990s there was a brief flickering of interest in *Anno Domini 2000* written, in some financial desperation and to give life to his still fertile imagination, over 100 years before. "By the year 2000 women have achieved equality with men, the empire has federated, and poverty has been eliminated." [10] The novel is, like many of Vogel's ideas, prophetic, even if the style is over-blown and the characterisation minimal.

It is ironic that the book, like most of his money-making ventures, failed, while many of his political ideas lived and markedly changed life in his adoptive country. In the 1870-80 decade £20 million – double the original amount – was actually spent on Vogel's public works and immigration schemes; the country's population doubled, there were 4,000 miles of new telegraph lines, and over 1,000 miles of railway line were laid.

David Hamer has written: "His public works programmes were of critical importance not only to workers but also to small farmers who very often could survive only through the additional income earned by working on local road and bridge construction. Speculators and landowners generally liked the increased land values brought about by spending on roads, bridges, and railways. Business people welcomed the extra business generated by the expenditure of loan money." [11]

William Pember Reeves, often a trenchant critic of New Zealand politicans, was an admirer of Vogel: "Imaginative and not afraid of a new thing that seemed likely to be useful in a practical way, Sir Julius Vogel had a hand in establishing State Life Insurance, the Public Trust Office, and the State Transfer of Land." [12] He also noted, Vogel's attempt, well in advance of the actual event, to establish a forestry department and his moving, in 1887, of a Women's Suffrage Bill.

Vogel was outward looking as well. "He was one of the few colonial politicians who took an active interest in affairs outside New Zealand, forging new links with the Australian colonies, the United States of America, and the Pacific Islands." [13]

During the last three years of his life the New Zealand government avoided the mutual embarrassment of penury by paying him £300 a year as a 'financial adviser'.

He died in Surrey in March 1899; his wife Mary died in 1933, aged 84.

Julius Vogel, who spent only 18 of his 64 years in New Zealand, was, as Raewyn Dalziel observed, a complex and colourful man: "His contemporaries both acclaimed and condemned him. He was described as brilliant, a far-seeing strategist, and a clever politician; he was also called a dangerous financier, a snob, a carpet-bagger, and a corrupting influence in politics. Even his enemies found him a man of rare vitality and power." [14]

Returning to the colony. *Vogel, now in London, seriously ill and stretched financially, renewed a claim for commission on loans he had raised in the past. William Blomfield,* New Zealand Observer & Free Lance, *August 2 1890. (ATL ref: H-722-066)*

9

DANIEL POLLEN
1813-1896

"He never had great faith in popular opinion; and in that case distrust is often reciprocal"

Considering he had a long and distinguished career in New Zealand public life it is surprising that Daniel Pollen is practically unknown, not even rating an entry in the *Dictionary of New Zealand Biography*.

Certainly little is known about his early life, except that he was born in Dublin, Ireland, in June 1813, the son of Hugh Pollen, a builder, and Elizabeth O'Neill. It is possible he spent a portion of his childhood in Washington DC, where his father played some role in the building of the Capitol. Daniel Pollen studied medicine, but the record is blank about where and when he qualified.

He apparently arrived in New South Wales in the late 1830s, continuing onto North Auckland. His signature, 'D. Pollen MD.' appears on the address of welcome presented to Captain Hobson in Kororareka on February 1 1840 and he was among the pakeha 'extras' at the signing of the Treaty of Waitangi.

Shortly afterwards he began a half century of business activity when he joined the provisional committee of the New Zealand Banking Co.

Chicane (Mark Winter), 2003. (ATL ref: A-230-044

In September 1841 Pollen bought land in and close to Auckland, living in Parnell and practising medicine. He became coroner in 1844, holding the post for four years. In 1846 he married Jane Henderson, daughter of a naval officer, and the next year they moved to Kawau where he was a copper mining company's medical officer. While there he began contributing to the *New Zealander*, writing with flair and perception about self-government, and taking a lead in community affairs.

Following the passing of the 1852 Constitution Act,

Pollen played a variety of roles in the Auckland provincial government. He was chief clerk in the superintendent's office, was appointed to the executive and then, in 1856, elected to the Provincial Council, serving through to 1865. He acted as deputy for the superintendent on two occasions.

By this time Pollen's public and political interests, with some business involvements that later included successful brick and pottery works, left little time for the practise of medicine. He was Auckland's commissioner of crown lands from 1858 until 1862, and was unfashionably sympathetic to the Maori perspective. He was later receiver of land revenue in Auckland and, in 1867, appointed agent for the general government in Auckland province.

Pollen's abilities had been recognised nationally for some time. In 1861-62 he was appointed to the Legislative Council where he represented the Fox ministry. He resigned from the Council when he accepted the Auckland agent's position in 1867, holding it only briefly before returning, in 1868-69, to represent the administration of his friend Edward Stafford in the Council.

Edmund Bohan, Edward Stafford's biographer, has described Pollen as "genially urbane and level-headed". [1] He and Stafford shared an Irish sense of humour and they wrote to each other regularly over the years. In one letter, after Pollen's salary as government agent in Auckland had been reduced, he asked if Stafford could restore it: "If you do I shall be thankful if not I will be only diligent." [2]

In 1869, Pollen was initially a candidate for the Auckland superintendency, but withdrew after a hostile meeting. Resigning from the Legislative Council again, he returned to the Auckland agent's role, holding several other positions relating to land revenue and confiscation at the same time.

Land purchase scandals were frequent during the early 1870s. Pollen was involved in Thomas Russell's 1873 offer to buy 80,000 acres of confiscated Maori land in the Waikato. Raewyn Dalziel wrote: "The whole transaction was carried out in secret and was illegal for confiscated land was supposed to be sold at auction, after it had been surveyed and gazetted. Russell had initiated the purchase with Pollen, then acting as agent for the central government in Auckland, and had discussed it with Vogel, who approved it." [3]

Later that year, at Vogel's behest, Pollen was back in the Legislative Council, this time joining the executive as colonial secretary. At the end of the 1874 parliamentary session Vogel left, for reasons that convinced neither the press nor the public, for another trip to Britain. When illness prevented him returning early in 1875 he resigned and the Governor asked Pollen to re-form the government. Pollen, isolated in the Council, might have been premier, but Harry Atkinson, in the House of Representatives and colonial treasurer, effectively led the administration. Vogel, taking the waters in Germany, was named postmaster-general.

When Sir Julius, as he now was, returned to New Zealand in February 1876, "Pollen happily surrendered the Premiership to Vogel, making it necessary to reconstruct the Ministry once again." [4] Pollen continued as colonial secretary until October 1877, serving in the Vogel and Atkinson-led governments.

Pollen was happiest in the Legislative Council. As he remarked on one occasion: "I have, I am happy to say, no constituents, and when I talk I address myself to this Council." [5] He continued as a member of the Legislative Council for another 19 years until his death in 1896.

William Gisborne wrote: "…. Dr Pollen's character, though rather frothy on the surface, has a strong undercurrent of common sense. …." [6]

Guy Scholefield: "He had a faculty for quick decisions and accurate perception without any political bias, and had a remarkable knowledge of detail and legislation. As agent in Auckland he showed great vigour and ability. As an administrator he was eminently safe and trustworthy, with a distinctly Tory belief that what was best administered was best." [7]

Although a supporter of the women's franchise league, he became markedly more conservative in later life, his good humour turning to trenchant sarcasm when he spoke out about the 'radicalism' he disliked and distrusted. According to William Gisborne: "As a statesman …. he never impressed the public mind with much confidence in himself. Among other reasons, one, probably, was that he never himself had great faith in popular opinion; and in that case distrust is often reciprocal." [8]

The Native Question. Sir G-e B-n: 'My dear Septimus, what am I to do with these troublesome Natives?'
Septimus Punch: 'Since they have taken to preserving us, Your Excellency, suppose we pot a few of them.'
Pollen was deeply involved, particularly in the Auckland region, with land purchases and sales, the root cause of deteriorating relations with Maori. Cartoonist unknown, Auckland Punch, *1868. (ATL ref: H-686-014)*

10
SIR HARRY ALBERT ATKINSON
1831-1892

"He never attracted a large personal following, nor did he seem to want one"

Atkinson was New Zealand's first truly 'colonial' premier – a man who had cleared land and built a home with his own hands, and took a frontline part in the land wars as well.

Although Harry Atkinson was born in Cheshire, England, it was not really surprising that he would live his life in New Zealand. He was the son of John Atkinson, an architect and stonemason, who believed strongly in education and in encouraging independence and self-reliance in his family. He and his wife Elizabeth Smith had 13 children; Harry was the seventh.

Walter Leslie, Parliamentary Portraits, 1887-1890.
(ATL ref: H-697-001)

While Harry Atkinson was still at school an elder brother departed for New Zealand and friendship with the Richmond family cemented the decision of Harry and brother Arthur to follow suit.

A party of 10 Richmonds and Atkinsons sailed for New Zealand in the *Sir Edward Paget* in December 1852, reaching their final destination, New Plymouth, in June 1853.

The closely connected and distantly related Atkinson-Richmond families were to early colonial New Zealand what the Kennedy clan was to the United States in the 1960s. Their close-knittedness and power caused some resentment and was all the more remarkable given they were based in the smallest and most impoverished of the country's provinces. Harry's sister Emily had married C W Richmond before leaving England; his brother Arthur later married Jane Maria Richmond; and Harry's second wife, Anne Smith was a cousin via Richmond connections. Arthur Atkinson was a lawyer and newspaper editor; C W Richmond was provincial councillor, member of parliament, minister and supreme court judge; his brother, James Crowe, served in provincial politics and the Weld and Stafford ministries and another brother, Henry Robert, was Taranaki superintendent. The letters and diaries they and their wives wrote, published in 1960 as the *The Richmond-Atkinson Papers*, provide sharply observant detail about political and everyday colonial life in New Zealand from the 1850s to the 1890s.

The Atkinson brothers had a limited amount of capital. However John Atkinson had, when the emigrating idea took hold, prepared his sons for the rigours of colonial life by having them tutored in useful trades like carpentry, tinsmithing, bootmaking, and blacksmithing, and Harry immediately put his trade skills to use, making six dozen pairs of boots for a local cobbler. By the end of 1853 the brothers had purchased 200 Grey block acres for 10s an acre. As well as clearing, fencing and ploughing the land, Harry built, from timber he had sawn, his 'Hurworth' homestead so by 1856 he and his new wife, Amelia Jane Skinner, daughter of a Rochester banker, had a suitable home. By this time the Atkinson and Richmond cousins were well underway with breaking in nearly 1,000 acres near New Plymouth.

In November 1854 Harry Atkinson had written to an aunt: "Upon landing you see at once that you mistake the country if you thought it aught but a land flowing with milk and honey. It is this in a literal sense, honey is most plentiful, and so indeed is everything that is good. The land in this province is as fine as anywhere in New Zealand … we have this great advantage over most of the other provinces that we have large quantities of good land altogether – in fact all our land is available …" [1]

However, growing land problems – ambitious settlers pressing unwilling Maori owners – affected the young couple's immediate life and significantly fashioned Atkinson's subsequent political career. He shared the view of most Taranaki colonists that land sales must continue, with local Maori assimilated by force if necessary.

Atkinson was an energetic farmer and enterprising colonist: by 1857 he was raising cattle, pigs and various table birds and had set up a butter and cheese-making dairy; he was also supplying firewood to troops garrisoned in Taranaki and was contracted to carry mail between New Plymouth and Wellington.

The same year he was elected to the Taranaki Provincial Council and in 1858 he received a commission in the Taranaki Rifle Volunteer company as Maori-pakeha acrimony slid towards open warfare. Harry Atkinson was a resourceful, but prudent officer skilled in bushcraft, and he led a company of volunteers with distinction throughout skirmishes and pitched battles in 1860.

Harry Atkinson was elected to the House of Representatives the next year, but it was not the end of his military career. Two years later, when hostilities broke out again, he organised an irregular force of 'bushrangers', leading them bravely, with several 'mentioned in despatches' and promotion to the rank of major.

Although several times Taranaki's deputy superintendent, Atkinson's political horizons had broadened. He left provincial politics early in 1864, apart from a brief involvement again in a decade's time, and later in the year joined Frederick Weld's 'self-reliance' ministry as colonial defence minister. Sending the British troops home was something he agreed with both philosophically and practically, and as a practical minister he spent more time in the field than behind his desk.

The Weld ministry was defeated in October 1865 and Atkinson resigned his seat the next year, largely for personal reasons. Amelia Jane Atkinson had died in June 1865, having borne four children during their nine year marriage. In June 1866 Atkinson married again, his cousin Anne Smith, and they subsequently had three children. His second marriage seemed a particularly happy one.

Jane Maria Atkinson wrote to her sister-in-law Emily Richmond in May 1866: " … I quite feel in this case that tho' a more affectionate and devoted wife than poor Jane was could not be found, she was

Driving them home. Whitaker (loq.): 'Don't hurry them, Harry! They are bound to pass them.' Atkinson (loq.): 'We've got 'em; but they require pushing.' *Atkinson was treasurer in Whitaker's 1882-83 ministry. William Hutchison,* Wellington Advertiser Supplement, *September 9 1882. (ATL ref: A-095-051)*

The last straw breaks the camel's back. *Atkinson's 'national insurance' scheme was well before its time. William Hutchison,* Wellington Advertiser Supplement, *July 22 1882. (ATL ref: A-095-045)*

no companion to Harry and that it was natural that he should at once attach himself to a woman who was his equal ..." [2]

Atkinson was not out of politics for long, returning to represent New Plymouth following the member's resignation in early 1867. He resigned again the next year, when he and his new wife traveled to England. When they returned in 1871 he was still, at a healthy 40 years of age, a comparatively young man with a number of options. The time away had convinced him that the future lay in further developing a now-prosperous 'Hurworth' property surrounded by his expanding family.

But in 1872 the pull of politics and the prospect of a stirring election fight in a nearby seat against William Moorhouse, previously superintendent of Canterbury, could not be resisted, particularly as his opponent was a supporter of William Fox, no friend of Atkinson's.

Back in the House as the member for Egmont, he was to become closely associated with Julius Vogel and his borrowing policies. His watchwords were restraint and moderation; he was fearful of reckless borrowing and spending and he shared Vogel's concern about the provinces' competitive excesses.

In September 1874 he joined Vogel's administration as minister of crown lands and immigration. When Vogel was delayed in England by illness the next year Atkinson was, as colonial

treasurer, effectively in charge during Pollen's brief premiership. And he became premier himself in September 1876 when Vogel departed to become agent-general in London.

Vogel left Atkinson with a great deal of unfinished business, notably the final abolition of the provincial system and its replacement with a complex jigsaw puzzle of boroughs and counties.

He was, though, as William Gisborne explained, the man for the job. "He was intensely self-reliant; he had great moral courage, and he had great faith in his own capabilities." [3]

Despite no formal training, Atkinson mastered the complexities of the finance portfolio and was to be colonial treasurer for 10 years between 1875 and 1891, in his own and two subsequent governments. It was no easy task to firstly try to keep borrowing in some sort of balance with the country's ability to pay and then, through tough depression years, to steer a careful, prudent course.

His biographer Judith Bassett has written: "Atkinson was almost a copybook exemplar of colonial rural virtues. He liked to describe himself as a 'country settler'. He had planted his roots in Taranaki and saw hard work, thrift and moderation as the keys to success. ... he saw money and finance not as the stuff of romance but as the fabric of

Sir Harry: 'They say resignation is a virtue, and when a fellow is so far reduced, what is he to do?" *Atkinson's fourth and final ministry was between 1887-91. William Blomfield,* New Zealand Observer & Free Lance, *May 4 1889. (ATL ref: A-316-6-1)*

morality." [4] He was middle-of-the-road in most of his thinking, particularly on financial matters. The borrowing had to be curtailed, but it would be irresponsible to turn off the tap completely.

It was not an approach that courted popularity, in or out of Parliament, and Atkinson's ministry ended in October 1877. He was in opposition during the two years of Sir George Grey's ministry, but was then paid the considerable compliment of being appointed treasurer by John Hall and Frederick Whitaker between 1879-83.

Atkinson was to be premier three more times: for 11 months in 1883-84, a week in August 1884, and from October 1887 to January 1891.

Conscience and, increasingly, circumstances ensured that Atkinson was financially conservative. But from time to time he surprised his colleagues with much more liberal views on a range of subjects. He favoured perpetual leaseholds to get more people on the land. He supported deferred payment for settlers on crown land, women's suffrage, proportional representation, and a one-man-one-vote electoral system. He even suggested that bachelors should be taxed as they were avoiding family responsibilities! But he was still the Taranaki 'farmer settler', supporting the detention of Te Whiti's supporters without trial after Parihaka's passive resistance was broken in 1881.

Even while penny-pinching as much as possible, Atkinson was a promoter of local industry, protecting with a tariff in 1888, and active in settling more small farmers as North Island dairying country became available.

Probably his most significant scheme, which he called 'national insurance' and proposed while he was treasurer in 1882, would have paid pensions to the needy from a central fund with money from a compulsory levy on workers, topped up with income from crown leases. Atkinson wrote to a correspondent in July that year: "…The principal object I have in view is to secure the independence and improve the condition of the working classes and so to extinguish pauperism. …. Nothing is further from my intention than to drive any one from the Colony or to demand a premium from the wage earning class which cannot be paid." [5] It was thinking too advanced for colleagues and electorate; conventional wisdom had it that charity was a private rather than a public matter. It was to be another 16 years before the Liberals had the numbers to pass the Old Age Pensions Act, the tentative beginning of the 'welfare state' era.

Sadly, Atkinson did not have the rhetorical skills to 'sell' his ideas. He was one of the country's first professional politicians, doing little else for 20 years, but he was not a persuasive communicator, like Vogel

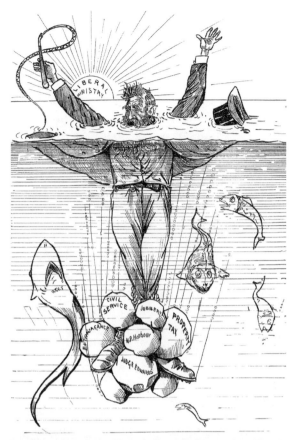

The Downfall of Sir Harry. The Old Man of the Sea is in the Sea at last …. *Atkinson was defeated by Ballance and his Liberals at the 1890 election. William Blomfield,* New Zealand Observer & Free Lance, *December 20 1890. (ATL ref: J-056-002)*

before him and Seddon later. He appeared unwilling, or unable, to court favour with anyone; his blunt, matter-of-fact pronouncements rarely produced either emotion or enthusiasm. As premier, he did not attempt to appease his supporters among the fluid political alliances in the House.

Bassett wrote: "He never attracted a large personal following, nor did he seem to want one. If members wished to support his policies on their merits they were welcome to do so; if not, not." [6] It is, of course, a mistake to think that 'personality' politics is an invention of the TV age; there might not have been a 'sound-bite' obsession, but it was still important in the late 19th century to explain ideas and policies, on the stump and in Parliament, in colourful, emotive language and in pithy slogans.

His great opponent over the years was Sir George Grey who entered the political fray on behalf of the provinces and remained to fight many other battles, often against Harry Atkinson. Politician and writer William Pember Reeves wrote: "This chief of Grey's opponents was as unlike him in demeanour and disposition as one man can well be to another. The two seemed to have nothing in common, except inexhaustible courage. Grey had been trained in the theory of war, and any part he took therein was as leader. Atkinson had picked up a practical knowledge of bush-fighting by exchanging hard knocks with the Maori as a captain of militia. Grey was all courtesy; the other almost oddly tart and abrupt. Grey's oratory consisted of high-pitched appeals to great principles, which were sometimes eloquent, sometimes empty. His antagonist regarded Parliament as a place for the transaction of public business." [7] Outside the House, said Reeves, Atkinson was a working colonist; inside it a practical politician.

It is an oversimplification to label Atkinson as a conservative and the lynchpin of a succession of conservative ministries. As Bassett wrote: "On most issues he held the middle ground – even on the question of finance he was considered dangerously expansionist by the right-wing retrenchers." [8] He might have been a laissez-faire free-trader in theory, but, in practice, he understood the need for state intervention.

In 1888, during his fourth and last premiership, Atkinson finally received the KCMG. He was now old for his years, worn out from carrying much of the burden of government for so long. However, the 'Scarecrow' ministry, as it is disparagingly known, was not the last gasp of conservatism before the Liberal revolution. Bassett wrote: "The first great reforming government in New Zealand's history did not succeed a pack of rank reactionaries, as some later liked to imagine, but a shaky, fad-ridden, middle-of-the-road administration headed by a man who was known to sympathise with most of the Liberals' ideas, though he lacked the power to put them into effect." [9]

One of Sir Harry Atkinson's final political acts, following defeat by Ballance at the 1890 election, was to appoint a number of anti-Liberals to the Legislative Council.

He was one of them and became speaker, collapsing and dying in his office in June 1892.

Above all else, Atkinson was, in today's parlance, 'open-minded'. As Bassett says: "It places him among the self-educated, eclectic, practical Prime Ministers of the twentieth century rather than the pastoral and professional gentry of the nineteenth. He is closer to Coates and Savage than to Whitaker and Hall." [10]

The retiring Premier, and possible successors. Young New Zealand (to honest John Bryce): 'Poor old Sir Harry will soon have to give up, but these fellows need not be in such a hurry to step into his shoes .... *Atkinson was worn out – old for his years – long before his final ministry ended. William Blomfield,* New Zealand Observer & Free Lance, *14 June 14 1890. (ATL ref: H-722-058)*

11

SIR GEORGE GREY
1812-1898

"He was never moderate, and his mind was lost to a proper sense of proportion"

Among a parade of premiers, some of them remarkable and few uninteresting, George Grey was extraordinary.

He was the only person to be both governor of New Zealand and its premier. And he was governor of two other colonies – South Australia and Cape Province. Besides this, he was a soldier, explorer, a notable writer of prose, linguist, naturalist, anthropologist and early recorder of Aborigine, African and Maori customs and mythology.

George Grey was also as deeply flawed as he was prodigiously talented. Today's psychiatric

Walter Leslie, Parliamentary Portraits 1887-1890.
(ATL ref: H-697-002)

profession would have found him a challenging study. Although he was liberal and humanitarian, it seems likely that these impulses took second place to his pride and ambition. He was supremely confident and arrogant, and obsessed with being right.

Edmund Bohan, his most recent biographer, sees Grey as a hero, even if a far from perfect one. Bohan writes: "Grey was a mass of complexities and contradictions: a democrat and rebel who was also an autocrat; an idealist of simple but deep religious convictions, yet calculating and devious; a man of almost irresistible personal charm and kindness, whose courtesy, fondness for children and private generosity became as legendary as his ruthlessness towards those

who crossed or thwarted him." [1] Others have seen him in a very different light. Bernard Cadogan, working on a further Grey biography, has described Grey as a "tormented and tormenting man." [2] He believes Grey aspired to being a great man – the Warren Hastings of the white settler second British Empire – rather than a 'hero'.

As a colonial governor George Grey's performance was spotty; as premier he was a failure. Perhaps he had been an autocrat too long to adapt successfully to the give and take of parliamentary politics. David Hamer has written: "Grey was ill-suited to the role of colonial politician, having just become one after a lengthy career as colonial proconsul. He had a paranoid attitude to criticism." [3]

George Grey was born in Lisbon in April 1812, a week after his father, a lieutenant-colonel in the Duke of Wellington's army, and a cousin of Lord Grey of Groby, was killed leading his regiment during an attack on Napoleon's troops in a Spanish fortress. His mother, Elizabeth Anne Vignoles came from a prominent Irish family. George Grey was educated at boarding school and by private tutor and with recurring entreaties from a large and affectionate family to live up to his father's heroic example.

When Grey enrolled at the Royal Military College, Sandhurst, in 1826, as a 14-year-old officer cadet, he was anything but a typical student. Richard Whately, who became his uncle-in-law and later Archbishop of Dublin, had already stimulated the teenager's intellectual curiosity about natural history and political ideas. Four years later, when Grey graduated, a soldier and talented linguist, there were no heroic battles to be fought, only garrison duty in Glasgow and Ireland as an ensign in the 83rd Foot. Peasant poverty in Ireland appalled him as he searched for answers in Edward Gibbon Wakefield's colonisation theories and the philosophical writings of Thomas Carlyle.

Lieutenant Grey returned to Sandhurst for advanced studies, leaving with glowing commendations. Despite this promising start to a military career, he was tiring of army life. An avid reader of the exploits of explorers like Captain Charles Sturt, and about the *Beagle's* voyage of scientific discovery, he was particularly fascinated by the largely untapped potential of Australia for exploration and subsequent settlement.

Perhaps surprisingly, the Colonial Office agreed to Grey's proposal that he should lead a small party to Western Australia to search for a rumoured inland waterway north of the Swan River colony that would open up new areas for settlement.

Grey led two unsuccessful, badly planned and executed expeditions during the 1837-39 period. On the first, Grey was speared by an Aborigine; on the second the party nearly perished. Nevertheless, Grey was promoted to captain and named resident magistrate at King George Sound to the south. His predecessor, Sir Richard Spencer, a naval hero, had died at his Albany post; Grey comforted Eliza Lucy Spencer, Sir Richard's daughter, and married the 16-year-old shortly afterwards. They had one child, a son, who lived only five months.

In 1840 the Greys were recalled to England. On the voyage back, and sensing an opportunity to create a favourable impression in Whitehall, Grey wrote and despatched on route a report to Lord John Russell, secretary of state for the colonies, with suggestions about how Aborigines might be successfully assimilated. Russell was sufficiently impressed to circulate the report to the governors of the Australasian colonies and then offer Grey the governorship of South Australia.

Grey was only 28 years old, and with practically no relevant experience, but immediately accepted the position and resigned his army commission. Grey's explicit instructions were to put a brake on the colony's spending; his predecessor George Gawler, a distinguished soldier, had spectacularly exceeded his budget. When the Greys arrived in Adelaide in 1841, the new governor carried out his orders to the letter. He slashed public works, wages and relief payments to cut costs, but also to drive the newly unemployed into the country where there was plentiful work. Adelaide's difficulties were compounded by Grey's refusal to accept his predecessor's considerable debts. It was now that two aspects of Grey's operational 'style', which were repeated again and again, became obvious. There was always to be someone else to blame for his difficulties, in this case the hapless Gawler. And Grey, aided by huge distances and poor communications,

The Cold Shoulder Reception as it would be if carried out as formerly promised. *By 1867 Governor Grey was as unpopular with southern settlers as he was with the Colonial Office. Cartoonist unknown,* Otago Punch, *January 19 1867. (ATL ref: H-686-009)*

could follow his own course by misrepresenting, just slightly, the intentions of the Colonial Office and, in turn, by subtly distorting settler views and aspirations.

In the beginning Grey was roundly loathed, castigated in the press and petitions and at public meetings and demonstrations, for both his economic stringency and an Aboriginal policy which attempted assimilation rather than retribution after the murder of European 'overlanders'. But by 1845, South Australia had bounced back from near bankruptcy, aided by a boom in farming and the discovery of mineral wealth. Grey had even found time to further his scientific studies, sending thousands of seeds, fossils and preserved mammal, snake and bird specimens to the appropriate London institutions. The governor was farewelled with heart-felt regrets and memorials.

The next challenge – to be even more demanding – was New Zealand. The colony's first governors had struggled financially and there were increasingly violent land disputes between settlers and Maori from North Auckland to Nelson. Arriving in Auckland in November 1845, Grey acted decisively, seizing the powerful chief Te Rauparaha while promising Maori there would be no land confiscations. Grey viewed some New Zealand Company land purchases with concern and the land-grabbing appetites of northern missionaries with distaste. There was no more open conflict between the races for over a decade.

Grey's measured and meticulous conduct of Maori affairs in the 1845-53 period was possibly his greatest achievement as a colonial governor. He observed the terms of the Treaty of Waitangi, constantly reassuring Maori that their land rights would be scrupulously observed. He charged the chief land purchase commissioner, Donald McLean, with negotiating land sales at tribal meetings. If a meeting agreed, the land passed to the Crown which sold it to settlers, profit from the transaction giving the colonial coffers a much needed 'top up'. A total of 33 million acres were purchased, all but three million of them in the South Island.

Keith Sinclair wrote: " ....he was the only able governor sent out while governors possessed any considerable influence; and the shape of New Zealand life in the nineteenth century owed more to him than to any other individual." [4] However, as in South Australia, Grey's attempts to 'Europeanise' Maori were not as successful as he claimed. He introduced British law to and built several hospitals in Maori districts, subsidised mission schools, and encouraged Maori agriculture. But he did not have the money to do much more than set a well-intentioned example. Personally, though, he became fluent in Maori and studied their traditions, legends and customs with his

Schoolmaster Grey: 'Is that your financial statement, Sir? Why, any little schoolboy in Wellington could do better than that'. *Grey and Atkinson, treasurer in Whitaker's ministry, disagreed on most things. William Hutchison,* Wellington Advertiser Supplement, *June 24 1882. (ATL ref: A-095-040)*

usual energy and thoroughness. Not surprisingly, his mana among Maori was high.

William Pember Reeves wrote: "With his Brown subjects, Grey after once beating them, trod the paths of pleasantness and peace. The chiefs recognised his imperturbable courage and self-control, and were charmed by his unfailing courtesy and winning manners." [5]

Grey's knighthood (the KCB) in 1848 – when he was only 36 – stuck in the collective craw of the settlers. They believed he had obstructed progress towards representative government. While it was true that Sir George wanted minimum interference it was also undeniable that the first complicated New Zealand constitution, written in the Colonial Office in 1846, would have seriously disadvantaged Maori and fermented trouble.

While Grey used his autocratic powers to the full, he was largely responsible for the country's much more enlightened 1852 constitution, with its provision for representative assemblies in both the provinces and nationally. The first provincial council elections were held before he left the country in late 1853, but the General Assembly did not have its first meeting until mid 1854.

Co-incidentally, at about the same time, the first Cape Parliament met in Cape Town, where Sir George Grey had recently arrived to be governor of the Cape Colony and the neighbouring British Kaffraria protectorate. Again, race relations were to be the defining feature of his governorship, which lasted until 1860. He planned an assimilation process, similar to his approach in South Australia and New Zealand. He attempted to convert frontier tribes to Christianity, he supported mission schools and built hospitals, but the policy foundered with his failed attempt to encourage thousands of Europeans to settle in British Kaffraria, where they would be agents of 'civilised' change. Also, the extraordinary millenarian movement, which prompted the Xhosa people to destroy their cattle and crops, decimated both livestock and human populations, and Grey's brutal response compounded the disaster.

Grey was increasingly out of favour at the Colonial Office; the British government's ledger-keepers accused him of overspending and, ignoring the official line, he proposed a union of the Cape, Natal, Kaffraria and the two Afrikanner republics, the Orange Free State and Transvaal. He was recalled to London and would have been sidelined had not an admirer, the Duke of Newcastle, returned to the Colonial Office.

On the voyage back to Africa, Grey's strained relationship with his wife worsened irretrievably when he accused her of a shipboard romance. Lady Grey was put ashore at Rio de Janeiro and he did not see, or speak of, her for 36 years; there was a reconciliation of sorts in London in 1897.

Late in 1860, with the first shots having been fired in New Zealand's land wars, Grey offered to return, believing he was the only man who could achieve peace. The Colonial Office agreed, and possibly regretted doing so. Grey was already criticising his predecessor, Gore Browne, before setting sail.

New Zealand now had responsible government but the governor still controlled native affairs. Grey later informed the Colonial Office that he was acting through his ministers in *all* matters; in fact he did retain control of native affairs, sometimes acting in an egocentic and arbitrary manner.

Raewyn Dalziel wrote: "Grey retained as much personal control over events as possible while trying to force successive governments to accept political and financial responsibility for the war. A series of ministries foundered on the handling of the war and the question of responsibility." [6]

Grey's ploys were largely unsuccessful. He tried to negotiate with the powerful Waikato tribes without success; the military road he built into the Waikato, in 1863, to placate apprehensive Auckland settlers further incensed the tribes. Military campaigns, in which Grey was more than a spectator, were ultimately inconclusive in Taranaki and the Waikato. He agreed to the confiscation of three million acres of Maori land in 1864 and this, along with his deteriorating relationship with the commander of British troops in New Zealand, General Cameron, made for continuing instability. In this inflammatory environment, Grey did his best to ignore very clear instructions to return the regiments to England. In 1867, with Te Kooti and other Maori generals reducing settler morale to a low ebb, the Colonial Office roused itself, and thoroughly exasperated, sacked Grey in the bluntest possible manner.

Grey's colonial career had not ended in the splendid fashion he had envisaged, but he never wavered from the firm conviction that circumstances and people had conspired against him. Sir George Grey had been a colonial governor for 28 years and was still only 56 years old, his intellect and powers of concentration undimmed.

He returned to England in 1868 but, after failing to win a seat in the House of Commons, it had little appeal after half a lifetime in the Southern Hemisphere, and he was soon back taking up again his wide-ranging scientific enquiries at his beloved Mansion House on Kawau Island, bought in 1862 and subsequently transformed.

"Kawau became his private world, where he ruled a small and devoted household and luxuriated in the peace and beauty of the Hauraki Gulf." [7] Grey planted trees from around the world and introduced exotic animals with an abandon impossible today. His niece and adopted daughter Annie Matthews, her husband Seymour George, who managed the estate, and their

Hanging onto the Grey horse's tail. Forecast of the parliamentary election. 'It is by the priest's skirts that the Devil climbs into the belfry.' – Spanish proverb. *Grey saw himself as the 'father' of Liberalism, the later Liberal leaders riding on his coat-tails. William Blomfield,* Observer & Free Lance, *April 26 1890 (ATL ref: H-722-054)*

The Political Jupiter & the Lesser Deities. The Colony is waiting to hear the thunders from the Grey clouds overhead, instead of the tin-trumpetings and toy-gun volleys of the so-called leaders. *Despite his rhetoric and oratory, Grey was a spent force by the 1890 election. William Blomfield,* Observer & Free Lance, *October 4 1890. (ATL ref: H-722-074)*

expanding family lived with Grey on Kawau for nearly 20 years.

It was the threat to the provincial system he had helped create that brought Grey out of his self-imposed semi-retirement in 1874. In a flurry of activity, he was elected superintendent of Auckland province and then an Auckland member of parliament. It was a doomed crusade but he had become its leader and when the Atkinson administration faltered in October 1877 he was asked to form a government.

The consultative and persuasive roles of premiership did not sit easily with Grey. As Reeves noted: "He learned to work apart, and practised it so long that he became unable to co-operate, on equal terms, with any fellow-labourer. He would lead, or would go alone." [8] He assembled a cabinet of individuals, some conservatives and two – John Ballance and Robert Stout – who shared his radical political views. Although Grey and Stout attempted to introduce manhood suffrage – 'one man one vote' – and some important trade union legislation was passed, the ministry was largely dysfunctional and survived just under two years.

Grey acquired a popular reputation as a 'Liberal' and his 1877-79 administration as the first 'Liberal' ministry. As David Hamer wrote: "Grey did much to give it the status of a myth through his oratory; he was one of the first New Zealand politicians to appeal to mass audiences, and his rhetoric implanted in their minds this version of what had happened in 1877-9." [9] When it suited them later Liberal leaders – Seddon particularly – paid lip-service to the myth.

Hamer again: "Grey ….worked hard at the time of his government and later to foster the myth that what was happening was a conflict between 'Liberals' and 'Conservatives'." [10] It may have, if nothing else, give a nudge to the idea of two distinct parties, a government and an opposition, in the House.

Grey retired to the back-benches but did not leave Parliament. He remained, a gadfly and irritant, until 1894, his intellectually democratic impulses very often swamped by an autocratic temperament that did not mellow with age. He returned to England in 1894, dying four years later.

He would have been pleased that his final resting place was St Paul's Cathedral.

William Gisborne, who first met Grey in South Australia in 1843 and served in his 1877 cabinet, had long observed him at close quarters: "He was never moderate, and his mind was lost to a proper sense of proportion. He overdid everything. His praise was flattery, and his blame was vituperation; he saw no merits in what he opposed, and no faults in what he supported. This moral excess was prejudicial in the highest degree to his practical influence and usefulness. His orbit as a statesman took the curve of an hyperbole. His precious gifts – and they were far beyond those ordinarily accorded to man – and his vast stores of political knowledge and experience were to a great extent dissipated into space." [11]

Fickle Sir George. All women of Auckland demand that 'their member', Sir George Grey, shall return from England at once to look after their legislative interests in New Zealand…. *In 1894, Grey requested leave of absence to travel to England. He was lionised by London society, visited Queen Victoria at Windsor, and did not return. William Blomfield,* Observer & Free Lance, *March 23 1895. (ATL ref: J-056-003)*

12
SIR JOHN HALL
1824-1907

"He looked on the transaction of departmental business as a labour of love"

John Hall was New Zealand's first middle-class premier, but he became the standard-bearer for some of the country's richest men. Essentially a conservative politician who was far happier administrating than politicking, it was, nevertheless, his radical legislation which secured the vote for New Zealand women.

Hall was born in 1824 into a respected local family in Hull, the English midlands port, His father, George Hall, was a master mariner and shipowner; his mother, Grace Williamson, who died in 1827, came from a prosperous mercantile family. John Hall first went to a local dissenting school and then, at 10, to Europe, his father believing the mastery of foreign languages essential to a maritime trading career.

He worked for a German merchant in London for several years, but then joined the General Post Office in 1845. At first his promotion was rapid, becoming private secretary to the permanent head. But when further advancement was blocked because others had more powerful connections, Hall cast around for opportunities that would better reward his personal abilities.

He liked what he read about the Canterbury Association in New Zealand; there the 'old boys' network' would be less developed and the climate good for his uncertain health. The new settlement's

Walter Bowring, Press Portraits No 42, Weekly Press, *December 4 1901. (ATL ref: B-094-003)*

farming opportunities and Anglican underpinnings also appealed. He decided to emigrate and arrived at Christchurch on the *Samarang* at the end of July 1852.

Hall was conscientious in his surveying of the pastoral possibilities, travelling to Hawke's Bay and Wairarapa before opting for Canterbury. In partnership with his two brothers who had followed him to New Zealand, he bought the leases of two 'runs', later taking over all the land and, with judicious freeholding, consolidated it into a 30,000 acre property. Although Hall owned other property, particularly in Christchurch, the 'Rakaia Terrace Station' made his fortune, moulded his political philosophy and was his refuge from the pressures of political life.

W J Gardner wrote: "His basic political aim was the preservation of private property rights in a society in which they appeared insecure. His political philosophy was defence of Terrace station writ large." [1]

Almost immediately, Hall began his long association with Canterbury politics. Apart from periods when he was out of the country he was a member of the Canterbury Provincial Council for the next 20 years, and he was three times a member of the executive. He proved to be particularly adept at protecting the interests of his fellow runholders. He was also active in church and community affairs – a magistrate in Lyttelton and Christchurch and first chairman of the Christchurch City Council.

He was 31 years-old when elected to the House of Representatives in 1855 and within months was colonial secretary in William Fox's first fleeting ministry. There followed a lengthy period in opposition and he spent 1860-61 in England where he married Rose Anne Dryden, a childhood friend, relative by marriage and daughter of a prominent Hull solicitor. They were to have five children, one daughter dying in young adulthood. Back in New Zealand, Hall was appointed to the Legislative Council in 1862, resigning nearly four years later.

In 1866 he contested and won a Canterbury seat and joined the Stafford ministry until June 1869. The passed-over postal official in England was now New Zealand's postmaster-general. For the next decade he combined periods as leader of the Legislative Council and colonial secretary with close supervision of his sheep station – his cross-breed merino flock climbing to 29,500 animals in 1869-70 – and a lengthy visit to England.

In 1879, back in the House as member for Selwyn, he was elected leader of the opposition when William Fox lost his seat. When premier Sir George Grey's administration collapsed acrimoniously some months later, Hall was called to form a ministry.

Hall wanted to be rid of Grey but had no particular enthusiasm for the premiership. As Jean Garner wrote: "He enjoyed the recognition his achievements won him but he was not vainglorious…. His talents …. were administrative rather than charismatic so that he preferred to hold executive and cabinet office rather than occupy the more conspicuous positions of superintendent or premier." [2]

However, the next 31 months were among the most significant in New Zealand's early parliamentary history. Like so many premiers in the pre-party era Hall had to hold together a cabinet of opposing personalities and policies and withstand the vitriolic and bitter attacks of the deposed George Grey. With his flair for compromise and consensus, Hall managed to garner enough support to blunt the opposition onslaught by picking up and enacting ground-breaking legislation – including universal male suffrage and three year parliamentary terms – that Grey had foreshadowed but been unable to pass. With an eye to his own constituency, he also adjusted the country quota system, giving even more weight to rural votes.

He was, as Gardner has written, very clear-sighted about his objectives: "Established interests could not be defended by confrontation; radicalism might be contained and diverted by flexible, low-profile tactics." [3]

The invasion of Parihaka in November 1881, the arrest of Te Whiti and the repressive measures that followed, was the most divisive issue of his ministry. Gardner wrote: "Hall was pulled one way by his natural caution and the need for economy, another way by the need to maintain the government's authority and the demands of angry settlers." [4]

The Parihaka crisis did not diminish Hall's standing at the time; in fact it probably provided some electoral advantage as he struggled to hold an uneasy coalition of competing interests together, largely by giving his ministers their heads, while his 'prudence' policy of moderate borrowing for moderate growth helped financial recovery take root. One of Hall's strengths was his administrative ability and, during his premiership, he greatly improved an inadequate civil service, streamlining the operation of government departments and centralising them in Wellington.

William Gisborne, that perceptive observer of New Zealand's 19th century premiers, wrote of John Hall: "He is, perhaps, more an official than a statesman …. His official aptitude was wonderful, and he looked on the transaction of departmental business as a labour of love. Correspondence on public service, files of former papers, memoranda, returns, despatch-boxes, and pigeon-holes were to him what a gymnasium is to an athlete, and unascended Alps are to a member of the Alpine Club." [5]

Hall, whose health had deteriorated with the strains of premiership, used cabinet squabbling as an opportunity to end his ministry in April 1882, receiving his KCMG shortly afterwards. Sir John left the House early the next year for a lengthy visit to England. When he returned in 1887, he was dismayed to see that private property was a principal target of the radical politicians who had growing support in and out of the House. He was soon back in Parliament and, although he did not take office, Premier Atkinson relied on him for advice that, his conservatism more engrained, was now not as astute as it once had been.

Edmund Bohan wrote: "In the House of Representatives he was always one of the readiest and best prepared (if not the most interesting) of speakers; a man others consulted in the cigar-smoke laden air of Bellamy's where factions negotiated and from which the coalition ministries of the pre-1890 period emerged." [6]

Oddly enough, it was at this point in his long political career that Hall played a leading part in legislation viewed as amongst the most radical of the era. His support of the female suffrage movement

The Veiled Prophet of Liberalism. 'Here judge, if hell, with all its power to damn, can add one curse to the foul thing I am.' *Hall, the guardian of property rights, became premier in early October 1879. Arthur Palethorpe,* New Zealand Punch, *(Wellington), October 25 1879. (ATL ref: H-693-009)*

the House of Representatives or Legislative Council, that stretched over a 38 year period. His fragile health suffered when he accepted the mayoralty of Christchurch during its 1906 exhibition year and he died in June 1907, his will including substantial bequests for charitable and religious projects.

Despite lengthy visits to the 'old country' John Hall had put down sturdy roots in New Zealand and sensed in the colony the beginnings of a separate and distinct identity. He made this clear when he represented New Zealand at an Australian conference debating federalism in Melbourne in 1890. His "Nature has made 1,200 impediments to the inclusion of New Zealand in any such Federation in the 1,200 miles of stormy ocean which lie between us and our brethren in Australia" [9] was stronger on rhetoric than reason, but a fair summation of his countrymen's views.

Bohan wrote: "For 40 years he was at or near the centre of New Zealand politics and Canterbury's public affairs, having built his distinguished public career on soundly organised business interests and a thriving pastoral estate. He survived the economic storms which sent so many of his contemporaries into bankruptcy, and he died in 1907 one of the most successful of all pioneer pastoralists, leaving an estate and a family which still holds a secure place in Canterbury life." [10]

combined a personal view that women had a right to the vote with a conviction that they would exercise their vote conservatively, derailing some of the Liberals' most dangerously radical policies.

In 1889 Hall stated: "We cannot afford to bid women stand aside from the work of the nation. We need all their spirit of duty, their patience, their knowledge in abating the sorrow, sin, and want that is around us." [7] In 1891, Hall's bill passed the House but the Legislative Council baulked at the idea. An 1892 bill introduced by Premier Ballance also bogged down. Finally, in 1893, when Hall presented a third petition with nearly 32,000 signatures, his female franchise bill passed both houses, although its passage was facilitated by some voting miscalculations by its opponents.

Subsequently, Hall's role in securing the vote for women in New Zealand has been downplayed, but Garner believes he was the key figure in the campaign. She wrote: "He was one of the politicians who had backed votes for women in 1878 and from 1888 he led the suffrage initiative in the General Assembly. Furthermore, his advice to [Kate] Sheppard to use mass petitions was crucial and his subsequent counsel to her and the other women helped shape the women's campaign to meet the requirements of the parliamentary arena." [8]

The legislation safely passed, Hall now largely retired from public life after a political career, in either

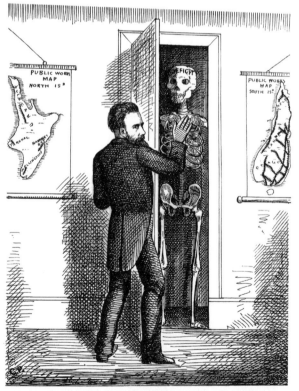

The Skeleton in the Cupboard . *Hall's 'moderate borrowing for moderate growth' policy kept the deficit at bay. C P,* New Zealand Punch, *(Wellington), April 24 1880. (ATL ref: H-693-029)*

13

SIR ROBERT STOUT
1844-1930

"He read widely in social and political theory and was passionately interested in ideas"

Like many well-educated Scots in the 19th century, Robert Stout was a man of varied accomplishments. His premiership of New Zealand was possibly the least of them. Stout was an effective attorney general, an outstanding chief justice and a pioneer of the country's university system, serving 20 years as the chancellor of the University of New Zealand.

Robert Stout was born in September 1844 in the Shetlands, the small cluster of islands in the North Sea noth-east of Scotland, the son of Thomas Stout and Margaret Smith. Stout's father was a merchant and he was the eldest of six children. His schooling began at kindergarten when he was five and continued at the local grammar and parish schools. More valuable to the wide-ranging political, scientific and theological interests he developed were the endless discussions among his extended family that he was encouraged to take part in. Books, magazines and newspapers also filled the long winter nights.

When he was 14 Stout qualified as a teacher, specialising in science and mathematics, and became a pupil-teacher at Lerwick's parish school. Thinking of a future elsewhere, as so many young Scotsmen of his generation did, Stout also qualified, two years later, as a surveyor.

Reading about the discovery of gold, he decided

Walter Bowring, Press Portraits No. 8, Weekly Press, *July 1899. (ATL ref: J-058-005)*

to emigrate to New Zealand's Scots-inspired Otago settlement in late 1863, but the links to the Shetlands were never broken, and he was to become a one-man emigration service helping many Shetlanders make the journey to the bottom of the world.

Robert Stout arrived in Dunedin on board the *Lady Milton* in April 1864. Lerwick might have been the northernmost town in the British Isles but it was sophisticated compared to a very primitive Dunedin during its earliest years.

Stout had honed his considerable debating skills at bible classes in Lerwick where discussion about the dogmatic attitudes of competing religious sects made him into an agnostic. His views, with an emphasis on morality rather than sectarian religion, soon became well known in Dunedin, whose Presbyterian foundations were being shaken by goldmining arrivals of a very different stripe. Stout edited a freethought paper, *The Echo,* and was a regular on lecture hall stages.

Robert Stout's hope of surveying work on the goldfields came to nothing, so he fell back on his teaching experience. He taught at two schools and was one of the founders, and first secretary, of the Otago Schoolmasters' Association. But when Stout was turned down for a headmastership in Oamaru, he decided on a third and much more enduring career.

To practise law in those days, a neophyte lawyer was articled to a legal firm for five years. Beginning in 1867, Stout completed his articles in just three years in the office of William Downie Stewart, father of a prominent politician in later decades. He was called to the Bar in 1871 and quickly gained a formidable reputation as a barrister.

Also in 1871, he was one of the first students at the University of Otago. He studied subjects ranging from moral science to political economy, was the university's first law lecturer and then a member of its council for some years late in the century.

It was probably inevitable, given his interests and training, that Stout would feel the strong pull of politics. He was 28 years old in 1872 when he was elected to the Otago Provincial Council, quickly becoming provincial solicitor. Robert Stout might have avoided national politics but for the 1875 threat to the provincial system. He was elected to the House in August 1875 and took an active, but frustratingly unsuccessful, part in the fight against abolition.

There was a sense of desperation in some of his arguments. According to Judith Bassett: "Stout said that abolition was a plot hatched by the 'monopolists and capitalists' to avoid closer settlement of the land." [1]

In 1876 in Dunedin Stout married Anna Paterson Logan, later an activist in the feminist and temperance movements and a child health pioneer. They were to have four sons and two daughters,

Politics was still for those with a private income; Stout had to earn his, and support his growing family, at the law. In part this explains his stop-go political career over the next quarter century. William Pember Reeves wrote: "His difficulty was that he was unable to devote himself to public life continuously. He had to try and serve two masters, both equally exacting. No sooner had he made his mark in the House than the claims of Advocacy took him back to the law courts." [2]

With his advocate's skills and legal knowledge, Stout soon impressed in the House, and on the public platform as well. Reeves again: "When facing a public meeting his strong physique, good presence, and obvious courage put him on terms with his audience at once. He wasted no time over circumlocution, went straight to the case that he had to state, and stated it in good plain English, delivered with plenty of action and vigour." [3]

Stout became attorney general in Sir George Grey's administration in March 1878, and shortly after, minister for lands and immigration. Sharing with Grey a number of liberal views, notably about land reform, his ideal was a land of small holdings, secured by the state, and he strongly favoured state leasing of land. Unfortunately, Stout's relationship

with Grey worsened, and was never repaired, when he and close friend and colleague John Ballance became involved in plans, along with Julius Vogel, to float the New Zealand Agricultural Company in England, an ambitious scheme to subdivide rabbit-infested Southland estates for considerable profit. Stout and Ballance, provisional directors of the company, had given the impression that the government endorsed the scheme.

Edmund Bohan wrote: "When Grey discovered the extent of this fraud, his shocked rage cowed even the irrepressible Vogel and forced Ballance and Stout to resign their directorships forthwith, although each protested his innocence of any deliberate wrongdoing." [4] They had, Grey fumed, compromised the probity of the great liberal cause.

As Raewyn Dalziel notes, such conflicts of interest were not uncommon: "In the days before payment of members of Parliament and with a restricted pool of potential parliamentarians, some of the political talent necessarily resided in the country's businessmen and speculators. These men did not draw the distinction between their various interests too finely." [5]

Stout resigned from the ministry and the House in June 1879, three months before the struggling Grey ministry succumbed. Dysfunctional cabinet relations aside, Stout's legal partner was ill and after a year in the government he needed more time to earn a living. But out of the House his political concerns remained and, in Otago, he forced inquiries into the practice of 'dummyism', used to acquire land people were not entitled to.

While Stout's legal practice prospered, with numerous Court of Appeal appearances, he grew increasingly concerned about the ineffectual performance of the untidy coalition of liberal parliamentarians opposing the essentially conservative Hall, Whitaker and Atkinson administrations. His personal coffers sufficiently replenished, Stout was back in the House again in July 1884, the member for Dunedin East.

Despite their many political differences, after one false start Stout and Vogel formed an administration that survived from September 1884 until October 1887. "A major reason for this seemingly bizarre connection was the association of all three men [Vogel, Ballance and Stout] with the Waimea Plains Railway and New Zealand Agricultural Companies. One purpose of the formation of the Stout-Vogel government was to rescue these companies from impending disaster." [6]

At first, as Waterhouse and Pollen had before him, Stout effectively played second fiddle to Sir Julius Vogel who was treasurer. Back in the country after five years in England, part of the time as New Zealand's agent general, Vogel had been welcomed in the hope that he would turn around a flagging economy. Privately, he hoped to give a similar boost to the failing fortunes of the New Zealand Agricultural Company.

As Vogel's health worsened, Stout played a more assertive role in the government, that was really no more liberal than its predecessors. It clung to power, buying the support of Canterbury members with a railway link to Westland, but had no answers for the growing economic malaise. Strongly influenced by the self-reliant philosophies of Herbert Spencer, a

Highly affecting. 'It was the late Premier's request and dying wish that I should come and lead the party.' – Sir Robert Stout at Wanganui women's political meeting. *Stout did not have a seat in the House when Ballance died, and Seddon was confirmed as premier before he did. William Blomfield,* New Zealand Observer & Free Lance, *August 11 1894. (ATL ref: H-722-184)*

hero of his teenage years, Stout was not prepared to provide relief for the growing numbers of unemployed. The ministry's few achievements – a far-reaching hospital act, legislation to remove political patronage from the public service and the introduction of probation for first offenders – all bear Stout's personal stamp.

Stout was a long-time supporter of equal rights for women and, most practically, in 1884, largely responsible for legislation allowing married women to acquire, hold and sell property in their own right.

Stout and Vogel had very different views on New Zealand's role in the Pacific and other international issues. As Dalziel wrote: "Stout was less of an expansionist, more of an internationalist than an empire man, something of a pacifist." [7] Stout wanted to consider federation with Australia; Vogel opposed doing so.

But they did share an apprehension about Germany's Pacific intentions and wanted to annex Samoa, Tonga and the Cook Islands. However, as Keith Sinclair wrote: "The Colonial Office was too shrewd not to see that the colonists were calling on Great Britain, in the name of the British Empire, to pursue imperial interests of their own." [8] William Gisborne wrote about the unhappy Stout-Vogel ministry: "Two statesmen who had been former rivals and who still held opposite views and principles in large political questions were yoked together to carry on government. Such a coalition of antagonism was a source, not of strength, but of weakness, and was foredoomed to failure." [9]

Stout lost the September 1887 election, and his seat. Possibly his acceptance of a KCMG the year before had contributed; certainly his links to an increasingly unpopular Vogel had. Still, Sir Robert remained true to his liberal conscience, supporting a campaign against 'sweating' in the clothing trade and acting as a conciliator during the 1890 maritime strike. Belatedly, Stout was coming to see that state intervention in the economy was the only way to change deeply entrenched injustices.

Sir Robert did not contest the election in late 1890, but the new prime minister, John Ballance, consulted him on personnel and policy. By early 1893 Ballance was dying. R M Burdon wrote: "Sir Robert Stout, who had been present at Ballance's deathbed, alleged that the Premier had expressed a wish that he should be his successor. Though not in Parliament at the time he was expected to find a seat before long at a by-election." [10]

It was not to be. Ballance died in April and Stout did not manage to scramble back into the House until early June. By this time, Richard John Seddon, Ballance's deputy, had consolidated his position as Liberal leader.

Out of step with Seddon's populist form of liberalism, Stout became a sterner critic of the government than the opposition. Now his long-time support for prohibition provided a convenient cudgel for a sustained attack on Seddon.

According to Burdon: "As a champion of prohibition it was inevitable that he should fall foul of the man who, in his opinion at least, showed undue favour to the liquor interest, but as time went on he became more and more prone to oppose every Government measure as a matter of course, and to reject all legislation tainted with Seddon's touch, quite regardless of its merits." [11]

Stout was returned to the House by the electors of Wellington City in 1893 and again in 1896. He and his family moved to Wellington in 1895, as did his new, young partner at law J G Findlay, subsequently a prominent politician. Stout's still considerable energies went into building another law practice, his presidency of the New Zealand Alliance, the principal prohibitionist organisation, and the founding of Victoria University College, subsequently serving on its council for 15 years.

Sir Robert's political career came to an end in 1898 when Seddon appointed him chief justice of the Supreme Court. Burdon again: "Born to excel in any chosen sphere of action, he had vexed and harassed Seddon at every turn for nearly five years. Man for man he was the Premier's match; as party leader or political strategist he could in no way compare with the rival who had ousted and supplanted him." [12]

Seddon might have been removing a political irritant, but Stout's distinguished quarter century as chief justice fully justified the appointment. Stout's prodigious number of decisions had a distinctly liberal flavour to them; he was closely involved with the consolidation of the New Zealand statutes; and he was appointed a Privy Councillor in 1921.

Following his retirement from the bench in 1926, Stout was promptly appointed to the Legislative Council. Until his health began to fail in 1929, it was a further and final platform for an indefatigable stream of opinions, and moralising, about the major issues of the day. Sir Robert died in July 1930, his wife less than a year later.

Hamer, who made a particular study of New Zealand's thirteenth premier, wrote: "Stout was that rarity in New Zealand life: an intellectual in politics. He read widely in social and political theory and was passionately interested in ideas, although he had no original political ideas of his own.... There was a strong moralising tone to his liberalism. It was to the inculcation of new morality rather than to legislation that he looked for the improvement of society. In the gradual evolution of his political views he was guided by his opposition to a class society." [13]

The Opposition goes a-fishing. *Stout became one of Seddon's principal critics, but could not outsmart the wily premier. William Blomfield,* New Zealand Observer & Free Lance, *March 30 1895. (ATL ref: H-722-196)*

14
JOHN BALLANCE
1839-1893

"Retiring, modest, courteous, willing to compromise, he won the affection and loyalty of all his colleagues"

John Ballance was the leader of the first real party government in New Zealand, but he did not live to see it in its glory days.

He was born in March 1839 in County Antrim, Northern Ireland. His tenant farmer father, Samuel Ballance, was a descendent of Puritan immigrants from England and his mother, Mary McNiece, a Quaker.

Until he was 14, Ballance was educated at the local Glenavy school and in nearby Belfast; he then found work at a hardware firm in the city. The eldest of 11 children, young John took an unusually strong interest in his father's political activities. At 18 he moved to Birmingham and a job as a travelling salesman. Birmingham was a centre of radical thought in the mid-19th century, so it is not surprising that, with his interest already whetted, Ballance attended politics classes at the Midland Institute, joined literary and debating clubs, and began contributing articles to local newspapers. In the course of his job, travelling to other cities and towns, he saw at first hand the conditions in which the poor lived in industrial England.

It was with his marriage to Fanny Taylor, in June 1863, that the emigration seed was sown. She was in poor health and it was hoped a more equable climate would help; she also had a brother living in Wanganui.

John Ballance was 27 when he and Fanny sailed

William Blomfield, New Zealand Observer & Free Lance, *December 19 1891. (ATL ref: H-722-100)*

for New Zealand and Wanganui in 1866. With little capital he was unable to buy land as he had hoped. After a brief period as a jewellery retailer, he was more confident about his next venture, a three times a week evening newspaper. He began the *Herald* with a printer as partner, but was soon the sole owner as well as an editor with a growing reputation for his spirited, independent views.

Titokowaru's attack on Wanganui in 1868 tested both these attributes. Ballance used the columns of his newspaper to promote the formation of a cavalry unit. He was then arrested for denouncing a universal militia call-up. Later he served in the cavalry, earning a commission that was cancelled when, wearing his war correspondent's hat, he criticised the government's war policy.

Politics was a logical next step, and in this he was fully supported by his second wife. Fanny Ballance had died in early 1868, only 24 years old; two years later he married Ellen Anderson, daughter of a Wellington merchant. Ballance was nominated for Egmont in 1872, but stood aside for Harry Atkinson, a future opponent, who also favoured Edward Stafford's 'centralist' approach. However, Ballance was in the House of Representatives three years later when his vote and voice contributed to the demise of the provinces. In 1877 he ended his loose alliance with Atkinson and joined George Grey's liberal grouping.

'Over the Garden Wall'. *Ballance lost his seat in 1881 and was forced to observe Parliament from the outside until 1884.William Hutchison,* Wellington Advertiser Supplement, *January 7 1882. (ATL ref: A-095-014-1)*

When Grey took power late that year he rewarded this support with several cabinet portfolios. Edmund Bohan: "Grey and Ballance had little in common except a fear that the old world's social evils might be replicated in this new country. Locked into essentially British problems, both were convinced that New Zealand was crowded with indecently rich capitalists intent on preying upon an abject working class sunk in miserable poverty and in need of succour." [1] It was in his first budget as colonial treasurer that John Ballance introduced the land tax, a then controversial revenue-raising measure which taxed the unimproved value of larger estates. Both Ballance and Grey badly misjudged the countrywide unpopularity of selective taxation that put a brake on much-vaunted 'enterprise'. He resigned from the government shortly afterwards following bitter personal arguments with the premier but, a committed liberal by temperament, he continued to support the Grey administration in the House for the rest of its term. While Ballance was to be successor to Grey's 'liberal' mantle, the dislike the two men shared for each other did not lessen.

Ballance lost his seat in 1881, in part because he criticised native affairs minister John Bryce's occupation of Parihaka, but was back in 1884, representing Wanganui as he continued to do for the rest of his political career. The same year he was also back in cabinet in the ostensibly liberal Stout-Vogel ministry. The lands portfolio allowed him to continue his promotion of closer land settlement and leasehold tenure and he sought to limit further sale of crown land and to curb the purchase of vast additional acreages by wealthy landowners. His villager settlements scheme, to cut unemployment and get more people on the land, was only partially successful. Future generations benefited from his foresight in facilitating the Maori gifting of the initial land for the Tongariro National Park. As native affairs minister he took a more conciliatory line than a number of his predecessors, beginning negotiations in the King Country and using police rather than the military to keep law and order.

According to David Hamer: "The Stout-Vogel government was not all that different from the Liberal government of the 1890s, especially after Ballance's death. The two halves were in effect re-combined – pragmatic, experimental reform, a doctrinaire gloss at the rhetorical level, and loan-based developmentalism." [2] After the Stout-Vogel government's defeat Ballance emerged, during the 1887-90 period, as the clear leader of a much more focussed opposition in the House. Hamer again: "The election of Ballance was of considerable significance because it was done by an Opposition 'caucus' comprising members from many parts of the country. This was not how leaders had been found in the past." [3]

Ballance thought of, and talked about, the opposition as the alternative government. And, not content with quoting liberal theorists from England and elsewhere, he adapted their ideas to the solving of real social problems in New Zealand and began to consciously woo the growing numbers of industrial workers in cities and towns around the country.

Judith Bassett wrote: "The reform programme he advocated was not unlike programmes which Atkinson had sympathised with for years, but Ballance's tone of urgency and desire for action could by no means be confused with Atkinson's weary diffidence." [4]

There was a general election at the end of 1890 – a year in which industrial workers had flexed their frustrations in strikes in England, Australia and New Zealand – and Ballance's Liberals, with the first torchbearers of an emerging Labour grouping and some sympathetic independents, were able to form the country's first fully-fledged party government.

R M Burdon wrote: "The habitual moderation and restraint of Ballance's language while addressing the House, his persistent courtesy both to friends and foes, had given rise to the fallacy that he was weak …. Ballance had never sought to lead, but when leadership devolved upon him through sheer force of merit he displayed strength of character hitherto unsuspected." [5] Ballance became premier and colonial treasurer; despite the wealth of talent he had available he was the only Liberal member in the House with previous ministerial experience. However, over the years R J Seddon, J McKenzie, W P Reeves, J G Ward, and J Carroll were to gain plenty of that, and change the face of politics and the nation. It was certainly a cabinet of 'big' personalities, as Michael Bassett observed. "Ballance, Seddon, Buckley and McKenzie were giants, each six feet tall and eighteen stone or more. A press gallery reporter described Ballance as 'large all over. Head well developed, hair smooth and iron grey; eyes pale .... which look out cautiously, sometimes, suspiciously, at times timidly, from beneath penthouse brows; features massive and marked'." [6]

With Ballance, New Zealand was moving to a new breed of premier and a new kind of leadership. Guy Scholefield wrote: "As a speaker Ballance was forceful; sometimes eloquent, always effective. He had no resource of Latin or Greek tags; but Parliament was beginning to value these things less or to notice them not at all." [7] William Pember Reeves, a close colleague at the time, later wrote:"A kind, courteous, considerate chief, always ready to listen, he was regarded by most of those round him with a feeling of personal friendship, in some cases amounting to affection." [8] While he has acquired a reputation more as a facilitator than an innovator, Ballance quickly set the scene for his pioneering administration with a boldly framed Land and Income Tax Bill which introduced direct taxation and repealed the unfair property tax.

Ballance was equally determined to attack a serious economic depression with self-reliance rather than more borrowing and to introduce legislation to ease the harsh living and working conditions of so many poorer New Zealanders. If this was 'state socialism', as their opponents called it, then so be it. Of course it was no more nor less than a carefully constructed bridge of practical measures, each policy plank leading the Liberals' disadvantaged supporters towards a better life. And, as treasurer,

he dulled the edge of the opposition's attack by producing a record budget surplus in 1892 after years of depression. The epithet, the 'Rain-Maker', was well deserved, but not to be long enjoyed.

In 1891 Ballance's government had passed a welter of reforming tax, land, labour and electoral legislation in the House of Representatives. "The Liberals' success, however, did not extend to the Legislative Council, where members enjoyed the comforting security of life appointments," wrote Burdon. "To them reform was anathema and progress a horrid spectre. Regarding it as their bounden duty to preserve the colony from self-inflicted wounds during a period of temporary insanity, they threw out or amended beyond recognition every Liberal measure sent up to them." [9]

Successive governors refused to appoint new Liberal members to the Council so Ballance appealed to London and the secretary of state for the colonies, winning both the argument and an important constitutional point.

Labour difficulty in the House. Strike of members for an increase of pay. *In 1891, MPs received only £100 per annum, plus £50 expenses; the amount was upped to £240 in 1893. William Blomfield,* New Zealand Observer & Free Lance, *August 1 1891. (ATL ref: H-722-091)*

Ballance strongly supported the female franchise, encouraged by his wife who was a prominent feminist, but he shared the common view that women were intrinsically conservative in outlook. His biographer, Tim McIvor, has written: "Once female enfranchisement passed the House of Representatives . ... he sought to delay its implementation until after the 1893 election, believing that the majority of women were politically uneducated and that their vote in the coming election would not be to the Liberals' advantage." [10] One of Ballance's enduring legacies was the nationwide party organisation, the Liberal Federation, he established; this and his effective leadership of caucus produced a cohesive political party that would remain in power an unprecedented 20 years.

During 1892 John Ballance was an increasingly ill man. "Unhappily," Reeves wrote, "he lacked one most necessary part of a leader's equipment, robust health." [11] He had wanted his old friend and confidante Sir Robert Stout to succeed him; with hindsight it is clear that it was to the Liberals' advantage that Stout was not a member of Parliament when John Ballance died, only 54 years old, in April 1893. His wife lived a further 42 years until 1935.

Sinclair has described John Ballance as "a man who has often been underestimated, largely because he died after two years in office. Retiring, modest, courteous, willing to compromise, he won the affection and loyalty of all his colleagues. This was no inconsiderable feat, for not only was his cabinet, in political, intellectual and administrative ability, probably the strongest ever formed in New Zealand, but it also contained masterful individuals quite incompatible without his presence." [12] Ballance was radical by inclination but also believed that reform must run in tandem, not ahead, of public opinion. It called for skilful political management.

"In these early years Ballance kept the party united through the ambiguity of the 'evolutionary' interpretation of progress towards policy goals." [13]

David Hamer has identified what is possibly his greatest achievement. "During Ballance's premiership a Liberal party gradually consolidated itself both in the House and in the country." [14]

Reinforcing the crew of H.M.S. 'Legislative Council'. *Ballance had to appeal to London before more sympathetic appointments were made to the Legislative Council. William Blomfield,* New Zealand Observer & Free Lance, *October 10 1892. (ATL ref: H-722-135)*

15

RICHARD JOHN SEDDON
1845-1906

"He alone could bridge by his personality gaps that were politically unbridgeable"

Richard John Seddon was a great many things. Constitutionally he was New Zealand's last premier, but sometimes called himself 'prime minister'. He was also a larger-than-life character, the first politician with the sort of charisma that could extend across the Tasman to Australia. While Grey used his immense prestige to become a timid populist, Seddon was a populist born and bred. With his blustering, bullocking style and rough manners his more patrician opponents underestimated him at their cost.

Seddon was born at Eccleston in Lancashire, England, in June 1845. With his father, Thomas Seddon, the headmaster of the local grammar school and his Scots mother, Jane Lindsay, also a teacher, it was more of a middle-class family than he would always admit to years later on the West Coast of the South Island in New Zealand.

His parents must have felt disappointment and some sense of personal failure when it was decided there was little point in

Walter Bowring, Press Portraits No 1, Weekly Press. *(ATL ref: A-312-005)*

schooling him beyond 12 years of age. For a while he worked on his paternal grandfather's farm and then, more happily, as an apprentice at an engineering works and iron foundry in nearby St Helens. There and at another company in Liverpool he gained a Board of Trade engineer's certificate.

In 1863, after a serious bout of smallpox, with employment prospects gloomy and news about the Victorian goldfields promising, he decided to emigrate to Australia, working his passage on the *Star of England*.

Melbourne was not a great success, but he did meet his future wife Louisa Jane Spotswood there. He worked in the Victorian government railway workshops, leaving for a spell of prospecting on the Bendigo goldfields. The Spotswood family, their pretensions bolstered by a number of army officers in their lineage, allowed Louisa to become engaged but not married until Seddon's 'prospects' improved.

Richard Seddon, again chasing a pot of gold, sailed for Hokitika, New Zealand in February 1866. He quickly made a reputation as a boxer and athlete and appears to have prospered sufficiently over the next three years, hydraulically sluicing for gold at the Waimea diggings, to set up several stores and, in January 1869, to return to Melbourne and marry his patient fiancée. They returned to the West Coast where Seddon had to muster his considerable stocks of energy and enterprise to make a living to support both his growing family and penchant for politics. A publican's licence to sell liquor boosted sagging receipts at his Big Dam store and this was later transferred to Kumara and the Queen's Hotel; mostly, though, he made his living as a miner's advocate in the goldfields' warden's court.

Given the confidence with which he was to stride the world stage, it is perhaps surprising that Seddon's political ambitions remained firmly focused on the West Coast for some years. He went from road board to provincial council, mastering speech-making and meeting procedure along the way, and, after 1876, to the Westland County Council. He became, and remained, chairman until 1891.

Also in 1876, the Seddons began their long association with Kumara and the next year he become the town's first mayor. Two years later, after an unsuccessful earlier attempt, Seddon won a seat in the House of Representatives, representing Hokitika. Seddon entered Parliament as a supporter of Sir George Grey, a favour Grey was to return over a decade later. The two men could not have been more different – in appearance, manner and, very often, political ideas. Grey, by now elderly, but still suave, polished and with a silver tongue; Seddon, 34 years-old, nearly six feet tall and large in physique, voice, and gesture. Initially, the association with Grey had him marked down as a radical; he wasn't and this became increasingly obvious. He was viewed, during those first years, if he was much noticed at all, as an uncouth country bumpkin. He excelled at long-winded stonewalling of legislation he didn't like, but contributed very little in the way of new ideas. His concerns, mainly the well-being of miners, remained very parochial, but he was a 'centralist' because

central government money was needed to build West Coast roads and bridges. Money rather than philosophy guided his conversion to 'state socialism'.

Seddon was a comparatively minor political figure during much of the 1880s. As historian David Hamer has written: "Seddon knew little of New Zealand beyond the West Coast, and it knew little of him." [1] After 1887, with Atkinson leading the government again, he was more prominent and widely accepted as an authority on mining legislation.

In January 1891 it was predictable enough that Ballance should entrust Seddon with the mines and public works portfolios in his Liberal cabinet. Suddenly, Seddon's 'commonness' had translated into the 'common touch' and a decided boon to his and the Liberal Party's fortunes.

It was Seddon's quiet mastery of parliamentary procedure, though, rather than his rumbustious style on the hustings that gave him the party leadership and premiership. With Ballance's health ebbing, it was logical for Seddon to take charge of the legislative programme. Ballance had wanted Stout to replace him but he died before his old friend could find a vacant seat and get back into the House. By the time he did, Seddon was firmly in control, having bolstered strong South Island support with the judicious leaking of telegrams from Sir George Grey. R M Burdon wrote: "When news reached him that Seddon was wavering he at once telegraphed, urging him if possible to form a government, and then, lest the first message should fail in effect, he despatched a second more fervid exhortation." [2]

When Seddon became premier in May 1893, the detail of many of the Liberals' major reforms had been decided, even if they had not been passed into law. Early in his premiership Seddon showed his skill in finding some common ground in the implacably fought liquor licensing issue and acting decisively to rescue the Bank of New Zealand from collapse, as well as ably facilitating the passage of a raft of pioneering financial, social and industrial legislation. And he was shrewd enough to subsequently extract political advantage from

On The War Trail. *Seddon met any political or personal charges with a well-honed vengeance. William Blomfield,* The Observer & Free Lance, *1899. (ATL ref: H-723-013)*

one major miscaluation, the passing of the 'votes for women' legislation in the upper house when he was sure a majority would oppose it.

Seddon used the 1893 election to consolidate his 'legitimacy'. As Len Richardson has written: "He required from candidates a pledge of support in return for official recognition. This practice, known as the 'hallmark', was widely condemned but extremely effective." [3]

Seddon's own contribution to the Liberals' legislative programme has probably been under-estimated. He was personally involved in laws that provided worker housing and teacher superannuation and, of course, he was the principal advocate for the Old-Age Pensions Act, the stimulus being his concern for ex-miners on the West Coast.

Keith Sinclair wrote: "In 1898, after a famous parliamentary battle in which 1,400 speeches were made, Seddon wore out the opposition in an uninterrupted ninety-hour sitting. The aged poor received their small pension – providing that they were of good repute, sober, and had not deserted their family or been recently in gaol." [4]

On the West Coast Seddon had developed the effective technique of constant campaigning, always on the stump, 'pressing flesh' at meetings and banquets; it was a style of politicking that, in the pre-mass media era, translated successfully to the national stage. It was also exhausting and doubtless contributed to his early death.

Guy Scholefield wrote: "No sooner had Parliament prorogued than Seddon would commence his perambulation of the countryside, tours which took him, by horse, buggy, coach, train or steamer to every corner of the country. They were a masterpiece of democratic practice." [5]

Of course, Seddon's close involvement with most things his government did was the inevitable corollary of his obsession with concentrating as much power as possible in the premier's office. He was minister of defence and public works until 1896, and minister of native affairs from 1893-99. More importantly, he became minister of labour when William Pember Reeves moved to London as agent-general in 1896, the same year he also replaced Joseph Ward, forced to resign because of personal financial problems, as colonial treasurer. He held these positions, plus the education and immigration portfolios acquired in mid-1903, until his death.

Scholefield again: ".... in addition to his numerous departments, he thought it necessary to keep a close watch on the work of all the others. He insisted that all major transactions and appointments should come before him; and so from major to minor." [6]

Following the November 1902 election, which

The Passing Of Democratic Dick Seddon. *Seddon's deputy Joseph Ward accepted a knighthood in 1901, but 'King Dick' was too shrewd a politician to follow suit and risk alienating his core support among the country's battlers. William Blomfied,* The Observer, *1902. (ATL ref: H-723-015))*

introduced the first-past-the-post system with only one member per electorate, the title of premier was replaced by 'prime minister', and Seddon lived the role to the hilt.

William Pember Reeves wrote: "It is noteworthy that his great popularity began after he had been Premier for five years. Of most Premiers it may be said that before they have been in power for five years they have no popularity left." [7]

As he barnstormed around the country in permanent election mode he carefully cultivated a genial man-of-the-people image. His sartorial signature, picked up by the cartoonists who were the press photographers cum TV cameramen of the day, was a frock-coat complete with flower in the button-hole and PC (privy councillor) fob watch.

There had never before been a leader in New Zealand like Seddon. Generally, premiers had been the most acceptable, or least unacceptable, politicians available at the time to cobble together and chair a temporary coalition of interests. Seddon stamped his personality and authority on Parliament, the Liberal Party and the country. Premier and prime minister for 13 years – longer than anyone else, before or after – he was 'King Dick' to everyone, the sobriquet said with either a sneer or an affectionate chuckle.

Seddon's frenetic political style and his very simple political philosophy owed a great deal to a basic insecurity. He was not, and felt it keenly, a member of the establishment that had controlled the

New Zealand government since the 1850s. As Burdon wrote: "Through all the days of his life Seddon spoke with a Lancashire accent; he dropped aitches from places where they should have been and inserted them in places where they should not have been." [8] He had "an awareness that he could never take his political position for granted, that constant effort would be required to maintain it, that there was nothing in his class situation and social background that would help him to survive in politics." [9]

His response was to reach out to ordinary New Zealanders like himself, to be, uniquely in the colony's history, 'a man of the people'. It sustained him and maintained his hold on power through a catalogue of attacks and scandals that would have crushed most politicians of any era. As Hamer wrote: "Seddon was New Zealand's first successful democratic leader." [10]

As his confidence and domination of New Zealand politics grew, Seddon's horizons broadened. A South Pacific imperialist, he rejected federation with Australia, casting a covetous eye at Samoa and Fiji. The annexation of the Cook Islands in 1901 was some small consolation.

Burdon wrote: "King Dick might rule New Zealand; the interests of Imperial policy forbade that Emperor Dick should rule a scattered oceanic federation, stretching from the tropic of Capricorn to the fringes of the Antarctic." [11]

Seddon achieved something like celebrity status at the 1897 and 1902 colonial conferences and at Queen Victoria's diamond jubilee celebrations, and his tough war talk, and sending of troops, prompted an invitation from Lord Kitchener to visit South Africa just as hostilities ended there in 1902.

While Seddon enjoyed strutting the international stage, his close attention to the local political scene never wavered. He had felt a sympathy for the views of the Labour politicians first elected in 1891 and the Liberal and Labour Federation he forged gave them and their concerns a carefully controlled place in the government's plans. It was an arrangement that extended the Liberals' hold on power and appreciably slowed the full-blown development of the Labour Party. Seddon was equally shrewd with his handling of the wider Liberal Party, ensuring that its more radical views did not dispute his cautious consolidation of the government's gains. He was acutely aware of public opinion and the limits to the acceptance of change.

Increasingly, the country's conservatives had little to fear from Seddon's Liberal government. Richardson wrote: "Although Seddon's methods were an affront to the social sensibilities of the old propertied elite, the legislation of his party did not

Fills The Bill. *Seddon's dream of a South Seas empire was thwarted. Scatz,* NZ Graphic, *1900.*
(ATL ref: H-723-014)

seriously disturb them. The lease-in-perpetuity was an optional tenure and posed no threat to existing freehold; the chief beneficiaries of the Advances to Settlers Act were established farmers who were able to re-finance existing debt and improve their farms." [12]

Seddon, his wife and nine children had moved from Kumara to Wellington in 1895, but his family did not see a great deal more of him. Louisa Seddon, who had largely attended to his West Coast electorate business, now founded the influential Women's Social and Political League.

Politics was Seddon's life, all day and much of each night. William Gisborne wrote: "Like Mr Gladstone, Mr Seddon is a devourer of work. He does not, however, devote his spare half hours to studies of Homer, versification of Horace, or lucubrations on Locke." [13] He had no time for, or interest in, the abstract. As Reeves wrote: "Seddon was not encumbered with either theories or ideals. If you had spoken to him of Utopia, he would have asked where it was." [14]

He was a skilful if domineering administrator who closely supervised all departmental work. The calibre of the Seddon cabinet declined as his power over it increased; less independently-minded ministers were unlikely to buck his increasingly conservative fiscal and social policies. Patronage was a political tool he used to great effect – with Legislative Council and civil service appointments as well as in cabinet. As Sinclair noted: "Seddon's generous nature was not restricted by too nice a conscience, and he habitually went beyond the stricter dictates of political morality in helping his friends, filling the Civil Service with 'temporary clerks' of the right political colour and handing out other favours when expedient." [15]

Never one to stint food or drink, Seddon's weight ballooned to nearly 20 stone in later life. Not surprsingly, this and his punishing schedule affected his health; from about 1897 he had a worsening heart condition.

After an impressive, and fifth consecutive election victory at the end of 1905, Seddon travelled to Australia to discuss trade and other issues. There was now increasing pressure from his back-benchers to promote more able people and he had dangled the carrot of his retirement, after another Colonial Conference in 1907. However, it was not to be. After 24 exhausting days in Australia, and his famous telegram to the Victorian premier, " Just leaving for God's own country", he set sail for New Zealand on board the *Oswestry Grange*. He died from a massive heart attack shortly afterwards. His widow lived another quarter century, dying in 1931. Their eldest son, Captain R J S Seddon, was killed in action in August 1918 and another son, Tom, held his father's

Nailing His Colours. *In 1905, Seddon was still dominant as opposition leader Massey struggled to make an impression in Parliament . EF Hiscocks*, NZ Graphic, *1905. (ATL ref: H-723-016)*

Westland parliamentary seat for many years.

It is perhaps inevitable that comparisons have been made between Richard John Seddon and Robert David Muldoon. Both were populists: Seddon stumped the country dispensing public works largess; Muldoon called on 'Rob's Mob' to win support. Both were prodigious workers with amazing memories. Both controlled the financial levers of power. Both tackled accusation with counter-accusation. As Hamer noted: "[Seddon] indulged in what a later practitioner of the same political style termed 'counter-punching'." [16] Both were aggressively loyal to the supporters they promoted beyond their levels of competence. Both made, unlike most premiers and prime ministers, a lasting impression.

W J Gardner wrote: "Seddon had bridged the gaps between the Liberal city, town, rural, and Maori votes by manoeuvre within a wide range of policy and with a wide range of men. It was a marvellously versatile, non-stop performance, unrivalled in our history, but it killed him at sixty, in spite of his unique physical and nervous resources. What greater triumphs could a politician have than that trade union leaders should be eager to shake his hand, and Maori chiefs proud to rub noses with him, while Hall praised him to his face, and Rolleston privately accepted him? He alone could bridge by his personality gaps that were politically unbridgeable." [17]

16
SIR WILLIAM HALL-JONES
1851-1936

"Staunch adherence to principle marked his whole public life"

William Hall-Jones, New Zealand's first officially gazetted prime minister – if only for a month in 1906 – kept the seat warm for Sir Joseph Ward. All the same, it is possibly unfair to consider him a 'Clayton's' prime minister.

Hall-Jones was born in Folkestone, Kent in January 1851, the son of William Hall Jones and Margaret Hall. His father was a cabinet-maker and William was, in today's parlance, 'home-schooled'. After a brief brush with the financial world, William Hall-Jones became a carpenter, moving to London to practice his trade when he was 20 years old.

In October 1873 Hall-Jones married Londoner Fanny Smith, and the newly-weds promptly emigrated to New Zealand, having heard there was no shortage of building work in the young colony. They landed at Port Chalmers in April 1874 and William plied his trade in Dunedin, Oamuru and then Timaru where Fanny died of cancer in early 1876. A little over a year later, Hall-Jones married again. He and his second wife, Rosalind Lucy Purss, were to have six children.

Before long Hall-Jones began his own building company and, once it was successfully established, he put his name forward and was elected to the Timaru Borough Council in 1884 and subsequently to the Levels Road Board. He was then invited to contest a parliamentary by-election and became

Walter Bowring, Press Portraits No. 9, Weekly Press, *1899. (ATL ref: J-058-001)*

member for Timaru in August 1890. He was to hold the seat for the next 18 years.

Hall-Jones joined Ballance's Liberal opposition and then, after the election, became government whip. "But he went through a difficult period after Ballance's death," wrote David Hamer. "He was a prohibitionist and supporter of Stout and resigned as whip rather than impose the Seddon line on the party." [1] He was particularly dissatisfied with the government's delay on key election promises, especially the subdivision of large estates and women's franchise. For the next three years he sat in lonely isolation as an independent, one of the government's sternest critics.

Seddon offered Hall-Jones a seat at the cabinet table, and the justice portfolio, when Reeves retired from politics in early 1896. In the event, Joseph Ward resigned shortly afterwards and Hall-Jones took his marine portfolio instead, together with public works. With typical shrewdness, Seddon had tamed an occasionally troublesome radical and gained an effective and increasingly respected minister.

Hamer wrote: "Public Works was not the kind of post in which a radical could find scope for controversial reforming activity. Hall-Jones made an instant and remarkable change of political identity. He dropped, in public at least, virtually all his old radical interests and even began voting against radical proposals which he had hitherto supported strongly." [2]

Hall-Jones ran the marine department for a decade and was minister of public works for even longer; at various times he was colonial treasurer and held the railways, labour and education portfolios.

William Hall-Jones was one of Seddon's ablest lieutenants, or 'safe pair of hands', during the second half of his lengthy ministry. He oversaw the completion of the main trunk railway in the North Island and, in the south, the building of the Otira tunnel through Arthur's Pass. Although Seddon is closely identified with the Old-Age Pensions Act, Hall-Jones's idea of 'non-contributory' pensions paid out of the Consolidated Fund was a critical component of the scheme finally adopted.

Seddon, who once said of Hall-Jones, "he is the best administrator I have in my Cabinet",[3] increasingly and publicly treated his ministers with barely veiled contempt and Hall-Jones was not entirely exempt from this. But unlike many of Seddon's later appointments, who were in cabinet largely to make up the numbers, Hall-Jones spoke his mind as well. In 1904, at a function before travelling overseas, Hall-Jones spoke frankly about Seddon's method of governing. " A Premier's role, he said, should be one of 'general supervision – not directing, but knowing what would be done'." [4]

Hall-Jones also displayed a degree of firmness with the governor, Lord Ranfurly, when he had wanted to extend a cruise of the sub-antarctic islands, in *Tutanekai*, the government steamer, to the West Coast sounds. John Hall-Jones, his son, wrote: "With supplies urgently required for the southern lighthouses Hall-Jones refused to grant permission for the extension. When the governor persisted Hall-Jones threatened to resign." [5]

Seddon came to respect and increasingly rely on him. "Towards the end of his life Seddon had relaxed to such an extent that he did not bother to brief Hall-Jones on the conduct of business while he was overseas and Hall-Jones was acting-Premier." [6]

A few months after his triumphant fifth election victory, Seddon made his fateful visit to Australia in May 1906. The ranking minister, Sir Joseph

Who shall rule? Lord Plunket: 'Take them. They belong to you now.' Hon. W. Hall-Jones: 'Only till Joe comes. I'll hold them for him.' *J C Blomfield,* New Zealand Free Lance, *June 23 1906. (ATL ref: J-056-004)*

Ward, was at a postal conference in Rome and James Carroll, nominally the next senior, did not push his claim.

Consequently, Hall-Jones was government leader when the shock news was telegraphed through that Seddon had suddenly and unexpectedly died on the ship returning from Australia. Lord Plunket, the governor, immediately asked Hall-Jones to form a new ministry. The acting-premier agreed but, in a breach of accepted practice, refused to be sworn in until after Seddon's state funeral 11 days later.

As Michael Bassett has written: "Hall-Jones assumed most of Seddon's portfolios for the time being and made almost no other changes to Seddon's ministry."[7] The government then marked time.

Some colleagues and supporters urged Hall-Jones to continue in office but, as John Hall-Jones later wrote: "It is easy to see what would have happened had he been a man of ambitious type and done so. The party would have divided into factions and quickly destroyed itself by civil war."[8] But Hall-Jones was quite clear that the only honourable course of action was to resign as soon as Ward returned to the country. This he did and Ward was promptly sworn in as prime minister.

In the Ward administration, Hall-Jones reverted to his previous role as minister of railways and public works. In 1907, after a period as acting prime minister while Sir Joseph was overseas, he suffered a serious heart attack. The next year he resigned from cabinet and replaced Reeves in London, the agent-general now known as high commissioner.

Later, Hall-Jones claimed that his greatest contribution during his years in Britain was when he persuaded the 1910 International Congress of Refrigeration in Vienna to ease restrictions on the entry of frozen meat into Europe. This was to prove of incalculable benefit to a generation of New Zealand farmers. He was awarded the KCMG the same year; most unusually the honour was on the recommendation of the Colonial Office rather than the New Zealand government.

There was high general regard for Sir William's ability and integrity in New Zealand too. When he returned in 1913 the Liberals were, after over 20 years, out of power, but William Massey, the new prime minister and a long-time opponent, asked Hall-Jones to become a member of the Legislative Council. This he did, and remained there, respected by politicians of all persuasions, for another 23 years until his death in 1936. His wife died in 1942.

Guy Scholefield wrote of William Hall-Jones: "Staunch adherence to principle marked his whole public life; and his personal character was distinguished by courtesy, consideration and a singular lightness of heart even into advanced age."[9]

Trying it on. *Hall-Jones was acting premier during Seddon's last, fateful visit to Australia. E F Hiscocks,* NZ Graphic, *May 1906. (ATL ref: A-315-1-015)*

17

SIR JOSEPH GEORGE WARD
1856-1930

"He was free of fads and radical theories, a practical man of business"

Joseph Ward was the ultimate survivor – in politics and in life. He was to become prime minister a second time a record number of years after his first administration and no other New Zealand politician has ever been a cabinet minister for a longer period.

Ward's beginnings could not have been more  unpromising. His parents, William Ward and Hannah Dorney, had emigrated from Ireland to Australia with two small children. Seven more were born in Melbourne; all but Joseph George Ward died of dysentery or diphtheria. Joseph was only four and a half when his father died in 1861, his liver succumbing to a sustained alcoholic battering.

The next year, with her three surviving children all at school, his mother became licensee of a North Melbourne hotel. Less successfully, she also

Vyvyan Hunt, Auckland Weekly News, *December 14 1895. (ATL ref: A-122-003)*

remarried; she was to carry John Barron's name for the rest of her life but he disappeared out of it soon after they and the three children arrived in Bluff, New Zealand in 1863.

The move was based on a fact and a promise: the cheapest fare anywhere from Melbourne was to Bluff and gold had been discovered in the area.

With the sort of energy and determination that was to characterise her son's career, Ward's mother opened a small goldfields store and then, the short-lived rush

over, leased a guesthouse on the Bluff waterfront. Joseph ended his formal education at Campbelltown School in 1869 when he was 13; his mother needed all possible financial assistance to purchase the guesthouse's freehold for £150 prior to converting it into what was to become the imposing Club Hotel.

Young Ward worked as a Post Office delivery boy for two years, then for a local merchant and as a Railways Department clerk. In 1877, and only 21, he was ready to begin his own grain merchant company, which he did with an £800 loan from his mother. The firm prospered and in time Ward built large grain warehouses on land he had bought in both Bluff and Invercargill.

Joseph Ward's involvement in politics was equally precocious. In 1878 he was elected to the Bluff Borough Council. Four years later he was mayor and a member of the Harbour Board. He had two spells as mayor and chaired the Harbour Board for a number of years.

In 1887, when Ward was elected to Parliament as the member for Awarua, he had a handsome wife, Theresa De Smidt, two young children and one of the larger merchant companies in Southland. The Wards had seven children, with twins dying at birth in 1900.

Ward stood as a supporter of the Stout-Vogel ministry, which did not survive the election. While the incoming government saw retrenchment as the only response to a deepening depression, Ward, who inherited a risk-taking brand of optimism from his mother, saw more merit in expansion aided by the new communication technologies that would lessen New Zealand's isolation.

Ward quickly made an impression in the House. He was knowledgeable about tariffs and mail shipping contracts, personable, and an effective debater. When the Liberals won the election at the end of 1890, Ballance immediately offered Ward the postmaster-general portfolio. He accepted, but only on the understanding that he could spend much of his time in Invercargill as his business interests still needed his close attention.

In a way that would have raised eyebrows even in the 'wild west' corporate era of the 1980s, Ward seemed to find it difficult – or possibly did not even try – to draw a line between politics and business either in principle or practise. This blind spot came close to wrecking both careers.

It was no co-incidence that Ward reduced the cost of tolls calls and telegrams and that his company was Southland's biggest user of both.

Ward's loyalty to Bluff's – and his own – interests was unequivocal. In 1891 when the Southland Frozen Meat Company decided to build a new freezing works

'Tis the pace that kills. Treasurer Ward: 'For pity's sake, Seddon, come take these reins yourself, or we shall be capsized. This young man Reeves is too reckless…' *W P Reeves' labour legislation was too radical for his colleagues. William Blomfield,* New Zealand Observer & Free Lance, *July 21 1894. (ATL ref: H-722-182)*

at Mataura, in his view far too close to Otago, Ward immediately set about clearing the way for a competing works at Ocean Beach, Bluff. He persuaded the local council to sell reserve land, rushed a necessary amendment to an Act through Parliament, and influenced railway freight rates. At the same time he did his best to stop moves that might inhibit Bluff's development.

Michael Bassett, his biographer, has written that Ward believed, throughout his career, his own prosperity was the key to success for all around him. " It was but a short step from this attitude to a belief that in the cause of Southland's economic progress there was no such thing as conflict of interest. Public office was the companion to private enterprise, not its enemy, nor its regulator. Probably no politician in New Zealand's history so blurred the distinction between his own business interests and the wider public interest." [1]

After Ballance died in April 1893, Joseph Ward became Seddon's colonial treasurer. Bassett again: "No ideologue, Ward was a technocrat with a passion for getting maximum value from government expenditure." [2] His business dealings convinced him that closer land settlement was essential, and the Government Advances to Settlers Act in 1894 made it possible for farmers to borrow 60 percent of the value of a property. Ward personally oversaw the London float that successfully raised the funds to launch the scheme.

Now that Ward was rarely in Southland he restructured his financial interests. His company became a farmers' co-operative, the J G Ward Farmers' Association, with managers making most of the decisions. There were links to the Ocean Beach works which had opened in 1892 and Ward part-owned. Local farmers were less enthusiastic investment risk-takers than Ward so he became heavily indebted to the Colonial Bank of New Zealand as cash was paid for stock to boost production at the freezing works.

The crunch came in 1895. Joseph Ward owed the Colonial Bank £100,000 and commodity prices had slumped. In London on government business, Ward borrowed heavily to prop up the Farmers' Association and take some pressure off a teetering Colonial Bank. In the event, the Bank of New Zealand, recently bailed out of trouble by Ward as colonial treasurer, took over the Colonial Bank. And, ironically, it then forced the Farmers' Association into receivership. Ward's only chance to avoid bankruptcy himself was for business friends to buy the Association; in mid-June 1896 a Supreme Court judge refused permission, declaring Ward "hopelessly insolvent" and, rubbing more salt in the wound, said he "should no longer be permitted to roam at large through the business world". [3]

Even Ward realised he could not continue under these circumstances and resigned his portfolios. Ward's natural optimism was now badly dented; he was re-elected to Awarua at the December 1896 election, but the prospect of bankruptcy still loomed. Only the deft manipulation of a legislative loophole saved Ward's political skin. A member of parliament's career was over if declared bankrupt, but there was nothing, at the time, to stop a bankrupt being elected. In July 1897 Ward resigned his seat, filed for bankruptcy and was promptly voted back in at the Awarua by-election.

David Hamer wrote: "To a modern-day observer it seems incredible that a politician making such a flagrant attempt to use political influence to rescue himself from financial disaster should have achieved so dramatic a comeback so soon." [4] Ward's cabinet comeback took longer. It was helped by his 1888-89 efforts to resurrect his business credibility. He was discharged from bankruptcy; Theresa Ward and friends bought back properties from the official assignee; money was borrowed to re-start J G Ward and Company; and share sale windfalls enabled Ward to repay all his creditors in New Zealand and England. Hamer noted: "His success in repaying his debts counted for more in their [business community] opinion, it seems, than the original bankruptcy." [5]

After the December 1899 election the rehabilitation was complete. Ward was back in cabinet, Seddon's deputy and with an impressive clutch of portfolios – colonial secretary, postmaster-general, industries and commerce, railways, and public health. The fact that Seddon did not hand back the treasurership may have had more to do with his control mania than any sense of propriety.

Ward resumed his political career with the same drive and intensity as before, but with his optimism now tinged by a degree of paranoia, always on the watch for those who, because of his past business dealings or his Roman Catholicism, wanted to bring him down. Certainly he had vocal detractors. One, A R Barclay, wrote that Ward "might be more aptly described as a 'juggler with figures' than a financier." [6]

Yet the Post and Telegraph Department, and the New Zealand public, benefited greatly from his belief in the economic advantage of better communications during his long tenure as postmaster-general. Universal penny postage – within the country and to many others besides – caught the public imagination and 13 million more letters were posted the year after the scheme's introduction at the beginning of 1901.

Ward reduced railway fares in 1900 and usage and revenue climbed steeply. He was the British Empire's first minister of public health and set about improving sanitation and hygiene; he also opened the first public maternity hospitals and required midwives to be properly trained.

Ward was never a typical Liberal Party politician, and he seemed less so as time passed. Hamer wrote: "He was free of fads and radical theories, a practical man of business." [7] He remained dapper even after too many years of banquets and too little exercise, his waxed moustache at least always slim and trim. The knighthood he accepted during the royal visit in 1901, ostensibly in recognition of universal penny postage, was not popular in egalitarian Liberal circles. It was remarkable that some still considered Ward a champion of the 'little people' after a baronetcy, at the time of the 1911 Coronation, and a second knighthood shortly before he died in 1930. The ministerial residence in Tinakori Road, occupied by the Wards from the beginning of the new century, and christened 'Awarua House', was the scene of many fashionable garden parties and soirees. Today it is 'Premier House'. As Bassett wrote: "Ward was the Liberals' opening to the upwardly mobile, just as Seddon reassured the static that someone cared for them." [8]

The Colonial Treasurer is torn by the financial wolves. *Ward, declared "hopelessly insolvent" by a Supreme Court judge, was obliged to leave the government. William Blomfield,* New Zealand Observer & Free Lance, *June 13 1896. (ATL ref: H-722-197)*

When Seddon suddenly died in 1906 the Ward family was overseas, the Postal Union Congress in Rome providing the devout couple and their children the opportunity of a private audience with Pope Pius X, an occasion marred by a total language impasse. Ward hurried back to New Zealand as fast as available sea transport allowed, William Hall-Jones serving as 'caretaker' prime minister until he arrived.

Close colleagues and confidantes they might have been, but Ward and Seddon could hardly have been more different personally or in their approach to politics. Seddon was the rowdy ex-miner who was blunt, brutal and vulgar on occasions; Ward was genial, polite, socially adept, and frequently enigmatic. It was abundantly clear what Seddon thought, sometimes uncomfortably so; with Ward an outpouring of words often obscured any real meaning, and he carefully maintained an impenetrable façade. E F Hiscocks, with his perceptive cartoonist's eye, said of Ward: " 'There is no such man, no such human soul'. He was merely 'a thick surface'. " [9]

Seddon had a special rapport with people from all backgrounds. "Ward, on the other hand, could manoeuvre measures, but not men," wrote W J Gardner. "He could persuade a caucus to swallow a contradictory policy of ingenious devising. On the platform, his torrent of facts and figures left in the main the impression – 'the wizard of finance' – he desired to create. But, at the point where party unity is fundamentally maintained, Ward was a failure .... Hence all his brilliant manoeuvring of 1906-12 won battles but helped to lose the Liberal empire for want of confidence between the

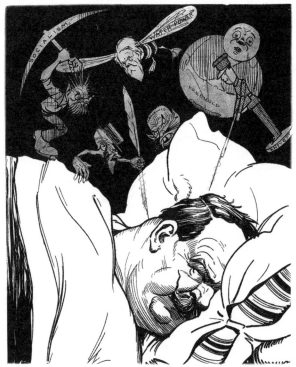

A myriad of ideas and schemes jostling for space in Ward's mind. David Low, ca 1907-11. (ATL ref: B-025-026)

Premier and his party marshals." [10]

Together Ward and Seddon were a formidable political combination appealing to a broad electoral spectrum. Ward, on his own, had little rapport with unions, nor was he sufficiently attuned to the growing importance of working class urban electorates. There were strikes – the first for many years – in the freezing and mining industries and it was clear that his government was losing the support of the labour movement which until then had been happy enough to hitch a ride on the Liberals' bandwagon.

Ward won the 1908 election, but the Liberals also lost seats in farming areas where its insistence on leasehold was beginning to provide a 'freehold' rallying call for the opposition led by William Massey.

Hamer wrote: "Ward was now the dominant figure in the government in a way that he had not been prior to 1909. The general election had given him a mandate and an authority independent of Seddon's." [11]

Ward appointed a cabinet more to his personal liking; and it became a rubber stamp for decisions made away from the cabinet table. His administration might have run out of steam domestically, but there were exciting challenges in the wider world: regular trips to London and new communications technology to explore, the championing of imperial federation and trade preferences, and the offer of a battleship to the British Navy to bolster the empire's defence.

At a time when Australia was wanting its own naval force, Ward sought to maintain the British Navy's south Pacific presence. As he put it: "There is but one sea around our shores and .... with one sea and one Empire, there should in reality be but one Navy." [12]

Ward was devastated, but should not have been, when there was no clear winner at the December 1911 election. Parliament next met in March 1912, and he resigned as prime minister before a confidence motion could be put. Thomas Mackenzie, his minister of agriculture, briefly succeeded him before Massey's Reform Party occupied the treasury benches in July.

After a period as a back-bencher, Ward led the Liberals to a creditable performance at the 1914 election. With only the narrowest of majorities, and a world war in progress, Massey asked Ward to join a national government. Massey, an Ulster Orangeman, and Ward, a devout Irish Catholic, tolerated each other as prime minister and deputy for the next four years. Reform won the 1919 election comfortably and, after 32 years, Ward lost the Awarua seat. It looked like the end of the political road; for anyone other than Joseph George Ward it would have been.

After an unsuccessful tilt at Tauranga in a 1923 by-election, Ward won the Invercargill seat narrowly in 1925. He returned to the House as the only Liberal; surviving former colleagues were in a National party grouping. Politics was now a deeply engrained habit for Ward and the prospect of power again, however unlikely, the only driving force. After Theresa Ward, his greatest supporter and valued adviser, died in February 1927, Ward's health declined markedly, and his speeches in Parliament seemed as irrelevant as his presence there.

Then, miraculously, Ward was asked to lead a new United Party, a motley patchwork of groups including the remnants of the old Liberal Party. In fact, the party was largely controlled by right-wingers appalled by Gordon Coates' 'excessive' borrowing. It was doubly ironic that Ward should lead such a grouping at the November 1928 election and that it should defeat Coates' Reform government when Ward, by accident or design, opened his campaign with the promise to borrow a massive £70 million in a single year to bolster a faltering economy. Bassett wrote: "The most credible explanation of Ward's £70 million loan, around which the whole election campaign came to focus, is that he had simply made a mistake during his speech, and that United's campaign officials decided …. to allow a degree of ambiguity to rest in the public mind." [13]

With the support of 19 Labour Party members, Ward had the numbers to complete the most remarkable comeback in New Zealand political history – fully 22 years after he first became prime minister he held the warrant again. But not very securely or for very long. Little of the £70 million materialised and a sick old man who had long ago run out of answers was no match for a depression that was tightening its grip on the world.

For much of 1929 Ward's colleagues ran an administration buffeted by contracting economic activity and growing unemployment. Ward suffered heart attacks and was in and out of hospital but it was not until May 1930 that, at a bedside conference, he finally agreed to retire as prime minister. He was dead six weeks later.

Sir Joseph Ward's reputation has suffered from the length of his political career and the farcical aspects of its latter stages. But, as Michael Bassett says, the modern infrastructure of New Zealand life owes far more to Ward than he is given credit for. "The rural economy and New Zealand's transport and communications networks carried the direct imprint of his imagination." [14]

Further, Bassett doubts whether any other politician has had a greater impact on so many aspects of the country's development. "Holding as he did nearly every portfolio of state, few areas escaped his energy, enthusiasm or stubborn determination. In new countries struggling to establish themselves, confidence radiating from high places could often be as important as specific policy initiatives. No one equalled Ward in that department." [15]

Coalition. Reform, Liberal and Labour join political ranks against a common enemy. *William Blomfield,* New Zealand Observer & Free Lance, *ca 1915. (ATL ref: B-055-019)*

18
SIR THOMAS NOBLE MACKENZIE
1853-1930

"His greatest contribution to New Zealand lay in his stout support of the cause of conservation"

Thomas Mackenzie made a significant contribution to New Zealand in several fields – but not as the country's prime minister. As a politician Mackenzie is probably better remembered as a conservationist and explorer. He was also a marketer and diplomat of some repute.

He was born in 1853 in Edinburgh, Scotland, to David Stewart Mackenzie, a gardener, and Rebecca Noble. Five years later, with parents and siblings, he left for Dunedin, New Zealand, on board the *Robert Henderson*.

Mackenzie attended primary and secondary school in Dunedin and then, after several years working as a clerk, headed for the outdoors, the lower North Island and survey work with his brother, James, who later became the country's surveyor-general. A surveying assignment took him south again and in 1877 he changed course, becoming a

George Finey, Smith's Weekly *Special Supplement (Sydney), ca 1925. (ATL ref: A-051-023)*

Balclutha storekeeper and succeeding well enough to marry Ida Nantes, from Geelong in Australia, in September 1884. The marriage produced five sons and two daughters.

His political involvement began in Balclutha where he was a borough councillor from 1881-87. His support for local farmers over various issues was the springboard for his election to Parliament in 1887 as the member for Clutha when he was still in his mid-30s. He supported the Atkinson ministry because it was expected of him by his constituents, and then

sat in opposition to the Liberals. He was an avowed freeholder but sympathetic to the Liberals' lease-in-perpetuity, which he saw as much the same thing, and he agreed with their closer settlement policies.

Exploring Fiordland and the Catlins was a welcome antidote to the sedentary boredom of the House of Representatives; in 1888 he led a party inland from Milford Sound to estimate the height of the Sutherland Falls. He helped open up the Milford Track and discovered the Mackenzie Pass to Dusky Sound. As early as 1894 he canvassed the idea of Fiordland becoming a national park. He reserved some of his most trenchant criticism of the Liberals for their lack of interest in protecting endangered bird and animal species and he introduced a forest and bird protection motion in 1893. Mackenzie wrote a lengthy report to the government in 1896, when his serious exploring days were over, detailing the fauna, flora and geology of the wild, remote areas he had visited many times during the previous decade. In 1898 Thomas Mackenzie was made a fellow of the Royal Geographical Society.

With the Liberals and Seddon at the height of their popularity Mackenzie gradually wearied, despite being an effective debater, of the largely negative opposition role. He resigned his seat in 1896 and embarked on another very different career.

MacKenzie spent the next three years in London where several farmers' co-operatives employed him as their marketing agent. On the one hand he made strenuous efforts to stop New Zealand meat being misrepresented as English; on the other he worked with the Department of Agriculture to ensure New Zealand dairy and meat exports did not suffer from poor branding and quality control. Another of his roles was to negotiate more favourable shipping and insurance arrangements for the co-operatives he represented.

Back in New Zealand in 1900, Mackenzie returned to the House as an independent at the Waihemo by-election. Still on the opposition benches, he was diligent in his advocacy of Otago causes as the once dominant province began its long and slow economic decline. He was mayor of Roslyn from 1901-05, and served on education and schools' boards in Dunedin.

As early as 1900, Mackenzie had made it clear he was much more favourably inclined to Ward than Seddon and in 1908 he joined – and it caused considerable controversy at the time – the Liberal Party. Possibly he was tired of perpetual opposition, but it was also true that he had agreed with the Liberals on a number of issues and, by then, there was little hint remaining of their early radicalism. Following the 1908 election, as Tom Brooking explains, the prime minister returned the compliment, naming him to the agriculture, industries and commerce and tourism portfolios. "…. Sir Joseph Ward hoped that appointing a freeholder to cabinet would help stop the drift of farmers away from the Liberal Party, and revitalise the old alliance of urban labour, small town businessmen and small farmers." [1]

In turn, Mackenzie hoped a Liberal revival would hold in check the Labour Party's socialist intentions.

Mackenzie's appointment ruffled feathers. As David Hamer wrote: "For many years Mackenzie had been a strong critic of the Liberal government, although he was regarded as an independent and something of a maverick rather than as a leading member of the Opposition …. His choice as a Minister was deeply resented by many Liberals because of the recency of his 'conversion' to Liberalism which had all the appearance of having been made solely in order to gain office." [2]

Mackenzie was an effective minister of agriculture, remembered for the beginnings of herd testing and the long-lasting *Journal of Agriculture*.

Ward was sufficiently concerned about the outcome of the 1911 election – when Mackenzie contested the Egmont seat – to introduce the second ballot, which he saw as a sort of security blanket. The theory was that in those seats where Massey's Reform candidate was ahead but short of an outright majority, the combined votes of second and third-placed Liberal and Labour candidates would swing the vote the government's way. The election produced a stalemate with neither Ward nor Massey a clear winner.

Ward, from 1909, and Mackenzie in 1912 appointed 'consensus' cabinets, the doubtful theory being that a diverse group of ministers with widely varying views would best reflect the diversity of public opinion in the country. Instead, as Hamer noted: "The emphasis on

Always moving on – the serious plight of a southern member of the N.Z. government. *After three South Island electorates he represented were abolished, Mackenzie contested a North Island seat in 1911. Trevor Lloyd,* Auckland Weekly News, *October 1911. (ATL ref: J-054-102)*

Whistling in the dark to keep his pecker up.
Mackenzie's ministry was a brief pause between two of the country's longest-lasting governments. William Blomfield, New Zealand Observer, *June 29 1912. (ATL ref: J-054-077)*

consensus paralysed the Liberals into almost total immobility." [3]

When the House met early in 1912 the Liberals survived, but only on the Speaker's casting vote. Ward resigned and Mackenzie replaced him ahead of John Millar, whose ambition was equalled only by his unpopularity.

Hamer wrote: "To many old-fashioned Liberals the choice of Mackenzie as head of what had been their party, the party of Ballance and Seddon, seemed proof of the final bankruptcy of the Liberal tradition." [4]

Although an able administrator, Mackenzie was no fire-in-the-belly politician or shrewd political tactician. As Michael Bassett wrote: "Mackenzie misread the political message from the 1911 election, which had seen the Liberals lose more heavily in North Island urban seats. He put aside the rash promises in the Governor's speech of February, and set his ministry's face firmly in the direction of the countryside." [5]

Further, shortly after becoming prime minister, Mackenzie took up "an old theme of the Liberal right: 'The country wanted political rest, more administration, less legislation'." [6]

Significantly, he was almost immediately engaged in secret correspondence with opposition leader William Massey and, after a limping three months, he seemed relieved when another confidence vote toppled his ministry in July.

The plum appointment as high commissioner in London was doubtless reward for going so quietly. But when war was declared in August 1914, Mackenzie suddenly had a busy and challenging role to play. The

welfare of the large number of New Zealand soldiers involved was a principal concern. He served on the royal commission into the ill-fated Dardanelles campaign, in which his son Clutha had been blinded. He supported Ettie Rout's campaign against venereal disease and was a member of the Imperial War Graves Commission. His KCMG in 1916 was an entrée to society circles, further enhancing his success as a negotiator on New Zealand's behalf. At war's end he was a delegate at the Paris peace conference.

His diplomatic career over, and with a GCMG to add to his other decorations, Sir Thomas was appointed to the Legislative Council in 1921 and re-appointed in 1928. He suffered a fatal heart attack in early 1930, his wife having died four years previously.

Conservation concerns dominated his last years on the political scene. He worked to add several birds to the protected breeds list and helped Captain Val Sanderson establish the Native Bird Protection Society, which later became the Forest and Bird Protection Society.

Brooking has summed up Thomas Mackenzie and his career: " [he] was a lively if somewhat enigmatic politician and a competent and caring diplomat. His later political career exemplifies some of the forces at work in the transition from Liberal to Reform. He rose to be prime minister almost by accident, and his greatest contribution to New Zealand lay in his stout support of the cause of conservation." [7]

Prime Canterbury. *Mackenzie has been appointed high commissioner in London. David Low, ca 1912 (ATL ref: C-047-017)*

19

WILLIAM FERGUSON MASSEY

1856-1925

"He turned a tattered opposition rump into a powerful political party"

William Massey is one of New Zealand's most under-estimated prime ministers. This is probably because he was a bluff, stolid conservative whose skills were more organisational and pragmatic than charismatic and inspiring. Yet he moulded a small, dispirited opposition into an effective alternative government and was then, against continuing odds, to share the prime ministerial longevity record of 13 years with Richard John Seddon.

David Low, Bulletin *(Sydney), 1915*
ATL ref: MNZ-0738-1/2

The eldest child of John Massey and Mary Anne Ferguson, William Massey was born near Londonderry in Northern Ireland in March 1856. His mother was Scottish, but his father had well-established local tenant farming connections. Despite this, John Massey sold his small freehold property to pay his family's way to New Zealand in 1869. Fourteen-year-old Bill remained in Northern Ireland a further year to finish his education at a private secondary school, arriving on the *City of Auckland* in December 1870.

John Massey must have pondered the brave decision to emigrate when he saw the unpromising bush section he was granted near Puhoi as part of Auckland's free land scheme. But by the time his son arrived he had leased land at west Tamaki. Bill Massey worked there for two years before a three year stint on John Grigg's 32,000 acre 'Longbeach' station near Ashburton. The young Massey would have heard radical land-reform talk in 'Longbeach'

bunkhouses. He would have also observed at first hand – and this seemed to make a greater impression – a successful and innovative farmer and a prominent member of Canterbury's landed class, which provided some of the colony's notable 'conservative' politicians during the early self-governing decades.

Back in Auckland Bill Massey soon leased a 100 acre farm at Mangere and also bought a threshing machine for contract work. In 1882, he married Christina Allen Paul, daughter of a neighbouring farming family of Scottish origin.

The young couple thrived – farming successfully and producing seven children – and Bill Massey was a prominent local figure by the early 1890s. School committee, Presbyterian church, Freemasons' lodge, debating society, and Mangere Road Board were the grassroots organisations that provided the solid community foundations to the slow building of Massey's career as a politician. More specifically, his chairmanship of the Mangere Farmers' Club, and presidency of the Auckland A & P Association, meant a spokesman's role for farmers in the Auckland province which, in turn, led to the vice presidency of the National Association of New Zealand, an attempt to organise rural and urban conservatives to provide more than token opposition to the Liberals.

Massey's first unsuccessful tilt at national politics was at the 1893 election, losing narrowly to the Liberal candidate in the Franklin electorate. A few months later there was a by-election for the Waitemata seat. In later years, Massey liked to tell the story about the telegram arriving, asking him to stand, while he was on top of a haystack, the message passed up to him on a pitchfork. As W J Gardner wrote: "Once called from the stack, he returned less and less to it." [1]

After winning the seat in April 1894, and beginning a 31 year parliamentary career, there was to be little more time for the practical day-by-day routines of farming. From the beginning he was a conscientious, hard-working member of a small,

91

discouraged opposition, many of its members still seeing themselves as temporary politicians doing their stint of public service in Wellington, while attempting to promote and protect their interests. W J Gardner wrote: "Canterbury Oppositionists could only be got together in Race Week, and even then they could hardly be persuaded to talk politics." [2]

Massey may not have had much in common with some of his colleagues but they recognised his solid debating and organisational skills and appointed him opposition whip in 1896.

As the 1896 election neared, Massey, away from his family for long periods and finding politics financially difficult without an assured private income, contemplated an early retreat back to the farming life. In the event, he won his home constituency of Franklin, and was further buoyed by the opposition nearly doubling its numbers in the House of Representatives.

There was now a little more coherent opposition to the government's land and labour legislation, Massey taking the lead with his clear, unequivocal support of freehold land tenure. His 'every man his own landlord' was very different from the Liberals' 'bursting up the big estates' cry. But what halting

progress was made vanished in 1899 as the Liberals rode the popularity of their old-age pensions scheme to an electoral landslide, and opposition numbers halved again to 15 members. In 1900, as Gardner explains, an extraordinary decision was made. "On the grounds that the colony had decided so overwhelmingly for Seddon, they agreed to do without a leader, and to act as independent members, there being no further mandate for an organised Opposition." [3] As much as a parliamentary opposition could be said to exist, Bill Massey was now its de facto leader.

Little changed at the 1902 election but the next year sufficient opposition members finally decided that, in the new century, squattocracy status was no longer a leadership attribute, and William Massey was officially appointed to the job he was already attempting to do. Keith Sinclair wrote: "Massey was prepared to adopt Seddonian electioneering tactics; was ready, so it seemed to the older generation of conservatives, to stoop to conquer. Moreover, though not one of the unpopular and discredited estate owners, he was a farmer who could be identified with the rural virtues." [4]

Minor gains were made at the 1905 election, but it was the death, in mid-1906, of a seemingly invincible Seddon that provided Massey with his first real opportunity. The new prime minister, Sir Joseph Ward, did not have the almost superhuman force of personality needed to hold together a coalition of small farmers, townspeople and workers that was, in reality, beginning to unravel after an extraordinarily productive 15 years. There was some political capital to be made from claiming Ward was stacking the public service with fellow Catholics, but more substantial gains from warning the growing number of urban and rural property owners that militant unionism was a threat to their hard won prosperity.

With more than a little help from the 'country quota', which gave a greater weight to rural votes, Massey's opposition performed well at the 1908 election. According to Len Richardson: "The link between rural and urban property was cemented in 1909 when Massey chose an urban title

Slow Poison. *In fact, Massey and his opposition party was finally emerging as a viable alternative government. David Low,* Canterbury Times*, June 24 1911. (ATL ref: C-047-047)*

for his predominantly rural party." [5] The Reform Party, with 27 seats, now had a significantly larger presence in the House.

By the 1911 election Massey was finally a political figure of some national substance. As well, a distinctive moustache replaced the beard and his middle-aged frame filled out to something like Seddonian proportions. Gardner wrote: " ….with the help of a razor, Massey gave himself a new persona, emerging as what he had claimed to be – the representative of New Zealand's new generation of small farmers. His enemies tried to christen him 'Bismarck Bill'; his friends, 'Farmer Bill'. [6]

Massey was Reform's first full-time politician. Richardson wrote: "He stumped the country, fashioning a reputation as a credible alternative to Ward. Fear of the socialist menace united the Opposition and attracted the Liberal right-wing." [7]

Reform won six more seats than the Liberals, with the ultimate balance of power resting with a quixotic collection of independents, Labour members as yet without a party caucus, and Maori MPs.

There was unseemly political jostling and accusations of bribery before the Liberals survived a no-confidence motion in February 1912 on the speaker's casting vote. The reprieve was short-lived and Massey was installed at the head of the country's first avowedly conservative government for a generation when another vote gave a clear majority to Reform in July. Sinclair wrote: "With the election of a small farmers' Government, the southern predominance in politics was also at an end." [8]

Sinclair again: "One virtue which Massey possessed and which in Seddon was quite lacking was modesty …. His first cabinet contained five graduates, three from Cambridge, one from Oxford, and one, Maui Pomare, with an American doctorate of medicine." [9]

Although 18 long years in opposition had given

Massey something of a reputation for cautious reasonableness, events were soon to cast him in a rigid, right-wing mould.

A particularly able cabinet aside, Bill Massey soon dominated his caucus and party organisation. His policies, defined by a restricted political and religious outlook, were quickly in place: no quarter for the industrial militants, elimination of political and religious cronyism from the public service, and the freeholding of crown leases. R M Burdon wrote: "Slow to make up his mind, but having once done so, tenacious in action, he could improvise boldly when the need arose. Uneventful times exposed the poverty

Political Bliss. Tom Mackenzie: 'My dear Willie, do eat this sweet apple just to please me. Willie Massey: 'No, my darling Tom, I cannot rob you even of a bite. You eat it all if we cannot share it.' *A prominent politician suggested the Liberals and Reform should co-operate, not struggle for power, but it was not to be. William Blomfield,* The New Zealand Observer, *May 4 1912. (ATL ref: J-054-018)*

of his political enterprise, but in periods of stress or calamity he invariably rose to the occasion." [10]

His tough, uncompromising response to the Waihi miners' strike in 1912 and to the waterfront and general strikes a year later won him the enduring support of the farming community. But the use of special constables, 'Massey's Cossacks', largely recruited from rural areas, earned the equally enduring hatred of urban workers and helped convince an indecisive labour movement that a united political approach was essential.

One of Massey's cabinet appointments was crucial to the success of his administration. As Gardner wrote: "The new Prime Minister made no better appointment than when he called F H D Bell to lead the Legislative Council. In a real sense, this was to be a Massey-Bell Ministry, for the two men came to work together in a relationship of respect and trust ...." [11]

It was, as Gardner has written, an extraordinary political friendship. "Massey generally deferred to Bell's judgment on measures; Bell generally deferred to Massey's on men, and was strictly correct in his relations with 'Mr Prime Minister'. Massey and Bell together became something greater than they would have been separately; it was a partnership unique in New Zealand politics. The two men had sat together on an Opposition back bench in 1894-6, and had formed a strong mutual regard." [12]

Given the divisiveness of some of his policies, it was not surprising that Massey fell a seat short of a working majority at the December 1914 election. The resulting parliamentary deadlock, and a world war already showing signs of being a long, drawn-out affair, pressured a reluctant Massey into a wartime coalition government with Sir Joseph Ward and his Liberal MPs. Richardson wrote: "In August 1915, after several months of mean-spirited jockeying for party advantage, Ward and Massey reluctantly formed a joint war-time administration." [13]

Massey and Ward, who was finance minister again and effectively *de facto* joint head of the government, were now colleagues. However, the national government, which lasted from August 1915 to August 1919, was largely paralysed by the personal, political and religious antipathy between the two leaders, and the decision to legislate only when both parties were in agreement. As Michael Bassett wrote: "....Ward disliked Massey intensely, considering him to be little more than an uncultivated bigot." [14]

Gardner wrote: "Each regarded himself as unequally yoked with his special *bête noire*, yet refused to trust the other out of his sight. Like political Siamese twins they travelled to Britain held together by the ties of mutual suspicion." [15] On the first lengthy visit in 1916-17, Massey attended an Imperial Conference and meetings of the Imperial War Cabinet. (Interestingly, the politician of limited education accepted two honorary doctorates; yet the staunch imperialist turned down both a peerage and a knighthood.) Massey spent time with wounded New Zealand soldiers, visits made all the more poignant because his youngest son had been seriously wounded at the battle of the Somme.

The two enemies-in-arms returned from another Imperial Conference just as the war was ending, but celebrations were muted by the outbreak of a vicious

The death of leasehold. *Massey was in power at last and strongly committed to freehold land tenure. Trevor Lloyd, New Zealand Herald, August 31 1912. (ATL ref: A-315-2-023)*

influenza epidemic that struck down New Zealanders in battlefield numbers.

Almost immediately, Bill Massey headed back to Europe to represent New Zealand at the peace conference in Paris and subsequent signing of the Treaty of Versailles. His devotion to the British Empire and New Zealand's place in it blinkered his view of the League of Nations.

Massey won the December 1919 election, despite a country more divided than for many years: employer versus worker; farmer v. town dweller; conservative v. radical; Protestant v. Roman Catholic. With the national government being blamed for everything from very high war casualties, to profiteering and the influenza epidemic, Sir Joseph had withdrawn from the coalition in August. The New Zealand Labour Party, formed in 1916, was beginning to flex its political muscles, but not in time to rob Massey of the one clear majority of his career.

At the beginning of the 1920s New Zealand's economic prosperity was faltering. Richardson again: "The prosperity that sustained the rural policies of the Reform Government came to an abrupt end in 1921-2. Dairy farmers, especially those on recently acquired marginal pumice and bush land in the Auckland province, demanded cheaper credit, marketing controls, and reduction of mortgages." [16] As the country slid into recession Massey set up meat and dairy producer boards in response to Britain slashing the prices it paid for agricultural products. After the 1922 election Massey was back in the familiar but stressful position of relying on the uncertain support of independents.

In retrospect the next two years, as he prepared the ground for the 1925 election, were his most successful in office. Tom Brooking wrote: "Much of Massey's political success was related to his promises to improve North Island roads. In office he tried to keep these; but despite his efforts many roads, especially in more isolated areas such as Northland, existed only in the imagination of departmental cartographers." [17]

With the able assistance of Gordon Coates and William Downie Stewart, Massey took action against inflation and climbing interest rates; on the other hand he put more money in pensioners' pockets. He introduced tax cuts and upped public spending. Export prices began to improve again and Massey established agricultural banks to assist with the farming recovery. It was also clear to Massey that, as Labour's influence strengthened, remaining Liberal voters had to be persuaded to vote Reform.

He did not live to see how well his strategy worked. R M Burdon wrote: "Towards the end of 1924 his health began to fail. He grew irritable and ever more dictatorial. The constant vigilance imposed upon him by the Government's small majority put an intolerable strain on his waning energy. 'If members want to die they must die in the House', he snapped when told that one of his party was absent because of sickness." [18]

Massey had to give up most of his prime ministerial duties before year's end. He died in May 1925, some months before Reform swept to a memorable election victory, winning 70 percent of the seats.

Today Bill Massey is mostly remembered for the

Trophies. Massey: 'Friends, this is only a few of the fearful odds I had to fight during my term, but I'm proud to say I finished the lot with credit.' *A month later Massey won the general election so narrowly that a joint wartime administration was inevitable. William Blomfield,* The New Zealand Observer, *November 21 1914. (ATL ref: A-312-1-079)*

Heaven helps those who help themselves. *Massey tackled the deepening depression by setting up meat and dairy producer boards. Tom Ellis (Tom Glover),* Free Lance, *October 19 1921 (ATL ref: J-044-003)*

Holy Writ and that Moses was the first and greatest of all freeholders, Massey was always ready to support his assertions made in the course of parliamentary debate with some quotation from the Bible. A Presbyterian, he also subscribed to the British Israelite contention that the Anglo-Saxon race, as one of the lost ten tribes, had inherited the state of being God's chosen people, and no doubt his staunch imperialism derived largely from this belief." [19]

Massey considered himself a conservative but Barry Gustafson says, "...both his personal instincts and his practise while in office place him in a tradition of humanitarian pragmatism." [20]

Sinclair has attempted to assess his place in the country's political history. "Massey was Seddon's equal as a parliamentary tactician; he was as verbose; he bore quite as excessive a load of portfolios; he was similarly peripatetic in pursuit of voters; he was as hearty and as genial in manner, but he cuts rather less of a figure in New Zealand history. Unlike Seddon he never overcame the limitations of his education and upbringing. 'King Dick' was as unlettered as 'Farmer Bill' but in some respects his boundless ambition carried him to a wider vision." [21]

imposing Massey Memorial at the entrance to Wellington Harbour, where he is buried, together with his wife who died in 1932. (She *did* accept honours, a CBE and then a DBE for her war and epidemic work.) Yet he was one of New Zealand's most important political figures. With a combination of stubborn patience, hard work and generally sound political judgment he turned a tattered opposition rump into a powerful political party that gave New Zealand a considerable degree of stability through a world war, unprecedented industrial action, a growing urban-rural split, the country's worst epidemic, and a sharp recession.

As Burdon has written, Massey's political career was underpinned by steadfast religious beliefs. "Firmly convinced that authority for his land policy could be found in

Yes, we have no plums today! *Better export prices underpinned the farming recovery, but Massey did not live to see the success of his policies at the 1925 election. Jack Gilmour,* New Zealand Truth, *March 15 1924. (ATL ref: H-705-002)*

20

SIR FRANCIS HENRY DILLON BELL
1851-1936

"It is difficult to find a parallel to so many-sided a man in New Zealand public life"

Francis Bell might have been a caretaker prime minister, but he was one of the most distinguished legal practitioners of his era. He was also the first New Zealand-born prime minister.

Cartoonist unknown, The Observer & Free Lance, *September 22 1894. (ATL ref: H-722-188)*

Bell was born in Nelson in March 1851. His father, Francis Dillon Bell, had come to New Zealand in 1843 as a New Zealand Company agent. He married Margaret Hort in 1849. He was later a member of provincial councils and the House of Representatives and Legislative Council at various times, and served in several ministries. Commissioner of Land Claims during the critical 1856-62 period, he was Speaker of the House of Representatives from 1870-75.

It was hardly surprising 'Harry' Bell became a politician; it is possibly more puzzling that it took him so long. One obvious reason was his early and sustained success in the legal profession.

After schooling in New Zealand, Francis Bell studied at Cambridge and was called to the English Bar in 1874. There were tempting legal and political opportunities in England, but he returned to Wellington to become junior partner in C B Izard's legal practice.

Bell's legal career was as glittering as it was diverse. He quickly made a reputation as a Supreme Court and Court of Appeal barrister. In 1886 he became senior partner in the law firm that has had various changes in names through the decades, but is still widely known as Bell Gully. Crown solicitor in Wellington for 12 years until 1890, he took a particular interest in Maori land and fishery issues. He also pioneered, with some colleagues, the publishing of law reports and commentaries in New Zealand.

For several years from 1899 he took a leading part in the disposal of the large 'Cheviot Hills' estate owned by his father-in-law William Robinson. He had married Caroline Robinson in 1878 and they were to have eight children. Ironically, sale of the estate, to resolve family difficulties under new 1891 land legislation, gave impetus to the Liberals' state land settlement programme.

Bell's first political forays were into local government. In the early to mid-1890s he was twice mayor of Wellington where his initiatives ranged from a modern drainage system to free public library, public baths, crematorium and water works.

After two unsuccessful campaigns Bell was elected to the House of Representatives as an 'oppositionist' in 1893. He remained for three years without much satisfaction or success. W J Gardner wrote: "He could not refrain from addressing the House as he would a not-very-intelligent jury – indeed, he had treated juries in the same way. The House soon had enough of him, and he of the House." [1] Of most lasting importance was the fast friendship he formed with William Massey.

Bell went back to a role he shone in – as one of the country's ablest and busiest lawyers. He regularly appeared before, and impressed, the Privy Council in appeal cases; he was again Wellington's crown solicitor; he was president of the New Zealand Law Society for an extraordinary 17 years from 1901; and he was named as one of the country's first king's counsels in 1907.

If Massey had not won his long, stubborn battle for the treasury benches, it is unlikely Francis Bell would have been persuaded to reprise one of the least memorable periods in a glittering career. But in 1912, when his friend Massey asked, Bell accepted both the leadership of the Legislative Council and a place in cabinet.

In time he was arguably the most effective and dominant personality in the Legislative Council's 96 year history, but his early attempt to reform the upper house fell victim to forces beyond his control. Gardner wrote: "Bell was the leading advocate of an elective Council, based on proportional representation; he apparently regarded this as a bulwark against the possibility of the power of appointment falling into the hands of a radical government." [2]

Bell engineered the passage of the Legislative Council Act 1914, despite the objections of a Liberal-stacked Council. War intervened and with it the National government, Liberal leader Sir Joseph Ward making a halt to Legislative Council reform one of the conditions of his co-operation. After the war the impetus to change had ebbed. Bell's biographer William Downie Stewart later wrote: "Had he foreseen that for years he would carry this measure like the Ancient Mariner's albatross tied round his neck, it might have quenched his zeal for reform." [3]

Bell's friendship with Massey quickly deepened into a close working relationship and he played an important administrative and legislative part to the point where the government was often known as the Massey-Bell ministry.

Downie Stewart discounted the view, which gained some currency at the time, that Bell was a sinister, behind-the-scenes manipulator. "....great as Bell's influence was, it was never the case that he dominated Massey. He recognised that on all questions of political strategy and tactics Massey had a flair for knowing the trend of public opinion and what measures he could induce Parliament to adopt. .... On the other hand, when it came to a question of finding a solution to some difficult problem, or of drafting an intricate Bill, or of giving advice on legal and constitutional problems, Massey realised that Bell was a consummate master." [4]

Awarded the KCMG in 1915, Bell continued as attorney general in the National government and the myriad of wartime laws and regulations bear the stamp of his close scrutiny. While a supporter of Empire, he threatened to resign if New Zealand

On the mend. The rising barometer of New Zealand's prosperity. *There was an air of optimism when Massey and his Reform colleagues replaced a tired and tattered Liberal government. Trevor Lloyd,* New Zealand Herald, *August 3 1912. (ATL ref: A-315-2-021)*

troop convoys did not receive adequate Royal Navy protection and, from a family with long standing Quaker associations, he inserted a clause allowing exemption on religious grounds into the Military Service Act 1916. (Nevertheless, three Bell sons and the four daughters were actively involved in the war effort. W H D Bell, the third generation of his family in national politics, was killed in action in France in July 1917.) Following the granting of New Zealand's mandate in 1919, Sir Francis drafted the legislation setting up the new government in West Samoa, and he retained an enlightened interest in the affairs of the embryonic South Pacific nation.

Bell prided himself on his indifference to public opinion and, as Downie Stewart put it: " …. he never studied the art of popular appeal". [5] The less public role as a Legislative Council appointee clearly suited his personality and manner better than any dependence on electors for a seat in the House of Representatives. Gardner wrote: "He could not suffer fools gladly, and possessed quite devastating powers of personal abuse. Some sensitive men, after a torrid interview, regarded him as a blustering bully." [6]

In the Reform administration after the war, Bell's advice and legislative skills were increasingly critical. He mastered a number of portfolios and was acting prime minister during several Massey absences overseas.

Bell foresaw the importance of forestry and laid the foundations for its successful growth and management. He summed up his views in a 1921 speech: "If we can keep a supply of timber for our children's children and their children's children, that will effect my aim." [7]

Sir Francis Bell visited Europe in 1922, representing New Zealand at League of Nations conferences, his enthusiasm for the British Empire paralleled by a strong belief in the role of the League. Now honoured with the GCMG, Bell, on the home front, finished tidying up New Zealand's conveyancing and land transfer systems, a task too daunting for less able legal minds.

When Massey died on May 10 1925, Bell, who had been *de facto* prime minister during his friend's long terminal illness, was the obvious temporary successor. Although entirely without political ambitions, on May 14, at the age of 74, he became the country's first New Zealand-born prime minister. He brought none of his well-honed skills to his brief prime ministership; he was a caretaker and did not intend to give the impression of being anything else.

Gardner wrote: "The most recent precedent for a Prime Minister in the Legislative Council had been Whitaker in 1882-83, hence it could only be a question of Bell's holding office until the Reform Party chose a leader from the House." [8] When the Reform party favoured Gordon Coates over W Downie Stewart, Bell resigned immediately, his ministry lasting 16 days. However, Coates was anxious to retain his most experienced minister and they went together to the Ottawa Imperial Conference in 1926; there, Bell opposed the Balfour Report because, strangely, given his far-sightedness in many fields, he did not believe the dominions should be equal with Great Britain then or in the future.

Bell was leader of the Legislative Council until 1928, but continued to be consulted by his political friends until his death at his much loved Lowry Bay, Wellington, estate in March 1936. His wife had died six months before. As Gardner wrote: "He lived to see the disintegration of the Reform Party, and Labour's coming to power, an event which Bell both feared and resisted with half his mind, yet regarded as inevitable with the other." [9]

In addition to his impressive legal and political careers, Sir Francis Bell held office in a large number of sporting and other organisations. He was, for example, president of the Wellington Cricket Association for 43 years and, at one time, grand master of the Freemasons. Gardner again: "It is difficult to find a parallel to so many-sided a man in New Zealand public life." [10]

W Downie Stewart wrote of his friend and mentor: "Bell's work in Cabinet revealed his great qualities as an administrator, and his astonishing grasp of the problems that arose in all departments. Just as photographs taken by an infra-red lens penetrate the fog and show up the distant landscape with absolute clearness, so Bell's mind saw all aspects of a question in high relief and with objective clarity." [11] Stewart also quoted the view expressed by a Labour member of parliament in 1921: "This man is the uncrowned King of New Zealand, he is one of the ablest men in the Southern Hemisphere." [12]

21

JOSEPH GORDON COATES

1878-1943

"He had never craved power, and was personally unambitious – a curious trait in a prime minister"

Gordon Coates was an unlucky prime minister. A depression, the vagaries of elections and a world war have obscured the fact that he was one of New Zealand's ablest, most forward thinking and selfless leaders. His reputation has also suffered because he was a better administrator than he was calculating politician.

More than most people, Coates was moulded by his background and early life. His grandparents were respected members of Herefordshire gentry, but his father, Edward, and uncle, Thomas, decided to leave England and seek their fortunes in New Zealand. Through family connections the young men were able to lease, then own, land on the Hukatere peninsula in North Auckland's Kaipara Harbour. In 1877, 11 years after arriving in the country, Edward married Eleanor Kathleen Aickin, a young, well-educated, Auckland woman of Irish extraction.

J T Allen, Parliamentary Portraits, *1936. (ATL ref: H-700-005)*

The next year Gordon Coates, the eldest of seven children, was born.

Gordon Coates relished the freedom and outdoor life of a rural backwater with a significant Maori population. From an early age he was an accomplished horse rider, a good shot and proficient Maori speaker. His adventurous nature led to riding accidents: one gave him a distinctive walking gait and another an upper lip scar he covered as soon as a moustache was possible. He attended a local school for a while, but mostly he received a catholic education at home from his mother and several governesses. The result was both a cultured accent and a lifetime liking for salty language.

Responsibility came early. His father suffered from manic depression, so at 21 Gordon Coates was running the family property with a younger brother. His first-hand experience of trying to raise loans on leased land made him an uncompromising supporter of freehold. As his biographer Michael Bassett has written: "For the rest of his life securing and maintaining the freehold became Coates's first and pre-eminent policy plank, one that determined which party he would ultimately join." [1]

In 1900 Coates joined, and soon led, the Otamatea Mounted Rifle Volunteers and held other commands before becoming a reserve officer. In 1905, the same year he was elected to Otamatea County Council, his father died. He later chaired the council, a government in microcosm, with efficient administration, and an emphasis on infrastructure, particularly roading, the key to success.

Tall, good-looking and successful from his early twenties, Coates was, and remained, attractive to women. There were rumours of two children fathered during a lengthy liaison with a Maori woman. Certainly, he was engaged to a young teacher, with marriage subsequently forbidden by her father who feared hereditary psychiatric illness; Eva Ingall did not marry and, years later, arranged for a red rose to be placed on Coates' funeral casket.

Gordon Coates entered Parliament in December 1911 and was to remain the member for Kaipara until he died. In the early years there were few indications that he would play such a prominent political role over two decades; his interests were parochial, concentrated on the 'roadless north', and he was never better than an average public speaker.

He began his political career as an independent Liberal and his vote was crucial to Sir Joseph Ward's shaky administration surviving a no-confidence motion in February 1912. He turned down a ministerial appointment when Thomas Mackenzie replaced Ward as prime minister and his lukewarm support for the Liberals wavered further as they vigorously promoted leasehold. Accordingly, he switched his vote to the Reform Party when it forced and won a no-confidence vote in July.

With Reform unequivocal in its support of freehold land tenure, Coates' principal political concern was satisfied and by 1914 he had joined the party and was its official Kaipara candidate at that year's election. Also in 1914, now 36 years-old and one of the country's more eligible bachelors, he married Marjorie Grace Coles who, 13 years his junior, was to be a decorative and supportive partner the rest of his life.

Physically active and adventurous by nature, Gordon Coates attempted to enlist in the army early in the First World War but Massey, constrained by a minimal majority, did not release him until November 1916. He lost little time in proving his leadership qualities and bravery. At war's end he had been awarded a Military Cross and bar, been promoted to major and was second in command of a battalion.

Back in New Zealand in May 1919, Coates was a hero in his Kaipara electorate and provided Massey with an opportunity to add some colour and youth to the jaded Reform administration that romped home at the December 1919 election. He became postmaster-general and added the justice, telegraphs and public works portfolios to his workload – all important departments at a time when the country's infrastructure and communications were still being developed.

His capacity for hard work, grasp of practical problems and willingness to grapple with priorities enhanced his reputation. While previous ministers had dithered, he concentrated on finishing three main trunk railway lines, centralised hydro-electric construction and set up a main highways roading system. Previously, as W B Sutch wrote: "Roads at their worst were dirt, bogs and boulders along a surveyed line, unlikely to be uniform from one town to another …" [2]

Also, between 1921-28 he held the sensitive position of native minister. It was an inspired appointment because Coates had grown up among Maori, spoke the language with some proficiency, and his casual and gregarious manner suited the role.

By late 1924 when it became clear that Massey's health was failing, there was little argument, either in the media or among his colleagues, that Coates was most likely to succeed him. Those Reform members who had doubts about his toughness, political astuteness and devotion to private enterprise were reassured by his no-nonsense handling of a short-lived rail strike earlier in the year.

After Massey died, and Sir Francis Bell served a brief caretaker period, Gordon Coates became prime

The Menace of Socialism. The Hon. J.G. Coates: 'Not while I'm Prime Minster!' *Fear of socialism struck a chord in the electorate, with Coates gaining a sweeping victory at the 1925 election. A S Paterson, Dominion,* October 14 1925. *(ATL ref: J-057-001)*

minister at the end of May 1925. Michael Bassett wrote: "The 47-year-old Coates was associated with no distinct philosophy or faction. He had no love for party politics or political theories, endured 'the cumbersome machinery of Parliament' simply because it must be endured, and cared only for practical achievements." [3]

Coates should have been able to chalk up an impressive list of such achievements, but he lacked the necessary political skills and the economy conspired. The 1925 election campaign, which gave a resounding victory to Coates, was the first in New Zealand to sell politicians as products. Coates was a tall, debonair man with, as it is now called, 'charisma'. Reform promoted the man rather than policies, with slogans like 'Coats off with Coates' and 'Coates and Confidence'.

After the election Coates missed the opportunity to replace at least some of his care-worn cabinet. Farm produce prices dipped disturbingly as the British economy went into recession. Attempts to license urban public transport and introduce town planning regulations had merit but they, along with payment of special allowances to larger families, exasperated the Reform government's natural constituency.

Coates made a favourable impression at the 1926 Imperial Conference in London, his lack of enthusiasm for the dominions becoming 'autonomous communities within the British Empire' contrasting with his energetic promotion of 'imperial preference' for empire trade. Back home the impression was increasingly unfavourable. Perhaps the most heat was generated by the government's indecisiveness when the Dairy Board attempted, as a minority supplier, to fix the price of butter in Britain. Predictably, the ploy failed with the fall-out denting the government's credibility.

By 1927 Coates' administration was drifting, unable or unwilling to explain its policies or philosophy. According to Michael Bassett: "He was full of vigour, active, virile; he was a kind, considerate person, always popular with the House. But he had never craved power, and was personally unambitious – a curious trait in a prime minister. He lacked direction. His weak Cabinet did not know how to disguise this failing, or to compensate for it." [4]

Coates showed little interest in the New Zealand Political Reform League, the organisation behind the party and had little in common with A E Davy who ran it and had devised the highly effective 1925 election campaign. By the end of 1926 Davy had left, armed with membership lists, in search of a political party more appreciative of his skills.

Reform's political fortunes worsened. W J Gardner wrote: "The electorate's reaction was to blame the Government, especially one headed by the political Moses of 1925. Coates was caught in the backwash of Davy's campaign and as harshly cried down as he had been extravagantly praised." [5]

About the same time, Sir Joseph Ward, physically ailing but with his political shrewdness intact, was persuaded of the opportunity to revive the rump of the old Liberal Party. With a lick of promotional paint, the United Party, using Davy's marketing savvy, picked up enough conservative, commercial and urban votes to deliver the government a crushing defeat at the November 1928 election.

With the rapidly worsening world economic situation and Ward's powers of financial wizardry long since spent, United fared no better than Reform. Ward, who was now dying, resigned in favour of George Forbes. Sharing a fear of Labour's free-spending, socialist

A Helping Hand. *Finding work for large numbers of unemployed did not save Coates from a crushing defeat at the 1928 election. Trevor Lloyd,* New Zealand Herald, *February 18 1928. (ATL ref: A-315-2-155)*

policies, Forbes and Coates were forced, personal preferences aside, into coalition in September 1931 with Forbes, his dourness disguising a calculating political brain, contriving to remain prime minister. Officially, Coates was his deputy, but Reform ministers controlled the key ministries, particularly Downie Stewart who kept a tight grip on the country's purse-strings.

The coalition won the December 1931 election, with Labour's vote continuing to grow. As minister of public works, and with responsibility for employment, Coates was the target of increasingly bitter criticism as unemployment soared to about 80,000 by September 1933. Conventional thinking in the early 1930s, as it had been during earlier crises, was to meet depression with retrenchments, the severity of one dictating the harshness of the other. Coates wanted to assist redundant workers into small farms, but finance minister Downie Stewart refused the funds for this and other attempted initiatives.

This modern Horatius. *Coates was confident – too confident – that the merging of the Liberal and United parties would not affect the 1928 election outcome. Stuart Peterson,* Free Lance, *May 16 1928.* *(ATL ref: A-315-3-049)*

He was more successful at the Imperial Economic Conference in Ottawa in July 1932, playing a leading role in convincing Britain to give preferential trade treatment to a range of agricultural products from the dominions. Coates returned to New Zealand convinced that farm incomes must be boosted by a devaluation. W B Sutch has summed up the situation: "He was opposed by his own finance minister, by the Bank of New Zealand and by all those in the community who said that exchange rates had to be fixed by the banks and that legislation against banks was a blow to the whole private enterprise system." [6] Coates prevailed in cabinet and, when Downie Stewart resigned, added the finance portfolio to his other responsibilities. With a 'brains trust' of bright young economists in his office, he set up the Reserve Bank and the Mortgage Corporation to help farmers re-finance their loans. While of far-reaching importance, these initiatives further enraged conservative supporters who from their narrow perspective decried them as further examples of the state interfering where it should not.

By 1935 Coates' policies had contributed significantly to the New Zealand economy recovering. Gardner wrote: "Those who saw it cannot forget the way drowsy Labour benches awoke to alert hostility as Coates rose to speak in the House. It was the greatest compliment they could pay to the one man who was their master in the art of applying State power to practical, progressive ends, but who was the principal obstacle in their road to office." [7]

However, at that year's election, it was clear that the public were no longer apprehensive about giving Labour a chance to govern. It was a heavy loss for the coalition and Coates came the closest ever to losing his Kaipara seat.

Out of office, and with no official residence, it was difficult to support his family on an ordinary MP's salary. They shifted north, Coates converting a Public Works Department home and moving it onto the family farm. While only in his late fifties, and outwardly in robust good health, it looked as if Coates' political career was largely over. In 1936, the remnants of the Reform and United parties re-branded themselves as the New Zealand National Party. They wanted a new leader to go with the new image and chose Adam Hamilton briefly and then Sidney Holland ahead of the much more experienced Gordon Coates.

The Second World War changed what might have been a quiet winding down of his political life, spending more time with his close-knit family. But again, in 1939, he offered to serve his country in wartime. Peter Fraser, who became prime minister after Michael Joseph Savage died in March 1940, had known and liked Coates for many years and quickly drew him into the war cabinet, opting for this form of administration rather than the national government the National Party wanted. Soon, with his military background, organisational skills and love of 'hands-on' involvement, Coates was playing a leading role in defence preparedness, travelling to the United States, Canada and Australia negotiating for war supplies and strategic co-operation.

Coates was minister of the armed forces and war co-ordination during the brief War Administration in 1942 and continued in the war cabinet after its collapse, engineered by Holland. Mutual disenchantment had developed into a widening rift and Coates planned to contest the 1943 election as an independent National candidate.

However, the combination of a weakened heart,

that he had kept secret, a punishing workload and a lifetime of heavy smoking caught up with him suddenly and fatally in his office in late May 1943.

Coates' reputation has suffered because he was associated in the public's, and historians' minds, more with the massive unemployment of the early 1930s than with the imaginative and far-reaching policies he, almost single-handed, implemented to ease the depression. For totally different reasons, neither National, which grew out of Reform, nor Labour wanted to acknowledgement his achievements.

Economist Brian Easton has written: "Coates was New Zealand's greatest minister of finance." [8] W B Sutch concurred. "In 1934 he set up the Reserve Bank to provide funds for State activities, abolished the note issues of private banks and replaced them with Reserve Bank notes. He transferred the country's gold reserves from the trading banks to the Reserve Bank, reduced interest on the National Debt by one-fifth, reduced overdraft rates, provided machinery to reduce both interest and borrowed capital on farm mortgages to the levels the farms could stand, and set up a Mortgage Corporation (now State Advances) to help farmers get mortgages." [9]

Michael Bassett wrote: "Gordon Coates deserves to be seen as the politician who pushed the role of government beyond barriers that his fellow conservatives thought prudent, yet stopped short of what his Labour opponents saw as desirable." [10]

Perhaps the last word should be left to one of our luckiest prime ministers, Keith Holyoake. "Some men are lucky in the times in which they had the opportunity to govern or to help in the government of any country. I would think Gordon Coates was the most unfortunate of men in this respect .... Had he had the opportunity to exercise his powers and qualities of government and leadership and courage in better times, he would have been known as one of our greatest statesmen ..." [11]

Strays. *Coates and Forbes were an unlikely pairing, with only a shared fear of Labour in common. Kennaway (Andrew Kennaway Henderson) Tomorrow magazine, August 1 1934. (ATL ref: H-705-027)*

22
GEORGE WILLIAM FORBES
1869-1947

"A good honest man whose political merits will, one day, be uncovered by some dogged researcher"

"George Forbes was an amiable man but his lack of initiative and his intractability made him unsuited to the office of prime minister, especially at a time of national crisis."[1] W J Gardner's crisp opinion was, and remains, the prevailing view of the country's twenty-second prime minister.

Forbes was born in Lyttelton in 1869. His parents, Annie Adamson and Robert Forbes, lived in modest comfort and their son attended the local primary school and then had two years at Christchurch Boys' High School. He worked first for a merchant and then in his father's sailmaking business. A little improbably he had a passion, apparently stimulated by hearing Sir George Grey speak, for political history and he joined a Christchurch debating society.

Locally, though, George Forbes was better known for his sporting prowess. He was an accomplished athlete and rower, but particularly made

George Finey, New Zealand Artists' Annual, Christmas 1931. (ATL ref: A-315-3-053)

his mark at rugby, captaining the 1892 Canterbury side from half back.

The next year, when he was 24 years-old, Forbes had the good fortune to draw a 226 acre property in the first ballot held to subdivide the Cheviot estate. So began a chain of events that drew him into politics and defined his political beliefs. Forbes added a 1,377 acre grazing run to his leasehold farm in the third ballot. Quickly a farmer of some substance in the new community, he was elected to the Cheviot County Council and played a leading role in the Cheviot Settlers' Association. Some local success bred more substantial political ambitions.

Premier Seddon tried to discourage Forbes from standing for the Hurunui electorate in 1902; he stood anyway as an independent Liberal and came an ignominious fourth. However, his reputation was restored with his appointment, as a prominent Cheviot resident and steadfast supporter of leasehold, to the royal commission on Crown lands in 1905. The Liberal member for Hurunui did not contest the 1908 election and Forbes won the seat. He was to hold it, wearing a variety of political hats, until 1943.

Loyally supported by his wife, Emma Serena Gee, whom he had married in 1898, Forbes served unspectacularly as a Liberal MP, unwavering in his devotion to state leasehold as the political pendulum swung sharply in favour of Reform and freehold. For a decade from 1912 he was a Liberal whip as the once great party steadily declined in numbers and influence.

Casting around for a post-First World War role the Liberals changed their name back to Liberal-Labour but this did not halt the erosion of left-leaning support. Then, in 1925, leader T M Wilford tried to firm up support on the other end of the political spectrum by proposing a fusion with Reform under the new name of National. Prime Minister Coates rejected the overture out of hand but Liberal-Labour changed its name to National anyway. Wilford promptly resigned and, to general surprise, George Forbes was elected party leader.

The Press commented: "The people of Canterbury have reared him, they like him, they have seen him play magnificent football. But they have not begun to think of him yet as a political leader …. And Mr Forbes will have to help." [2] It was a doubt that lingered for the rest of Mr Forbes' political career.

"Introduced to the nation as 'a plain man without frills' Forbes soon revealed the fact that he was also without ideas or initiative. More fitted to preside over the quiet demise of liberalism than to herald its revival, he seemed neither able nor specially eager to play a major part in the election campaign," wrote R M Burdon. [3]

His first election campaign as party leader was inauspicious to say the least. On the hustings Coates and Labour's Harry Holland were dominant. When the votes were counted, National had only 11 seats. What might have been a terminal decline was halted by two things: Coates' plummeting popularity and the machinations of New Zealand's first, highly successful and seemingly unprincipled, spin doctor, the same A E Davy who masterminded Reform's crushing 1925 victory.

Motivated by ambition and desperation, a rag-tag of anti-Labour opposition elements were re-packaged by Davy as United, and Forbes, while still parliamentary leader, relinquished party control to Sir Joseph Ward, an ailing ghost from the Liberal past. At the 1928 election, the public's desire for salvation from a deepening economic crisis was met with seductive promises of better times. Amazingly, United swept to

Punctured romance, or Reform's refusal. *Coates and Reform were unwilling to join with Forbes and United, but a 'marriage of convenience' was inevitable as the depression deepened. Jack Gilmour,* New Zealand Free Lance, *May 13 1931. (ATL ref: H-705-003)*

power with Ward prime minister again nearly 16 years after he had resigned the position. Forbes became minister of agriculture and lands and, within the year, de facto prime minister, Ward then too ill to attend cabinet meetings. The charade continued until Ward resigned in May 1930.

Historian Keith Sinclair wrote: "… he was succeeded by New Zealand's most improbable Premier, G W Forbes, a good, honest man whose political merits will doubtless, one day, be uncovered by some dogged researcher." [4]

The tragedy was that Forbes found himself facing one of the greatest economic crises of modern times while heading a government of mediocre ability. "As minister of finance Forbes introduced orthodox deflationary measures, but in 1931 faced a heavy deficit," wrote Gardner. "He appeared to be simply marking time, waiting for something to turn up." [5]

Regardless of the situation at home, New Zealand prime ministers always answered the call to attend imperial conferences in London, as Forbes did in 1930. In his absence an unemployment act, approving some payment of relief, was passed. But when Forbes returned his attitude had hardened: no payments without work and 10 percent wage cuts. Labour refused to support United any longer and the unenviable task fell to Reform, preferring this to forcing an election.

As the depression deepened, with no end in sight, Forbes pressed Coates to join in a coalition and share responsibility for the draconian cuts and retrenchments that orthodox thinking deemed necessary. Coates, who had a low opinion of Forbes and his colleagues, resisted for some weeks before accepting the inevitable.

Forbes, known as 'Honest George', possibly because he lacked the imagination to varnish the truth even a little, remained prime minister. "The next three years harshly tarnished this public image of courageous integrity into one of short-sighted stubbonness," wrote Gardner. [6] In fact, Forbes played less of a role in the coalition government than was admitted at the time, with Coates and his Reform colleagues taking the key portfolios.

At first, with Downie Stewart a thoroughly orthodox minister of finance, Forbes was sufficiently encouraged to campaign vigorously and successfully for 'national solidarity' at the 1931 election. In time, though, Coates' growing disquiet with the administration's wallowing indecision led to the raising of New Zealand's exchange rate to assist the farming community. When Stewart resigned and Coates became finance minister Forbes reportedly said: "I consider it my duty to remain on deck and if necessary go down with the ship." In fact, to carry the metaphor further, Coates rarely left the bridge and Forbes stayed in his cabin, receiving occasional reports on the direction the ship of state was taking.

In part, Forbes coped with a situation he had little control over by taking several extensive overseas trips, to the International Monetary and Economic Conference in 1933 and the dominions' prime ministers meeting during George V's silver jubilee celebrations in 1935.

By this time the depression had eased, but the voters remembered, with considerable bitterness, the harshness of many of the coalition's policies. Labour was the only untarnished party. This was duly reflected in the 1935 election result with Labour's handsome first time win and the decimation of the National Political Federation. George Forbes stayed on for a year as leader of the opposition but was not wanted by the newly-minted National Party, launched in May 1936. Hurunui's favourite son continued to represent the electorate for a further eight years, retiring at the next, long-delayed election in 1943.

George Forbes died at his Cheviot farm, 'Crystal Brook' in May 1947.

Forbes might have been the least impressive of New Zealand's 20th century's prime ministers but, as W J Gardner has written, "Forbes was neither as good as he was sometimes painted in 1931, nor as bad as he was made out to be in 1935 .... As party halfback behind a beaten pack he was thoroughly hardened to going down on the ball in the face of dangerous rushes. Averting defeat was his main aim as leader; outright victory was beyond his powers and his expectations." [7]

Certainly he had qualities that were admired – by colleagues and opponents – before being swamped by the depression. He was personally friendly and courteous, and a well-developed sense of humour contrasted with his stolid appearance and political pronouncements. Gardner wrote: "Capable of summing up a situation quickly and effectively, he could often gauge the feeling of the House in difficult situations. Once he had made a decision he stuck to it and remained imperturbable under attack." [8] While he did not display the enterprise or imagination to cope with the depression crisis, Burdon believes he "was a man of great mental toughness and moral courage".[9]

Forbes was personally responsible for little that was positive during his nearly five years as prime minister, which made it doubly ironic that, having carried the flickering Liberal torch in Parliament for so long, he should preside over the abolition of two of its principal tenets – the graduated land tax and compulsory arbitration.

"Cruel circumstance had betrayed George William Forbes into the position of a pilot called upon suddenly to weather a storm of novel aspect and unpredictable severity – a position he had neither coveted, nor, until very recently, expected to fill," wrote R M Burdon. "The early promise he gave of growing up to be a worthy, public-spirited citizen, though amply fulfilled had never been transcended." [10]

Half-time. *The coalition struggled to find economic solutions. Sir Gordon Minhinnick,* New Zealand Herald, *December 9 1932. (ATL ref: H-705-005)*

23

MICHAEL JOSEPH SAVAGE
1872-1940

"He helped set the social pattern of New Zealand for two generations, and had become its icon"

Michael Savage was like no other New Zealand prime minister, before or since. He was charismatic before the term was invented, but with few if any of the ingredients that today define 'charisma'.

'Joe' Savage, as he was often known in New Zealand, was small, plain, softly spoken, modest, and selfless to an extraordinary degree. He was gregarious and enjoyed the company of women and children but never married; like a priest, he single-mindedly devoted himself to a compelling cause. When he was prime minister he delayed a potentially life-saving operation for nearly a year, worried that the government's programme might stall in his absence.

J T Allen, Parliamentary Portraits, 1936. (ATL ref: H-700-001)

A few prime ministers have been respected, some have been loathed. The relationship between Savage and many New Zealanders was special. As Keith Sinclair wrote, he was: " …. a benign, political uncle, cosy, a good mixer, with a warmly emotional appeal. He smelt of the church bazaar and not at all of the barricades. He became one of the few Prime Ministers who were loved by their supporters." [1]

There were several reasons. Politician and historian Michael Bassett has written: "The dimpled face, the glasses, the avuncular air, all conveyed rectitude and confidence after a generation of uncertainty." [2] After so much disappointment and disillusion, Savage, with his transparent simplicity and single-minded devotion to bettering the lot of working people, could not have been more perfect had he been genetically-modified to order. Also, wrote journalist Leslie Hobbs: "No one listening to Savage could have thought of him as the leader of a pack of property-confiscating 'Red Feds' such as its enemies had always claimed Labour would be." [3]

Michael Joseph Savage was born in Victoria, Australia, in March 1872. His Irish parents, Richard Savage and Johanna Hayes, had sought, but did not find, a more benign future on the other side of the world. Michael was the youngest of eight children and the family made an uncertain living on a small farm near Benalla.

Savage's humble, emotionally-scarring, and often grim early life did not produce the bitterness or ruthless pursuit of wealth and power that is a common outcome. Interestingly, bush ranger Ned Kelly grew up in uncannily similar circumstances in the same area a few years earlier.

Despite the unremitting hardship, it was a close-knit family. Richard Savage, who had briefly contemplated a life in politics when he arrived in Melbourne, helped neighbours who could not read or write; Johanna Savage was a devoted, protective mother who, even when close to death, had the children lined up at her bedside for evening prayers. She died when Michael was five and he was largely brought up by a older sister who died, along with Joe, the crippled brother he was closest to, when he was 19.

Michael was fortunate to have five years of primary schooling before, at 14, he began working at a wine and spirits shop in Benalla, where he was remembered for boxing and weightlifting prowess. He also took night classes in bookkeeping and other subjects.

He lost his job in 1893 as a lengthy depression blanketed Australia. Unsettled by the succession of family deaths Savage left home and, after a period as an itinerant labourer, found work on the vast North Yanco station in the Riverina district of New South

Wales. During his seven years there he became a member of the General Labourers' Union and absorbed the political theories of Americans Henry George and Edward Bellamy. Later, at Rutherglen, not far from Benalla, he was involved in both the local miners' union and Victoria's Political Labour Council (PLC). With British social evangelist Tom Mann now influencing his thinking as well, he was chosen as the PLC's candidate to contest the local seat in the 1907 state election. He withdrew when the Council could not support his bid financially.

The same year the Rutherglen mines closed and, after some prompting from miner friend Paddy Webb, Savage sailed for Wellington in October. His original intention was to join Webb, already at the Denniston coalmine on the South Island's west coast, but possibly influenced by a dislike of wet, cold weather he moved, and worked, northwards in easy stages, arriving in Auckland later in 1908.

He had now lived in a room and out of a suitcase for many years, so it was not surprising that he looked for somewhere to board. More surprising, but underlining the uncluttered simplicity of his way of life, he moved in and remained with Alf and Elizabeth French who, years later, shifted to Wellington to provide a prime ministerial roof over his head.

Savage soon had a job as a cellarman in a Newmarket brewery, with his spare time and money fully devoted to union matters. By 1910 he was president of the Auckland Trades and Labour Council, and a year later transferred his allegiance to the more radical New Zealand Federation of Labour. With friends, including Peter Fraser, who was to succeed him as prime minister nearly 30 years later, he distributed the 'Red Fed' newspaper, *The Maoriland Worker*, and organised an endless round of political and educational meetings. Standing for the Socialist Party at the 1911 election, his second place in the Auckland Central poll showed a promising level of support. Despite this Savage was preparing to return to Australia the next year when he became involved in a labourers' strike in Auckland and then the Waihi miners' strike.

In 1913, thoughts of returning to his extended family across the Tasman faded as he played a leading role, using the mild-mannered people skills he honed over many years, in getting a number of socialist and union organisations to support a new Social Democratic Party. But what progress was made was soon over-shadowed by a waterfront dispute that developed into an ugly general strike and then a comprehensive defeat of the union movement.

After unsuccessfully contesting the 1914 election, for the Social Democratic Party this time, Savage moulded a fragmented political labour movement in Auckland into the more coherent force that won a seat on the hospital board at the local body elections early the next year.

During the First World War Michael Savage spoke out against conscription – wealth should be called up before men – but he did not go to prison like his friends Peter Fraser and Robert Semple, in part because by the time his name came up in the ballot he was 45 years old. By now his economic thinking had matured, reinforced by the writings of Irving Fisher, and he was able to explain, in a simple and persuasive way, that only state control of money supply and credit could ease hardship and misery.

The year after the war Savage's name began to be heard more widely. In short order he was elected to the Auckland City Council and the Auckland Hospital Board. He then won the Auckland West parliamentary seat with a comfortable majority, joining seven other Labour MPs in the House of Representatives.

His biographer Barry Gustafson wrote: "From his first speech in Parliament in 1920, Savage concentrated on two basic interrelated themes: the ideal of a comprehensive social security system and the need to reform the country's financial system in order to provide the money for social welfare." [4]

Savage quickly played a prominent role in the Labour caucus, this being formalised with the deputy-leadership following the 1922 election. Now he could, and did, dedicate nearly every waking hour to achieving his political goals. As Hobbs wrote: "…Savage was one of the most uncomplicated politicians ever to play an important role in New Zealand. He had a one-track mind. He wanted to improve conditions for the worker and the underprivileged." [5]

A necessary intermediate step was to widen Labour's appeal beyond the union movement and in this cause Savage travelled tirelessly around the country. As Michael Bassett writes: "Almost alone in those early days the small dirt-farmer's son had a vision of a broadly-based party; such was essential if Labour was to win power in a country whose electoral system was slanted away from the towns." [6]

Harry Holland was party leader but Savage, in his quiet, unobtrusive way, was advocating pension changes and a free health service, successfully pushing the Reform government to introduce a family allowance, and persuading his colleagues that a freehold land policy was crucial to winning sufficient rural votes to occupy the treasury benches.

After the 1928 election, with its extraordinary re-incarnation of Sir Joseph Ward, Labour held the balance of power and, with United bumbling while the depression worsened, Savage wanted Holland to attack its performance more decisively. "By this time," wrote Gustafson," differences of opinion between Holland, the socialist theorist, and Savage, the practical politician, were starting to become apparent within the upper levels of the party." [7] Late in 1931, Savage was also coping with the first signs of an abdominal problem that puzzled doctors – and eventually killed him.

When Holland died in 1933, Savage quickly turned up the parliamentary heat on the coalition government, partly because it was important to be seen as a viable alternative government, but also because he was genuinely upset by the all too familiar signs of suffering among the unemployed and elderly as he criss-crossed the country with his message of hope. Savage and his closest colleagues had worked hard to make Labour acceptable to a largely conservative electorate. As Sinclair wrote: "In the years 1931-33, having shed socialism, the Party adopted credit reform in an all-out effort to win non-union votes and power .... But the leaders had no intention of practising anything more than mild inflation ... Socialist or Social Credit theories were alike cast aside .... The unions would not stand socialism and, the leaders judged, the economy would not stand Major Douglas." [8]

The next election, delayed a year, was finally held in December 1935. "In the months leading up to the 1935 election Savage came to personify the Labour Party's commonsense humanitarian approach," Gustafson wrote. "He spoke with sincerity, eloquence and power, convincing many voters that he and his colleagues not only understood their problems but could be trusted to solve them." [9]

The 1935 election was a momentous victory for Labour and their 63 year old leader. With the support of two Ratana MPs, Labour now occupied 55 of the 80 seats in Parliament. It was a mandate for bold and comprehensive change. While Savage's well-tuned political instincts warned against an avalanche of new legislation, the first Labour government's programme during 1936 made most administrations, before and since, look like timid procrastinators.

In line with long-held Labour views, it was critical to give people more purchasing power to stimulate a sluggish economy that would, in turn, boost employment and trigger further demand. State control of the newly-established Reserve Bank was at the heart of this economic recovery. An ambitious state housing programme, guaranteed prices for dairy produce, the nationalisation of commercial radio, and compulsory union membership linked to a 40-hour working week were some of the sweeping changes. And Savage, who had taken the native affairs portfolio, further consolidated Labour's position by forging a political alliance with the Ratana movement that he had farsightedly foreshadowed some years previously; for neglected Maori it meant education, health, employment, and land settlement initiatives.

Savage's prime ministerial predecessors had felt a strong emotional attachment to Britain and the Empire, enjoyed the pomp and circumstance in the regular visits to London, and rarely questioned Downing Street's motives or machinations. Perhaps because of his Irish origins, and certainly because of Labour's internationalist perspective, Savage took an altogether more detached and objective view of New Zealand's foreign policy interests. He attended King George VI's coronation and

On the warpath? *Savage's new reforming government was about to take decisive action. William Blomfield,* New Zealand Observer, *December 5 1935. (ATL ref: H-705-020)*

accompanying Imperial Conference in 1937 and made a singular impression criticising Britain's weak response to Japan's and Italy's foreign adventures and Germany's rearmament. He was unimpressed by Britain's claims about the effectiveness of the Singapore naval base, should Japan invade the Pacific, and said so bluntly.

While in Britain he wrote to his niece Eileen, as he did regularly over a 20 year period, that he was longing to be back home to get on with his "real job". "The amount of artificial humbug that one meets with here is astounding ," he wrote. "….If you could have seen me in Westminster Abbey decked out in the uniform of a Privy Councillor you would have wondered if I was the person who in 1893 carried his swag through the Riverina." [10]

In 1938 Savage introduced Labour's social security programme; "applied christianity" was the verbal shorthand he liked to use. The 'cradle to grave' legislation, the most comprehensive in the world, assured his place in history – and killed him as well. Shortly after the Social Security Bill was introduced to Parliament – providing a universal, free health system, a means-tested old-age pension at age 60 and universal superannuation from 65 – Savage was diagnosed with colon cancer. Immediate surgery was necessary but Savage delayed the operation for months: the social security legislation needed to be passed, there was an election to be won, and a war was looming. It was the most dramatic example, from a lifetime of them, of principles coming before his personal comfort or well-being.

Again, the 1938 election was a personal triumph for Savage, and Labour's share of the vote climbed to 56 percent. However, any euphoria was quickly dampened down by an increasingly malicious and personal attack on his leadership by John A Lee, once a close friend.

Lee was the antithesis of Savage in almost every way and, as a prolific and effective writer, spent the rest of his long life trying, with some success, to rewrite the history of the first Labour government to his advantage. Savage had personally selected

his cabinet after the 1935 victory and left out Lee, later being persuaded to give him an under-secretaryship. This snub plus several areas of policy and personal disagreement were sufficient for Lee, who saw himself as an alternative Labour leader, to mount an increasingly ferocious campaign to discredit Savage. After the 1938 election Lee persuaded his colleagues that they, not Savage, should select the new cabinet. Savage insisted that the decision be ratified by the next party conference and Lee, not in cabinet, saw his chances of contesting the leadership disappearing.

Savage struggled through the first months of 1939: he acted decisively to break doctors' resistance to the free health system and was acting finance minister when Nash, responding to an exchange crisis, travelled to England in search of loans to pay for Labour's expansive policies.

At the beginning of August, the day after reading the budget, he collapsed and finally, a year too late, had the operation that might have saved his life. A week after he came out of hospital, New Zealand was at war with Germany. He did not have the strength to travel widely, as he had in the past, so he spoke to his adopted countrymen via a series of 'New Zealand's Problems As I See Them' Sunday night radio broadcasts in late 1939 and into 1940. It was, in effect, an armed forces recruitment campaign, but in Savage's inimitable, folksy style. Yes, volunteers were needed to fight for the future of democracy but, no, there would not be conscription of men, should it be necessary, before the conscription of wealth. Terminally ill though he was, Savage still had his finger firmly on the New Zealand pulse.

The Medicine Man. *The medical profession resisted Labour's free health system. Sir Gordon Minhinnick,* New Zealand Herald, *August 18 1938. (ATL ref: H-723-005)*

Oh, wad some power the giftee gi'e us…! *Savage was compared, not always favourably, with Seddon. B E Pike,* The Monocle, *1938. (ATL ref: H-705-019)*

The spirit of his ancestors. *The conservative press tried to equate Labour's policies with those of the European dictators. Sir Gordon Minhinnick,* New Zealand Herald, *July 15 1938. (ATL ref: H-705-018)*

Savage's last weeks were haunted by the fear that the monetary reform faction headed by Lee, who had widened his attack to also slate Peter Fraser and Walter Nash for their financial orthodoxy, might gain sufficient support in caucus to put the government's achievements at risk.

Not long before the March 1940 party conference Lee's notorious article in *Tomorrow* magazine, inferring that Savage was mentally as well as physically ill, gave the prime minister one last opportunity to neutralise Lee. Savage was too ill to attend, but Fraser electrified the conference, reading his leader's description of the last two years of "living hell" as Lee attacked him "through the public press with all the venom and lying innuendo of the political sewer". [11] Lee was expelled from the Labour Party and Savage was dead within two days.

The country had not seen a funeral like it before; 50,000 mourners filing past the casket at Parliament, the solemn requiem mass, the ceremonial send-off from the Wellington Railway Station, the train stopping 20 times on its way north, thousands more lining Auckland streets to watch the gun carriage pass, and the burial at Bastion Point, with 200 boats bobbing at anchor nearby.

Bruce Brown wrote: "He had the ability to strike a chord in the average member of his audience. He did not impress with cleverness; the image was rather of humanity, sincerity, and a fund of common sense. His appeal was essentially that of the average man, not of the intellectual or the expert." [12]

With a simplicity that sometimes appeared like naivety, coupled with Lee's crusade to denigrate him, much has been made of Savage's 'ordinariness'. But he was more than a great communicator. He was a skilful chairman of cabinet, he was decisive, clearing his desk quickly and efficiently, he gave ministers their heads, supporting and praising their efforts, and he could be steely in his resolve when he felt his government's policies were threatened.

As Gustafson has written, Michael Joseph Savage was, " …. The architect of the first Labour government's achievements just as he had been one of the chief organisers of its rise to power …. He had helped set the social pattern of New Zealand for two generations, and had become its icon." [13]

24
PETER FRASER
1884-1950

"There has been no other prime minister who looked as good as his advisers did"

Peter Fraser may have been New Zealand's greatest prime minister, making very substantial and varied contributions to his adopted country, but recognition and acknowledgement of this has been belated, and it was not until 2000 that he was the subject of a major biography.

There are several reasons for this: he was seen as a cold, austere man; John A Lee and Bill Sutch, who wrote persuasively and at length about the first Labour government, were not friends; his promotion of peacetime conscription in 1949 was seen as a betrayal of his own and Labour's principles.

Fraser was a Scotsman who never lost his enthusiasm for things Scottish or, entirely, his soft burr. He was born in Fearn, a highland village in Ross-shire, in August 1884, second youngest of the six children of Donald Fraser and Isabella McLeod. Peter Fraser's father was a shoemaker with a passion for politics and a commitment to the strict Free Church of Scotland.

Noel Counihan, 1939. (ATL ref: H-705-021)

The family eked out an existence marginally above the poverty line. Peter was sent to the free elementary school when he was five but, despite his obvious intelligence and leadership qualities, left at 14 to supplement the family income.

Apprenticed to a local carpenter, Fraser was already a voracious reader with a precocious interest in Keir Hardie and other socialist writers. He joined the local branch of the Liberal Association his father belonged to, and was its secretary at 16. He spent several volunteer years in the uniform of the Seaforth Highlanders and helped begin a village debating society.

In 1907, Fraser moved to London, lack of work locally and a desire to be closer to the centre of political activity the two strong motivating factors. He found work as a carpenter, but it was the Independent Labour Party, which he joined in 1908, that was central to his life. Two years later, unemployed and impressed by what he had read of New Zealand's pioneering welfare legislation, he emigrated, arriving in Auckland early in January 1911.

Work and political involvement were immediately available. Tall and bespectacled, and his nose often in a book, he did not fit the stereotype of the labourer and wharfie that he became, albeit briefly. He was elected president of the Auckland General Labourers' Union and promptly initiated direct action that won significant improvements in wages and conditions from the Portland Cement Company. Only 27, he was clearly a coming man in union circles. Tim Beaglehole wrote: "An incisive and forceful orator with an instinctive combativeness, a ready wit, and a sarcastic turn of phrase, he was also a shrewd and tireless organiser." [1] The same year he was campaign manager for Michael

Joseph Savage's first, unsuccessful tilt at national politics; it was the beginning of a long and fruitful friendship and working relationship.

In 1912, Fraser, now on the executive of the NZ Federation of Labour (the 'Red Feds'), represented the organisation in Waihi during the bruising miners' strike which new prime minister William Massey lost little time in squashing.

The Waster – Peter removes the halo. *Fraser, by now a prominent parliamentarian, admitted that while the great majority of unemployed were genuine cases, there were some "wasters in the Labour class". Stuart Peterson, Free Lance, February 16 1927. (ATL ref: A-315-3-054)*

The next year Fraser moved to Wellington, finding work on the wharves. He was soon secretary-treasurer of the United Federation of Labour and Social Democratic Party that resulted from two 'unity' conferences of the fragmented, argumentative union and labour groups in the country. A failed general strike at the end of the year showed how fragile worker solidarity remained. Fraser and other strike leaders were arrested and bound over to keep the peace. More pragmatic than doctrinaire, Fraser was one of a number of prominent socialists who now decided more would be achieved via the ballot box than by direct industrial action. Eric Olssen wrote: "Peter Fraser, erstwhile Red Fed who had flirted with the small but influential New Zealand branch of the revolutionary Industrial Workers of the World in

1912, now studied parliamentary procedure." [2]

By mid 1916 there was sufficient agreement to form the New Zealand Labour Party just in time for its collective weight to be thrown into opposing the Military Service Act and the conscription it authorised.

Fraser, on the new party's national executive, was not a pacifist and less adamant than some of his colleagues, arguing that in-tandem conscription of men and wealth was acceptable. Nevertheless, in December 1916 he was arrested, charged with sedition for speaking against the legislation, and jailed for 12 months. On the positive side, the prison term gilded his growing reputation in labour circles and gave him the time for serious study, books courtesy of the recently formed Workers' Educational Association (WEA).

Fraser quickly made up for the period of enforced inactivity. In 1918 he organised Harry Holland's successful campaign in the Grey electorate by-election; briefly edited the *Maoriland Worker*, now Labour's official publication; displayed calm leadership and courage during the raging influenza epidemic; and won Wellington Central in an October by-election, a seat he held through a succession of name and boundary changes for 32 years.

The next year he was elected to the Wellington City Council and married Janet Henderson Munro, who had recently divorced his one-time friend Frederick Kemp. She had a son from her first marriage; their decision not to have children was, at least in part, because of Fraser's closely guarded concern about some hereditary mental problems in his family.

Over the next 16 years Fraser consolidated his senior position in the Labour Party; as secretary of the caucus he was an effective organiser and he mastered the demands of parliamentary life, both tactically and as a forceful debater. His intellectual ability and breadth of knowledge were vital to policy development. Together with the party, Fraser had lost his firebrand militant radicalism and any enthusiasm for communism. As Labour's ambitious social goals would now be won in the parliamentary chamber rather than on the streets controversial policies like land nationalisation and opposition to the arbitration system were quietly dropped.

Fraser became Savage's deputy after Holland's death and deputy prime minister after Labour's election triumph in 1935. It was the beginning of 13 years of self-imposed, unremitting toil which, with the added pressures of the 1939-45 war, eventually wore him out.

Michael Bassett wrote: "At 51, Fraser was nearly the youngest of the Cabinet, and more austere in his habits than all but Nash. He seldom socialised, and didn't drink. Chintzy hospitality held little appeal. He rarely went to dinner parties and these days had few leisure pursuits except reading and talking and the rare delight of a visit to the theatre or an art gallery." [3]

Fraser took the two portfolios that are today rated the most difficult, and are potential graveyards for ambitious politicians. Fraser's contribution in the education and health portfolios were two of the cornerstones of Labour's success and longevity in government.

He brought to the education portfolio a conviction, its beginnings embedded in his Scottish upbringing and developed through years of reading, that education was an essential foundation to wide-ranging social reform.

Brian Easton wrote: "In his first major speech as minister in 1936 …. he had explained what education should 'aim at' in human terms: 'the development of the personality of each individual child, in an atmosphere of comradeship, equality, and mutual help, and in an environment which offers abundant opportunity for constructive work and open-air activity'." [4] What might appear self-evident today was a huge, imaginative leap for most educators nearly 70 years ago.

Fraser moved quickly to restore depression cuts and closures, lowered the school entry age to five, encouraged curriculum innovations, and widened entry to secondary education by abolishing the Proficiency examination.

Fraser had more opposition with the health reforms Labour was committed to. The 1938 Social Security Act, which set up a mainly free national health service, was bitterly opposed by the New Zealand branch of the British Medical Association. It took the combination of Fraser's tough negotiations and Savage's softer approach to finally persuade doctors that the government was determined to proceed. In the health area particularly, where she had considerable experience, Janet Fraser was her husband's trusted adviser; for a considerable period she was also his research assistant, working from an office next to his.

Peter Fraser's workload surged with the tragic combination of the outbreak of war and Savage's last few months after a futile cancer operation. Fraser read the actual declaration of war in Parliament and he took charge of war preparations, including talks in London and the forging of a cordial and invaluable personal relationship with Winston Churchill; he also achieved an immediate rapport, that developed into close friendship, with Bernard Freyberg, who was subsequently appointed to command the 2nd New Zealand Expeditionary Force.

Despite the distraction of orchestrating John A Lee's expulsion from Labour at the 1940 party conference, and then the masterminding of Savage's elaborate, many-faceted funeral, Fraser, now prime minister, was intensely focussed on the war effort, the preparedness and welfare of New Zealand's troops and the 'mobilising' of the nation.

Ruthlessness, never far below the surface with Fraser, was justified by the threat New Zealand faced, particularly when Japan began to sweep down the Pacific. A raft of measures – censorship and emergency regulations that gave the government unprecedented control over people and property – were pushed through Parliament. By the time Fraser introduced the legislation, there was surprisingly little opposition to conscription.

With the war effort paramount, Fraser wanted a coalition government. Some opposition politicians, notably Gordon Coates, put the national interest first, but National, and particularly leader S G Holland, favoured politics over patriotism. Aside from a brief War Administration, that Holland joined and left, the war was principally run by a small war cabinet.

Fraser was determined that New Zealand troops would not again be on the receiving end of some of the War Office bungling that strained relations during the First World War. According to Keith Sinclair, "Freyberg took the same view as Fraser, writing later that the New Zealand Division was the expeditionary force of a sovereign state, the army of an ally, not part of the British army, but a 'partner in the British Commonwealth of Nations'." [5]

The importance of this stance became all the clearer when New Zealand suffered heavy casualties in Greece and Crete, a poorly planned campaign that Fraser and Freyberg had been pressured into without adequately consulting each other. One of the most difficult decisions Fraser had to make was whether to recall the country's troops from the Middle East – as the Australians did – following Pearl Harbour. In a brilliant display of wartime leadership Fraser persuaded a doubtful Parliament and public that the great bulk of the country's troops should remain in the Northern Hemisphere. Fraser paid several visits to Britain, attending war cabinet meetings in London, and to troops in the Middle East and Italy, these being morale-boosting and party political exercises in about equal proportions. With the wholehearted support of servicemen, Labour won the 1943 election Fraser had felt obliged to hold.

Concern about New Zealand's security eased following the arrival of American troops for r & r before returning to the bloody business of rolling back the Japanese, island chain by island chain. Prescient about the United States' importance in the post-war world, Fraser had already despatched Walter Nash to Washington to ensure New Zealand had some say in the Pacific war and in decisions that were already beginning to shape the post-war world. He was also concerned about improving trans-Tasman relations and the Australian-New Zealand Agreement was signed by the two Labour administrations in 1944.

By war's end, after his visits to London and Washington, Fraser had won the respect of the Allies' most senior politicians. His international stature was further boosted at the meetings that established the United Nations where, speaking for small countries, he vigorously opposed veto powers for the great powers. He argued, years ahead of his time, for the UN to have a greater peace-keeping role. He chaired the committee that established the Trusteeship Council, proposing Western Samoa as the first territory under the trusteeship system.

Alister McIntosh, the first secretary of external affairs when Fraser created the department in 1943, wrote about his boss's practice of looking for a principle to base decisions on. "This particular habit and capacity in a Prime Minister and a politician were to my mind almost unique; but I hasten to add this did not mean that he was not equally capable of following the customary lines of political expediency when needs demanded, and no politician could be more devious, or shrewder or more ruthless in achieving his desired end." [6]

While Fraser could usually inhabit the high moral ground in international affairs, at home he was bogged down by the sort of expediency that catches up with weary governments that have been in power for years. The 1946 election was a close run thing, the four Maori seats the difference.

Ever the pragmatist, Fraser promptly added the native affairs portfolio to his heavy workload. He changed the department's name to Maori Affairs and introduced legislation that addressed problems caused by the growing drift to the cities.

Fraser was exhausted and often sick; his cabinet colleagues were in no better shape. It had been a terrible blow when Janet Fraser died the year before. Bassett wrote: "First and foremost she was Fraser's soul mate. They loved nothing more than an evening at home by the fire reading aloud to each other and commenting as they went along." [7]

Fraser had few close friends. Within his own caucus he was intolerant of opposition and ruthless in maintaining authority. His formality was reflected

Why, Pete, you're blushing! *'Food for Britain' was still Labour's catch-cry, but the public was tired of shortages and the militant unions were stirring. Gordon Minhinnick,* New Zealand Herald, *April 11 1946. (ATL ref: H-723-007)*

in the fact that although the Frasers and Nashes had been friends for many years no-one ever heard him call his finance minister 'Walter'.

Labour had now run out of steam, the public was tired of continuing shortages and controls, militant trade unionists were flexing muscles, and a revitalised opposition sensed the mood change. As well, Labour's core support was shaken by Fraser's increasing dependence on union hard man F P Walsh and his determination, based on his gloomy assessment of the likelihood of peace in a world of belligerent superpowers, to introduce peacetime conscription. He tried, but failed, to deflect widespread criticism by calling it 'compulsory military training'.

Photographs of the time suggest that Fraser may have been more relieved than disappointed by Labour's crushing loss at the 1949 election. He was leader of the opposition when his indifferent health allowed and died a year later in December 1950, living long enough to see his old friend Walsh forming a cosy backroom relationship with the new National government.

"Fraser was a complex man," wrote Leslie Hobbs. "A humanitarian who did a tremendous amount for the poor and the sick, he was at the same time ruthless, even unscrupulous, in securing his political aims." [8] He was, though, less contradictory than often portrayed. Is it really surprising that the young idealist in 1916, believing war to be the exploitation of the poor by the rich, should many years later, and with the full weight of prime ministerial responsibility on his shoulders, decide it essential for the country to be better prepared for war than it had been previously?

"He had the kind of flair, instant reflex, instinct almost, which marks the born politician," says Sinclair. [9] Fraser was highly intelligent, and a political realist. He was cool and effective in a crisis, his political judgment and intuition usually impeccable. He was masterful in the House. As Hobbs remembers: "Fraser had an intuition which was almost womanly .... When things were going really wrong, he would switch from indignation to a kind of paternal Scottish good humour, illustrated with little quotations from Scottish writers, or perhaps Dickens." [10]

In his earlier years he was a spine-tingling, spontaneous orator; as prime minister, with his eyesight failing, he stumbled over prepared speeches, squinting at the specially enlarged type a few inches from his nose.

According to McIntosh, "Working with Peter Fraser was a rich but arduous experience." [11] He had an extraordinary ability to get to the nub of an argument or the key points in a report. As McIntosh remembers: "When confronted with a report or paper of more than a page, he would open it at random, reading a bit here and there and, like as not, he would by then have grasped the main points and thus proceed to give his opinion." [12]

The Old Vic Influence. *One of Fraser's few 'indulgences' was his love of the theatre; he rearranged his schedule to see Laurence Olivier and Vivien Leigh in* Richard 111 *in Auckland. Gordon Minhinnick,* New Zealand Herald, *September 14 1948. (ATL ref: H-723-009)*

He had an immense range of knowledge and interests but not, to the frustration of his officials and colleagues, an ordered or disciplined mind.

Fraser routinely worked 17 hour days (8 a.m. – 1 a.m.), often over the weekend as well, and expected his staff to keep to the same timetable. In part, the extraordinarily long hours were because he had no talent for organising his time and work; in part it was because he wanted to be involved in everything and he never learnt the art of delegating.

There was the same degree of chaos in cabinet meetings. McIntosh again: "An agenda was an affront, and any attempt by an official or a colleague to introduce order would only make him mulish and antagonistic." [13]

As journalist Keith Eunson had observed with interest, when Fraser was under pressure or particularly tired his temper could flair. "While his steel-rimmed glasses gave his short-sighted eyes a benign appearance, it was a sure sign of trouble if those eyes turned as cold as sleet, his balding head, surrounded by a receding half-circle of white hair, began to redden and his voice rose half an octave." [14]

Despite all this Fraser attracted, and kept with him, some of New Zealand's finest public servants, who gave order and, sometimes, substance to his ideas. Brian Easton: "From one perspective Fraser's achievements were based on their competence, but from another, his ability to judge and use such men effectively is a mark of his greatness. There has been no other prime minister who …. looked as good as his advisers did." [15] A partial roll call included Clarence Beeby, James Shelley, Alister McIntosh, and Joseph Heenan.

Fraser's relationship with Heenan was particularly creative. Easton wrote: "Among the institutions they created or which were developed out of their initiatives were a literary fund, an arts council, a national orchestra, and the Historical Branch …" [16]

As much as anything, Fraser's claim to greatness rests with the respect he garnered internationally for a small country, still tentative about cutting Mother Britain's apron strings. McIntosh wrote: "He was also a statesman of whom we have had so very few. Certainly no other leader ever attained such stature and reputation overseas. This is something that his fellow countrymen have never fully appreciated." [17]

But Peter Fraser also left an indelible impression on his adopted homeland. As Bassett puts it: "….the values underpinning today's civil society owe more to the first Labour government, in which he was the pre-eminent figure, than to any other administration of the twentieth century." [18]

Ghost of Ramsay : 'So…you too, fail them.' *Fraser is compared to Ramsay MacDonald, Britain's first Labour prime minister, whose national coalition government in the early 1930s was seen as a betrayal. Kennaway (Andrew Kennaway Henderson),* Fool's Carnival, *1949. (ATL ref: H-705-006)*

25

SIR SIDNEY GEORGE HOLLAND
1893-1961

"His importance was not primarily that of a prime minister, but that of a party builder"

Sid Holland was prime minister for eight years, his greatest achievement turning the unpromising, newly-formed National Party into the country's predominant political force. Unlike his immediate predecessors, his passion for politics developed late although his contempt for the left was as strongly developed as theirs of the right-wing establishment.

Holland was born in Canterbury in October 1893, the fifth of English-born Henry Holland and Jane Eastwood's eight children. Henry Holland prospered during the buoyant 1890s, moving his family to Christchurch and setting up a successful business that was his springboard to the mayoralty, with labour support, in 1912, and 13 years later to a parliamentary seat. Then much more conservative in his views, he won Christchurch North for Reform at three elections.

Sid Holland attended Christchurch West District High School, leaving as soon as he could. At 15 he was working in a hardware store; later he joined his father's transport company. He was 21 when war was declared and served in France in the NZ Field Artillery. He was a second lieutenant when he was invalided out of the army after the battle of Messines. He was struck down, not by enemy bullets, but by hydatids. Seriously ill, he spent six months in hospital and lost a lung.

Knight, Here & Now, *October 1949.*
(ATL ref: H-723-012)

Subsequently, he and a brother began the Midland Engineering Company which made spray pumps. Sid Holland became managing director in 1918 and he slowly built up an organisation known for its employee profit-sharing scheme. Not yet involved in politics, Holland was an enthusiastic sportsman. He represented Canterbury and the South Island at hockey, belying the bulky, double-breasted image he presented in later years. He was also a hockey test match umpire and, in 1932, manager of a New Zealand team that toured Australia.

In May 1920 he married Florence Drayton and his family (two sons and two daughters) and community involvements expanded. At various times he was president of the Canterbury Employers' Association, Chamber of Commerce and Christchurch Businessmen's Club. Intentionally or otherwise he was establishing his credentials as a solid conservative. Like another National prime minister he also had an enthusiasm for flowers, his specialities dahlias and gladioli.

Holland's serious political involvement began as a family affair, serving a useful apprenticeship as his father's campaign manager at the 1925, 1928 and 1931 elections. He flirted with the New Zealand Legion, approving of its opposition to both the Labour Party and Gordon Coates' interventionist policies in the United-Reform coalition, but did not join the associated Democrat Party. He now had close connections with Reform and was perfectly placed to step into his father's shoes when Henry Holland was persuaded to step down shortly before the 1935 election.

In many ways it was the ideal time for the young Holland to win the blue-ribbon parliamentary seat, later renamed Fendalton, that he held for 22 years until he, too, retired reluctantly. In the wake of Labour's crushing victory, there were only two new opposition MPs in the House. An energetic 42-year old, and with confidence born of his bluff, uncomplicated personality, he immediately stood out in the elderly, divided and depleted opposition ranks. Barry Gustafson wrote: "Determined, vigorous, with a good memory and naturally aggressive, he detested socialism, which he defined as equality of income, irrespective of capacity – 'the very antithesis of private enterprise'. [1]

He was an effective, sometimes humorous, debater. When Savage talked about Labour's social security legislation as 'applied Christianity', Holland made newspaper headlines saying that, in the current economic conditions, it was 'applied lunacy'.

New boy though he was, Holland played an important role in persuading the United, Reform and Democrat parties to reinvent themselves as National. One of the new party's most immediate challenges was the appointment of a new leader, not made any easier by having two former prime ministers, Coates and Forbes, among its ranks. Forbes, as the recently defeated prime minister, was the temporary leader of the opposition. But, as Gustafson explains, there was little enthusiasm for either Forbes or Coates: "They were yesterday's men, associated too closely in the mind of the public with the suffering of the Depression and the old party rivalries, which it was hoped would be submerged in the new party." [2]

Adam Hamilton, a tall, gangling man who had trained for the Presbyterian ministry before becoming a Southland grain and seed merchant, was eventually, if unenthusiastically, elected National's leader. With a drooping gait and a personality to match, and after another thumping at the 1938 elections, there were rumblings about Hamilton's leadership, but no decisive action.

There were three possible leadership contenders: Keith Holyoake who lost his Motueka seat at the election, Holland and Colonel James Hargest. Hargest, a Gallipoli veteran, was promoted to brigadier and commanded the Second Echelon when it left for Egypt at the beginning of

Return of Sid. *Holland and National were confident of winning the 1949 election; Labour was weary and divided after 14 years in power. Gordon Minhinnick,* New Zealand Herald, *May 4 1949. (ATL ref: H-723-010)*

the Second World War. (Much decorated, he was killed in Europe in 1944.)

Holland's opportunity came in July 1940 when Hamilton and Coates joined the war cabinet. How, he and his supporters argued, could Hamilton be part of the government *and* the leader of the opposition? In November Hamilton was asked to step aside and did so when Holland won a caucus vote convincingly.

Holland was no theorist and had limited education, but knew what he believed in. Barry Gustafson wrote: "In his speeches he stressed individual freedom, initiative, opportunity, enterprise, responsibility and reward." [3]

While Fraser put New Zealand on a wartime footing, Holland concentrated on consolidating National's centre-right position, persuading several right-wing groups to join it.

Following Japan's bombing of Pearl Harbour in December 1941, Holland pressed, and it was the second time he had, for coalition government. In June 1942 Holland eventually accepted Fraser's offer of a seat in the war cabinet and in a specially constituted war administration along with five National colleagues.

However, although he was given responsibility for all war expenditure, Holland saw more political capital in being the government's principal critic and, after just three months, used the court's lenient treatment of striking Huntly coal miners as the excuse to end National's grudging co-operation.

Holland went to considerable lengths to build National's voter base. He was aware that the party's natural rural constituency was fragile, with Social Credit theories in vogue and a country party flexing its backblocks muscles. So Sid Holland, businessman, attempted to reinvent himself as Sid Holland the farmer. He was also aware that farmers saw Coates and Keith Holyoake, neither a Holland favourite, as their particular champions. So, with advice and financial assistance from Stan Goosman, a wealthy National Party MP and successful racehorse owner, Holland bought a north Canterbury sheep and cattle farm. In the end, Holland was never very comfortable with, nor were farmers completely convinced by, the gumboot image-making.

'Goodness, my dear – Look what he is doing to that poor baa-lamb!' *Holland's aggressive approach to the watersiders' wage demands left Labour nonplussed. Keith Waite,* Otago Daily Times, *May 25 1951.*
(ATL ref: H-723-001)

It was at his farm, 'Greta Paddock', during the 1942-43 summer holidays that Holland wrote his booklet *Passwords to Progress* which tried to present National's approach more positively. As Gustafson explained its contents: "He argued that with a National government people could have economic prosperity and social welfare, and in addition individual freedom and a minimum of bureaucratic intervention and restriction." [4] Holland wrote: " …. The basis of New Zealand's material future was a little word with a big meaning – work.."

With these ideas presented more coherently, Holland made some progress at the postponed 1943 election and it was only the four Maori seats that separated National and Labour in 1946. In 1949 Holland was prime minister with a substantial majority. Two of his principal election planks were abolition of Parliament's upper house, the Legislative Council and, more controversially, of compulsory unionism. The first was something of a personal crusade; the second had all his caucus firmly behind it.

The ineffectual Legislative Council, its membership heavily weighted with pensioned off Labour MPs and sympathisers, was an obvious target for the first-term National administration. In 1950 Holland appointed to the Council sufficient National supporters, dubbed the 'suicide squad', to carry a vote for its dissolution.

The 1951 waterfront dispute generated far more heat, in fact, unprecedented levels of bitterness. At the beginning of 1951 a wage demand confrontation between shipowners and watersiders gave Holland the opportunity to impose emergency regulations. The Watersiders' Union was de-registered and its funds seized; the armed forces worked the wharves; freezing workers and miners struck in sympathy. Gustafson wrote: "Holland declared that the 'government intends to govern' and that 'law and order shall prevail'. The strike lasted until 11 July – a bitter 151 days of industrial disruption, social hardship, economic loss and political hatred." [5] Compulsory unionism remained, but the strength of the most militant and strategically important unions was broken and, most satisfactorily, while Labour prevaricated Holland contrived and won a snap election – and six more years in power.

Holland's role was now more to undo than to do. To general relief he ended wartime rationing of butter and petrol; freed up import licensing to

September Morn. *National's decisiveness and Labour's dithering gave Holland a substantial victory at the snap election. Keith Waite, Otago Daily Times, July 17 1951. (ATL ref: J-044-007)*

some extent; removed price controls on urban land; allowed tenants to buy their state houses; and gave majority control of agricultural boards to the producers.

An important foreign policy development was the 1951 signing of the ANZUS treaty with the United States and Australia. That aside, Holland's abiding philosophy seemed to be his mantra that he was "a Britisher through and through". Brian Easton quotes correspondence between two leading public service mandarins: "As McIntosh wrote [to colleague Carl Berendsen] – implicitly criticising Sidney Holland, Fraser's successor: 'We do miss Peter Fraser's farsightedness, astuteness, breadth and enlightened humanitarianism." [6]

Nevertheless, Holland was a shrewd, calculating politician who had comprehensively outwitted Nash during the 1951 waterfront crisis. As Sir John Marshall says: "He was not a thinker in the philosophical sense, but he learned quickly, from experience, from observation and from discussion." [7] Holland could be a tough and autocratic politician; personally he was a hearty, genial companion; a practised magician, he was easily persuaded to perform tricks for the children of colleagues and visiting royalty alike.

The 1954 election was won comfortably and Holland relaxed his control a little, passing the finance portfolio to Jack Watts. Journalist Keith Eunson has written: "Sidney Holland brought to his government organisation and system, reflecting his own earlier life in business, and while he could not compete with many of his Cabinet colleagues intellectually or academically, he nonetheless ran a tight ship and his reign was notable for the lack of schisms or coup attempts, perhaps because he had the good sense to delegate and to let his ministers get on with their tasks." [8]

By 1956 Holland's health was in decline but he delayed announcement of his retirement until August 1957 and National's annual conference, giving too short a time for his deputy Keith Holyoake to settle into the top job and raise his profile sufficiently before that year's election.

Sid Holland was knighted, and remained in Holyoake's short-lived cabinet as minister without portfolio until he retired at the time of the election. He died in Wellington in August 1961.

Some commentators, like Keith Sinclair, have dealt unsympathetically with the Holland era: "Sid Holland had immense self-confidence, determination and energy, but very limited intellectual horizons. He has been described as 'jaunty', 'ebullient', 'bouncy', 'aggressive'. He was notorious for a cheerful vulgarity which made sensitive citizens shudder, but was not disliked by the average voter. Although he ruled the country for eight years, he developed no great personal following. He was detested by his enemies while his party supporters failed to love him." [9]

Others see him as a major party political figure, if not a national leader of the first rank. Historian Bill Oliver wrote: " … his importance was not primarily that of a Prime Minister, but that of a party builder. During his eight years of office very little was actually done, either by the Prime Minister or by the government as a whole, apart from the day to day administration of the country as the Labour Party had remade it." [10]

Or as National Party historian Barry Gustafson puts it: "His major contribution was undoubtedly the role he played in the creation and establishment of the National Party, which was to dominate New Zealand politics during the latter half of the twentieth century." [11]

From Auckland to the Bluff… *Holland, enthusiastic monarchist, basked in the reflected glory of the 1953-54 royal visit. Neville Colvin,* Evening Post, *December 23 1953 (ATL ref: C-132-868)*

26
SIR KEITH JACKA HOLYOAKE
1904-1983

"He was the chairman of the board of directors of the biggest business in New Zealand"

Keith Holyoake was one of New Zealand's most successful prime ministers, winning four elections on the trot. Not only was he the longest serving since William Massey but, after retirement from the prime ministership, he carried on in cabinet and then, controversially, served three years as governor-general.

Holyoake had close connections with the two electorates he represented during his 40 years as a parliamentarian: his great-grand-parents settled near Motueka in the Nelson district in 1843 and he was born near Pahiatua in February 1904.

Henry Victor Holyoake and Esther Ives had seven children; Keith was the third born. His parents, at the time estranged from Victor's father, ran a small general store at Mangamutu, and later moved to Hastings and Tauranga. Keith was nine when his grandfather died and the family moved back to run the farm – with its hops, tobacco and fruit – at Riwaka.

Older and younger brothers and sisters went on to secondary school, but Keith left at 12 to work on the farm. His mother, a teacher and "a clever woman of resolute personality", [1] gave him further tuition at night after long days in the fields. By the time he

Sid Scales, Otago Daily Times, *February 16 1974.* (ATL ref: H-384-060)

was 20 he was running the 32-acre property in partnership with his father and was active in the local community. He played for the district at rugby and cricket and his voice was beginning to be heard at local producer organisation meetings.

Holyoake's first political foray was briefly unsuccessful. He stood as Motueka's Reform Party candidate against the incumbent MP in the 1931 elections, then took the seat some months later following the member's death. At 28 he was the youngest MP in the House. He won again in 1935, already seen as a coming man for his effective advocacy of the raft of farming organisations he was associated with. Now representing National, he lost his seat in 1938, boundary changes, Labour's powerful showing and the opposition's weak performance all contributing factors.

It looked for a while as if Holyoake's promising political career might be over. Fortuitously, Pahiatua's MP signaled his retirement at the next election and Holyoake accepted nomination after he was helped to buy a sheep and cattle farm, conveniently located near the centre of the electorate. After the Motueka property was sold, Holyoake moved his family – he had married Norma Jean Ingram in 1934 and they now had four children – back to the area where he had been born. It was a long wait, until the September 1943 election, before he could get back to Parliament. He was immediately welcomed onto the opposition front bench and four years later became National's first deputy leader. During these years he was nationally prominent in the Farmers' Union and on the council that, in 1944, established Federated Farmers.

When National won the treasury benches in 1949, the Holyoakes and their five children moved to Wellington and, not surprisingly, Keith Holyoake was given the demanding portfolio of agriculture which he held for eight years. In that time remaining marketing controls were removed, rabbit plagues were brought under control, farm mechanisation was encouraged, and meat and dairy prices were renegotiated under the bulk trading agreements with Britain. In agricultural circles, at least, Holyoake's reputation as an efficient, pragmatic and well-informed minister grew steadily.

Holyoake was acting prime minister when Holland was overseas but it was not until after the 1954 election that he was officially named the country's first deputy prime minister.

Ill though he was, Sid Holland clung to power, giving up the prime ministership just two months before the 1957 election. National had been in power for eight years, Labour's Walter Nash was a national institution – and the election was narrowly lost.

Labour inherited a well-disguised exchange crisis and its response, import controls and the notorious Nordmeyer budget, showed courage, resolve and little political nous. Holyoake pounced. " … for the remaining two-and-a-half years of that Parliament, Holyoake made the Chamber and the town halls boom with denunciations of the 'Black Budget'." [2] National won by a margin that took years to erode.

Holyoake then presided over a 'steady as it goes' approach to the economy, with Harry Lake, his finance minister, playing a carefully circumscribed role. One of the few initiatives, the introduction of decimal currency, gave a boost to the career of Robert Muldoon, the newly appointed under-secretary of finance. Holyoake was something of a mentor to Muldoon as Gordon Coates had been to him, and appointed him minister of finance when Lake died in February 1967.

With liberally-minded senior ministers, and because of his own pragmatic approach, Holyoake's administration had few right-wing inclinations. As Ian Templeton and Keith Eunson wrote: "He is essentially a middle-of-the-road man, without strong philosophical goals, governing by consensus, an anti-doctrinaire conservative who nevertheless believes in the welfare state and in Government intervention if the need arises." [3] And, according to Hugh Templeton, " …. in the sixties, the Holyoake government shifted to social expenditure, maintaining and extending the welfare state and transforming the education sector with massive investment in the secondary schools and universities, which Holyoake had never enjoyed, and which he determinedly supported for succeeding generations." [4]

With a major contribution from Ralph Hanan, the government was also active in the civil rights area. An impressive list of achievements was chalked up: the first ombudsman office in the Commonwealth; the abolition of capital punishment; the removal of censorship and broadcasting from direct political control; public acknowledgement of the Security Intelligence Service (SIS) for the first time; the Hunn Report's telling catalogue of disadvantages faced by Maori in New Zealand; and support for the 'No Maoris No Tour' view forced change in the NZ Rugby Union's blinkered perspective.

Keith Sinclair wrote: "Holyoake's view of the role of a Prime Minister was that he was chairman of the board of directors of the biggest business in New Zealand. He saw his duty to be 'leadership by

Holyoake was back in government again after just one term on the opposition benches. Gordon Minhinnick, New Zealand Herald, *November 25 1960. (ATL ref: B-056-104)*

consent'. Similarly, in the country at large, he sought 'consensus politics'." [5]

He was more actively involved, as minister, in 'External Affairs', as it was then called. G A Wood has written: "The Holyoake years were notable for [his]continuance of the progressive assertion of a distinct New Zealand identity, and for the expansion of New Zealand's contacts, notably in South East Asia." [6] New Zealand was to have its first locally born governors-general; New Zealand's national song replaced the British national anthem on official occasions.

Two major challenges during Holyoake's time as prime minister were Britain's intention, known from 1961, to seek entry to the European Economic Community (EEC), and New Zealand's involvement in the Vietnam War.

There had been no reason for New Zealand to seek other markets for its agricultural products when one country would take everything, but this would change markedly when Britain joined Europe. Holyoake's calm and studied response, with most of the international legwork done by his deputy John Marshall, was to sign a free trade agreement with Australia (NAFTA), negotiate the best possible quotas into Britain for the post-EEC era and begin the business of developing new markets.

Also, as Anthony Wood writes: " .... New Zealand joined the International Monetary Fund (IMF). It marked the end of reliance upon Britain as a source of loans." [7] The initiatives were successful, securing New Zealand against massive economic disruption.

Involvement in the Vietnam War, as a United States ally, was debated at the 1966 election. The public accepted Holyoake's reasons: the threat of communism spreading through Asia, defence commitments and trade repercussions. Away from the public platform Holyoake had his doubts, and ensured New Zealand's participation was as limited as possible. At the same time the Holyoake government showed a degree of independence by declaring New Zealand a nuclear free country.

Sir George Laking, former secretary of foreign affairs, worked as closely with Holyoake as any public servant: "I knew that I was dealing with a high order of intelligence and subtle complexity and I admired the apparent ease with which he guided and controlled the business of government." [8]

Holyoake was the consummate political manager, exercising firmness, authority and good humour in various combinations. According to Hugh Templeton: "Holyoake was a master at managing caucus and Parliament. All members had their say, but inexorably the caucus would move to the conclusion the Prime Minister wanted." [9]

Holyoake worked closely with John Marshall, although there were eventually tensions as his deputy's leadership ambitions became more overt. And Holyoake gave a talented and diverse line-up of ministers their heads in portfolios they usually held,

'It won't come!' *Holyoake carefully distanced himself from industrial relations, leaving the thorny compulsory unionism and arbitration system issues to Tom Shand, his minister of labour. Gordon Minhinnick,* New Zealand Herald, *April 12 1961. (ATL ref: B-056-106)*

Why, how nice! *There was considerable concern expressed when Muldoon named 'Kiwi Keith' Holyoake governor general. Malcolm Walker,* Sunday News, *1977. (ATL ref: A-305-053)*

and became expert in, over long periods. Templeton and Eunson wrote: "He has always had an extraordinary ability to delegate, rare in a New Zealand leader. Whenever he issues an instruction for some proposal to be drafted, he does not want to see it again until it has been thoroughly worked over and thought through to the conclusion." [10]

For much of his time as prime minister Holyoake had an uncanny ability at sniffing shifts in public opinion, but he never did master the powerful new TV medium. Holyoake appeared to his fellow New Zealanders as a strutting, pompous man, with a plum in his mouth and an inexhaustible supply of cliches. Barry Gustafson wrote: "Through his political career, Holyoake was painfully aware that in public, and especially from 1960 on television which he never mastered, he appeared somewhat aloof, even supercilious, and sounded pompous. …. In later years his accent became worse because of a physical difficulty in keeping his upper denture in place, especially when giving an address." [11]

In fact, Keith Holyoake was an unassuming man who walked to work from his unpretentious home close to Parliament, chatting to shopkeepers along the way. His home phone number was in the telephone directory – and he was likely to answer calls there himself. He fought 16 election campaigns without indulging in personality politics nor was there ever the arrogance that can sometimes be the by-product of a long political career. He had a "profound

if not easily fathomed influence on his colleagues and younger contemporaries." [12]

Keith Eunson recalled Holyoake as a man who knew and was comfortable with his limitations. "He was loyal to those around him, staff and colleagues, and ready to support unpopular courses if he thought they were right. And because he was a sensible, basic fellow not given to wild swings of optimism or pessimism, he had an innate ability to absorb setbacks or successes with equanimity ….and never publicly appeared overly elated or downcast." [13] The private Holyoake was, Gustafson writes, very different from the public persona: "Despite first appearances, Holyoake was a sensitive and privately rather lonely and almost insecure man who kept his inner thoughts very much to himself and remained remarkably modest about his role in New Zealand politics." [14]

Predictably, National began to run out of steam after a decade in power. The politics of consensus bogged the government down in endless policy consultation while, internationally, the cold war blocs were breaking up and, locally, women and Maori were more assertive, opposition to the Vietnam War mounted and environmental concerns multiplied. The political landscape was changing but Holyoake and his ministers did not see it.

Holyoake was probably a more controversial figure during the last few years of his career than he had been for the previous two decades. He stayed on too long as prime minister, doing what Holland had done to him, and giving John Marshall too short a time to revitalise an administration that looked old and tired. John Roberts wrote about the lead up to the 1972 election and "…. the muffling consensual platitudes which made National appear, finally, and fatally, indecisive." [15]

Holyoake did not retire from politics; he was minister of foreign affairs until the Marshall government was roundly beaten late in 1972 and then minister of state in Muldoon's cabinet when National surged back into power at the 1975 election. Most criticised of all was his appointment as governor general early in 1977, the first politician to be named to this non-political and largely ceremonial position. Constitutional experts and opposition MPs tut-tutted, but Holyoake and his wife Norma served the shortened, three-year term with appropriate dignity.

Sir Keith Holyoake died in December 1983, one of the country's most decorated politicians, the rare appointment to the Order of the Garter only one of a number of awards garnered in the years following his first knighthood in 1970.

Looking back, Gustafson commented: "Most

people …. saw his Government as a capable one that was reluctant to intervene unnecessarily in the economy or in the affairs of individual New Zealanders and that believed in and practised cautious but liberal government by consensus." [16]

Ross Doughty, author of an early biography, wrote: "Of all recent prime ministers Keith Holyoake was the best prepared in his personal abilities. His preparation had been long and deliberate. He is in many ways a composite character: he has the geniality of Seddon, the chairman's ability, though tempered, of Holland and the shrewdness in the House of Peter Fraser." [17]

Gustafson again: "As a hard-working Prime Minister, who often worked until 2 a.m., he displayed leadership skills of shrewd judgement and uncanny timing, a sound pragmatic commonsense, a sensitivity to other people, and an intuitive rather than intellectual grasp of conservative political philosophy – all of which in retrospect appear even more impressive and formidable than they did at the time." [18]

The King Maker. *Some saw the appointment of Holyoake as governor general as a further consolidation of Muldoon's power. Bob Brockie,* National Business Review, *1977. (ATL ref: H-705-013)*

27
SIR WALTER NASH
1882-1968

"He led the band from the front but he led it as a one-man band"

Walter Nash was the third of the triumvirate of remarkable Labour Party politicians who transformed New Zealand in the 15 years after 1935. But unlike Savage and Fraser he had to wait until he was 75 years-old, in 1957, to become prime minister.

He has been called the country's greatest finance minister but was a seriously flawed prime minister.

Nash was born in Kidderminster, an industrial town in the English Midlands, in February 1882. He was the fifth of six children born to Alfred Arthur Nash, who worked at various times as a rug weaver and clerk, and Amelia Randle, a weaver in the town's woollen mills.

The family was close to the poverty line and there were two other influences in the young Walter's life that made a permanent impression: he had an early introduction to politics, helping his father who was a part-time Conservative Party agent, and his steadfast Christianity was anchored in his mother's devout Anglicanism which sustained her through her husband's drunkeness and early death.

Walter Nash was sent to a nursery school at three but, despite winning a scholarship, there was insufficient money for him to attend the local grammar school. So his long working life began when he was 11 years old. He was office boy for a local solicitor and then, when the family moved to Selly

Oak, near Birmingham, he mainly worked in a bicycle factory, becoming an analysis clerk, and accountant in all but name and qualifications.

He met Lotty May Eaton at the local post office where she worked and they married in June 1906. The Nashes were, and remained, a devoted couple. Lotty had an early introduction to Walter's boundless energy and ambition when he opened two shops, one selling tobacco and the other confectionery, and became secretary of several local clubs and associations, organised a debating society and attended night classes where his interest in Christian socialism blossomed.

This busy, well-ordered life was interrupted by a sequence of setbacks. Lotty and their first child were both sick, a daughter died shortly after birth and, in early 1909, a severe economic recession battered Selly Oak businesses. The Nashes decided to emigrate and arrived in Wellington in May that year.

On the other side of the world, they quickly settled into a familiar routine, family life centred on a rented house in Brooklyn. Walter Nash became secretary and shareholder in a small tailoring business, the family attended the local Anglican church, and two more sons were born.

Nash's religious life prospered even if his business

Noel Counihan, Caricatures, *1939. (ATL ref: J-058-011)*

one spluttered along, and he developed deeply felt and largely unwavering views. It was, he came to see, "a Christian's duty to work to bring about God's kingdom on earth."[1] His religion centred on practical morality and ethics rather than spirituality and ritual. This dovetailed with his enthusiasm for John Ruskin's view that the distribution of wealth in the interests of the majority was, or should be, at the core of economic thinking.

As his biographer Keith Sinclair wrote: "To Nash, socialism quite literally was applied Christianity."[2]

Nash was briefly involved with the first Labour Party during the 1911 election campaign, but he had the more immediate task of rebuilding his own family's livelihood when the tailoring business faltered badly. He cut his losses, losing job and an investment, and the Nashes moved to Palmerston North in early 1913, restoring his self-confidence and family bank balance as a successful commercial traveller for a woollen merchant and cloth importer.

During the next three years Nash further developed his wide-ranging educational interests at WEA classes, where he met socialist radicals including Peter Fraser, Bob Semple and Harry Holland. He, too, was a pacifist during the First World War, but Christian teaching rather than socialist doctrine guided his thinking.

In 1916, Nash and a partner established a co-operative tailoring company in New Plymouth and the family moved north to the Taranaki town. The business was a success but Nash's partner did not share his altruistic instincts. The business relationship soured, but during his three years in New Plymouth Nash was active in the Anglican church. He was also prominent, as Fraser was in Wellington and Savage in Auckland, during the 1918 influenza epidemic, and formed the local branch of the second, and enduring, Labour Party. In 1919 he attended his first party conference and was promptly elected to the national executive.

At the beginning of 1920 Nash was 38 years old. It was time to take stock: his church involvement was satisfying and he was beginning to make a name for himself in Labour Party circles, but he still did not have a secure livelihood. The next venture would be a bookshop, an unsurprising choice given Nash's interests and the voracious appetite of the growing Labour Party membership for information. To prepare for this, the Nashes then took the unusual step, given the time and their circumstances, of a 'working holiday', with the boys sent to boarding schools.

Walter and Lotty sailed for England in March but there was very little holiday. Apart from visiting family, Nash hurried around securing agencies from publishers and manufacturers and met several Labour leaders, the first signs of what became a compulsive urge to rub shoulders with the politically famous. He travelled to Geneva where, as the NZ Labour Party's observer, he met more illustrious names including Ramsay MacDonald and Sidney Webb at the Second Socialist International Conference. Lotty, who had little interest in politics and an active distaste for the radical sort, stayed in England.

Nash's reputation among the 'Red Fed' element in the Labour Party would have been enhanced when, on their return home, he was fined for importing a 'seditious' book found in an unwrapped parcel of samples. But the fine simply added to the serious financial problems awaiting them – his former partner was jibbing at paying the agreed amount for Nash's share of the New Plymouth business. If 1920 had been an exciting and mind-expanding year, 1921 was a hard grind to set up the Clarté Book Room, which also handled magazine subscriptions, with friends helping with money and somewhere to live.

In 1922 Nash was elected national secretary of the Labour Party, the £130 salary helping considerably. For some years Nash maintained a sample room displaying the diverse range of goods he had secured agencies for – cutlery, rag dolls, model aeroplanes – but the Labour Party took over the bookshop in 1924.

By then Nash had paid off the party's debts and established a smoothly running head office. He remained national secretary until 1932, three years after he had won a by-election in the Hutt electorate, his third attempt to win the seat. Nash had greatly increased the party's membership and secured its finances during the 1920s and in his final party position, as president in 1935-36, he contributed significantly to the resounding election victory.

There was little surprise when Nash was named minister of finance following the 1935 election. As third ranking member of the first Labour government it was his responsibility to find the money to fund a rush of legislation to stimulate jobs and production following years of depression paralysis.

Nash may have made a limited contribution to policy formulation, but his was a masterful performance, juggling the introduction of far-reaching economic measures with the raising of income and land tax to pay for them. The ability to control the economy was greatly increased with the immediate nationalisation of the Reserve Bank and the combination of guaranteed prices for butter and cheese, cheap loans for farmers and home-buyers, and the restoration of state sector salaries to previous levels all stimulated confidence and growth.

Nash's prodigious appetite for work and some less admirable attributes both awed and irritated those who observed him. Les Hobbs wrote: "No Minister in New

Zealand history could compete with Nash in the number of hours he spent working. First to arrive at Parliament Buildings in the morning, he was invariably the last away. Night after night, year after year, the light in his big room could be seen burning hours after most Wellingtonians had gone to bed – and when he left he still had to go to his home in Lower Hutt." [3]

Bernard Ashwin, who became secretary of the Treasury early in 1939 wrote: "His greatest failings are indecision and a passion for detail. He wastes hours every day over matters [that] he should not consider at all, while urgent matters of national importance are laid to one side. I sometimes feel that he turns to small things for relief from big ones." [4]

Sadly, and this possibly resulted from his earlier, unhappy business relationships, he found it difficult to trust the people he worked with. Ashwin wrote: "While personally pleasant to meet and a likeable person in many respects, he is suspicious and does not really trust anyone very far ....." [5] This, of course, affected his working methods. Journalist Keith Eunson has written: " ... he always checked figures. 'It meant I always kept

things for quite a long time,' he admitted, 'because I wanted to check everything. I didn't believe anything until I believed it." [6]

Although sometimes considered vain and even egotistical, Nash also lacked self-confidence in some crucial areas. As Sinclair says: "He distrusted his own instinctive judgement. Since he would not rely on the judgements of others, the result was inevitable – delays. When he did make decisions they were usually right – common-sensical, politically sound, morally acceptable, successful. But he had to keep and master every file to ensure that his decision was, in fact, right." [7]

Nash's addiction to work was firmly rooted in "a sense of hours filled by important duties – a sense of significance." [8]

Gathering around him some of the brightest young public servants in the country, it never occurred to him that they might be less driven than he was. Harold Innes, a former member of his staff, later wrote: "As far as his treatment of staff was concerned , 'unthinking' rather than 'ruthless' would be a more accurate description. He automatically thought that the same intensity of

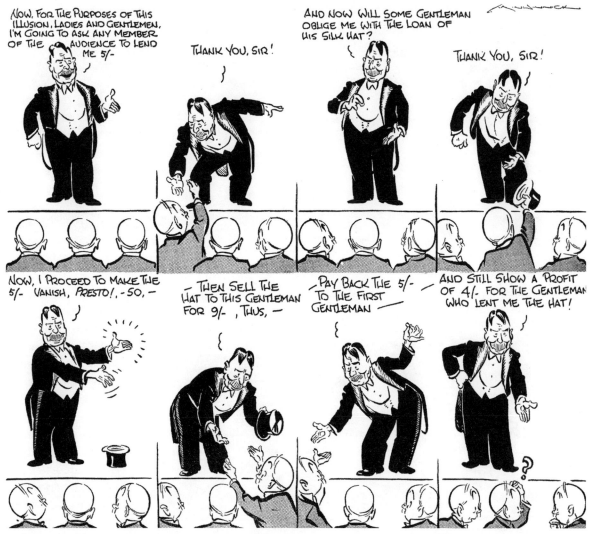

Budget magic. *Nash's financial wizardry was questioned in some quarters. Gordon Minihinnick, New Zealand Herald, July 23 1938. (ATL ref: H-723-003)*

131

response to work at all hours would come just as naturally from us as it did from him." [9]

There was considerable suspicion of the new Labour government in Britain, where Nash, at the end of 1936 and on the first of many official visits, attempted to negotiate bulk trading agreements to underpin his guaranteed price scheme. The British were unhelpful and patronised the former Kidderminister clerk. Nash was still persisting when, in May 1937, he attended George V1's coronation, with his wife and Savage, and then the linked Imperial Conference. An honorary LLD from Cambridge University, the Freedom of Kidderminster and the opportunity to meet political and business luminaries were some compensation for achieving very little from his trade talks. On the way home, via the United States, he met President Franklin D Roosevelt, an acquaintanceship that was to be particularly valuable.

In the months he was away Nash's cautious approach had been increasingly under attack from Labour caucus members attracted to social credit monetary views. But Nash, with the support of Savage and Fraser, refused to be swayed by 'funny money' arguments and the social security legislation he introduced in August 1938 bore the stamp of his conservative and prudent approach. The country obviously agreed because the 1938 election, with the legislation a major debating point, returned Labour with an increased share of the popular vote.

Cautious though Nash was, the government's expansive social programme was a drain on the country's sterling reserves in London, which had dipped alarmingly to exchange crisis proportions. Financiers and politicians were no more welcoming when Nash returned to London in April 1939. Loans were given grudgingly and with tough terms.

Two days after Nash got back to New Zealand the country's immediate economic problems were solved, and the nation thrown into upheaval, with the declaration of war on Germany. The British government, which had recently disdainfully dismissed Nash's bulk sales pleas, now wanted to buy every last ounce of meat and dairy products the country could produce.

Divisions within the Labour caucus eased in March 1940 with John A Lee's expulsion almost immediately followed by the death of Michael Joseph Savage. Peter Fraser became prime minister and Nash his deputy, two former pacifists in charge of a country at war. His working habits did not change. Alister McIntosh, then in the prime minister's department, later wrote: " [he] would, after some delay, always receive you with the greatest of courtesy and sweetest of smiles, but he would never, never want to give an immediate answer. 'Leave it with me,' he would say or, worse – the indecisive Minister's favourite delaying gambit – 'Let me have a report' on some aspect or other." [10]

Walter Nash was to have a thoroughly unusual war. He was acting prime minister for several months in 1941 and then spent most of the remaining war years out of the country. Labour's leaders, long doubting the effectiveness of Britain's naval base in Singapore, decided, before Pearl Harbour, that New Zealand needed a closer relationship with the United States. One man – even though he was minister of finance – seemed ideally suited to the task.

In January 1942, the Nashes arrived in Washington; as 'resident minister' he was the country's first overseas representative. For 16 months Nash attended meetings of the Pacific War Council, chaired by Roosevelt, and energetically stumped the huge country talking about New Zealand and the post-war need for a United Nations organisation.

Nash returned home in April 1943, presented the budget, attended the party conference and campaigned in the election that Labour won by a smaller but still comfortable margin. He had returned to the United States

'We hope he'll be OK for the big fight'. *Labour was ill-prepared to fight the 1951 snap election. Keith Waite,* Otago Daily Times, *July 27 1951.* (*ATL ref: H-723-002*)

by December, spent several months in London in early 1944 and, back again across the Atlantic, he was elected president of the International Labour Organisation (ILO) and then took part in the Bretton Woods conference that set up the International Monetary Fund (IMF).

It is questionable how much Nash could really run the finance ministry from so far away. Ashwin's comments are illuminating: "I wrote all the budgets and although he arrived to present them there was never any time for him to alter anything of basic importance. I let him play with a few words to make him feel that he had contributed to the budget, for Nash had a great love of the theatrical and made a great show of presenting 'his' budget to the House." [11]

After the war, Nash continued to travel at every opportunity, no doubt comforted by New Zealand's relative prosperity, underwritten by Britain's continuing bulk purchase of farm produce, and the positive effects of the wide-ranging pre-war legislation. He attended the Commonwealth prime ministers' meeting in London in 1946 and, over the next two years and in diverse locations, a number of conferences debating the proposed General Agreement on Tariffs and Trade (GATT).

While Nash flitted, Labour's popularity sank. The wartime restrictions remained, inflation ate into purchasing power, there were strikes by militant unions, and the stars of an ageing cabinet – Nash and Fraser – were too often out of the country. The 1946 election was narrowly won, the four Maori seats making the difference.

By 1949, with militant unions flexing waterfront muscles and a plan for peacetime conscription, there was a souring of relationships between the industrial and political wings of the Labour Party and, to no-one's great surprise, National won the end-of-year election.

When Peter Fraser died in December 1950, Nash, now 68 years old, was finally Labour Party leader. Bruce Brown, his secretary, later wrote: "Despite his intellectual capacity and energy, he lacked organising ability – or even any real sense that a parliamentary team needed to be organised. He led the band from the front but he led it as a one-man band. Once every three years, so it seemed, he looked over his shoulder at election time to see if his followers were still there. Not all of them were." [12]

Attempting impartiality during the 1951 waterfront strike, Nash said, famously, 'We are not for the waterside workers, and we are not against them'. This tarred him as an equivocating fence-sitter, contributing to the political climate in which Labour lost further ground electorally at the snap election later that year.

'Somebody's going to pay for this!' *Labour increased the child allowance substantially in the 1958 budget, better known as The 'Black Budget'. Neil Lonsdale,* Auckland Star, *September 1958. (ATL ref: A-309-037)*

Nash weathered challenges to his leadership but made little progress at the 1954 election. In 1957, the imminent introduction of Pay As You Earn (PAYE) income tax, provided the two parties with the opportunity to tempt voters with tax concessions. Labour's £100 tax rebate, coupled with the promise to abolish compulsory military training and 3 percent loans for housing, resulted in the narrowest of victories and, at 75, Walter Nash became New Zealand's oldest incoming prime minister.

His insatiable enthusiasm for travel belied his age, but did nothing to enhance his government's reputation which was effectively sunk after Arnold Nordmeyer's principled, but politically naïve, June 1958 'Black Budget' grappled with serious balance of payments difficulties inherited from National.

Around the world about 80 times. *Despite his age, Nash's enthusiasm for travel did not slacken. Gordon Minhinnick,* New Zealand Herald, *August 13 1958. (ATL ref: H-705-009)*

When not touring the world "lecturing conferences and individual leaders on the importance of international understanding, disarmament and peace", [13] Nash led an administration committed to industrialisation and two projects – an aluminium smelter and cotton mill – proved particularly controversial. But even more damaging electorally was Nash's support of the Rugby Union's decision to send an 'all-white' team to South Africa.

Nash was leader of the opposition again after the 1960 election; he carried on, despite the severe blow of his wife Lotty's death in December 1961, in part because politics was his life but also to stop Nordmeyer becoming leader. Finally, in February 1963, the party president precipitated a leadership vote and Nash resigned.

He continued as the member for Hutt, a seat he was to hold for 39 years despite considerable boundary changes over the years. Amazingly energetic for his age, it was the "bustle of business", [14] as Sinclair called it, that kept him going. The impulses that made him an inveterate collector of files and a function attendee never waned. Later, when Keith Sinclair reduced the Nash collection of papers by about half, there were still 10 tons of material left. As Sinclair wryly noted: "It could be that he was the greatest lover of paper, and not merely documents related to himself, in history." [15]

Keith Eunson is one of many who have commented on his compulsion to accept invitations: "Walter Nash was as much a peripatetic traveller at home as he was abroad, and would attend the opening of a letter if he knew of it!" [16]

Now the elder statesman of New Zealand politics, Sir Walter, knighted in 1965, devoted much of his time during the final years to his enduring passion for international affairs. The man who was a founder of the Wellington branch of the New Zealand Institute of International Affairs in 1934 was, from 1965, a prominent and compelling voice in the protest movement opposing the Vietnam War and New Zealand's involvement in it.

Walter Nash died, 86 years old, and still a parliamentarian in June 1968.

Loyalty was one of Nash's strongest characteristics and trust, when given, was unconditional. Michael Bassett and Michael King captured Nash's importance to New Zealand's political history when they wrote about the early years of his relationship with Peter Fraser. "A trusting friendship that would endure until Fraser's death 21 years later had been cemented; although their temperaments were different, the two men were henceforth regarded as Labour's best brains and shrewdest tacticians. Their capacity to work together in war and peace was to be the making of the first Labour government." [17]

28

SIR JOHN ROSS MARSHALL
1912-1988

"For many he was and remained the National Party's conscience"

John Marshall, or 'Gentleman Jack' as he was known, will have an enduring place in New Zealand political history, but not for his brief prime ministership. It was his patient perseverance over a gruelling decade that ensured New Zealand's relatively unruffled economic survival when Britain joined the EEC.

Marshall was born into an urban, middle class family. His parents, Allan Marshall and Florence May Ross, had Scottish ancestry and were active in the Presbyterian Church. Born in Wellington, John was the elder of two children. His childhood years were spent in Whangarei and Dunedin where his father was public trustee. Marshall's successful schooldays, in the classroom and on the sporting field, set the pattern for a life of steady, well-adjusted achievement.

One of the few shadows over Marshall's early life was his father's sudden death

Sid Scales, Otago Daily Times, *February 1974.*
(ATL ref: H-384-037)

in October 1930, the year he began law studies at Victoria University in Wellington. He worked part-time for a law firm, common in those days, steadily passed his exams and participated in the busy religious and social life of St John's Presbyterian Church. The hours were long and the living frugal, but Marshall was fortunate to observe the depression from a distance, completing his LLB in 1935 and his law masters a year later.

In early 1939 John Marshall travelled to Europe, meeting his future wife in Perth on the way. He toured Britain and several European countries, leaving Germany a week before the beginning of the Second

World War. Jim Eagles and Colin James later wrote: "A devout Christian, he was once a dedicated pacifist – before Nazi Germany changed his mind for him." [1] Marshall returned to New Zealand via North America, arriving home for Christmas. He enlisted early in 1940 and, after officer training school, served in the Pacific. In November 1943 he rejoined the New Zealand Division in the Solomon Islands as Major Marshall following several months at a military staff college in the United States.

Marshall married Jessie Margaret Livingston in Perth while on leave in July 1944; their brief meeting five years previously had blossomed into romance, a blizzard of letters resulting in their December 1939 engagement. Newly married and with his employer asking for his release from the army, Marshall might have escaped further war service, but he chose otherwise and sailed for Europe in January 1945, commanding a squadron of the Divisional Cavalry Battalion. Marshall and his squadron took part in the battle of the Senio river and then the liberation of Trieste.

There were opportunities waiting in postwar Wellington. He decided to practice as a barrister, renewed his involvement with St John's, attended lectures to complete a BA in political science begun some years previously, and was approached by a delegation urging him to stand for National in the new Mt Victoria electorate at the 1946 election. As Marshall recalled in the first volume of his autobiography many years later: "They had apparently calculated that in the state of public sympathies just after the war, the kind of candidate most likely to win votes and influence people would be a young man with an adequate war record. If he could also read, write and speak, that would be an advantage" [2] He accepted the challenge and won what was considered a marginal seat by nearly 1,000 votes.

Marshall had once considered himself a Christian socialist; now he was a committed liberal, and he set out, in his maiden speech, his beliefs with more certainty and clarity than most neophyte politicians attempt to do. In this speech, as National Pary historian Barry Gustafson has written: "He affirmed four aspects of liberty – national, political, personal and economic …. He argued that economic liberty and social security were not alternatives, but warned that allowing governments too much economic power to achieve security was dangerous. His goal as a politician was a prosperous and just property-owning democracy, not an unrealistic socialist utopia." [3]

During his first parliamentary term, Marshall

continued to practice law part-time, but National's convincing win in 1949 abruptly ended a promising legal career.

Labour had been in power for 14 years; National would now be on the treasury benches for 20 of the next 23 – and John Marshall in cabinet all those years.

Marshall was one of the most junior ministers in Holland's first cabinet, but as an assistant to the prime minister he was much closer to the action than he might otherwise have been. As minister of the State Advances Corporation he built more state houses but also made it easier for lower-income families to buy, build or improve homes.

After the 1951 snap election Marshall jumped a number of places in cabinet ranking and in responsibilities which now included the always challenging health portfolio. His Mount Victoria electorate disappeared at the 1954 election but he moved across town to the safe Karori seat, holding it until his retirement in 1975.

He was now minister of justice and attorney general,

A willing horse. *Marshall had a heavy workload through the 1960s, despite a serious heart attack in 1964. Eric Heath,* Dominion, *December 23 1969. (ATL ref: H-725-023)*

liberal in many of his views but a supporter of the death penalty for murder. It was not until 1961 that the issue was put to a vote, with Marshall supporting the death penalty for 'aggravated murder'. He later wrote about his stand: " …. My sympathies lay with the victims of murder, and not with the brutal or calculating murderers who, in some cases, I believed, would be deterred by the fear of the death penalty." [4] It was one parliamentary battle Marshall lost.

When Holyoake replaced Holland as prime minister in August 1957, Marshall defeated a more senior colleague, finance minister Jack Watts, for the deputy's position. He was deputy prime minister for less than three months.

During the next three years in opposition, Marshall supplemented his reduced parliamentary salary with some legal work and visited the United States on a foreign leader exchange programme. Labour's tenure in office was short, in part because it had inherited an overseas funds crisis from the out-going government, this precipitating the very unpopular 'Black Budget'.

Jack Marshall had a particularly heavy workload in the second Holyoake ministry. In December 1960, as well as the deputy prime ministership, he became minister of industries and commerce, minister of overseas trade, and minister of customs. There were some major challenges for Marshall: the balance of trade with Australia, 4:1 against New Zealand, was worrisome and there were already signs of Britain's interest in joining the EEC. There was also the challenge of dealing with two of the most controversial senior public servants of their era – W B Sutch and J P Lewin – and their ideas on industrial development. Ian Templeton and Keith Eunson later wrote: "The Sutch-Lewin philosophy struck no answering chord in the National Party, and it was Marshall's task first to blunt it …. and then gradually to eliminate it." [5]

During the early 1960s Marshall led the New Zealand effort to revolutionise trade with Australia. The result, in 1965, was the New Zealand-Australia Free Trade Agreement (NAFTA) which gradually corrected New Zealand's adverse trade balance.

NAFTA honed Marshall's negotiating skills for the even more important defence of New Zealand's export trade to Britain. It was to be an epic 11 year saga of countless trips to Britain and Europe to argue New Zealand's case for continued access, EEC membership notwithstanding, to the British market. France's Charles de Gaulle said "non" to Britain's application in 1963 and 1967. A third application, in 1971 succeeded, but by this time New Zealand's case was well known. Eunson wrote: "He worked year after year, country after country, to overcome enormous and formidable difficulties, and objections from nations who had no traditionally filial association with this country, and to convince them that New Zealand was 'special' and had a case that deserved 'special' consideration." [6] The final agreement was, as Gustafson has pointed out, as much as could be hoped for and more than most expected. "Prior to the final agreement between Britain and the six [EEC] members, Marshall in tense negotiations with the British persuaded them, and through them the EEC negotiators, to agree to a five-year transition period, subject to review, allowing 80 percent of New Zealand's butter and 20 percent of New Zealand's cheese in exports to Britain. Together with continued concessions for lamb

'You'll learn to love the great NEW taste…' *Marshall was the 'face' of New Zealand's effort to avert economic disaster when Britain joined the EEC. Peter Bromhead,* Truth, *1971. (ATL ref: H-705-023)*

exports to Britain, the agreement saved New Zealand from a massive economic disaster and gave it time to diversify its products and find new markets." [7]

It had been a masterful performance over a long period. Rita Ricketts wrote: "By laying down the ground rules for preserving markets in Europe and encouraging diversification elsewhere, Sir John showed himself to be a great strategist; with one eye to the past and present and the other to the future." [8]

During the 1960s Marshall encouraged the setting up of New Zealand Steel and the Tiwai aluminium smelter and was the driving force behind major export and national development conferences.

But even more demanding was Keith Holyoake's insistence, following the 1969 election, that Marshall should also take on the labour portfolio and attorney general role following the deaths of Tom Shand and Ralph Hanan. Marshall had nearly died himself, suffering a serious heart attack in Tehran in 1964, but there was to be no let up for him.

The Court of Arbitration's 'nil wage order' in 1968 had unsettled the industrial scene, with employers and unions involved in bitter direct bargaining. The situation was not helped by Robert Muldoon who had no inhibitions about involving himself in colleagues' portfolios. He had become minister of finance following Harry Lake's death, and after Marshall had turned down the job.

Interestingly, Marshall was on better personal terms with union leaders like Tom Skinner and Jim Knox than with a number of the employer representatives, although he did not hesitate to deregister the seamen's union and introduce stabilisation of remuneration measures in 1971. Of more personal satisfaction was his introduction of the Accident Compensation Bill in December the same year; it was ground-breaking legislation that gave income-related compensation to all employed people when injured, regardless of cause or fault.

Jack Marshall became prime minister when Keith Holyoake stepped down in February 1972. As Robert Chapman wrote: "….John Marshall had little prospect of reversing the downward political impetus in the ten months remaining before the election. He reshuffled his Cabinet fiercely but it was to no avail. After twelve years National stood exhausted and half-prepared for defeat." [9] Marshall's beavering away within National's ranks – shaking up cabinet, caucus, research unit and party – did little to alter hardening public perceptions. At the time Colin James and Jim Eagles wrote: "Marshall is ill-at-ease with the common man and lacks the ability to stir an audience with rhetoric. Neither could he command the caucus with Holyoake's or Kirk's authority. He is a chairman rather than a leader." [10] Much later Hugh Templeton observed: "On the Queen's visit to New Zealand Marshall spoke and acted like a statesman. But as

'Congratulations, Jack!' *Marshall's deal for continued access to the British market was better than many expected. Neil Lonsdale,* Auckland Star, *June 24 1971. (ATL ref: H-725-001)*

leader of a government party under siege, he failed to lift his performance. He did not make the grade in Parliament. Not only was this fatal to his standing in his own caucus but worse, it gave heart and confidence to the Labour Opposition." [11]

National had won narrowly in 1969; three years later the electorate was more than ready to endorse Labour's 'It's Time' slogan at the ballot box.

Marshall was not a successful leader of the opposition. After 20 years

'Feels like a good fit…' *A prophetic cartoon, when Holyoake finally stepped down. Nevile Lodge,* Evening Post, *1972. (ATL ref: H-705-022)*

as a minister, and a senior one for most of those two decades, he did not enjoy the largely negative role the opposition plays under the Westminster system. Hugh Templeton again: "As Leader of the Opposition Jack Marshall seemed to find the full-time grind of the House unpleasant, if not oppressive. Of course he took his place for the formalities and for the set pieces but he continued to live his own life, as if he were still one of Trollope's 19th century parliamentarians. He went home most nights to dinner; and away to his retreat at the weekend." [12]

Marshall was no match for prime minister Norman Kirk in the House and, a patrician by New Zealand parliamentary standards, he made little effort to cultivate his colleagues. As Gustafson has written: "Late at night, long after the somewhat aloof Marshall had gone home, Muldoon sat drinking and chatting with the other members of the caucus, reviving their flagging spirits." [13]

By July 1974 a substantial majority of National's caucus saw his deputy Rob Muldoon as more likely to revive the party's position in Parliament and around the country. Rather than lose a caucus vote, Marshall resigned. Hugh Templeton again: "He was too proud to take a vote and risk that humiliation. Today there seems a certain inevitability in someone of Jack Marshall's lineage and manners standing down in the interests of the party to which he had given so much service and which he had rebuilt after a shattering defeat." [14]

Jack Marshall was knighted later in the year and left politics at the 1975 election. In time he gave studied but pointed expression to his distaste for Muldoon, his manner and some of his more expedient policies; for many he was and remained the National Party's conscience.

Marshall's life remained full and varied: he was a consultant partner in a major law firm, lectured in public policy at his old university, sat on company boards, and was patron or trustee on scores of charitable and community bodies. He took a prominent part in two Christian organisations, as patron of World Vision and president of the Bible Society in New Zealand. He also wrote, turning a number of children's stories he had read on the radio in the mid-1930s into a best-selling series of *Dr Duffer* books.

And Jack Marshall was one of the very few New Zealand prime ministers to write his autobiography, the first volume being well received and the second finished but not published when he died suddenly in England in August 1988.

Marshall showed toughness as a negotiator and administrator but, as National party historian Barry Gustafson has suggested, he may have been out of his time as a politician. "As New Zealand politics became more divisive and robust in the 1970s Marshall's calm, quiet dignity appeared to many to be weakness, and his colleagues and the electorate turned to more aggressive leaders. As a result Marshall never really had the opportunity to prove that in different circumstances he could have been one of New Zealand's great prime ministers." [15]

29

NORMAN ERIC KIRK

1924-1974

"He spoke from the heart, believing the electorate aspired to more than 'consensus'"

Norman Kirk was prime minister for just 21 months. When he died the public outpouring of grief was unrivalled since Savage's death in 1940 and a shell-shocked Labour government disintegrated in the face of a ferocious Muldoon attack. Yet he will be remembered for renewing New Zealanders' faith in themselves and their small country and what they could achieve together.

Tom Scott. (ATL ref: H-705-024)

Kirk was as contradictory as any prime minister before or since. He had a broad sweeping vision but he was narrowly suspicious of his colleagues. He promised a great deal and achieved far less. He became a significant international figure while the domestic economy worsened, bequeathing his successors as long a period in opposition as Nash's ineffectual 1957-60 government had.

The first Labour prime minister to begin life in New Zealand, Norman Kirk was born in Waimate in South Canterbury in January 1923. He was the eldest of the three children of Norman Kirk, of Scottish origin, and Vera Janet Jury, whose Cornish forebears had settled north of Christchurch in the 1840s. Margaret Hayward later wrote: "His mother, Vera, was a strong, rawboned, determined woman whose ability .... was limited only by her fear of stepping out of her class. She had none of the usual maternal yearnings for children and from an early age he was aware she had never wanted him." [1]

Norman Senior was a cabinet-maker but the family's precarious existence depended more on odd-jobs, sustained by strong Salvation Army beliefs. Hayward again: "As a child, he didn't have very joyful Sundays. The Kirks lived two and a third miles from the Christchurch Salvation Army Citadel. In the morning, dressed in their best clothes, they'd walk to church and back in time for lunch. After lunch they'd return to church for afternoon services and back in time for tea. After tea they'd walk back to church for evening service – 14 miles of walking." [2]

With the hope of more work there, the family had moved to Christchurch in 1928, where young Norman became a foundation pupil of the only school he went to – Linwood Avenue. His father spent most of the depression years on relief schemes, the indignities and bureaucratic bunglings vividly remembered by Norman Kirk in later life.

A large child, Kirk was not good at sport and found escape and solace in books, developing a strong interest in history and geography. This was tempered by an equal enthusiasm for the outdoors, rabbit and possum shooting and fishing, often with his father, on trips back to Waimate and when visiting Kaiapoi relatives. He also developed a life-long love of swimming.

Norman Kirk left school before his 13th birthday, his proficiency certificate no guarantee of work in 1935. A spell helping a roof painting gang and learning something of gas welding led to work as an apprentice fitter and turner and then a job, when he was 16, with New Zealand Railways hundreds of miles to the north at Frankton Junction in the Waikato. He began as a cleaner but was soon an acting fireman, working with boilers. In a 1972 campaign biography, John Dunmore wrote: "When he was working for New Zealand Railways, he estimates that for four years he read about seven books a week – over fourteen hundred books – nearly all of them non-fiction and most of them during the long hours of the night shift." [3]

In 1940 he was transferred to Paeroa where he

met Ruth Miller, daughter of the local postmaster. She was his first girlfriend, a blind date to the movies developing into an 'understanding'.

Kirk was a strapping, strongly built man, over six feet tall, but was rejected for military service in 1941 because of a goitre problem. Later that year he joined a nearby dairy factory as a 'separator-boilerman'. In August 1942, having passed his engine driver's certificate, second class, by correspondence, he was employed at the Martha goldmine in Waikino. With marriage planned, Kirk moved to Auckland in early 1943, working for the Devonport Ferry Company, and gaining his river engineer's certificate. He was briefly vice-president of the ferry workers' union. Dunmore later quoted Kirk: " 'This wasn't the wisest move if you really wanted to get ahead in the ferry company. Promotion was for the penitent and the puritanical, not for those who tried to force the curate's hand when payday came round.' " [4]

The Kirks married in Auckland in July. He earned less than £5 a week, sometimes supplemented by 'seagulling', casual waterfront work, usually unpleasant jobs regular watersiders avoided. In 1944 the Kirks returned to the Bay of Plenty with their first son Bob, Kirk now employed as a boiler engineer at a Katikati dairy factory. They lived in a public works hut near the factory, and during this period Margaret, their first daughter, was born. As Norman Kirk remembered years later, rats were a winter problem: "Rats got into the cots where the children were sleeping. We clobbered rats with hammers, we trapped rats, we fed them poison, we did everything one can do to rats, and still they kept coming." [5] Action was taken when Kirk delivered a dead, flea-infested rat to a directors' meeting.

The Kirks remained at Katikati until 1948, leaving when management did not honour the promise of a house.

With a growing family – the Kirks were to have five children over a 16 year period – a house to call their own was now of sufficient importance for them to move back to Kaiapoi. A section was bought for £65 and Norman Kirk poured his considerable energy into building a house, even making the cinder blocks himself, at weekends and after cycling back and forth to his job as an engine driver at the Firestone Tyre and Rubber Company factory in Papanui. He studied and passed his engine driver's certificate, first class.

Kirk had joined the Labour Party five years previously, an involvement he continued at Katikati, but he now took a much more active role. As chairman, he built the membership of the faltering Kaiapoi branch and in 1951 was elected chairman of the Hurunui Labour Representation Committee. At this time, though, his interests were strictly local. He organised a team of Labour candidates to stand in the October 1953 local

body elections, campaigned vigorously and effectively, and swept away the mayor and several councillors.

As Kirk's friend Ken Sinclair told biographer Dunmore: "What surprised his opponents was how much he knew; Norm knew about building, about engines, about water, transport, every little problem, from his own experience. They'd criticised him as a young man with no experience, but local body matters are mostly works – roads and the like – and he knew more about the practical side of all that than all the accountants, lawyers and shopkeepers who'd been running the Council before." [6]

At 30 years of age, Kirk was the youngest mayor in the country. He was beginning to be seen as 'a man in a hurry', a line that cartoonists and columnists were to use increasingly over the years. With an enlarged heart the legacy of childhood illness, Kirk was keenly aware of his own mortality. Later he would tell embarrassed friends that he was not likely to live past middle age. With his love of food, and especially meat, Kirk's weight had ballooned to over 20 stone, yet his unremitting routine of job, scrub cutting and patching up of old cars to supplement the family income, and political chores would have tested the health of a much fitter man.

Kaiapoi was transformed over the next few years – a new sewerage system, better roading and footpaths, revival of the small river port, the building of pensioner housing, and a change in the rating system – and Kirk was unopposed at the next local elections in 1956. Michael Bassett has written: "He lacked social graces and could sometimes be rude; at meetings with local businessmen he would tongue-lash them, then smooth ruffled feathers – a technique that he used to good effect throughout the rest of his life." [7]

When Kirk stood for his second term as Kaiapoi mayor, to finish the work he had begun, he had turned down the opportunity of a safe parliamentary seat. His organisational and leadership abilities had been noted in Wellington and he was encouraged to stand for the Hurunui seat, a National stronghold, at the 1954 general election. His effective, hard-grafting campaign there led to the declined offer of Riccarton, with one of Labour's largest majorities, when the incumbent MP died in 1956. But Kirk did contest the 1957 general election, standing in the marginal Lyttleton electorate when his friend, Tom McGuigan, decided not to contest the seat again.

Kirk took time off work, knocked on nearly every door in the town of Lyttelton, and held a series of house meetings. He won with a majority of nearly 600, defeating sitting member Harry Lake, a future minister of finance, and Wilfred Owen, Social Credit's leader.

With some regret, Norman Kirk resigned the Kaiapoi mayoralty and the family moved to Christchurch. His maiden parliamentary speech in June

1958 talked about New Zealand's place in the world but his focus during that first term was a far-flung electorate that included the Chatham Islands, specks in the vast Pacific that he developed a particular affection for. He held his seat in 1960 despite the Nash government's comprehensive loss, consolidating his reputation as one of the opposition's leading debaters, rattling the rafters or talking with quiet authority as the occasion demanded. He was also developing other skills. As Garnier, Kohn and Booth noted: "He had spent hours studying Sir Keith Holyoake's handling of the House. The importance he attached to understanding and the reading its subtleties were sequels to the times he had seen Holyoake win through in difficult circumstances because of his tactical abilities." [8]

Kirk was now being talked about as a future Labour leader. He had much in common with the 'old guard'; he was a conservative on moral and law and order issues who talked about families and full employment rather than socialism, and he was a self-made man of limited formal education who had known hardship firsthand. At the same time he was a young man with a broad vision for his country who could hold his own intellectually with the university-educated candidates Labour was now attracting. He grew up in the depression but he was on the same wavelength as the values-centred postwar generation.

Kirk was elected Labour Party vice-president in 1963 and president a year later. He was still heading the party organisation in December 1965 when, with customary efficiency, he successfully challenged a disbelieving Arnold Nordmeyer for leadership of the parliamentary wing. He was 42 years old, the youngest ever Labour Party leader by more than a decade.

Kirk was leader of the opposition but there was still a long, hard slog to the treasury benches. Ian Templeton and Keith Eunson wrote in 1969: "He has changed the whole atmosphere of caucus. Instead of holding the stylised meetings Kirk encountered as a young back-bencher, the Labour caucus today encourages dispute; everyone with an opinion is encouraged to ventilate it." [9]

However, Labour's 1966 election advertising talked about a dynamic new leader with a photograph of Kirk looking, as Colin James described it "like a gauche, moon-faced oaf, with jug-handle ears, thick lips, and jowls evidently made up to disguise a four o'clock shadow." [10] Finally, though, National's comfortable win was mostly due to Labour's opposition to New Zealand's involvement in the Vietnam War, briefly a popular cause.

The labour movement's frustrated recourse to direct action over wages in 1968 did not help, but Kirk was a much more commanding figure during the 1969 election campaign, rising above the humdrum as he drew on his own practical experiences unencumbered by theory or doctrine. Templeton and Eunson wrote: "He has a philosophy that has a larger ingredient of idealism than materialism, that depends largely for its inspiration on the family unit and on the idea of full nationhood for New Zealand free of unnecessary overseas ties." [11] He had also accepted that he and Labour had to be 'sold' to the electorate. Garnier, Kohn and Booth wrote: "The meeting between Kirk and a young, fast-talking, extroverted ad-man, Bob Harvey, opened a new era for New Zealand politics. It launched the packaging and selling of politicians and policy to the public by professional advertisers. Politicians became products. The politician's soap box oratory was

The 'It's Time for a Change' campaign slogan was a neat summation of public opinion. Peter Bromhead, New Zealand Truth, 1972. (ATL ref: H-705-025)

The Springbok Tour: the hardest decision. *After much procrastination Kirk finally decided a racially selected Springbok rugby team would not get entry visas. Gordon Minhinnick,* New Zealand Herald, *April 1973.* *(ATL ref: H-705-026)*

taken from the street corner and into the voter's living room through television."[12] Although Kirk was more natural on the new medium than Holyoake, National narrowly won the election.

Kirk the political pragmatic knew he could not lose three elections in a row and remain Labour leader. While he took no pleasure in the process, he submitted himself to a complete 'makeover'. He now made a conscientious effort to lose weight, let his curly silver hair grow, and dressed in snappy new suits. He expected the same dedication from his colleagues as they faced down a wilting Holyoake and time-worn National front bench. Kirk stumped the country, quoting from a policy document, detailing promises and their costs, like an evangelist finding inspiration in his bible. Kirk had left organised religion behind during his early independent years, but he now showed a passionate belief in a reforming government's ability to create a society of genuinely equal opportunity in New Zealand. He spoke from the heart, believing the electorate aspired to more than 'consensus'.

Sensing the tide running against it, National changed leaders early in 1972, but Jack Marshall was no match for Kirk in the House or on the hustings. Kirk left nothing to chance. The trade union movement was persuaded to work collaboratively with Labour. The campaign theme, 'It's time for a change', brilliantly encapsulated both Labour's ambitions and public sentiment.

In late November Labour swept to victory, its 23 seat majority considerable consolation after 12 long years in opposition. It was very much Kirk's personal triumph and for a 'honeymoon' period he basked in both public and press approval. 'Big Norm' was now an affectionate nickname and, improbably, the campaign song made the pop charts.

In retrospect, Labour's first months in power contained the seeds of another one-term administration, but the public perception was of progress and pride in principled government. There was an immediate Christmas bonus for pensioners, an injection of money for a stagnating house-building industry, and a freshly-minted interest in the world beyond New Zealand's shores.

Kirk might have been new to government, but he had travelled widely during his years as opposition leader and had a clear vision meshing perfectly with the views of his foreign affairs bureaucrats, about how New Zealand should conduct itself on the world stage.

Garnier, Kohn and Booth again: "Where National had seen New Zealand's lack of size as a hindrance to developing an assertive foreign policy, Kirk saw it as an asset. Because New Zealand could be no threat to other nations, there was, he believed, an opportunity for a bridging role between the super-powers and small countries."[13]

Rob Muldoon, National's deputy leader, liked to call Kirk the 'stationary engine driver', but the epithet seemed particularly inappropriate as, in short order, his government established diplomatic relations with the People's Republic of China; he made a lasting impression at a Commonwealth PMs conference, forging close personal relationships; he announced, in April 1973, that visas would not be granted to a racially selected South African rugby team; the government pressed the French to stop nuclear weapon testing in the Pacific; he authorised a New Zealand frigate to sail to Mururoa, the French test area. However, a record surplus, and subsequent revaluation of the currency, coupled with Kirk's impatience with economic detail, gave the government a false sense of domestic security. As Garnier, Kohn and Booth wrote: "Kirk saw economics in terms of symptoms rather than causes. He projected catchy phrases but appeared to have little detailed grasp of the complexities." [14]

The situation changed rapidly early in 1974. The world economy slowed, the first oil shock bit, government expenditure soared. Kirk's preoccupation was with delivering election promises – holding milk, postage and electricity prices – and inflation rose dramatically. There were large wage increases and, belatedly, an ill-conceived Maximum Retail Prices (MRP) price justification scheme.

Kirk was respected and admired; but few of his colleagues were close to him, and they were not exempt from a deepening paranoia. As Keith Eunson wrote: "There was a black side to the personality of this man, an innate inability to trust even his closest colleagues, seeing too often in them images of Brutus come to kill Caesar. He tended at times to suffer a deep melancholy and loneliness which caused him to walk lonely parliamentary corridors late at night ..." [15]

Kirk's gruelling schedule continued through the 1973-74 holiday period. A rapid swing through five Asian countries left him emotionally drained and ill. There was a well-hidden heart scare in New Delhi and the dysentery he contracted stayed in his system.

The first few months of 1974 were particularly hectic with the Commonwealth Games in Christchurch in February and accompanying royal and head of state visitors. Inflation continued to worsen bringing industrial strife with it. Abortion and homosexual law reform, which Kirk opposed, were divisive items on the legislative agenda.

In April Kirk had painful varicose vein surgery on both legs, ignoring medical advice that one leg should be treated at a time. There were blood clot and heart complications and delegates were

Kirk's radicalism was reserved for foreign – not domestic – policy. Peter Bromhead, Auckland Star, May 9 1973. (ATL ref: A-261-021)

shocked to see a gaunt, struggling prime minister at the mid-May Labour Party conference. By now his behaviour had grown more erratic, focussing on trivial issues as major economic problems engulfed his administration, already hampered by confusing overlaps in ministerial responsibilities. The last of his flagging energy ebbed away in occasional verbal jousts against a rampant Robert Muldoon, who had deposed Jack Marshall as leader of the opposition. According to Hugh Templeton: "Without Kirk in the House, Labour under the soft-hearted deputy leader, Hugh Watt, became a leaderless rabble." [16]

Kirk attended his last cabinet meeting on August 19, returning home exhausted. Unable to rest, he was constantly on the phone to staff and colleagues; he was saying goodbye to many of them although they did not realise it at the time. Finally he was persuaded to enter a nearby hospital where he died, aged 51, on August 31 from congestive cardiac failure and heart disease.

The suddenness of Norman Kirk's death, and the age at which he died, have encouraged theories, similar to those following the disappearance of Australian prime minister Harold Holt while swimming in 1967, about the involvement of foreign powers and secret service agencies. There has even been a thriller written on the subject of Kirk's death. Perhaps more plausibly, Norman Kirk had a weak heart and had a series of heart problems going all the way back to 1958, he was ultra secretive about these and his final illness, he carried too much weight and drove himself unmercifully.

Certainly his loss was deeply felt, particularly for what he achieved internationally.

Frank Corner, a former secretary of the foreign affairs ministry has written: "The gap that Kirk left was occupied by people who presented to the world no coherent vision and by other, very different, faces of New Zealand." [17]

Michael Bassett has written: "He was Labour's last passionate believer in big government, someone whose commanding presence and extravagant rhetoric introduced a new idealism to political debate in New Zealand. [18]

'Is there some reason why we can't all support a nuclear free zone, gentlemen?' *Kirk was the first New Zealand politician to advocate a South Pacific nuclear free zone. Eric Heath,* Dominion, *February 27 1974.* *(ATL ref: C-132-124)*

30
SIR WALLACE EDWARD ROWLING
1927-1995

"He was probably the most typical New Zealander of all Labour leaders"

Bill Rowling was never a prime minister in waiting. The prime ministership was not something he had expected or even wanted and it hardly seemed likely he would succeed Norman Kirk who, at only 49, became prime minister in 1972.

Rowling was also one of the unluckier prime ministers. In any other era his mild manner, light voice and short stature would have been un-remarkable and barely remarked upon. But, as Russell Marshall wrote: ".... he suffered what you might call a triple whammy – the treble misfortune to be preceded by Kirk, opposed by Muldoon, and to have Lange breathing down his neck – three of the all-time larger-than-life Prime Ministers of New Zealand politics." [1] Bill Rowling was also unlucky enough to win the popular vote in 1978 and 1981 but lose both elections.

He was born on September 15 1927, the youngest of Arthur and Agnes Rowling's four children, and inherited or learnt many of his enduring characteristics from his father. The grandson of Thomas 'Hop Ashore' Rowling, a Cornishman, and reputedly the first European to set foot in the Motueka district in October 1841, Arthur was a small, tough, reserved, hard-working and humble man. Rowling was christened 'Wallace Edward', but his father began

Bob Brockie, Sunday Times, *September 1974. (ATL ref: H-705-028)*

calling him 'Bill' when he was a teenager, and as they grew closer. The name stuck and it was certainly the one he preferred.

Bill Rowling grew up on a pioneering apple orchard in Motueka's Moutere Hills and, with his siblings eight to 14 years older, he absorbed the family's work ethic from an early age. The depression made a lasting impression. While the family was poor by modern standards, and lived very frugally, there was always a welcome for 'swaggers'. It was expected, and accepted, that he would work on the farm after school – at Lower Moutere and then Nelson College – and during holidays. He enjoyed his school years, but did not excel particularly in the classroom or on the sports field, and was not fondly remembered by teachers as a leader in the making. It was a happy childhood, with holidays at local beaches with the extended Rowling clan.

Arthur Rowling's political views were moulded in West Coast coal mines and on Queensland canefields where he worked and saved to buy his land, but it was not until later in life, with the orchard established, that he was active in the Labour Party. He ran the election campaign that saw his candidate C F 'Gerry' Skinner beat incumbent Keith Holyoake, whose parents lived next door to his.

Bill Rowling absorbed the political influences like blotting paper; with his father he listened to the parliamentary broadcasts, recently introduced by the new Labour government, he read the pink-covered copies of Hansard that arrived regularly by mail, and he listened, literally at their feet, to leading politicians like Michael Joseph Savage, Peter Fraser and Walter Nash when they visited the Rowling home.

Bill Rowling decided he wanted to teach, attended Christchurch Teachers' College, and studied part-time at university as well. In 1947, he volunteered for J Force, the New Zealand military contribution to Japan's post-war occupation. After the Army discovered he was only 17 shortly before his planned departure, the year of Japanese adventure was spent on much more familiar ground, as a probationary teacher at Motueka District High School. Teaching and studies continued and, after finishing an economics degree in 1949, he accepted a sole-charge position at Lake Rotoiti, the outback and deer shooting particular attractions. He was briefly downcast at the result of the 1949 election, but his Labour Party involvement was still only a ballot box tick.

It was in 1950, staying with his parents during the August school holidays, that Bill Rowling met Glen Reeves, also a teacher, and daughter of a sea captain who came ashore to be harbour master at Motueka. Their friendship blossomed and, over the Christmas period, they applied and were accepted for positions at Waverley District High School, hundreds of kilometres to the north, not far from Wanganui. It was the early 1950s, so they boarded separately in Waverley, an arrangement ending with their marriage later in 1951. It was a pleasant interlude, with time for sport and a social life.

Back in Christchurch, Rowling sat the papers for his economics masters and did casual work to supplement his wife's teaching salary. His thesis, on the history of pip fruit marketing in New Zealand, was completed while the Rowlings were at Whangape in Northland. Early in 1953, they joined the Maori Education Service, choosing to teach in a Maori school in one of

the country's remoter areas. It was here that Bill Rowling's life-changing involvement with the Labour Party really began, his enthusiasm surviving an unsuccessful tilt at selection as the party's Hobson candidate in the 1954 election. He did not see himself as a 'socialist', but at the core of his practical and pragmatic approach to politics was a commitment to improve the lot of the underprivileged.

Rowling was awarded a Fulbright Fellowship for 1955-56; he taught and the family, now including a baby daughter, travelled widely around the United States. In Northland again, Rowling was elected chairman of the Hobson LRC.

After a decade's school teaching, and more promotions than most of his contemporaries, Bill Rowling changed direction and joined the Army's Education Corp. He spent over four years in the Army, becoming assistant director of the Education Corp with the rank of captain. Mainly based in Christchurch, he almost completed a second, commerce degree and was a part-time economics

AUSTRALIANS TAKE TOUGH STANCE ON
NAFTA TRADE IMBALANCE ~NEWS

AUSSIE EXPORTS

NOW THERE'S A NOVEL TWIST!

"PLEASE SIR, I DON'T WANT ANY MORE!"

The trade balance which previously favoured Australia had now swung New Zealand's way. Bill Wrathall, New Zealand Truth, September 23 1975. (ATL ref: A-289-054)

lecturer at Canterbury University.

This promising career ended when, unexpectedly, Rowling was asked to contest National's 'blue-ribbon' Fendalton seat for Labour shortly before the 1960 election. Campaign photographs show a young, thoroughly composed army captain puffing away at his pipe. Bill Rowling enjoyed the experience and had the opportunity to do so again when Gerry Skinner, Labour's deputy leader and MP for Buller, died in April 1962. He contested the by-election, winning narrowly. The Rowlings swapped their new Christchurch home for a rented house in Westport, their obvious commitment to the electorate, which included Motueka, reflected in majorities that had increased seven-fold by the 1969 election

Bill Rowling was rarely at home, either visiting distant electoral outposts or representing Buller's interest in the House in Wellington. His ability was apparent from his maiden speech, but there was no rush to portray him as a future party leader.

Very aware of how politics affected family life – and there were now four children – Rowling made a special effort to spend Sundays at home. As John Henderson wrote: "Often he would leave Motueka – or even the more distant Takaka – after a Saturday night meeting and drive home to Westport, arriving at three or four in the morning. It was a hard and difficult drive involving long stretches over unsealed roads. But he was determined to be with his children when they awoke." [2]

His focus now shifting to finance after an early preoccupation with agriculture, Rowling wanted an involvement with Labour's organisational wing as well. When, after four successive annual challenges, he finally won the vice-presidency in 1969, he took charge of the party's public image, hired Bob Harvey, a bright and enthusiastic adman, and together they masterminded an efficient and professional election campaign that year.

Bill Rowling had made a favourable impression and was elected party president in 1970. It was the first time in 54 years the position was uncontested and, at 42, Rowling was the second youngest president ever. He served unchallenged for two further years, working closely with John Wybrow, the party's new general secretary. Jim Eagles and Colin James wrote: "Between the two of them they chipped the rust off the party machinery, replaced useless parts ruthlessly, oiled where necessary and got the thing moving properly in time for the 1972 election." [3]

The lopsided election victory was also a personal triumph for Rowling. After the redrawing of boundaries, his electorate, now named Tasman, was highly marginal and Norman Kirk wanted him to shift to a safe Christchurch seat. Rowling refused, to Kirk's considerable displeasure. He campaigned as single-mindedly as ever, a camper van his mobile headquarters, and won Tasman with a handy 1,800 plus majority.

There was some surprise when he, and not opposition spokesman Bob Tizard, was named minister of finance. The country had a trained economist as its finance minister for the very first time!

After the 1975 election rout. Tom Scott, ca 1975. (ATL ref: H-705-011)

However, although the economy had a prosperous surface sheen to it, with little unemployment, record export returns and large overseas reserves, just under the surface inflationary pressures were building dangerously. National had written an expansionary budget in 1972 as an election sweetener; now Labour was hell-bent on implementing its election manifesto in the shortest possible time. Rowling was caught between the rational need to systematically invest in faltering economic growth, after years of 'stop-go' policies, and the new government's impatience to implement its social agenda.

As Henderson wrote in his Rowling biography, Norman Kirk did not "accept that valid economic reasons could exist to prevent necessary social actions being taken. His strong humanitarianism did not sit easily with economic reality. He was, as Bill Rowling has reflected, unwilling and sometimes unable to compromise between the desirable and the attainable." [4]

Attempts to dampen down rising prices and inflation were largely ineffectual, even before the massive oil price rises following the Yom Kippur war in October 1973. In short order, the record overseas reserves were gone, with import costs sky-rocketing and export prices sagging, and New Zealand was signing up for the largest single overseas loan in its history. The underlying fragility of the economy had been exposed, but Rowling rejected the traditional, knee-jerk, retrenchment option and attempted to juggle Labour's promises, like holding government charges, while encouraging economic growth.

Bill Rowling was working 18 hour days, six days a week, attempting to keep an over-heated, 'oil-shocked' economy from foundering and championing Rural Bank and Overseas Investment Commission legislation and the New Zealand Superannuation Scheme which, although overly complicated, was much sounder than its politically-motivated successor.

When Norman Kirk's health steadily worsened, during the early months of 1974 cabinet and caucus drifted, with vital economic measures postponed. Rowling did not panic and it was as much for his strength of character as his able stewardship of the finance portfolio that a clear majority of his colleagues wanted him to take charge after Kirk's death, rather than deputy PM Hugh Watt. At 46, he was the youngest leader of government since 1884. Russell Marshall later wrote: "He was probably the most typical New Zealander of all Labour leaders. He was certainly a typical New Zealand male. He

All God's chillun got left wings... *The 'Citizens for Rowling campaign – and its 'Clergy for Rowling' and 'Lawyers for Rowling' offshoots – backfired, being seen as elitist. Sid Scales,* Otago Daily Times, *November 20 1975. (ATL ref: A-319-025)*

played rugby, and he was very keen on and knowledgeable about cricket." [5]

Rowling took on Kirk's foreign affairs responsibilities, finance passing to his deputy Bob Tizard.

Rowling chaired cabinet and caucus efficiently and inclusively and decisions were made rather than avoided. Despite a co-operative and consultative political style, Rowling could also be tough and determined. As Jim Anderton later wrote: "At a personal level he was a tough machine politician and by no means the wimp that his enemies sought to depict." [6] The public misunderstood his tendency to turn the other cheek. While not a churchgoer he strongly believed in the Christian ethic of service and in the inherent decency of people. He could even shrug off Muldoon's notorious comment – "You could see the cold shivers running around Mr Rowling's body seeking a spine to run up – unsuccessfully" – as an inevitable part of the political game.

Rowling was possibly overly cautious; he was certainly not a risk-taker. With hindsight, he should have called an election after Kirk's death. Viewing this from an opposition perspective, Hugh Templeton wrote: "[Labour's] strategic error, however, was not to go to the country for a mandate. Rowling would have won easily on a sympathy vote; this would have given him a full three years to consolidate." [7] Instead he remained a caretaker, trying to keep alive the spirit of Kirk's vision as economic reality bit.

Nevertheless, Rowling remained consistent in his economic philosophy – borrowing rather than retrenching, keeping people and industry at work. In fact, although inflation reached 15 percent and unemployment and prices shot up, New Zealand weathered the global crisis of a threefold increase in oil prices better than most other countries. Muldoon, however, called it "borrow and hope" and the expression stuck.

While preoccupied with the domestic economy, Rowling safeguarded New Zealand's butter and lamb interests as Britain re-negotiated its EEC terms, maintained the country's high reputation at the Commonwealth Prime Ministers' Conference in Jamaica, and stoutly re-affirmed his government's anti-apartheid and anti-nuclear stands.

Bill Rowling did not expect to lose the 1975 election and neither he, nor Labour's confidence in him, fully recovered from a loss that turned a 23 seat majority into an equally large minority. A number of reasons have been debated: the vicious Capital Club campaign, led by political gadfly Bob Jones, was insidiously effective in portraying Rowling as a 'mouse' and 'weak'; the retaliatory 'Citizens for Rowling' was ill-judged, the elite roll call not impressing heartland New Zealand; the oil shock and dropping export returns turned boom-time into grim recession; and Muldoon's aggressive campaign, linked to scare-tactic TV commercials, hammered

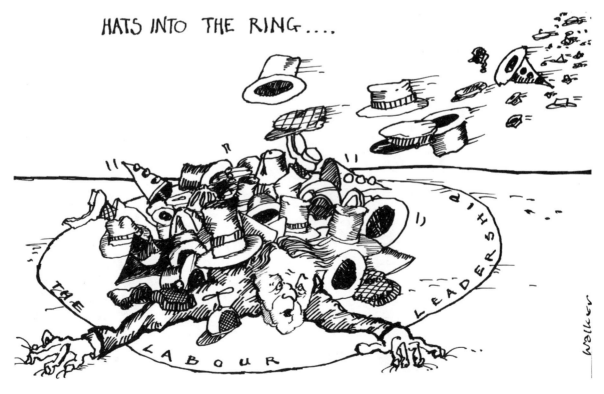

HATS INTO THE RING....

Through 1982 there was the expectation that Rowling would resign, but he left the decision until late in the year.
Malcolm Walker, Sunday News, *September 13 1982. (ATL ref: A-305-066)*

away at this and traditional Labour bogeys.

According to Keith Eunson: "In Rowling's view the Jones campaign of denigration with the 'mouse' symbol made the difference, and because Jones had the money and the platform to maintain the momentum of his cause." [8]

The 1980s might have been very different had Rowling won. John Henderson has written: "A case can be made that under Rowling's careful management style New Zealand might have avoided the extremes of both Muldoonism and Rogernomics." [9]

Rowling showed steely strength to then survive over six years as opposition leader, sometimes with a rebellious caucus, and chalk up more

ERIC HEATH

Rowling increasingly walked in the shadow of David Lange who finally replaced him as Labour leader. Eric Heath, Dominion, October 12 1982. (ATL ref: B-145-634)

votes than National in both the 1978 and 1981 elections. And he did so in an increasingly distasteful political environment. There was, for example, the November 1976 parliamentary exchange between Muldoon and Labour's Colin Moyle, homosexuality claims, a flawed commission of inquiry and Rowling's heart-wrenching decision to persuade his close friend to resign from Parliament.

Rowling believed this new divisiveness and meanness of spirit in politics, and the country generally, contributed to the suicide of his 18 year-old daughter Kim in March 1978. Her death nearly brought his political career to an abrupt end; instead he re-dedicated himself "to getting rid of some of the stench in politics that ought not to be there".

Clearly, the electorate did not share Rowling's convictions. The 1978 election result might have been a moral victory for Labour, but too many anti-government votes went to Social Credit and National was back with a six seat majority.

Inevitably, Bill Rowling had to fight for his political life before the 1981 election. An attempted coup in December 1980 came close to replacing him with the charismatic David Lange, who won the Mangere by-election following Moyle's resignation and became deputy party leader after less than three years in Parliament.

Labour should have won in 1981 but the balance was tipped by a divisive Springbok rugby tour that shored up key marginal provincial seats and National's 'Think Big' promise of economic salvation. Also, Muldoon's masterful use of television, beamed straight into the nation's living rooms, was more persuasive than Rowling's traditional, 'on the road' campaign.

Rowling did not concede defeat on the night, but finally National had 47 seats, Labour 43 and Social Credit two – a majority of one after appointing the Speaker.

As Barry Gustafson wrote: "If fewer than 500 voters had changed their minds in any two of six seats, Labour might have become the Government." [10]

Bill Rowling did not resign the leadership immediately, stepping down a year later. He was only 56 when he retired from politics at the 1984 election after 22 years in Parliament.

Now Sir Wallace, he remained in public view as ambassador in Washington and then as the driving force behind the building of Te Papa, the new national museum. Politics gave him less pleasure. He was openly contemptuous of 'Rogernomics', driven by an ideology that hurt traditional Labour voters most in need of help. More typically, he quietly let his Labour Party membership lapse when his nemesis Bob Jones became Sir Robert during protégé Geoffrey Palmer's short prime ministership.

Unfortunately for Bill Rowling, in the late 1970s and early 1980s it was not enough to be liked and respected. As John Henderson commented: "It is a pertinent commentary on recent New Zealand politics that features which are widely admired and applied when making personal judgments – honesty, friendliness, understanding, respect, co-operation – have not been regarded as important attributes for a prime minister."

Bill Rowling died of a brain tumour on October 31 1995.

31
SIR ROBERT DAVID MULDOON
1921-1992

"He missed the opportunity to save by more pragmatic reform the mixed economy and the welfare state"

While there are sharply divided opinions about the political significance of Robert David Muldoon, it is widely agreed that he was the 20th century's most controversial prime minister.

Robert Muldoon was, as it has been aptly put, "in the National Party but not of it". His family lacked the usual farming or middle-class business connections and were only a generation away from the slums of Liverpool. He was born in Auckland on September 25 1921 into a poverty-line household dominated by two women devoted to each other, the new arrival and the Labour Party.

Jim Muldoon was 39 years old and his wife Annie Rusha 33 when they had their only child. Rob Muldoon's father, an unqualified accountant, was badly gassed in France during the First World War. He struggled to find work until his health deteriorated so badly in the late 1920s that he was permanently hospitalised for the 20 years before he died.

The strongest influences during Robert's growing-up years were his mother, notable for her bristling personality and well-developed work ethic, and her mother, Jerusha Browne,

Chicane (Mark Winter), Southland Times, *1984. (ATL ref: A-323-004)*

also a single-parent after her husband had deserted her. Mother and daughter were passionately committed to the Labour Party, Annie Muldoon cutting back on her Sandringham branch activities only when son Rob was appointed to the National cabinet many years later.

Of necessity, the young Muldoon acquired an early familiarity with gardening, a bountiful vegetable plot supplementing a budget that rarely stretched to new clothes.

It was an accident in this garden, and no money for medical treatment, that resulted in Muldoon's trademark dimple-scar on his left cheek.

Rob Muldoon won a prestigious scholarship giving him the three years of secondary education he might have otherwise missed. He was the youngest and smallest boy at nearby Mt Albert Grammar School in 1933, the bullying meted out to him stimulating a latent pugnaciousness later refined into a potent political weapon. His school results were only average but the result of an IQ test, a new educational technique at the time, gave him a 'genius' rating. Muldoon scraped through the university entrance examination at 14, but further study was a dream beyond his family's reach.

Nothing about the next few years suggested a spectacular political career. He worked as a junior clerk at the Auckland Electric Power Board until, just 19, he enlisted in the army in November 1940, serving as a non-commissioned officer in New Caledonia and Italy. The one 'war story' told about Muldoon was that Major Jack Marshall, who he much later replaced as National's leader, supervised his final cost accountancy examination in a tent at Trieste. It was the finale of a single-minded study programme during the war years. He was New Zealand's first cost accountant, with the immediate reward a year-long accountancy scholarship in England.

Back in New Zealand he joined an accountancy firm and the National Party. At Young Nationals meetings he refined his debating skills and met Thea Flyger, the cosseted daughter of a successful builder, and five years his junior. They were 'going steady' in 1948 and finally married in March 1951.

Thea Muldoon might have been expecting a relatively anonymous, middle-class life as housewife and mother of their three children, but Rob Muldoon's political ambitions were already stirring. He was chairman of the Young Nationals in 1949 and in 1954 contested the first of the three general elections it took to reach Parliament. Mount Albert and Waitemata were Labour strongholds but, in 1960, Tamaki was more marginal. He won and then held the seat, with majorities ranging from adequate to very substantial, for the next 31 years.

Muldoon quickly made an impression, prime minister Keith Holyoake choosing him to move the Address in Reply at the opening of the 1961 parliamentary session. As Spiro Zavos wrote: "The uneasy schoolboy, the soldier who didn't fit in, the fiancé who wasn't from the right side of the tracks, the local body employee who had no future in a dead end department – all these experiences were left behind." [1]

A loose grouping of new National MPs – Peter Gordon, Duncan MacIntyre and Muldoon – became known as the 'Young Turks' and the name stuck as their political careers flourished. In 1963, Muldoon became chairman of the powerful Public Expenditure Committee, but the other two made cabinet first.

In many ways Keith Holyoake was Muldoon's mentor, next appointing him under-secretary to the minister of finance, Harry Lake, after the 1963 election. But Holyoake held back from giving the outspoken member for Tamaki full ministerial responsibilities. He was, though, given the task of introducing decimal currency and had acquired a national reputation by the end of the process.

Muldoon was not named to cabinet after the 1966 election, but Holyoake relented at the beginning of 1967 with the lowly tourism portfolio and a boost in his financial role to associate ministership. When Harry Lake died suddenly barely a month later Muldoon lost little time in staking his claim and Holyoake acquiesced.

Muldoon soon put his distinctive stamp on the finance portfolio, with his abrasive manner, accessibility to the media and few inhibitions about interfering in his colleagues' portfolios. Muldoon

looked more and more like a leader in waiting, particularly as deputy PM Jack Marshall spent so much time in Europe shoring up New Zealand's agricultural export future.

Keynsian economics suited New Zealand and Muldoon when he began his marathon stint as minister of finance. But the halcyon days of living comfortably off the sheep's back were nearly over, and Muldoon was slow to accept – as economies underwent huge technological and structural change and reeled from surging inflation and oil shocks – that New Zealand had to change too. "He willed upon a younger generation with new ideals and ideas," wrote Colin James, "the values of his own youth." [2]

It suited Muldoon for Holyoake to remain leader as long as possible but he thought he had the numbers to comfortably beat Marshall when the prime minister finally stepped down at National's first 1972 caucus meeting. In fact, although Marshall won easily, Muldoon, now deputy prime minister, was perfectly positioned to move after the new prime minister lost an increasingly unwinnable election.

National had run out of steam – farmers unhappy with inflation rates and businessmen angry about the payroll tax Muldoon introduced in 1970 – and this was reflected in the size of Labour's victory late in 1972.

Muldoon and Marshall had little affection for each other. Their backgrounds, political beliefs and personal styles were too different. It was inevitable Muldoon would challenge for the party leadership; surprisingly it was not until July 1973, and Marshall seemed blithely unaware he had lost his caucus's confidence. As Muldoon later wrote: "...I think that the thing that concerned our Caucus members most was that he stuck very close to his office and seldom mingled with either front or backbenchers." [3] Muldoon did not make the same mistake and late night drinks in his or colleagues' offices were an important part of his daily routine.

While Muldoon and his lieutenants had been counting heads, Jack Marshall, suffering indifferent health and without his deputy's savage ambition, made no attempt to lobby his colleagues. When Marshall finally realised he was likely to lose a leadership vote, and Holyoake was actively supporting Muldoon, he stepped down at the July 4 caucus meeting.

Marshall's defeat was not universally welcomed. As Gustafson noted: "More refined National Party supporters used to the courteous Holyoake or Marshall personifying their party now regarded with some disdain the 'roughneck from Tamaki' and his verbal assaults on Labour MPs, journalists, Polynesian overstayers, unionists with Clydeside accents, 'trendy lefties', ivory tower academics, and seemingly anyone else who crossed his path." [4]

But in late 1974, and through election year, what his colleagues saw was a total commitment to the campaign trail, indefatigably repeating in memorable phrases New Zealanders responded to, on television and in packed halls, that only National could repair the country's 'shattered economy'. Labour was beaten as comprehensively at the 1975 election as National had been humiliated three years before. National won 48 percent of the popular vote and the margin of 23 seats was its largest ever parliamentary majority.

Muldoon was now prime minister, arguably the most powerful ever. While his combativeness was usually held in check, it was always sufficiently close to the surface to subdue most colleagues and public servants. In 1975, as Gustafson noted, "His dogmatic stance was seen as the virtue of decisiveness, not the vice of intolerance." [5] He strengthened the prime minister's department so he had advice independent of the treasury and foreign affairs mandarins. He interfered, as he saw fit, in his ministers' portfolios. Critically, after eight years in the job he continued as minister of finance. Prime Minister Sid Holland was also finance minister for three years and both Ward and Forbes held the two positions briefly in the late 1920s and early 1930s but none had been so completely in command as Muldoon.

He was a rare political phenomenon. Gustafson again: "A superb debater, Muldoon had the ability to comprehend, synthesise and simplify complex material and combined a clear analysis with a sense of emotional outrage when required." [6] He also had a remarkable capacity to deal with the avalanche of paper that crossed his desk, reading everything and remembering most. He did not forget, or forgive, the prominent New Zealanders who added their names to the 'Citizens for Rowling' campaign before the 1975 campaign, nor did he forget, or fail to reward, some of his more mediocre colleagues whose loyalty had never wavered. Most controversially, in 1977 Muldoon insisted on Keith Holyoake's appointment as governor general, the first and only time a former prime minister and serving cabinet minister has been so elevated.

Possibly most important, as Templeton wrote: "…. Muldoon was a master of television …. Instinctively he knew the importance of short, sharp statements: the sound bite came naturally to this politician. People loved his quirkiness, his outspokenness, his willingness to knock down idols …. Age, drink and power had not yet distorted that face." [7] His staring down-the-camera-lens interview technique produced mesmerizing television performances and his ability to communicate with the 'ordinary decent bloke' made him a talkback radio favourite.

A Muldoon accusation in the House in November 1976 led to the unravelling of Colin Moyle's political career. Peter Bromhead, Auckland Star, *February 12 1977. (ATL ref: A-328-036)*

New Zealand was firmly in the grip of 'Muldoonism'; however, while the myth of 'economic miracle worker' grew, others saw 'Piggy' Muldoon as a dangerous threat to the country's democratic tradition.

The contradictions in Muldoon's nature and performance were already in evidence. He was, as Templeton later wrote, " a genuine, combative, populist demagogue. Yet in action he proved profoundly conservative ...." [8] At the same time, the man who supported New Zealand's involvement in the Vietnam War and was opposed to abortion achieved a certain rapport with the Black Power gang. And the rowdy rhetoric aside, he was particularly cautious and careful when it came to making decisions. Hugh Templeton was, for example, repeatedly frustrated by the halting progress as he edged Muldoon towards acceptance of closer economic relations with Australia in the early 1980s. Also, Muldoon's intimidating manner masked a not inconsiderable social conscience. Gustafston wrote: "He believed in, and indeed excelled in, operating the levers of power but took time to get used to new ideas. Many he could not accept because of what he judged to be the human cost." [9]

Muldoon was more at ease with hecklers in a crowded hall than with dinner party repartee; his rudeness was, in part at least, a way of hiding an innate shyness and insecurity; he was ruthless with those, opponents or colleagues, obstructing him yet sought solace growing lilies.

For the next eight years Rob Muldoon was rarely off the front pages of the nation's newspapers. Political pronouncements aside, there was a rash of incidents like the prime ministerial party's riotous night at the Crazy Horse strip club in Paris, public spats with 'nitpicking' TV journalists and the memorable occasion when Abraham Ordia, from the Supreme Council for Sport in Africa, was told to "stew in his own juice".

The cause célèbre of Muldoon's first term as prime minister, and a nastier example of 'counter-punching', was the 'Moyle Affair' which began in the House on November 4 1976. During an evening of testy exchanges Muldoon accused Colin Moyle of being "picked up by the police for homosexual activity". The matter – handled poorly by all involved – escalated out of control, wrecking Moyle's career, added another substantial blot to Muldoon's spotty reputation for unacceptable invective and brought David Lange into the House at the resulting Mangere by-election, to the subsequent political embarrassment of both Muldoon and Bill Rowling.

Muldoon had made it clear during the 1975 election campaign that there would be no political interference in sport. But with the Soweto riots shortly before the 1976 Springboks visit, it was also a stance increasingly out of kilter with international opinion. African nations withdrew from that year's Montreal Olympics in protest. Serious disruption of the 1978 Commonwealth Games – with New Zealand the villain – looked likely until the Gleneagles Accord, accepted at the Commonwealth Heads of Government meeting in 1977, provided Muldoon with an escape clause short of an explicit reversal of National's policy.

As Zavos wrote: "Foreign policy is about nuances, shades of meaning, protocol – and none of these have much appeal to Muldoon." [10] Relations with the United States were distinctly cool after Muldoon said of President Jimmy Carter, "He's only a peanut farmer from Georgia" and the remark that New Zealanders emigrating to Australia raised the IQ in both countries was neither original nor likely to warm Muldoon's frigid relationship with Malcolm Fraser.

After the second oil shock, Muldoon's tinkering, reactive approach to managing the economy could no longer patch over some fundamental problems. Bob Brockie, National Business Review, ca 1978-79. (ATL ref: B-128-009)

If Muldoon's reputation for 'economic wizardry' had any substance, it was most in evidence during the 1976-78 period. He inherited an economic mess: the 1973 oil shock and a lengthy slide in commodity prices had conspired to produce a balance of payments crisis and high double-digit inflation.

While his overly generous, but election-winning National Superannuation scheme may have been a departure from his usual fiscal caution, Muldoon was openly contemptuous of Rowling's 'borrow and hope' attempt to keep New Zealanders in work and safeguard living standards. His objective, now as before, was to have the economy on a short, closely guarded leash, 'fine-tuning' with mini budgets his modus operandi. He reined in economic activity in an attempt to control inflation and reduce the overseas deficit, and engaged in wholesale state intervention to lessen dependence on imported oil and boost export income. Templeton wrote: "His first three budgets were as important as any he ever wrote and laid the basis, particularly in the energy, forestry and tourism sectors, for the development of a broad-based New Zealand economy in the next 20 years." [11] Economist Brian Easton agrees: "His presiding over the great export diversification of the 1970s was his greatest economic achievement." [12]

The situation looked a little brighter in 1978, but it was primarily a restructuring of the tax system – giving relief to both low and average wage earners – that persuaded the electorate National was, as the election slogan said, keeping its word. National's majority was cut to 10 seats, Labour won the popular vote, Social Credit's success underlined the electorate's volatility – but Muldoon began his second term with a firm grip on cabinet, caucus, party and country.

The second oil shock, following the Shah of Iran's overthrow early in 1979, quickly showed that Muldoon's interventionist, reactive, tinkering approach to economic management no longer worked. New Zealand's oil bill doubled virtually overnight, but while his caucus wanted to restructure and free up the private sector, Muldoon retreated to his old formula of incentives and the imposition of counter-productive sales taxes. Then, with an eye to

the 1981 election as well as the deepening energy crisis, he threw himself and a great deal of government money into a 'Think Big' programme of major diversification and import substitution projects, the most grandiose of them energy-related.

Muldoon's administration was increasingly divided. Issues like abortion caused friction, but the last straw for his caucus, already frustrated by increasingly dictatorial behaviour and unwillingness to open up the economy, was the shock loss, in September 1980, of the East Coast Bays seat to Social Credit after he allowed the sitting member, a personal friend, to resign with a year of the parliamentary term to run.

Shortly afterwards, in what was dubbed the 'colonels' coup', Muldoon came close to being unceremoniously dumped by his colleagues. The coup leaders had the numbers to defeat Muldoon, but both he and his deputy, and likely successor, Brian Talboys were overseas. On his return Muldoon fought tenaciously, including a television appeal to the 'Rob's Mob' admirers of his populist politics, Talboys procrastinated and the crisis passed. The unforgiving Muldoon promptly forced Talboys' resignation.

'Think Big' and the cynical manipulation of a Springbok rugby tour won Muldoon his third term at the end of 1981. National had reiterated its opposition to apartheid, but Muldoon insisted that the final decision in a free country had to be made by the sporting body concerned and not the government.

Again National failed to win the popular vote in a deeply divided country and survived with an uncomfortable one seat majority. Anti-Muldoonism was now widespread, within as well as outside the National Party.

Muldoon's caucus was increasingly fractious. A welcome to nuclear-armed warships from the United States and a frigate offered to Britain during the Falklands war, voluntary unionism and the special legislation to circumvent Clyde High Dam holdups troubled National's more 'liberal' back benchers, notably Marilyn Waring and Mike

Muldoon's reining in of economic activity had predictable consequences. Bob Brockie, National Business Review, *November 9 1981. (ATL ref: H-725-004)*

Minogue. Cabinet minister Derek Quigley questioned the government's growth strategy and was forced to resign. With the explicit purpose of defeating Muldoon at the 1984 election, property magnate Bob Jones formed the New Zealand Party in protest at interest rate controls and the lengthy, back-to-the-wall wage and price freeze imposed in June 1982.

The election was four months early, triggered by Muldoon's belief that he could no longer rely on Waring's support. His justifications were largely spurious, but weariness, serious health problems and increasing evidence that his band-aid economic tinkering was failing may have been behind his snap election decision.

It was a crushing loss for Muldoon, National winning only 36 percent of the vote. While Labour would have won comfortably without the New Zealand Party, its 12 percent support from traditionally National voters turned rejection into rout. Then, in a final act of defiance, Muldoon brought New Zealand to the edge of an unprecedented constitutional crisis when he briefly defied the incoming Labour government's instructions to devalue the dollar.

Characteristically, Muldoon did not accept responsibility for the election loss and clung to the leadership until the end of November when he was beaten decisively by his deputy Jim McLay. If his knighthood was supposed to usher in retirement, the thought had not occurred to Muldoon; politics was, after all, his life. He retreated to the back benches when denied a front bench position, as intent on destabilising McLay's leadership as opposing Labour.

When Jim Bolger replaced McLay in March 1986, Rob Muldoon returned to the opposition front bench until the 1987 election. More respected elsewhere, he spoke at a number of international economics forums during the 1988-90 period; at home his speeches, newspaper columns and talkback radio sessions reflected his growing

distaste for National's monetarist policies. Although not fully recovered from a serious illness he contested Tamaki for the 11th time at the 1990 election, recording his largest-ever majority and attacking the right wing of his own party and Labour with equal vehemence. When National swept back to the treasury benches Muldoon's highly personalised attacks on finance minister Ruth Richardson were extraordinary even by his standards. He finally retired, to National's great relief and without the traditional farewell party, in December 1991. Increasingly unwell, Muldoon died in early August 1992.

No other New Zealand prime minister has ever written as much about himself as Muldoon. His four autobiographies, beginning with *The Rise and Fall of a Young Turk* in 1974, were largely exercises in self-justification. Muldoon knew John A Lee well and saw how that colourful politician had written himself favourably into the historical record. Muldoon's books also provided further evidence that his political philosophy was narrowly based and that he rated pragmatism above principle.

Famously, Rob Muldoon once told a television interviewer that his ambition was to leave New Zealand no worse than he found it. Possibly too much has been made of the remark; his desire to

Freeze. *The price and wage freeze was part of Muldoon's armory of devices to avoid economic reality. Tom Scott. (ATL ref: B-128-007)*

hold on to the 'golden weather' days of post-war New Zealand was surely admirable, if ultimately impossible. Colin James wrote: "In economic policy he clung to protection, regulation, public enterprise, subsidies with public money and deficit financing in the belief that these policies would protect jobs. He relaxed only in tiny, safe ways and in crisis reverted to control." [13]

Muldoon controlled New Zealand's economic policymaking for nearly 17 years with his views frozen in early 1960s protectionist thinking while the rest of the world opened up dramatically. Templeton wrote: "The concept of more market-orientated policies and deregulation did not enter his mind. He had no faith in Friedmanism. His task was to get control of the economy and then fine-tune its ups and downs." [14] Canute-like, and with his mini-budgets and financial tinkering, Muldoon ignored economic reality to the point that massive, disruptive change was inevitable. Regrettably, as Gustafson pointed out, " .... he missed the opportunity to save by more pragmatic reform the mixed economy and the welfare state to which he was so genuinely attached." [15]

Prior to the Muldoon era, New Zealand had been developing an enviable reputation internationally as a principled country with influence in world forums disproportionate to its size. By allowing the 1981 Springbok tour to proceed, Muldoon put marginal provincial seat prejudices before the country's international standing.

Undoubtedly, a meanness of spirit and aggressive self-interest developed in New Zealand in the late 1970s and into the 1980s. While international influences, and television particularly, were significant, it is also true that the Muldoon style and practice of politics gave legitimacy to a climate of personal denigration and polarisation of issues in a country more comfortable with consensus.

It is too early to be certain of Robert David Muldoon's place in New Zealand history, but the omens are ominous. As Easton wrote: "Muldoon's reputation has been caught in a double bind. The right loathed his economics: the left his politics." [16] Perhaps most positive has been the reaction to the negatives of the Muldoon years: concern about prime ministers again holding the finance portfolio, the weaknesses of the first-past-the-post parliamentary system, the dangers of dividing a small, fragile society, and the destructive power of 'populism'.

The last word might be left to Sir John Marshall, who rarely had that luxury at the time. "He failed because his unrestrained verbal antagonism stretched beyond the limits which decent people are prepared to tolerate in a prime minister." [17]

Muldoon's decision to call a snap election in 1984 had very little support from colleagues or party officials. Malcolm Walker, New Zealand Herald, *1984. (ATL ref: B-095-009)*

32
DAVID RUSSELL LANGE
1942-

"His charismatic appeal ensured Labour two terms in government"

Few prime ministers have had political careers that skyrocketed so dazzlingly and then fizzled so dramatically. During a period of profound economic change, unequalled for half a century at least, he often appeared more spectator than committed participant.

David Lange was born in August 1942, the first child of 40 year old Dr Roy Lange and his wife Phoebe, 10 years his junior. He inherited his surname from his German great-grandfather, his verbal fluency from his mother and sharp wit from his father.

His father, despite Edinburgh qualifications as a surgeon, was beginning a career dedicated to general practice in South Auckland when he met Phoebe Reid, a highly trained nurse. Living and working in a large house at a busy Otahuhu intersection, the Langes were to become local institutions; he the traditional family doctor who was as un-businesslike in keeping appointments to time as he was collecting his fees, she supporting up to 10 families at a time and helping run Maori Sunday schools. As his biographer Vernon Wright wrote: "Lange ….grew up in a liberal Christian household where the twin injunctions of charity and duty kept the parents busy in the service of others. You were, in a sense, defined by what you did for others" [1]

Life in the Lange household was rumbustious,

Trace Hodgson, New Zealand Listener, *July 22 1989. (ATL ref: H-725-012)*

particularly at meal times. And proof, should it be needed, that meals on trays in front of television have done as much as anything to damage family relationships and children's development. Meals were rowdy affairs, the children encouraged to be funny and play competitive word games. Another, less fortunate, legacy of the lengthy meals and lashings of food was the weight problem that later affected Lange and his siblings.

Although Lange could read fluently in the primers, his primary, intermediate and secondary schooldays were unspectacular. If a topic did not appeal he was quickly bored. He never failed, but the potential of his high IQ was rarely realised. He played sport until his size and other interests intervened. He had a passion for public speaking which dovetailed conveniently with a growing enthusiasm for world affairs, travel and politics. As early as his intermediate years he was listening to parliamentary broadcasts. Roy Lange, who was known as 'a bit of a left', took his elder son to a number of political meetings to hear the great issues of the early 1950s – including the waterfront lockout and Korean War – passionately debated.

Lange's first full-time year at Auckland University, in 1960, when he lived at Trinity College, a Methodist theological college and hostel, was financed by long, physically hard summer weeks at a freezing works. From 1961, for another six years, Lange studied part-time, mostly repeating the pattern of just-adequate performance he perfected at Otahuhu College. For most of these years he clerked in a law firm that was, unconventionally, committed to acting for the less privileged and protesters against apartheid, Vietnam and the nuclear arms race. Lange had joined the Labour Party in 1963 and found the work interesting and satisfying.

Nevertheless, shortly after graduating in March 1967 he left for England, where he relished the debates in the House of Commons, Speakers' Corner in Hyde Park, and the discussion of issues in newspapers and on television. Most significantly, he stumbled across the Kingsway West London Mission. The initial attraction was its cafeteria, but he then heard the Methodist theologian Donald Soper, later Lord Soper, preach a sermon.

Although the Langes were Methodists he had turned away from the church's restrictive, negative practices. But now Lange heard a message, about Christian socialist action and the importance of the Labour Party in giving effect to it, that answered some unresolved questions for him. "At the core of Christian socialism," wrote Wright, "is the conviction that the best work the ambulance at the bottom of the cliff can do is to go to the top of the cliff and stop people falling off." [2]

He began to visit the West London Mission regularly, as did Naomi Crampton, a young woman from Nottinghamshire, the county of his forebears.

Despite differences in background and education, they were attracted to each other, their church involvements cementing the relationship. They married the day before Lange's 26th birthday and immediately left for New Zealand, honeymooning in India on the way.

In a little over a year Lange had travelled to the other side of the world, married and taken over a run-down law practice in Kaikohe. He concentrated on court work in a circuit of Northland towns, sometimes combining this with lay preaching, which he had qualified for some years previously. The work was interesting and varied; the remuneration was minimal. Fortunately, David and Naomi Lange also shared a complete lack of interest in the trappings of materialism. The Langes moved back to Auckland at the end of 1969 and the next year he studied for his LLM, passing with first class honours while tutoring in the law faculty.

Although the law masters was to prove to himself that he could excel academically, it was certainly of little use in his subsequent legal career. In November 1970 Lange took over the law practice of Alan Nixon, Auckland's 'poor man's lawyer', well-known for representing the poorest, least-likely-to-pay clients.

David Lange continued the tradition; with his bulk, ballooning suits and lengthy lists of cases he was to become the dominant legal personality at the Auckland Magistrate's Court in the early 1970s. While Lange was constantly engaged with the way the 'system' dealt with his clients, he was also edging towards a more direct political involvement. He became chairman of the Council for Civil Liberties and stood unsuccessfully in 1974 for the Auckland City Council seat Michael Bassett, a distant cousin, was retiring from to concentrate on his parliamentary career.

The decision to stand for Labour in Hobson, a safe National seat, at the 1975 election was a far bigger commitment. For much of 1975 Lange juggled Auckland court work with taking his family (Roy, four years old, and Byron, born in 1974) on caravaning adventures cum electioneering forays around the far north of the North Island. It was, of course, a hopeless task, but Lange had the satisfaction of holding the

Lange's one-liners were invariably witty at the time, but sometimes caused him, and the government, embarrassment later. Peter Bromhead, Auckland Star, *March 4 1987. (ATL ref: H-452-001)*

swing below the countrywide average as National won by a landslide.

In 1976 nothing was further from the Langes' minds than another tilt at national politics; their second daughter, Emily, was born in May with a cleft palate, necessitating two major operations before her first birthday. (There had been a still born daughter in 1969.) But then Parliament and the country were rocked by the 'Moyle Affair'; Colin Moyle resigned and later decided not to contest the by-election in Mangere, Lange's home turf. In the end 16 candidates, including former MP Mike Moore and David Lange, sought selection for the safe Labour seat. It was clear that the party leaders wanted someone else, but Lange's selection speech changed all that. Wright wrote: "Lange's selection was like Kiwi entering and then winning the 1983 Melbourne Cup. He was so much an outsider that he was barely recognised by the Labour Party people involved in the by-election." [3] The actual poll was an anti-climax, Lange romping home with an impressive majority.

His physical presence, booming voice and compelling way with words meant that Lange was immediately a national figure in a political world of few dominant personalities other than Robert Muldoon. After his May 1977 maiden speech the political pollsters began to record the potency of the Lange chemistry. Hugh Templeton wrote: "Few could know that this loud fat man, with the pudding-basin haircut, would instantaneously make a mark in Parliament with his scintillating wit and eloquence." [4]

Extraordinarily, barely a year after Lange entered Parliament there was an attempt, mainly by Auckland colleagues, to promote him to the deputy leadership. There was insufficient support then, but another election defeat later, David Lange replaced Bob Tizard in November 1979.

Through 1980, Labour's poll performance was lamentable; by December it had even fallen behind Social Credit. Lange, essentially a loner, remained aloof when his promoters forced a leadership vote at a December caucus, Rowling surviving on his casting vote. Lange was uneasy about personal ambition and, as Roger Douglas later wrote, "If he won the leadership he was not going to be beholden to anyone. It is a quality of Lange's, a fundamental integrity, few people have recognised." [5] It was a quality Douglas appreciated less in a few years time.

Lange faded into the background during 1981, his determination not to upstage Rowling reflected in a falling poll rating. Deeply weary after the 1981 election and Labour's third loss in a row, Lange decided his weight problem had to be addressed if he was to continue in politics. As he told Wright: ".... one ends up with a funny sort of selfish feeling about the '81 General Election. You know, if I'd been deputy prime minister I would be 28 stone by now." [6]

The stomach by-pass operation was a success and a much slimmer, more energetic, sunnier David Lange emerged. He performed well as acting opposition leader while Rowling was overseas and by November 1983 he was even tackling Muldoon in the House on economic issues, a field he admitted little background in. In his inimitable way, he described Muldoon as "an economic ignoramus unfit to oversee a 50 cent raffle". [7] Shortly afterwards Bill Rowling announced he would be standing down from the leadership in February 1983, and there was little doubt, within the party or the media, about who would succeed him.

Tactically, Labour was in better shape for the snap July 1984 election than National; its polling had shown the electorate's contradictory desire for reconciliation and strong leadership. And these were the key themes from Lange's inspirational opening

Rebel Labour MPs John Kirk and Brian MacDonell did not share their party's views on nuclear matters. Bob Brockie, National Business Review, September 26 1983. (ATL ref: H-725-008)

161

address through to the remarkable TV confrontation between the two party leaders a few days before the poll. In his well-fitting suits and carefully styled hair and fashionable spectacles, Lange played the part of the moderate, consensus-seeking prime minister elect. While the outcome was not unexpected, the margin of Labour's victory was.

In an extraordinary week, before Labour was officially installed, Lange and his key colleagues faced down Sir Robert Muldoon's initial refusal to devalue the currency, reached a temporary accommodation with the U.S. secretary of state about ship visits, and gave the South African consulate its marching orders.

It was truly a baptism of fire which Lange, the youngest prime minister for more than a century, survived coolly, his sense of humour undimmed.

Lange's major problem, now that he was actually prime minister, was the lack of a coherent political philosophy. As Bruce Jesson wrote in 1987: "Lange is not inclined to abstract systems of belief, either in religion or politics." [8] In his maiden speech he had described his politics as 'democratic socialism' which, after the nostalgic faith in traditional Labour values, the family and community, were peeled away, was of little concrete help in dealing with the economic problems that confronted the fourth Labour government.

As Jesson also wrote: "Lange's lack of policies – and his lack of political cronies – left him prey to the ambitions of other people." [9] One senior Labour politician, Roger Douglas, shy, colourless and single-mindedly determined, had given a great deal of thought to New Zealand's economic problems and had clear, simple answers and a body of international theory to back them up. While the Labour Party in opposition had been preoccupied with moral and foreign policy issues, Douglas had debated his free market views with like-minded people in business, the universities and the Treasury and Reserve Bank, long under Muldoon's interventionist thumb.

He had a monetarist – small government, low inflation – agenda but he lacked the opportunity to implement it. He was one step closer when Lange asked his then friend to be Labour's finance spokesman in 1983.

Barely a year later Douglas was minister of finance, the 20 percent devaluation, to stop the country's coffers emptying out, in turn justifying removal of the mechanisms that had protected New Zealand industry for so long. Douglas even had the blueprint at hand, a comprehensive briefing document prepared by treasury bureaucrats. Their shared goal was a radically deregulated economy, driven by market forces. It called for, as Jane Kelsey has written, " …. Less government, the privatisation of state assets and businesses, increased economic efficiency, reduced public expenditure, and rolling back the welfare state." [10]

Lange and Douglas were, in 1984, the perfect political team. As Colin James wrote: "Douglas was so determined on big changes to economic policy that he had several times put his career on the line rather than compromise. And Lange was temperamentally ideally suited to be his instrument." [11] There is no doubt about Lange's commitment to the government's economic reforms during its first term. The apparent rationality of Douglas's ideas appealed to him; the puritan streak to his Methodism reconciled him to the need for 'pain' before 'gain'; his most senior colleagues were young and receptive to new ideas and change; he was evangelical about 'selling' policies that were the antithesis of 'Muldoonism'.

In a major and very rapid restructuring of the New Zealand economy, that many agreed was long overdue, Labour deregulated the money and foreign exchange markets, introduced radical tax changes (including a goods and services tax, now embedded in the language as GST), eliminated agricultural subsidies and removed much of the

While speculative fortunes were being made, wage earners had little 'gain' to show for their 'pain'. Al Nisbet, Sunday Times, *January 25 1987. (ATL ref: H-725-009)*

manufacturing sector's protection.

"I was very enthusiastic about GST," says Lange. "For the first time a lot of people I loathed were going to pay tax because they had to eat." [12]

The 'efficiency' catch-cry was also behind the creation of nine state-owned enterprises (SOEs) carved out of former government trading departments. As Jane Kelsey wrote: " The public service was widely perceived as inefficient, privileged, self- perpetuating and in need of a good shake-up." [13]

Staid economic predictability vanished and everyone struggled to cope with the see-sawing ups and downs of inflation, interest rates, share prices and the Kiwi dollar as local and international 'market forces' buffeted the country.

While the economy dominated the headlines, Labour's eager-beaver cabinet was committed to other initiatives – a Bill of Rights, legal clout for the Treaty of Waitangi, official language status for Maori, a new environment ministry, homosexual law reform, the restructuring of local government – that were to be significant and, as they came to fruition, would garner their own share of controversy.

Despite growing economic concerns, the government's overall dynamism, coupled with National's stumbling performance, resulted in Labour winning again, and even increasing its majority, in 1987. But Lange's powerlessness in slowing Douglas's headlong pursuit of economic nirvana was a growing frustration as it became clearer there was little 'gain' to compensate for mounting 'pain', particularly among Labour's core constituency. The October 1987 sharemarket crash, barely two months after the election, was dramatic and ugly confirmation of the dangers of the totally unfettered market.

The concept of 'Rogernomics' might have been attractive, but Lange could no longer ignore the detail of its consequences. Keith Eunson wrote: ".... while he was initially able to accept the need and inevitability for what Labour began under the 'Rogernomics' label, he came to recognise the downside as his compassion began to gnaw at his beliefs as a Christian socialist." [14] His concern intensified as there was a mushrooming of company closures and unemployment.

The battle lines were being drawn. Douglas, his ideological lieutenant Richard Prebble and other

On economic matters at least, the fourth Labour government bore very little resemblance to the first. Eric Heath, Dominion, *February 23 1987. (ATL ref: J-013-001)*

Auckland MPs who had opportunistically masterminded Lange's rise to party leadership, and had needed him as the public face of 'Rogernomics', increasingly saw him as the principal obstacle to the introduction of a flat-scale tax system, an article of faith among 'supply-side' economists, the deregulation of labour unions and state sector privatisation.

Douglas was now well into his 'reform' stride. It was time to move from the halfway house of corporatisation to privatisation. The real purpose of corporatisation had been fudged in 1986; now there was talk of 'one-off' sales to reduce the overseas debt. But by early 1988 the boards of all the state corporations, and it was now a long list, were asked to identify any impediments to their sale. The sale of New Zealand's 'family silver' was underway, to underwrite the $2 billion surplus Douglas announced in his 'garage-sale' budget and, as importantly, in deference to the 'new right' tenet that private enterprise is always more efficient and flexible than state ownership.

Lange had halted flat tax planning early in 1988 and, as the 'Rogernomics' agenda looked to shift its focus to social policy areas, and put social spending at risk, he tried to further rein in Douglas in a September 1988 cabinet reshuffle, appointing two associate finance ministers. In November Lange was forced to fire SOEs minister Prebble when he called him dictatorial and irrational. The situation worsened, and Douglas followed a month later, having accused Lange of 'presidential-style' leadership that ignored cabinet's views.

Lange's problem, as his economic restructuring concerns multiplied, was his lack of a power base within caucus. He was a stranger to backroom politicking, had never lobbied for himself, was not a networker and the few friends he had among his colleagues were now his opponents.

Over a seven month period, Lange weathered a motion of no confidence and a Douglas challenge for the parliamentary party leadership in June 1989. The final straw, in early August, was caucus voting in favour of Douglas's reinstatement to cabinet.

A week later New Zealanders were astonished, but insiders less surprised, when David Lange resigned the prime ministership and took the precaution of publicly anointing loyal deputy Geoffrey Palmer as his successor. It was a rare event for a sitting New Zealand prime minister to go without being forced out by ill health, age or the certainty of losing a caucus leadership vote. After five years in the job, he was the youngest prime ministerial retiree for over a century.

After his resignation, Lange served as attorney general, but outside cabinet until the 1990 election; he then had two more terms on the opposition benches. Later he regretted he stayed on so long. As he said: "Once you've been in government, it is really like instant coffee being in Opposition. It's not the real thing. It's not a heady brew that spins you away and makes the senses whirl." [15]

David and Naomi Lange officially separated in November 1989, their marriage under increasing strain after her 1984 decision to continue living in Auckland. Lange married Margaret Pope, his former speechwriter in 1992, and they have one daughter. Over recent years he has written a newspaper column and several books and lectured extensively overseas despite serious health problems – Lange has been a diabetic for 20 years and had an angioplasty in 1988, and by-pass surgery in 1995 and 2001; in mid-2002 he was diagnosed with amaloydosis, an extremely rare, incurable disease that affected his kidney function. Treatment has included chemotherapy and regular blood transfusions.

Lange has also fought, then dropped after five years, an expensive libel action against a national magazine and its political columnist. Ironically, the action, perhaps another indication that Lange never developed a necessarily thick political skin, appears to have widened rather than diminished press freedom.

Richard Prebble's approach to the sale of government assets was uncompromisingly blunt. Bill Paynter, National Business Review, *November 3 1988. (ATL ref: H-725-011)*

David Lange will be remembered as one of New Zealand's most interesting prime ministers. His charismatic appeal ensured Labour two terms in government, six years that produced as much far-reaching change as the Liberals in the 1890s or the first Labour government elected in 1935.

After the 1987 election, he became the first prime minister in the modern era to hold the education portfolio. It was his way, Harvey McQueen has pointed out, to protect education from the zealots: "The New Right wanted to make it a marketplace commodity." [16] And, as minister, he presided over the major, 'Tomorrow's Schools' administrative changes.

Foreign minister during Labour's first term, he built on New Zealand's anti-nuclear reputation in a difficult environment: the sinking of Greenpeace's *Rainbow Warrior* by French agents in Auckland Harbour in July 1985 and the effective demise of the ANZUS defence alliance with Labour banning port visits by nuclear-armed or powered warships and the United States' unbending 'neither confirm nor deny' policy. Although initially ambivalent about banning nuclear-powered ships, he became an impressive advocate of New Zealand's stand, most memorably in the widely televised Oxford Union debate in March 1985. In addition, there was a greater focus on international aid, a less paternalistic South Pacific perspective and an end to equivocation about apartheid.

David Lange also had the political and personal courage to try to slow the "relentless juggernaut of the New Right", as he put it, when he recoiled from the damage being done to so many New Zealand lives.

As Helen Clark later said: "David saw what Roger was offering as a means to an end. But in fact, of course, the means utterly perverted the end. That was tragic." [17]

Lange's greatest skills were individualistic. With his devastating wit, he could destroy an opposition attack in the House or inspire a town hall audience. In part the self-defence mechanism of a one-time 'fat boy', Lange's effortless one-liners were often personal and cruel: Jim Bolger had "all the intellectual rigour of an amoeba" and Winston Peters was "the only member of Parliament named after a concrete block, and I can understand that". He was a loner, often lonely and easily wounded, not a team player or builder of alliances. At

times Lange inspired the nation; on a more personal level he often seemed unable to inspire his colleagues. The Lange government will be most remembered for its seismic changes to the New Zealand economy, yet his role in these was limited.

"Initially, Lange revelled in freeing the economy from the Muldoon straight-jacket," says John Henderson. "And he understood more economics than many people have given him credit for." [18]

David Lange has not, as some have claimed, tried to distance himself from the 1984-87 economic reforms. "In fact, I spent 10 years on the lecture circuit bragging about them," he says. [19]

The economic reformers who had pushed for Lange's elevation to the leadership were contemptuous of his mid-course change of heart; traditional Labour voters were dismayed that he had been a 'Rogernomics'

Lange, increasingly concerned at the direction 'Rogernomics' was taking, could no longer work with Douglas. Frank Greenall, Dominion Sunday Times, August 6 1989. (ATL ref: J-012-005)

fellow-traveller for so long. Now David Lange's appointment to the exclusive Order of New Zealand in the 2003 Queen's Birthday honours list shows that, with the passing of time, it is also possible to see him as a big man who gave new confidence to a small country.

As Chris Laidlaw wrote: "Labour's foreign policy, compared with the fawning sycophantism of the previous decade, was utterly refreshing. Here at last were a few statements of principle and a willingness to extend our psychological comfort zone out beyond the United States and Britain." [20]

33
SIR GEOFFREY WINSTON PALMER
1942-

"He was always more concerned about process than ideology"

In an era when politics was a profession, although not one highly rated by the public, Geoffrey Palmer was really an interloper, an enthusiastic amateur. He came to Parliament a successful legal academic, his passion for and expertise in the law and exceptional organisational ability wafting him to the political heights, and then he left, with barely a backward glance, for an even more successful career in another branch of the law. In essence, he was more interested in constitutional law reform than he was in being a politician or even prime minister.

Geoffrey Palmer was certainly not a typical Labour Party politician. Like David Lange, his upbringing was solidly middle class; unlike Lange his early years were not permeated with Christian 'do-goodism'. There was, though, always an awareness of and feeling for history. As Palmer has written: "There was some debate about the precise time of my birth. Adolf Hitler's birthday was 20 April. Princess Elizabeth, as she then was, had her birthday on 21 April. I arrived about midnight and my father and the doctor decided to give me the benefit of the doubt – so my birthday is 21 April." [1]

Geoffrey Winston Russell Palmer was born in 1942; his father, Russell, then associate editor of the *Nelson Evening Mail*, was an admirer of Britain's wartime leader.

The Palmers were early Nelson settlers and his father chose journalism as a career as there was

Trace Hodgson, New Zealand Times, *September 29 1985. (ATL ref: H-384-168)*

not enough land in the family for three sons to go farming. It was most unusual, in the 1920s, to begin such a career with an MA in history and diploma in journalism. At Canterbury University he met Jessie Patricia Clark and they married in 1928, by which time Russell Palmer was a Christchurch *Press* journalist. The Palmers were in Nelson, after several years in Wellington, when Geoffrey was born, 11 and nine years after their two daughters.

Russell Palmer effectively ran the *Evening Mail* for years before becoming editor, his ailing predecessor clinging to the position. He wrote the editorials – campaigning for the retention of the Nelson rail link, about the cotton mill controversy, and the unfinished cathedral – so he knew the local politicians well and was influential in the community. By comparison Geoffrey Palmer's mother was quite reclusive, compensating for her intense shyness with wide-ranging and voracious reading. It was a happy childhood of eeling, whitebaiting, hop picking, visits to family farms, and trolley racing down Nelson's hills.

Palmer did not shine at primary school but first noticed the long blonde pigtails of his future wife, Margaret Hinchliff, in Standard One. His mother, always a strong influence, decided early he would be a lawyer as he "had the gift of the gab". It never occurred to him to be anything else, even though the parental expectations meant he worked harder to excel at Nelson College than he might otherwise have done. The venerable college – a state school but with English public school pretensions – encouraged his interest in drama, public speaking, music and team sports. As prefect-in-charge-of-dancing there were visits to Nelson College for Girls, where Margaret Hinchcliff was deputy head girl, to arrange joint classes. Soon they were inseparable.

At the beginning of 1960, when he was 17, Geoffrey Palmer began law and arts degrees at Victoria University of Wellington. His mother died from cancer at the end of the year and his father, who never recovered from the loss, followed less than three years later. Palmer and Margaret Hinchcliff married in late 1963 and during the next three years, while completing his BA LLB, Palmer worked as a law clerk and, drawing on the experience of holiday stints reporting for the *Evening Mail*, wrote for and edited the university newspaper, *Salient*.

His interest in journalism and writing and enthusiasm for political science, his arts degree major, were to be enduring influences.

Palmer qualified as a solicitor in 1966 and was soon conducting court cases that attracted law report mentions. He was offered a Wellington law firm partnership and scholarships to law schools in British Columbia and Chicago. The Palmers, with the young son who was to become a law professor like his father, sailed for the United States, barely aware at the time that the University of Chicago's graduate law school was one of the best in the world. Thousands applied each year for 150 places. While in Chicago, studying for his law doctorate, Palmer met Sir Owen Woodhouse, chairman of a royal commission set up to recommend changes to New Zealand's personal injury law. It was a meeting that later led to some challenging and significant assignments. At the end of 1967, Geoffrey Palmer graduated cum laude – the highest possible distinction and the coveted passport to academic appointments around the world.

Back in New Zealand, Palmer lectured in political science at Victoria University and relished the opportunity to help the Labour Department draft a White Paper on the Woodhouse personal injury report.

In 1969, the Palmers were back in the United States, now with a daughter as well. Three years as law professor at the mid-western University of Iowa, specialising in personal injury law, was followed by a further year at the University of Virginia. In 1973, on Sir Owen Woodhouse's recommendation, Palmer was appointed principal assistant to an Australian committee of enquiry on personal injury. Then, in July 1974, he returned to his Wellington alma mater, spending the next five years as professor of English and New Zealand Law, broadcasting and writing, with visiting appointments back at Iowa and at Wolfson College, Oxford.

During this period, Geoffrey Palmer became actively involved in politics. His academic interest had deepened while at Chicago where he started going to political meetings and saw, at first-hand, the wretched living conditions of the city's poor blacks. Back in the United States in the early 1970s, Palmer was active in the Democratic Party and then, working for the Whitlam government in Australia, helped campaign for Labour at the 1974 election.

As he has admitted, Palmer could have stood comfortably enough for either major political party in New Zealand. His growing interest in entering politics was, he has written, because of a "desire to reform, do big reforms, particularly in the legal area. There was not a great deal of idealogical edge to my political thinking". [2] As much as anything, it was his personal observation of the vested interests opposing change in Australia that led him to join the Labour Party in 1975. The beginnings were not auspicious: involvement in the backfiring 'Citizens for Rowling' campaign and an unsuccessful 1976 attempt to win the Nelson candidature following the sitting member's death.

During the next two years Palmer was one of the talented group of young activists who helped Bill Rowling rebuild a badly demoralised Labour Party; the reward was the safe Christchurch Central seat in a 1979 by-election. With his intellectual capacity, administrative ability, legal expertise and solid debating skills, Palmer was soon Bill Rowling's special assistant and then sufficiently indispensable to be elected David Lange's deputy when Bill Rowling went in 1983. He carried no divisive Labour Party 'baggage'; on the other hand he had served a very modest apprenticeship and there was little sign then, or later, of instinctive political skills.

A deputy leader, or deputy prime minister, is often the ambitious No. 2 positioning himself for a putsch. But not Geoffrey Palmer. He was David Lange's loyal lieutenant through the 1984-87 period, to the extent of papering over the prime minister's diffidence in confronting problems, lack of interest in some areas of policy and his infrequent involvement in cabinet committees. Hugh Templeton saw the situation clearly: "In the New Zealand system, where the management of the House, the caucus and the party falls to the deputy, Palmer's capacity for work and mastery of detail made him ideal." [3] Or, as Palmer put it himself: "Success in the job is measured by what does not go wrong but could have." [4]

As the government's political manager, he also facilitated the Douglas economic revolution. He admired its neatness and logic, but he was always more concerned about process than ideology. Palmer played a central role in implementing Rogernomics, but was relatively untainted by it. As Bruce Jesson noted, it was as if he had "done these things on behalf of other people, rather like a lawyer carrying out his brief." [5] As well, Palmer was leader of the House, attorney general and minister of justice.

But Palmer was also loyal to the constitutional niceties that distinguish Westminster government from other systems. It was obvious to him, as it was to Lange, that, particularly after the 1987 sharemarket crash, the government's bold economic reforms were not producing the promised results. But to Palmer, cabinet decisions, like the December 1987 flat tax proposal, were, once made, sacrosanct; to Lange, the tax decision was a mistake that needed to be rectified, unilaterally if necessary.

Lange's disbanding of the troika of economic ministers – Douglas, Prebble and Caygill – was part of his largely ineffectual attempt to move the government's focus to social matters. Douglas and Prebble, original Lange backers, were now bitter opponents, despite Palmer's attempts at diplomacy. Privately, Palmer was furious. He later wrote: " …[Lange] destroyed his own government by going about changing the policy in the way that he did. He was always reluctant to argue for a position in cabinet.…Failure to follow the sound orthodoxies of cabinet government had an effect on David Lange's government from which it never recovered." [6] Palmer found his position increasingly difficult and after Lange's 1989 Anzac Day speech at Yale University, which did not reflect the government's defence views, he informed the prime minister he no longer enjoyed the confidence of cabinet.

David Lange resigned shortly after Labour's caucus reinstated Roger Douglas to cabinet in early August. Palmer had not expected or wanted to be PM. He later wrote: "I never really wanted the job of prime minister. I took it out of a sense of duty when David resigned. I did not think we could win the 1990 election after what had happened. But I was determined to do my best. In rugby parlance, what I got from Lange was a hospital pass." [7]

Ozone friendly. *Palmer chalked up significant achievements as minister of the environment. Klarc (Laurence Clark),* New Zealand Herald, *July 22 1989. (ATL ref: A-299-166)*

There was, as Bruce Jesson has written, "the fundamental contradiction between its [the government's] economic and social policies, between the removal of the state from the economic sphere and its continued role in social spending." [8]

Palmer's 13 months as prime minister were by far the most frustrating, and least satisfying, of the 11 years he spent as a politician. There were now two feuding camps within the Labour caucus, a growing popular perception that the reforms had not lived up to their ambitious expectations and a personal inability to project the sort of prime ministerial 'image' the media and public had come to expect. Palmer found it difficult to talk in the generalised sound bites that often blur the truth and offended his belief in moderate, balanced discussion of issues.

To him – although he was accused of being naïve and unworldly – truth and honesty were important. He was not going to change, but he recognised he was out of step, almost a throwback to the 19th century patrician politician doing his service. He later wrote: " It is better in politics to be confident than to be right …Sincerity is not important but the appearance of it is. Often the most successful politicians are the most cynical." [9]

He appeared a wooden and humorless academic – he was nicknamed, like Malcolm Fraser in Australia, 'The Prefect' – but his attempt to 'lighten up', tooting the trumpet he had played in the Nelson College dance band, was roundly ridiculed. Media relations were not helped by Palmer's clear lack of regard for much of the country's political journalism.

Keith Eunson wrote: ".... Palmer was almost always the lawyer .... somewhat aloof, austere and seeming judicial, certainly lacking the charisma his predecessor wore like a second skin." [10]

Further, Palmer had been more effective implementing colleagues' policies than avoiding political pitfalls with his own. Maori affairs initiatives "pursued for impeccable liberal objectives," as Colin James wrote, ".... put the government up a boulder-strewn creek without a paddle. They heightened expectations among Maori over land and fishing rights and the influence of the Treaty of Waitangi, heightened fears among pakeha, and were followed by muddle over devolution, messy negotiations and unilateral manoeuvres." [11]

Geoffrey Palmer had easily beaten Mike Moore in the leadership vote when Lange resigned, but his fiercely ambitious No 3 now positioned himself as a more populist, alternative leader. As Labour sagged in the polls, and the 1990 election neared, desperate caucus members in marginal seats saw Moore as their last, slim chance of political survival. With a cynicism that dismayed Palmer, his colleagues, including his deputy Helen Clark, were more concerned about Moore's ability to claw back a few marginals than his prime ministerial credentials. Gauging the feelings of his cabinet colleagues, Palmer resigned in early September.

Geoffrey Palmer was an activist politician. As Colin James wrote in 1989: "Palmer .... is consumed by the need for reform, to tidy things up. If the economy is in a mess, restructure it; if the criminal law or resource law is antiquated, modernise it; if there are inequities for Maoris, eradicate them; if social policy is not delivering what the people want, clean it up." [12]

Palmer introduced significant parliamentary reforms. "Although they represent the most significant reform of Parliament this century," Geoff Skene wrote in 1987, "they are best regarded

Palmer's original Bill of Rights was savaged, with legislation finally passed in 1990. Tom Scott, Evening Post, March 22 1986. (ATL ref: H-725-022)

as an evolutionary rather than a revolutionary step in the development of New Zealand's political institutions." [13] Palmer was the driving force behind a raft of major legislation, some of it enacted by National: State-Owned Enterprises Act 1985, Constitution Act 1986, Ozone Layer Protection Act 1990, NZ Bill of Rights Act 1990, and Resource Management Act 1991 and he set up the royal commission that recommended the MMP option. He also gained enduring satisfaction from his time as minister of the environment, taking up the portfolio at the beginning of Labour's second term and retaining it after becoming prime minister. Among his achievements were the outlawing of driftnet fishing in the South Pacific and ozone layer legislation. As Eunson wrote: "…he was an environmentalist who recognised early that this was to be a major legal and political issue internationally as well as in New Zealand, and he staked a claim then as a legislator and as a spokesman on the subject which continues increasingly to occupy the minds of world leaders." [14]

After leaving politics Palmer returned to academia – teaching law at Victoria University and at the University of Iowa in the United States – before founding New Zealand's first practice specialising in public law, in partnership with one of his Wellington faculty colleagues, Mai Chen. Chen Palmer & Partners has flourished, he has continued to write and broadcast widely and teach short courses at both universities, more comfortable in a role as constitutional adviser to the nation than a practising politician. He was appointed New Zealand Commissioner, International Whaling Commission in 2003.

In 1991 he was knighted (KCMG) and made an honorary Companion of the Order of Australia (AC).

By temperament and circumstances Geoffrey Palmer was not a significant prime minister, but as the manager of the reforming 1984-87 Labour government, and as justice and environment minister responsible for major legislative change during the 1984-90 period, he was certainly a significant late 20th century politician. And, as he liked to remind people, his dry sense of humour intact, he had one singular distinction among the country's modern day prime ministers – he was the only one who had never won or lost a general election.

Shortly after his resignation, Tim Grafton wrote in *The Dominion*: "In retrospect, Mr Palmer was an elegant wading bird unsuited to the mud of politics." [15]

Palmer – sometimes drawn as an Easter Island statue – resigned in September 1990. Bob Brockie, Evening Post, *June 6 1990. (ATL ref: A-298-165)*

34
MICHAEL KENNETH MOORE
1949-

"His urgent restlessness has always been infectious, his enthusiasms contagious"

Mike Moore was a mass of contradictions. He had a burning ambition to be prime minister and few of the necessary qualities. He was 'old-style' Labour and became a fervent proponent of the 'market economy'. He was a scheming political organiser who dreamed lofty dreams. He was a one-man ideas factory who rarely slowed long enough to get any of them into production.

He was certainly one of New Zealand's most colourful late 20th century politicians and one of the very few to ever have more than a brief, walk-on part on the world stage.

Mike Moore's beginnings, and much of his early life, were inauspicious. He was born in 1949, in Whakatane, the middle of three sons to parents of Irish heritage. He grew up in Kawakawa, North Auckland, where Alan and Audrey Moore owned a second-hand shop. The death of his father in 1955 was traumatic, in part because Moore spent the next years living with various family members and attending numerous schools. The most important of these was Dilworth, the well-funded private Auckland school that caters for boys from deprived or troubled families. Although Mike Moore was eventually expelled, Dilworth's high standards and dedicated teachers had a lasting influence. It was there Moore listened to Parliament on a crystal set and, being poor at sport because of a malformed foot, became a voracious reader.

Back in Northland, where his mother had remarried and moved to a farm at Otira, Moore took happily to

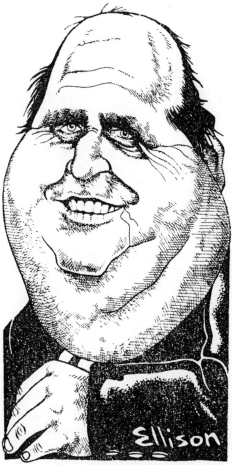

Anthony Ellison, Sunday Star, November 26, 1986. (ATL ref: H-384-153)

the country life but his reading also opened up worlds beyond Northland's teenage culture of cars and beer, often mixed in dangerous proportions. Holiday work at AFFCO's Moerewa freezing works made a profound impression, Moore later writing: "Fourteen is a vulnerable age and I was horrified to see men drink beer for lunch and bet their unopened pay packets playing poker. I kept my head down, banked my money and determined that I wouldn't spend my life working on the chain there, or anywhere near a freezing works." [1]

It had, of course, been the expectation, with Moore taking technical rather than academic subjects at school. There was too wide a gap to bridge when the family moved to Auckland and he began but did not finish the sixth form year at Papatoetoe High. With the impetuousness and self-confidence that became his trademarks, the 15 year old Mike Moore left school, found work as a brickie's labourer and saved £60 for corrective surgery on his foot.

A little later, settling into a new printing works job and living in a rented room at a down-at-heel Ponsonby boarding house, Moore joined the youth section of the Labour Party in Roskill. His parents had been Labour supporters, but the main reason was to meet people in a city where he knew very few.

In fact, Mike Moore's first direct political involvement was with the Printers' Union; he campaigned against the Vietnam War and then, only 18, found himself on the Auckland Trades' Council.

In 1966 Moore served a valuable electioneering apprenticeship, working for acknowledged political strategist Colin Moyle in his Manakau electorate and learning more from Roger Douglas, when he stood for the same seat in 1969. Moore became youth representative on Labour's national executive and travelled widely overseas, largely at his own cost, seeking out socialist party conferences on several continents.

By 1972 Mike Moore, now well-known in Labour Party circles, was asked to stand in Eden; it would be a suitable blooding until a safer Auckland seat became available. He took a year off work, conducted some of the country's first political polls, devoured every book he could find on campaigning, and devised a canvassing system that identified critical swinging voters. In the event, the 23 year old Moore astonished friends and opponents by winning the seat.

The campaign was exhilarating and the prospect of a Norman Kirk led-government exciting. But Moore had few illusions. As he wrote later: "My three year re-election campaign started the night I was elected." [2] Despite the energy he poured into electorate work the task grew demonstrably more difficult as Kirk's illness and death, falling produce prices and the first oil shock paralysed government decision-making. Meanwhile, Moore won the heart of Yvonne Dereany, daughter of Labour Party stalwarts in Eden, and they married in 1975; later in the year he lost the electorate.

Broke, out of a job and without tertiary qualifications to fall back on, Mike Moore now faced the most difficult years of his life with characteristic and stubborn determination. Initially, the only job he could find was as night watchman on a harbour dredge; he used the time to read and plot the future, deciding to focus on trade policy and tourism, key areas largely neglected by his former Labour colleagues. Then he was an untrained and highly unorthodox social worker at Oakley Hospital, a secure mental institution. He was, of course, marking time, but the Labour Party seemed loath to welcome back their junior vice president to parliamentary duties. He was not wanted again in Eden and he missed selection in Mangere and Papatoetoe. He was then diagnosed with cancer which responded well to radiotherapy. Despite 'carpetbagger' accusations, Mike Moore now won selection in the National-held Papanui electorate in Christchurch. Early in 1978 the Moores moved south, their financial problems eased when Yvonne was chosen to 'front' a children's television programme. Once again Moore campaigned all year, using a computerised system to specifically target key groups in the community. The result was a resounding win and the biggest swing to Labour in the country.

Two days later Mike Moore was told his cancer was back and the prognosis very poor. He began chemotherapy in Christchurch after Christmas. Amazingly, as he lost his hair and five stone in weight, the media did not discover how ill he was. In time the tumours retreated, Moore felt stronger and his hair began to grow back, but he was not well enough to return to Parliament until September 1979.

Late in 1980, Moore was on the fringes of the abortive attempt to replace Bill Rowling with David Lange, a leadership change that was inevitable after Labour lost again in 1981. When Rowling stepped down in February 1983, Mike Moore narrowly lost the deputy's position to Geoffrey Palmer but was confirmed as Labour's No 3 and opposition spokesman for overseas trade and tourism, supporting CER despite his party's rejection of the agreement and Roger Douglas's call for radical economic change. Labour was now the government-in-waiting and Moore's 'Wednesday Club', which brought in leading decision-makers to address caucus members, underlined the point.

Mike Moore was a member of the 'inner circle' that met at a Mangere hotel the day after Labour won a stunning victory at the July 1984 election. Faced with a major economic crisis, Lange, Palmer and Moore accepted Douglas's prescription to avert the crisis. But subsequently, Mike Moore played little part in the administration's most significant decision-making. He did not hold key portfolios and his evangelical devotion to the development of trade meant he was often out of the country, leading a seemingly endless succession of trade delegations – catholic mixes of business leaders, unionists, bureaucrats and politicians – to Australia, Japan, China, Southeast Asia, the Middle East, Europe, Russia, Latin America, Sri Lanka, India, Pakistan, Turkey, and Central Europe. Very often they travelled in modestly modified RNZAF 727 troop-carriers.

With his boundless energy – all the more remarkable considering his near fatal cancer – and his creative, if unstructured, enthusiasm he was successful and popular as New Zealand's No 1 trade and tourism salesman. There were repeated trips to Europe, continuing a well-established bi-partisan tradition, to renegotiate a new butter access agreement and he set up the Market Development Board to plan the country's trading future. Moore's enthusiasm for the General Agreement on Tariffs and Trade's (GATT) objective of reducing and eliminating international trade barriers sat comfortably with Labour's economic thinking, and he played a prominent role in launching GATT's Uruguay Round at Punta del Este in 1985, with agriculture on the agenda for the first time. As Moore wrote: "Subsidising agriculture and protecting markets is just a clumsy way of exporting social and political problems." [3] Moore was later a member of the International Eminent Persons Group on World Trade which lobbied for a successful conclusion to the Uruguay Round.

Mike Moore's priorities as tourism minister were entirely pragmatic: it made good business sense to let the government's Tourist Hotel Corporation compete more freely in the marketplace, but to end Air New Zealand's monopoly of flights in and out of the country. As minister of recreation and sport, Moore established the sports and cultural ambassador programme, set up the Hillary Commission and encouraged the beginnings of the America's Cup yachting saga.

Mike Moore was like the small, wide-eyed boy in a toy shop; to him the world is a wonderful toy shop of facts, figures, ideas and schemes to be picked over and sampled. He was on a never-ending search for ideas to increase the further processing of New Zealand produce, to attract more tourists, or to export our engineering and technical skills. He was, in business jargon terms, a lateral thinker. As he wrote: "I had always thought I was talented at seeing toothpicks not forests, surimi not hoki, and lamb burgers not frozen carcasses." [4]

Mike Moore was something of a mystery to his colleagues. He was clearly ambitious but his backroom politicking skills were being used to cajole trade ministers overseas or exporters at home rather than in the lobbying of his fellow MPs. They were confused by his seemingly irreconcilable political views and the torrent of ideas that spilled out of speeches and interviews. They admired his communication skills, but thought his woolly rhetoric too insubstantial and unfocused for him to be prime ministerial material Nevertheless, he had some support for the leadership in 1989.

His opposite number, National's Oxford-educated Hugh Templeton saw something his colleagues didn't. "Mike Moore in my view was the best natural politician in the House. He had an eye for our regional future, having already written about the need to link CER with a South Pacific community." [5]

Undeterred by his rejection, and with his trade and tourism goals either achieved or unachievable, Moore now turned serious attention to becoming prime minister. By the beginning of 1990 there was growing realisation, skilfully prodded by Moore's office, that the marginal seats of a number of government backbenchers were wobbling badly. Geoffrey's Palmer's uncertain performance included the dropping of experienced cabinet ministers and a poorly timed

visit to Australia. While he was away deputy PM Helen Clark polled her cabinet colleagues about a leadership change; it was a hint Palmer chose not to ignore. Moore, his colleagues now reasoned, had the 'good Kiwi bloke' image that worked across party lines and was a skilled campaigner. It was desperate stuff. As Keith Eunson wrote: "Even opting for Mike Moore as a hot-shot vote-getter was like trying to win Lotto without a ticket, especially in view of the time frame Labour was working to." [6]

Although Moore knew Palmer was likely to stand down after the election, it had always been his ambition to sit behind the big desk on the ninth floor of the Beehive. As his successor Jim Bolger later wrote: "Mike thought it better to be prime minister for a few weeks than never to have had the job at all." [7]

So, just 59 days before the 1990 election, Labour

Moore was New Zealand's No 1 salesman. Trace Hodgson, New Zealand Listener, *August 31 1985. (ATL ref: H-725-007)*

had its third leader in 13 months. Bruce Jesson was not impressed: "Moore's election as leader was one of the most cynical political actions that I can remember. In order for it to work everyone had to act out a charade. People who scoff at Moore in private had to take him seriously in public. Fellow MPs had to accept Moore's innovations in policy without demur. The union movement had to pretend that this was a worker-friendly government, despite having being battered beyond belief by Labour's economic policies." [8]

Predictably, National won at a canter, finishing with a massive 39-seat majority. Less predictably, Mike Moore, at his most disarming, admitted that the change in Labour leadership had made no difference at all.

New PM Bolger took Moore to GATT talks in Brussels early in 1991. It was both a calculated act of bi-partisanship and recognition of the important trade role his predecessor had played through the 1980s. (The Uruguay Round, finally concluded in December 1993, was critical to the transformation of the New Zealand meat industry – and the trebling of sheepmeat's export income over the last decade to $3.1 billion.)

During the next three years Moore led a seriously depleted Labour opposition with trademark verve. As Eunson noted: "Moore with those Panda-like black ringed eyes, big head and up-front personality had an ability to create and then contribute to his own mythology with an ebullience born of his innate political optimism."[9] The 1993 election was a close run contest. Jim Bolger later wrote about the strange, highly emotional late night speech Mike Moore made when it had become clear that National had narrowly survived as a minority government: " 'It will be a cold dark night for the Bolger-Richardson government,' he intoned in a voice that would have gone pretty well on the soundtrack of a Dracula movie. Before he had finished he had done everything short of claiming victory."[10]

Moore, who had now lost twice, was swiftly replaced by Helen Clark. To a man who lived and breathed politics more than most, rejection by his colleagues was as devastating as it had been predictable.

As Eunson wrote: "For a longish time he seemed to be in the Labour Party but not really of it, and whenever olive branches were held out to entice him inside the inner councils he tended to shuffle his feet, and mumble excuses without making the decision either to raise an independent standard outside the embrace of the party, or to stay."[11] In 1996, when other Labour Party colleagues were breaking away to position themselves for the new MMP environment, there were media stories about Moore forging alliances with several disaffected MPs and even starting his own party, but in the end he did not make the break and before that year's election he was back as foreign affairs and trade spokesman.

Labour was just behind on election night and then lost the first skirmish of the MMP era when, to general surprise, NZ First went into coalition with National instead. Mike Moore continued his strong advocacy of international trade from the opposition benches until, in 1998, he identified a new challenge: the director generalship of the World Trade Organisation (WTO), formerly GATT, based in Geneva. Supported by National prime minister Jenny Shipley and former PM Jim Bolger, then ambassador in Washington, Moore ran a typically energetic and innovative campaign. He

Moore threw all his considerable energy into the 1993 election, hopeless though the situation was. Garrick Tremain, Otago Daily Times, *September 28 1993. (ATL ref: A-299-113)*

Mike Moore became the director general of the WTO in September 1990. Jim Hubbard, Dominion, *March 25 1999.* (ATL ref: H-725-020)

began an outsider and finally wooed sufficient of the 130 plus WTO member countries to win a shortened term when the organisation could not decide between him and a Thai rival.

It was a tumultuous three years and catapulted Mike Moore into the international headlines like no New Zealand politician before him. The serious rioting at the WTO ministerial meetings in Seattle just after he took over in September 1999 could have derailed the organisation. But Moore – who was awarded the Order of New Zealand in December 1999 – worked tirelessly to restore confidence before launching a new round of multilateral trade negotiations in Doha, Qatar, at the 2001 ministerial meeting that also admitted China and a number of other countries to the WTO. As Dani Rodrik wrote: "Much of Moore's hard work between Seattle and Doha was directed at putting agriculture at the centre of a 'development' agenda that would not only capture the moral high ground but also make the momentum for agricultural liberalisation unstoppable by enlisting developing-country support on the issue …. This brilliant tactic bridged both of the divides that had led to the collapse of the Seattle ministerial meeting." [12]

Since his term ended in August 2002, Mike Moore has led a comfortable life of global consultancy and keynote speechmaking at international conferences. He can be excused a certain satisfaction, as a self-taught, self-made man, whose ideas were rarely taken seriously at home, that he has also been appointed to adjunct professorships at two Australian universities and is a visiting professor at a British one.

His latest book, more substantial than the number he wrote for largely political purposes during his parliamentary career, promotes globalisation and free trade, but he is not a blinkered apologist. In *A World Without Walls*, he wrote: "It's dangerous when free trade and the virtues of markets are lifted to a level of theology. No single idea solves everything." [13] He's also firm on the need for 'corporate social responsibility'.

Mike Moore might now be bustling around the world stage, but some things won't change. As Colin James wrote: "Moore will be a young man in a hurry when he's 70. His urgent restlessness has always been infectious, his enthusiasms contagious." [14]

35

JAMES BRENDAN BOLGER
1935-

"In some ways he was an interesting mix of Holland, Holyoake and Muldoon"

Jim Bolger was one of the more under-estimated of New Zealand prime ministers. His solid, even stolid, determination and unflappability had more in common with the Holyoake 1960s than the sound-bite frenetics of the 1990s, yet he was prime minister for seven years, longer than nearly all of his modern day counterparts.

It was remarkable that he became prime minister at all. The last six prime ministers, Moore excepted, all had tertiary qualifications. Jim Bolger, a farm boy, left school as soon as he could. As well, he was second-generation Irish, Catholic and father of nine.

James Brendan was the son of Daniel and Cecilia Bolger who had left County Wexford in Ireland in 1930, swapping depression privations for the faraway promise of New Zealand. By the time Jim Bolger was born in May 1935, the second of five children, they had parlayed work on a dairy farm near Hawera into a 94-acre leasehold farm on the Taranaki coast at Rahotu.

Jim Bolger and his siblings attended the local Rahotu primary school and then Opunake High. Farm work dominated his early life. Only 10, he went to live with a neighbour to help milk cows when a son joined the air force. He left school at 15 for a routine, common in rural New Zealand in the 1950s, of working on the farm, including another 99 acres of swamp that was gradually developed, playing rugby and occasionally going to country dances on Saturday nights.

The Young Farmers' Club provided Bolger, who had

Murray Webb, Otago Daily Times.
(ATL ref: H-384-123)

hazy aspirations of becoming a lawyer, with an opportunity for public speaking and to debate farming issues. It was on a debating trip to Palmerston North that he again met Joan Riddell, the red-haired daughter of a neighbour, who had left the district to train as a teacher. He was 28 years-old when they married in 1963.

Two years later the hard working Bolgers were able to buy a sheep and beef farm near Te Kuiti. Now a farmer in his own right, Jim Bolger was soon involved with the local Federated Farmers' branch. In time he became Waikato vice-president and a national councillor. He invited politicians to the district so they could see at firsthand the consequences of drought, freezing works stoppages and tumbling wool prices. He later told Warwick Roger: "I also worked to establish a co-op meat company with union involvement to try to stop the madness of a strike a week, and that really was the bedrock of my active political involvement." [1]

Bolger was now thinking through, without the benefit of textbooks or university seminars, his own political views. His Catholic upbringing had instilled ideas about family and community and his experience with meat industry unions convinced him that individuals should be free to make their own decisions. He rejoined the National Party, which he had belonged to in Taranaki, and sought, with seven other hopefuls, the King Country nomination in 1972. He won selection and the seat, one of a handful of new MPs to join National's decimated caucus. It was a good time for newcomers to be noticed and Bolger certainly was when his maiden speech ignored convention and strongly attacked the new Kirk government.

National leader Rob Muldoon clearly approved of the young, new backbencher with the forceful debating style, rewarding him with several under-secretaryships when National surged back at the 1975 election. Hugh Templeton wrote: "A powerful speaker in caucus, Bolger made a real impact with his political feel for the key issues. An example was his querying the wisdom of the 1976 All Black tour of South Africa."[2] Two years later Jim Bolger was in cabinet as minister of fisheries and associate minister of agriculture.

In 1978, Bolger was appointed to the critical labour portfolio. Although the job had blighted the careers of other up-and-coming politicians, Bolger became a serious prime ministerial contender during his six years in the role dealing with problems like the unfinished Mangere Bridge and BNZ building in Wellington, two very obvious monuments to a serious breakdown in industrial relations. In an era when most industrial matters ended on the minister's desk, Jim Bolger's calm, even-handed and pragmatic approach even earned some grudging admiration from union leaders. Bolger also weathered Muldoon's interference in his portfolio better than other colleagues and won kudos and brickbats for opening up Saturday trading and introducing voluntary unionism.

Muldoon followed National's disastrous loss to Social Credit in the September 1980 East Coast Bays by-election with an ineffectual cabinet reshuffle. Templeton wrote: "Worse for the ambitious was [Colin] McLachlan's move from ten to eight on the front bench, a green light for the disaffected like Jim Bolger who, still sitting at nine, was furious at being superceded by an old warhorse on the point of retirement."[3]

Bolger was one of the 'colonels' who mounted a coup attempt against Muldoon while he was on an extended overseas trip. The attempt faltered with prospective leader Brian Talboys' prevarication, withered under Muldoon's savage counter attack and ended when Bolger changed sides.

In 1981, although Bolger challenged for the vacant deputy leadership against Muldoon's friend Duncan MacIntyre, his cabinet ranking moved up to five, with a seat on the front-bench, in the pre-election reshuffle. Early the next year MacIntyre stepped down after suffering a heart attack, with Bill Birch, Jim McLay and Bolger contesting the deputy's spot. McLay, who appealed to a liberal, well-educated urban constituency, won on the first ballot. As Barry Gustafson wrote: "Although Bolger appeared to be a better balance to Muldoon than McLay in both occupation and geographic location, the balance National required was not so much geographical or sectional as attitudinal."[4]

Without doubt, though, Jim Bolger was a coming man. Gustafson wrote: "Self-confident, relaxed, with a

The Descent Society. *Some months before the 1990 election Bolger unveiled the 'Decent Society' theme that was to be something of an embarrassment. Klarc (Laurence Clark),* New Zealand Herald, *October 31 1989. (ATL ref: A-299-173)*

natural charm and a rather droll humour, Bolger rarely became flustered. In some ways he was an interesting mix of Holland, Holyoake and Muldoon." [5]

National was buried by Labour's 1984 avalanche and in November Muldoon was replaced by Jim McLay with Jim Bolger, representing the rural heartland, chosen as his deputy. McLay's leadership was undermined from the beginning by an unforgiving Muldoon and that, combined with dismal poll results and a reshuffle of opposition responsibilities that offended senior colleagues, meant he lasted barely 15 months. Gustafson wrote: "Gair and Birch, two of the most capable and experienced National parliamentarians, quietly set to work to change the leadership." [6] Bolger took over in March 1986.

Jim Bolger performed creditably at the 1987 election, with support for National climbing back to a respectable 44 percent. After Labour's already divided cabinet was dealt the double whammy of the October 1987 sharemarket crash and the bitter Lange-Douglas battle for control of the government's political agenda, Bolger, now with Don McKinnon as his deputy and Ruth Richardson as shadow finance minister, went to the 1990 election with a comfortable lead in the polls and a 'Decent Society' theme that later proved an embarrassment.

After the brief euphoria of the biggest electoral swing since 1935 and a 39-seat majority, Jim Bolger was confronted, as Lange had been in 1984, with a financial crisis. The Bank of New Zealand was insolvent. The subsequent $620 million bailout led to cuts in social spending and a backdown on the election pledge to remove the unpopular superannuation surcharge. Denied a cabinet role, Muldoon brooded on the back benches before precipitating a nail-biting by-election in the Tamaki electorate; the volatile Winston Peters was sacked after a year as minister of maori affairs, and used his Tauranga bulwark as the first building block in the creation of New Zealand First. Ruth Richardson, whose policies were unflatteringly labelled 'Rogernomics on steroids', led an enthusiastic 'razor gang' assault on the ballooning deficit; her "mother of all budgets" in 1991 was a slogan that haunted National for the next two years.

It was during 1990 that Jim Bolger first demonstrated the extent of his political pragmatism. Flexibility and opportunism, rather than a fixed philosophic viewpoint, were to be his watchwords. Often breathtaking and quite unrepentant shifts of ground or reversals of policy were to help him manoeuvre successfully through one of the most complicated and challenging decades in New Zealand history. As John Campbell later wrote: "First he attacks the ANC, or in 1981, belongs to the Cabinet which uses the Springbok Tour to win re-election, then he attends Nelson Mandela'a inauguration. First he is pro-ANZUS

Jim Bolger's nuclear views shifted from pro-ANZUS and pro-bomb to maintaining the ban on nuclear-powered US warships and protesting about French testing in the Pacific. Bob Brockie, National Business Review, *February 25 1990. (ATL ref: A-298-164)*

and pro-BOMB, then he is anti-bomb and giving the French hell. First he will stand by Ruth Richardson come what may, then gives her the sack." [7] Bolger, of course, saw it differently. The point of being in politics, he liked to say, was to be in power, pointing to three election victories in a row. Political conditions, circumstances or imperatives change and politicians have to change with them.

Nevertheless, this short-term success may have damaged National in the longer term. Some commentators, including Barry Gustafson, believe that National's about-faces in 1990 led to a level of disillusionment and a collapse of membership the party had not recovered from over a decade later.

Bolger's first ministry was not, of course, always on the back foot. The Fiscal Responsibility Act in 1993 might have done away with budget night excitement but it also put an end to unpleasant 'morning after' financial surprises for incoming governments. The Employment Contracts Act, premised on the belief that employers and employees shared a common interest in productivity and profitability, was bitterly opposed; nevertheless industrial stoppages fell away spectacularly and New Zealand climbed the world competitiveness charts. Jim Bolger had a commitment to settling major Treaty of Waitangi claims and the first, the Sealord deal, was signed in September 1992. Bolger's conviction was not shared by all his colleagues. "It was argued that it was too late in the day to start rewriting our history," Jim Bolger commented later. "It was not rewriting history but learning our country's true history we were afraid of." [8]

Like Holyoake, Bolger had considerable management and negotiating skills. And, as Keith Eunson has written, they "also shared that sort of prescience that enabled them to read storm signs before the rain and thunder arrived, and make some provision to get in out of the wet." [9] At the beginning of 1993 National's poll performance was as bad as it had ever been, but Bolger kept his nerve. 'Goodwill tours' around the provinces gave flesh and blood evidence of the economic recovery appearing in Treasury reports. The public, though, was sceptical and National lost nearly all of its large parliamentary majority on election night, governing with the unusual stratagem of appointing a Labour MP, Peter Tapsell, to the speakership.

Bolger ushered in MMP (Mixed Member Proportional Representation) and then showed he was the most skilled in adapting to the new political dynamics.

MMP was the recommendation of a royal commission that reported in December 1986, but Labour was soon too pre-occupied with its own internal problems to take the matter any further. Perhaps surprisingly, National decided there was an inherent unfairness in the 'first past the post' system that had provided it with such lengthy periods in office and made a commitment to hold two referenda. As Jim Bolger later wrote: "On this occasion, principle won out over politics; something that doesn't always happen." [10]

The first referendum, in September 1992, showed New Zealanders wanted change, with MMP the

Bolger never tired of underlining the importance of trade with Asia and that New Zealand was part of a greater Asian region. Malcolm Walker, Independent, *May 21 1993. (ATL ref: H-078-002)*

preferred option. In the second, at the 1993 election, MMP nosed out the status quo. There would be an MMP election in 1996.

The next three years were particularly challenging for Jim Bolger. Firstly, he replaced the country's first woman finance minister, believing Ruth Richardson's rigidity and divisiveness increasingly unhelpful. "We were entering the era of MMP, which would demand a very different style from what Ruth had shown in the past, he later wrote, "and I was certain it was not within her to change." [11] Richardson refused any other cabinet position and her resignation, and resulting by-election, put National's whisker-thin majority at risk. But this was only the beginning, with the jockeying among parliamentarians attempting to shore up their post-MMP futures stealing headlines from more substantial matters like a run of Bill Birch budget surpluses and Treaty of Waitangi settlements to Tainui and Ngai Tahu.

A major new political grouping – the United Party – included four National MPs and two from Labour. The MMP era had not officially begun but, as Bolger later wrote: "This constant changing of their political loyalties by MPs for whatever motives meant that for the three years …. it was necessary to negotiate new coalition agreements on a regular basis to keep the government's majority." [12]

In retrospect, it's debatable how well either the public or the media understood the new political realities during and after the 1996 election campaign. Certainly no-one knew better than Jim Bolger the need to keep all conceivable coalition options open; he even talked about a 'Grand Coalition' with Labour, an idea Helen Clark promptly rejected. National also ensured a parliamentary toehold for United's Peter Dunne by not standing a candidate in Ohariu-Belmont and lessened ACT's inroads into the party vote by virtually conceding Wellington Central to Richard Prebble.

On election night Labour, and much of the country, believed New Zealand had its first woman prime minister. In fact Labour had lost much more electoral ground than National, as had potential coalition partners the Alliance and New Zealand First. It was also assumed that personal antipathy between Jim Bolger and Winston

Peters ruled out National and New Zealand First joining forces. For six long weeks the final outcome hung in the balance as NZ First negotiated with both Labour and National. In the end Bolger's patience and pragmatism won out: Winston Peters would be deputy prime minister and deliver the budget, running finance with Bill Birch; compromises had been worked out about social spending and compulsory superannuation and, in a world in which there were no prizes for coming second, Jim Bolger remained prime minister. Perhaps the outcome should not have been such a surprise. As Warwick Roger wrote: "Peters and Bolger are natural allies in a way that Peters and Anderton, Peters and Prebble, Peters and Clark can never be. Both men are well aware of that." [13]

It was a textbook study of MMP politics in action and there was now grudging respect for the politician previously known as 'Gumboot Jim' and 'Spudhead'. Eunson wrote: "Bolger became known (and apparently quite liked the sobriquet) as the 'great helmsman', largely because it was some recognition of his skill in negotiating his National government through some tricky political waters." [14] The unlikely coalition survived minor personal scandals, a ministerial resignation, the Cave Creek tragedy and the referendum

Bill Birch was Bolger's 'Mr Fix-It', the prodigiously hardworking minister who took on some of National's knottiest problems. Bob Brockie, National Business Review, *May 1993. (ATL ref: A-296-021)*

on compulsory superannuation during 1997. Nevertheless, Jim Bolger returned from a Commonwealth heads of government meeting in Edinburgh at the beginning of November to find that Jenny Shipley, then transport minister, had convinced sufficient caucus colleagues concerned about National's relationship with NZ First that it was time for a leadership change. As Eunson wrote: "Bolger was being seen as being the dog wagged by its tail Mr Peters, and an October poll placed Jenny Shipley as the front runner in any challenge to leadership." [15] Bolger accepted the inevitable, but delayed his departure until after an APEC leaders' meeting in Vancouver and a visit to China.

Jim Bolger – awarded the Order of New Zealand in December 1997 – resigned from Parliament in early April 1998 to take up his next appointment. As a politician who enjoyed the international spotlight and rubbing shoulders with world leaders his major regret was not to be chairing the major APEC (Asia Pacific Economic Co-operation) leaders' meeting in Auckland in September 1999, but he was to be there after all, renewing those friendships, as New Zealand's ambassador to Washington.

After three and a half years in Washington, and not yet ready for King Country retirement, Jim Bolger became chairman of NZ Post and its new Kiwibank subsidiary, the brainchild of an old adversary, the Alliance's Jim Anderton. It was headline news, but it should not have really been a surprise that the man who sold the Bank of New Zealand to Australians with the utmost secrecy in 1992 should accept the invitation of a Labour PM to head a bank set up to partially redress the overseas ownership balance. He is also advisory board chairman of the World Agricultural Forum based in Missouri in the United States.

Bolger's unerring political pragmatism blinkered some observers to the point that they missed the other Jim Bolger. The man who could adapt to new political realities with great ease had humane and sensible ideas on a range of issues ranging from race relations to republicanism and the importance of 'social capital', the Robert Putman concept that Bolger applied to New Zealand circumstances in a series of speeches that deserved more attention.

Warwick Roger wrote: "Nobody from his background becomes prime minister without possessing a good deal of nous. He's also tenacious, clever, cunning and more liberal (within the bounds of his Catholic religion) and, yes, even visionary than a lot of people give him credit for." [16]

Bolger came home from a Heads of Government meeting in late 1997 to find Jenny Shipley had the numbers to defeat him in caucus. Tom Scott, Evening Post, *May 12 1997. (ATL ref: H-385-063)*

36
JENNIFER MARY SHIPLEY
1952-

"Her caucus elected her expressly to be high-handed with Peters"

In a short attention-span world, long-serving prime ministers start to pall, particularly if they are uncharismatic. In part, then, Jenny Shipley became New Zealand's thirty-sixth prime minister because Jim Bolger had been good enough at the job to survive seven long years.

But nothing can diminish the very considerable achievement of being the country's first woman prime minister, rising to the top of an occupation more male-dominated, even in the 1990s, than most in the land.

Jennifer Mary Shipley was born in Gore in February 1952, the second of Len and Adele Robson's four daughters. Len Robson was a respected, liberal Presbyterian minister and the family lived in Wellington and then Blenheim. Life at the manse was middle-class but the Robsons, like most clergy, lived frugally. Shipley remembers: "My father was on a very low income and I don't recall having anything new bought for me until I was at teachers' college." [1]

It was a close, supportive family in which everyone was encouraged to use their gifts and talents. Jenny Robson showed an early public speaking ability, winning the Victoria League prize for debating at Marlborough College, but she passed School Certificate narrowly and failed University Entrance. She was best known for her swimming prowess, winning many cups and competing nationally. Her commanding physical presence in later life owed something to her sporting talent.

It was traumatic but not entirely unexpected when Len Robson died at 52, after years of serious heart attacks. Adele Robson brought up their two youngest children on a widow's benefit and Jenny, only 18 when her father died, trained as a primary schoolteacher in Christchurch, making ends meet by working in hospitals and market gardens during the holidays.

She was still at training college when she met Burton Shipley, a fifth generation central Canterbury farmer. She then taught in the Christchurch area, latterly at Greendale School, near Darfield and the Shipley land holdings. The Shipleys married in 1975 and the first of their two children, Anna, was born two years later. As Shipley said later: "It was only after I had children and moved to a rural community that I realised you could become the chattel of your husband. At that stage I had to choose whether I was going to take on a role that was being imposed on me or continue to be myself." [2] Jenny Shipley gave up teaching before Anna was born and her community involvement deepened as she willed herself out of postnatal depression following Ben's birth in 1979. She was involved in both Plunket and the local playcentre, an early leadership path trodden by a number of New Zealand women of ability. Later, from 1983-87, she was a Malvern County councillor; she attended a confidence-building Kellogg rural leadership course at Lincoln College; she held a number of National Party positions at branch, electorate and divisional levels.

It was this last involvement – and specifically watching Ruth Richardson gain selection as National's candidate and then win the neighbouring Selywn seat – that was to transform

Murray Webb, ca 1997-99.
(ATL ref: DX-001-282)

her life. The Shipleys and Richardson and her husband Andrew Wright became close friends, many of their political and personal views meshing. Shipley later said: "When it was clear the Ashburton seat would become available, the four of us spent many a night in front of our fire going over why my excuses were not good enough for refusing to get into politics."[3] The decision was made easier by Burton Shipley's willingness to take primary responsibility for their two pre-teen children.

Jenny Shipley's Ashburton victory at the 1987 general election was one of the brighter aspects of a disappointing result for National that made no impression on Labour's substantial majority. She quickly made her mark in Wellington. As Jane Clifton wrote: "Shipley, as a post-Muldoon recruit, was unambiguous about her ambition. So much so that – and here's another unusual thing about her – she was marked out as a potential leader from day one."[4]

After only one term as an opposition backbencher, Jenny Shipley was in National's first cabinet for six years. As she said: "In politics people are harder on women than men. That provides opportunity and cost. The opportunity is that there are fewer of us and so our visibility is high. The cost is that you can be over-exposed and pushed quickly."[5]

Although ranked only 11th by Jim Bolger, the social welfare portfolio carried both considerable political responsibility and personal risk. Bolger later wrote: "I offered her Social Welfare because real change in the thinking behind and the delivery of social welfare was needed .... It's not a glamour job but as expected she was assiduous in putting forward programmes to refocus the spending of social welfare dollars to produce a better result."[6]

National's 1991 plan to remodel the welfare system resulted in the minister of social welfare becoming one of the country's most disliked politicians with her endlessly repeated mantras: the state simply cannot afford to fund an ever-growing welfare system; for every person working, another is on a benefit, whereas only a decade ago there were four workers for every beneficiary; and: resourcefulness is being submerged in a creeping mentality of dependency.

Jenny Shipley, as minister of social welfare, reduced the welfare budget and cut benefits. Chris Slane, New Zealand Listener, *May 15 1993. (ATL ref: H-103-008)*

She told *Time* magazine: "We can no longer assume that people know how to boil rice, dig a vegetable garden or sew on a button." [7] Although 'smart cards' to buy welfare services did not eventuate, she did reduce the welfare budget by $340 million a year, cut benefits by up to a quarter, made the unemployed wait six months for the dole after losing jobs, and set a minimum age of 17 before single parents could claim state support. She also initiated data-matching between state agencies to detect benefit fraud.

She and Ruth Richardson, an equally unpopular minister of finance, were now prime media targets. Rosemary McLeod wrote: "Popular cartoon

Shipley finalised her coup plans while Bolger was overseas and when he got back in early November she had the support to topple him. Malcolm Evans, New Zealand Herald, *November 5 1997. (ATL ref: H-725-016)*

images put them in dominatrix garter belts, wrap them in pinnies, present them cooking up potions flavoured by the poor and downtrodden. They've been burned in effigy, had nasty threats made about them, and they need police diplomatic squad protection in public wherever they go." [8]

As minister of health, following the 1993 election, Shipley now had the unenviable task of defending policies as unpopular as those she had presided over in the social welfare field. The designers of the 1993 health reforms believed there would be huge savings and reduced hospital waiting times when a split between care 'providers' and 'purchasers' replaced the Area Health Board system which had carried out both roles. Now, the providers, or Crown Health Enterprises (CHEs), would compete amongst themselves for funding from Regional Health Authorities (RHAs). As well, hospitals would be run more efficiently by private sector managers.

In reality, while thousands marched in protest, the CHEs were swamped by debt and waiting lists grew ever longer.

There were, of course, some positives from this period. As minister of social welfare she began the Compass programme for solo parents, social workers working closely with beneficiaries to map out viable futures. Also, as Minister of Women's Affairs from 1990-96 she cut prescription charges for contraceptive pills and campaigned against domestic violence.

Jenny Shipley was, in many ways, an impressive cabinet minister. She was never afraid to say what she thought. As she once put it: "This isn't a damn beauty contest. If you come into politics to be popular, then you've picked the wrong sport." [9] She was focussed, determined, hard-working and had an excellent memory. She also knew her limitations.

Clifton wrote: "Shipley also passed for articulate, in that she was well-spoken, confident and fluent. The content might have been Rogernomics cant, but the form – a strong, elegant woman – was new and attractive." [10]

By the 1996 election she was clearly a leading contender for the National Party leadership. Bolger, briefly secure after his third election victory in a row, handed a new raft of responsibilities to Shipley: state services, transport, state-owned enterprises, Radio New Zealand, and ACC. By now Jim Bolger was very conscious that she was a serious rival.

Bolger's grip on the prime ministership weakened as embarrassment with coalition partner New Zealand First increased and when the compulsory superannuation referendum, agreed in coalition talks, was lost by a large margin, Shipley was in the opposition vanguard. Bolger later wrote: "Given the vigour of her public opposition to what was finally put forward, she obviously saw the scheme she had helped to design as a bad one; or perhaps she saw the compulsory superannuation proposal as a popular issue on which to stake her identity and her ultimate claim to higher office." [11]

Jenny Shipley was a detail person and her coup planning was lengthy and meticulous. There were a number of reasons her lieutenants were able to gradually build support until a clear majority of caucus favoured a leadership change.

There was clearly respect for her organisational ability and a growing view that it was time for the next generation to take charge. As Ruth Laugesen wrote: "Mrs Shipley represents a generational change which will see the baby boomers move into the dominant positions in National, as they did in Labour as long ago as the early 1980s." [12] Most of all, though, there was the conviction that National needed to be more assertive with New Zealand First. Clifton wrote: "Her caucus elected her expressly to be high-handed with Peters. Peters was elected expressly because of his combative hatred of such establishment politicians as Shipley." [13]

In the tried and true manner, Jenny Shipley finalised coup details in October 1997 while Jim Bolger was overseas attending a Commonwealth heads of government conference. But the change of leadership was a mixed blessing for National.

The electorate had little affection for Jenny Shipley personally and her elevation did not reassure those hoping for a move back to more centrist policies. As Laugesen wrote: "Mrs Shipley will have no trouble being energetic or reforming, but her most difficult feat will be to convince a doubting electorate that a heart beats beneath her power suits." [14]

During Shipley's 'honeymoon' period, which lasted for about eight months, National climbed steadily in the polls. She focussed, in the spirit of early 1990s radicalism, on micro-economic reform and had some success, with ministerial 'teams', improving co-operation and prioritisation across ministries and programmes.

But then her prime ministership began to unravel. In August 1998, the sale of Wellington Airport ended the increasingly brittle alliance, New Zealand First ministers walking out of cabinet and Shipley sacking Peters, her deputy PM, for flouting the concept of collective responsibility. National's junior coalition partner fragmented, leaving Shipley with a minority government dependent on a ragtag collection of miniature parties and independents. Despite the automatic kudos from chairing the annual Asia-Pacific Economic Co-operation (APEC) forum, conveniently held in Auckland in September 1999 shortly before the general election, Jenny Shipley did not look or sound a confident prime minister. Colin James wrote: "Mrs Shipley has .... not made the transition from portfolio minister, where her formidable capacity to master briefs greatly impressed most public servants who worked for her, to Prime Minister, which demands a big-picture capability that briefs don't furnish." [15]

Shipley did not concede the 1999 election easily, but there had been too many mistakes. James again: "Mrs Shipley won deserved praise for her combative electioneering. But that does not obliterate her political misjudgments – in veering right in 1998 when the electorate was chorusing its wish for a new centre, in pinching pennies off pensioners and calling it 'progress', in time after time mismanaging micro-scandals into crises ...." [16]

Jenny Shipley was not an effective opposition leader, and looked even less so as Helen Clark blossomed as prime minister. Michael Laws wrote: "It is a completely different environment to that of government and requires a wholly different set of skills. Independence and intuition come into their own – those lacking either smarts or cunning are ruthlessly exposed. And Shipley was." [17]

Ironically, Shipley came home from an overseas trip in late September 2001 to find her

Shipley inherited Winston Peters as her deputy; it was not a relationship that ever warmed. Peter Bromhead, Dominion, November 17 1997.
(ATL ref: H-725-017)

185

days numbered. Her lack-lustre performance, a minor heart attack a year before and her dismal personal poll ratings underlined the point all too clearly. Barely a week later she made way, with a graciousness that disguised her anger, for her deputy Bill English.

Jenny Shipley left politics at the 2002 election, still only 51 years old and having built a flimsy majority in Ashburton, then Rakaia, into one of the country's most substantial. She had been an unusual politician: she had firm convictions, spoke her mind and knew she always had the support of a close-knit family.

The Shipleys, who left their farm when she took up her parliamentary duties, sold the Ashbuton smallholding they had subsequently developed. Now based in Auckland, Jenny Shipley is a director of an executive search and business development organisation which operates in New Zealand and internationally. She also runs her own consultancy business advising educational, agricultural and tourism clients, with an emphasis on business opportunities in China. She became a

Distinguished Companion of the New Zealand Order of Merit (DCNZOM) in December 2002.

It is not easy to be a woman politician and a very considerable achievement to have been New Zealand's first woman prime minister. Tears might have shown Australian prime minister Bob Hawke's humanity, but there was, and still is, the perception that the woman politician who shows emotion is weak. As Hubbard wrote: "Those close to Mrs Shipley say .... her cool manner, which can seem both patronising and chilling, is a mask which all women politicians have to wear." [18] So the New Zealand public rarely saw the other Jenny Shipley, the warm, friendly and unaffected woman liked and respected by those who know her personally.

Shipley and Peters attempted to work together until August 1998 when NZ First ministers walked out of cabinet when Wellington Airport was sold. Garrick Tremain, The Press, *March 30 1998. (ATL ref: H-483-032)*

37
HELEN ELIZABETH CLARK
1950 -

"Some new prime ministers struggle and others cope; she blossomed in the role"

Helen Clark was, in 1999, the first woman to be elected prime minister of New Zealand.

Born in Hamilton in February 1950, the first of George and Margaret Clark's four daughters, hers was a farming family, its roots in the New Zealand soil going back four generations, at a time when farming was profitable and highly respected and farmers were invariably conservative in their views and politics.

Helen Clark spent nearly 13 sheltered years on the family's Te Pahu farm, only travelling the 22 miles to Hamilton on special occasions. Suffering from debilitating allergies, there was a period of schooling by correspondence, supervised by her mother who had originally moved from the South Island to teach in the district.

Clark had limited contact with other children, apart from her sisters, so neither her shyness nor passion for reading was surprising. The decision to send her to board at Epsom Girls' Grammar school in Auckland was traumatic for both Helen and her parents, upset to see how unhappy she was.

Murray Webb, Otago Daily Times, *January 27 1989. (ATL ref: DX-001-600)*

The school has an excellent academic reputation, but little was expected of the hostel girls, mostly from remote country areas. As Helen Clark later remembered: "The headmistress used to come across to the hostel and tell us we were country girls and we'd go back to where we came from, that there wasn't much that could be done for us educationally, but we'd be better for the experience of rubbing shoulders with the other pupils."[1] In fact, there was little contact with the day pupils from the prosperous Remuera and Epsom suburbs, urban sophisticates by comparison.

However, with the resilience and determination that were later notable political attributes, Clark moved up classes until her 6A year provided the necessary passport to university. Like many of her generation, Helen Clark was, in 1968, the first member of her family to go to university. It was a development her father in particular watched with a mixture of pride and suspicion, the latter blossoming into concern when, in her second year, she concentrated on political studies. Her radical political views were more and more at odds with her father's National Party orthodoxy and there were increasingly bitter arguments on weekend visits home.

She found mentors among her lecturers, particularly Robert Chapman and Ruth Butterworth, and soul mates in the Vietnam War and rugby tour protest groups she joined. She joined the Halt All Racist Tours (HART) committee; her father later went on a rugby supporters tour to South Africa. Their estrangement lasted a decade.

Helen Clark was not quite 21 when she joined the influential Princes Street branch of the Labour Party and was soon its vice-president. Later, she said: "I joined Labour quite consciously because it had lost four elections in a row. It was obvious that the things I'd become really interested in, like rugby and

South Africa, or New Zealand slavishly following the Americans, as in Vietnam, weren't going to stop under a conservative government." [2] The branch, unique for its roll call of subsequently prominent cabinet ministers, had a penchant for writing party policy.

Her undergraduate degree completed in 1970, Clark started work on an MA topic – Political Attitudes of the New Zealand Countryside – that was of particular relevance given the dichotomies in her personal life. Despite some residual shyness and radical 'uniform' – long, flowing hair and drab clothes – she was now being noticed on and off campus. Professor Chapman, her MA supervisor, remembered her skill at sorting a mass of detail into analytical order that "constituted a proper argument" and Professor Butterworth her ability to combine "highly honed" intelligence with commonsense. [3]

Clark's life was focussed on her study and political activity – local body and general election campaigns, presidency of the Princes Street branch, chairing the party's youth advisory council, and a seat on the party's Auckland regional council. First class honours led to a junior lecturer's position at Auckland University, but by now she was more interested in a seat in the House of Representatives in Wellington.

Ideally, Clark wanted a safe urban seat but Auckland Central, the only one available before the 1975 election, chose Richard Prebble as its candidate. There was no competition to contest the heartland National seat of Piako – her home turf. She campaigned enthusiastically using canvassing techniques learned in previous city campaigns. Labour lost the election as comprehensively as it had won in 1972, with Piako one of the few seats where its vote increased.

Early in 1976, Helen Clark left for Britain and Sweden to develop her MA thesis into a PhD. Returning 11 months later, she was appointed to a political studies lectureship. There were no safe Auckland seats in the offing for 1978, so she concentrated on playing a constructive party role locally and nationally. Labour was seriously demoralised when it won the popular vote but lost the election in 1978 and Clark, now on the central executive, played a pivotal backroom role in the programme of morale and organisational rebuilding when Jim Anderton, an old friend, became party president in 1979.

Anderton and his then wife Joan were, along with Cath and Judith Tizard, Helen Clark's principal backers when she put her name forward for Mt Albert in April 1980. Because it was among the safest of Auckland seats, she had to beat six other candidates at the selection meeting. During the 1981 election campaign there were rather contradictory slurs about her sexuality and about 'living in sin'. She was persuaded to marry her partner, Peter Davis, the English medical sociologist she had lived with since 1979, but felt compromised. "I think legal marriage is unnecessary and I would not have formalised the relationship except for going into Parliament." [4] It was an early example of Clark's acceptance that compromise is a political reality that has to be accommodated in the furtherance of longer-term goals.

Clark's first term in Parliament was a little like her first years at Epsom Girls. She was lonely and isolated in an unremittingly chauvinistic atmosphere. Clark's political views were intellectual, absorbed from books and sharpened by debate, not formed by personal experience of poverty and disadvantage. Further, her concerns were traditional Labour ones, not shaped by a specific commitment to feminism. As she declared in her maiden speech: "We do not seek as our first priority to make the rich richer and the powerful more powerful." [5]

It was an 'old-fashioned' view that found little favour with the cabal of Auckland colleagues intent on replacing Bill Rowling with David Lange. Clark, a Rowling supporter, felt increasingly marginalised and even

Critics considered Clark dealt severely with ministerial colleagues – Dover Samuels, Phillida Bunkle, Marian Hobbs and Ruth Dyson – during her first term. James Waerea, New Zealand Truth, *2000. (ATL ref: H-617-014)*

contemplated premature retirement at one point. She remained on the party executive until 1989, her belief that the parliamentary wing should be more responsive to the wider party a further worry to some of her caucus colleagues.

Any frustration Helen Clark felt at not being elected to the incoming Lange cabinet following the snap 1984 election was soon replaced by relief as Roger Douglas's economic reforms set off in directions neither canvassed in party forums nor carrying the manifesto seal of approval.

As chair of the foreign affairs and defence select committee she had, and took, the opportunity to travel widely, attending anti-nuclear conferences and the United Nations End of the Decade for Women Conference in Nairobi.

The 1984-87 years were very difficult: she disagreed fundamentally with much of 'Rogernomics' and she saw, at first hand, its effect on the lives of her poorer constituents. But she kept her thoughts to herself, unlike Jim Anderton who had won the Sydenham seat at the 1984 election. Discipline, pragmatism and patience – not emotion – were her watchwords.

The result was a greater level of acceptance in Labour's caucus and, with it, election to cabinet after the 1987 election. Clark was given the conservation and housing portfolios, the latter much more challenging as Douglas was intent on selling state housing stock and mortgages. The new minister managed to delay a decision, appointing a slow moving working party with Heather Simpson her nominee, until Douglas left the ministry in December 1988. In the meantime she built 3,000 more houses and ensured better access for those in greatest need.

In February 1989, in the reshuffle that followed the Prebble and Douglas departures, Helen Clark became minister of health, jumped nine cabinet spots to No 8 and became the first woman in New Zealand to sit on a government's front bench.

Clark quickly gained a reputation for toughmindedness: demanding health boards stay within budgets and sacking the troubled Auckland Area Health Board on which, the media was quick to point out, Peter Davis sat. More positively, she emphasised public health with legislation establishing smoke free environments, more co-ordinated health research and autonomous status for midwives.

David Lange gave Clark a couple of days notice of his resignation intentions, suggesting she stand for the deputy position. She beat Douglas narrowly in the August 8 1989 ballot and, at 39, was deputy prime minister. Over the next, troubled 13 months, with Douglas and Prebble back in cabinet and the assets sales accelerating, she was deputy to both Palmer and, from September 4 1990, Moore.

Clark dropped housing in favour of the labour portfolio, her Employment Equity Act later repealed by National.

Labour was decimated at the 1990 election then, as National intensified the 'reform' process, moving into the social services and wages areas, won back a number of seats in 1993. The result was not good enough for Mike Moore to retain the leadership and the Labour caucus moved quickly to replace him with Clark. He did not go quietly, as Palmer had before, and poured some of his legendary energy over the next three years into destabilising the Clark/David Caygill leadership.

During 1990-93 Helen Clark had taken stock of the imbalances in her life; she renewed her arts interests and began a fitness regime – including cross-country skiing – that continues today. Over the next three years she was going to need every ounce of optimism, determination and energy to meld the two distinct caucus factions into a workable team. Acceptance of a woman leader was slow in coming, particularly one disinterested in the outward signs of 'femininity'. Third place in a by-election and poor polling results led to a May 1996 delegation of senior Labour members asking her to step down. She called their bluff, the only change being Caygill's replacement with Michael Cullen.

By now, persuaded that style and substance were not incompatible, Clark was getting grooming advice and her clothes from a leading fashion designer, and with the 1996 election approaching she reluctantly agreed to work on her television technique. More assured performaces led to better personal poll results, a confident campaign that focussed on her leadership, and a good haul of seats in the first MMP parliament. In fact, so impressive had Clark been that it was barely noticed at the time that Labour's 28 percent of the party vote was its poorest result since 1928.

Labour lost its Maori seats and the opportunity to form a coalition government when, after weeks of protracted negotiation, Winston Peters took his 16 NZ First colleagues into the National camp.

For the next three years – through the Bolger and Shipley administrations – Clark was able to study the problems and pitfalls of coalition government at close quarters. As Labour's popularity surged, National replaced Bolger and Shipley hastened the disintegration of its partnership with NZ First. Anticipating similar problems when the Jim Anderton-led Alliance openly attacked the senior opposition party at a May 1998 by-election, Clark was determined her differences with Anderton and between the two parties be patched up. Anderton acknowledged the unpopularity of his progressive tax policy and Clark received a standing ovation when she addressed the Alliance's annual conference in August. There was agreement about a post-election coalition.

As her confidence grew, and she looked more like a prime minister in waiting, Clark adopted an open, accessible approach with the media that contrasted sharply with Shipley's irregular, carefully staged press conferences. Easy familiarity with key journalists gave Clark an important early edge in the 1999 presidential-style election, focussing as it did on the two women leaders. Further, Clark was steeled by Shipley and National's unsubtle attacks on her lack of children and unconventional marriage.

Clark and Labour won a comprehensive victory, the Maori seats back again in the fold. With its 49 MPs and the Alliance's 10 in the 120-seat House, and with Anderton as deputy prime minister, the centre-left minority coalition was quickly in place with an undertaking that the Greens would support the government on matters of supply. A swag of legislation was passed – dealing with ACC, hospital services, industrial relations, student loans, the bulk funding of schools, defence, shop trading hours, energy conservation, the logging of indigenous West Coast timber – but the dominant political story of

She had long since abandoned the heady leftist enthusiasms of her university days; there were still ideals and aspirations, but they were more 'corporatist' in tone, with the state, employers and trade unions working co-operatively to modernise and diversify the New Zealand economy in tandem with measures that would minimise economic and social difficulties.

With her patient, analytical mind she had also used her 18 years of political apprenticeship to ponder the ingredients for successful, enduring leadership. They included: a watchful eye on, and regular contact with, all her ministers, a determination to nip problems in the bud, a low tolerance of mistakes and sloppy work by public servants, colleagues and board appointees, and a positive relationship with the media, including regularly programmed radio interviews.

Privately, Clark is compassionate, caring and funny but, she decided long ago, these were sides of her personality irrelevant to the serious business of politics. She dealt promptly, and sometimes severely, with a succession of bush fires that might have badly burned her administration. High profile public servants and board appointees left their jobs and she sacked four ministers, reinstating three of them later. Some see Clark's public criticism of her own ministers as domineering, autocratic and insensitive; others approve of her 'hands on' style and her formidable ability to identify and fix problems before they get out of hand. Barry Gustafson said: "Helen speaks out more than any prime minister in recent memory. It's a question of transparency …. Helen is not prepared to try and rationalise away incompetence or mistakes." [6] The much-vaunted 'Closing the Gaps' initiative was quickly 're-focussed' when it became an embarrassment.

A major shift in defence priorities, including the scrapping of the RNZAF's F-16 fighter planes, was roundly criticised by retired military chiefs and experts. Malcolm Evans, New Zealand Herald, *May 7 2001. (ATL ref: DX-002-039)*

National replaced Shipley with Bill English in September 2001 but this made no dent in the government's popularity which has been substantially aided by a benign economy that produced record export income, tourism receipts and surpluses.

that three year term was the prime minister herself.

Clark, the shy, uncertain opposition leader of 1994 was now, at the beginning of the new century, in control of Labour's agenda and respected by her generally capable cabinet. Some new prime ministers struggle and others cope; she blossomed in the role.

In an attempt to win the clear parliamentary majority the polls told her was reachable, Clark went to the country four months early in late July 2002 on the doubtful grounds that the split within the Alliance made it impossible to advance the government's legislative programme. The public was sceptical and, after 'Corngate' dominated the election campaign, the coalition parties managed only 54 seats, with the Progressive Coalition, Anderton's latest political vehicle, contributing two. Now Clark routinely needs a different coalition for every legislative measure, seeking support either from the Greens (9 MPs), to the left, or United Future (8 MPs), to the right.

In her second term, the 'Helengrad' era of aggressive micro-managing has faded. Her ministers are either competent, or more experienced than they were. Her primary requirement of them is still 'no surprises'; 'leaky buildings' caught minister George Hawkins off-guard and energy minister Pete Hodgson was embarrassed by the electricity crisis but both remain at their desks.

Today, an official from the Prime Minister's Department is assigned to most portfolios to ensure a desirable level of co-ordination. The hours she works are still crushing – up to 19 on the trot – but the priorities have changed. She now gets involved if the issue or problem is serious enough. Clark's two mobile phones are crucial to her way of working; she is in regular direct contact with ministers and it's rare that journalists don't hear back when they leave

a message. She is also as disciplined about keeping physically fit and having regular away-from-it-all breaks as she is with her daily work routine.

Clark now securely occupies the centre ground that middle New Zealand is most comfortable with, leaving the opposition parties disconsolate on the periphery. Ironically, her good working relationship with Peter Dunne's United Future, principal winners at the 2002 election, means her 'centre' now stretches further to the 'right' than before. She travels extensively throughout the country, listening to middle New Zealand, and this is more her weather-vane than the obsessive polling some Beehive-bound prime ministers have indulged in.

Two people make it easier for Clark to travel widely, both at home and abroad. There is a close, highly effective working relationship with deputy Michael Cullen. Colin James writes: "Cullen holds the fort in Wellington while she travels. He looks after her correspondence which is not strictly prime ministerial in nature. He convenes ministerial groups to deal with the tough issues: infrastructure, the Maori seabed claim, Air New Zealand, Tranz Rail." [7] And there is her chief of staff Heather Simpson who can now represent Clark's view as second nature.

Into her fifth year, Clark and Labour remain

Clark's attacks on the Business Roundtable were followed by an increasingly effective charm offensive aimed at the rest of the business community. Tom Scott, Evening Post, *October 25 2000. (ATL ref: H-647-038)*

comfortably ahead of English and National in the polls, with the minor parties generally bobbing slightly over or under the margin of error. There has been the inevitable list of problems – Clark's signing of other people's charity auction paintings, 'Corngate' and the GM moratorium, 'undiplomatic' remarks about the invasion of Iraq, Maori television, and the potentially explosive Appeal Court ruling on the foreshore and sea bed – but none have yet dented the government's credibility.

Clark is project-orientated, more comfortable as a manager than as a visionary. As James has written: "Clark cannot paint a picture of her promised land. If this nation is on a journey with Clark, it is one marked whistle-stop by whistle-stop, not mapped in grand vistas." [8]

Her government is busy with a programme of small changes that will add up to considerable regulatory law readjustments, more centralisation of health and education, more environmental protection, and an emphasis on sustainable development. And it is Clark's particular passion to further New Zealand's reputation as a small, independently-minded western nation.

Clark has a clear contempt for National's long-time conviction that it was the 'natural party' of government. As she says: I think that's a terrible thing …. No one has a divine right to rule." [9] At the same time one of her major goals is to put Labour in the position National occupied through much of the second half of last century.

It remains to be seen whether Clark will find an enduring answer, that accommodates the wishes of Maori and other New Zealanders, to the foreshore and seabed issue. It is probably all that stands between her and a third term as prime minister. It may call for a greater imaginative leap than Helen Clark is capable of, but it would certainly propel her into the first rank of New Zealand leaders.

Clark took the unusual step of becoming minister for arts, culture and heritage, and provided an early, unprecedented injection of $80 million into the arts sector. Jim Hubbard, Dominion, *May 19 2000. (ATL ref: A-350-044)*

REFERENCES

INTRODUCTION

1. Keith Sinclair, *A History of New Zealand*, London, 1959, p. 111.
2. Jeanine Graham, *Frederick Weld*, Christchurch, 1983, p. 121.
3. Mike Warman, *The White Swan Incident*, Masterton, 2002.
4. Raewyn Dalziel, 'The Politics of Settlement', *The Oxford History of New Zealand*, Wellington, 1981, p. 99.
5. Sinclair, p. 109.
6. Dalziel, p. 95.
7. Keith Jackson, *The Dilemma of Parliament*, Wellington, 1987, p. 161.
8. David Hamer, *The New Zealand Liberals*, Auckland, 1988, p. 14.
9. Dalziel, p. 101.
10. Hamer, p. 26.
11. Dalziel, p. 111.
12. Hamer, p. 9.
13. J O Wilson, *New Zealand Parliamentary Record* 1840-1984, Wellington, 1985, p. 57.
14. Sinclair, p. 171.
15. Tom Brooking, *New Zealand Journal of History*, Vol. 21, No. 2, 1987, p.277.
16. Interview with author, 1. 09. 03.
17. Judith Bassett, *Sir Harry Atkinson*, Auckland, 1975, p. 43.
18. William Pember Reeves, *The Long White Cloud*, Christchurch, 1950, p. 195.
19. Judith Bassett, 'Atkinson, Harry Albert', *Dictionary of New Zealand Biography*, Wellington, 1990, Vol.1 (1769-1869), p. 9.
20. Michael Bassett, 'The Essentials of Successful Leadership in Twentieth-Century New Zealand Politics', *Political Science*, Vol. 51, No. 2, December 1999, pp. 108-09.
21. Interview with author, 25. 08. 03.
22. John Henderson, 'The Prime Minister: Powers and Personality', *New Zealand Politics and Government*, (ed. R Miller), Auckland, 2003, p. 108.
23. Interview with author, 25. 08. 03.
24. Ibid.
25. Richard Mulgan, *Politics in New Zealand*, Auckland, 1997, p. 96.
26. John Henderson, 'The Prime Minister', *New Zealand Politics in Transition* (ed. R Miller), Auckland, 1997, p. 76.
27. Interview with author, 25. 08. 03.
28. Interview with author, 19. 08. 03.
29. Jonathan Boston, Stephen Levine, Elizabeth McLeay, Nigel Roberts, *New Zealand Under MMP*, Auckland, 1996, pp. 127-28.
30. Interview with author, 5. 09. 03.
31. Interview with author, 1. 09. 03.
32. Jonathan Boston, 'Advising the Prime Minister in New Zealand', *Politics*, Vol. 23, May 1988, p. 10.
33. Interview with author, 5. 08. 03.
34. Ibid.
35. Interview with author, 25. 08. 03.
36. Henderson, 'The Prime Minister: Powers and Personality', p. 110.
37. Interview with author, 5. 08. 03.
38. Ibid.
39. Interview with author, 26. 05. 03.
40. Ibid.
41. Alan Henderson, *The Quest for Efficiency*, Wellington, 1990, p. 21.
42. Hamer, p. 204.
43. Interview with author, 26. 05. 03.
44. Interview with author, 19. 08. 03.
45. Jon Jonansson, 'Muldoon Explanations: The Crucible of Character', *Muldoon After Gustafson*, (ed. M Clark), Palmerston North, 2004.
46. John Henderson, 'The Prime Minister', p. 76.
47. Interview with author, 25. 08. 03.
48. Ibid.
49. Geoffrey Palmer, *New Zealand's Constitution in Crisis*, Dunedin, 1992, p. 111.
50. Interview with author, 5. 09. 03.
51. Mulgan, p. 92.
52. Interview with author, 25. 08. 03.
53. Interview with author, 5. 09.03
54. Bassett, 'The Essentials of Successful Leadership', p.108.
55. Interview with author, 26. 05. 03.
56. Keith Eunson, *Mirrors On The Hill*, Palmerston North, 2001, p. 213.
57. Interview with author, 5. 08. 03.
58. Interview with author, 19. 08. 03
59. Ibid.
60. Interview with author, 11. 08. 03.
61. Interview with author, 5. 08. 03.
62. Interview with author, 5. 09. 03.
63. Bassett, p. 114.
64. Interview with author, 5. 08. 03
65. Interview with author, 10. 09. 03.
66. Bassett, p. 110.
67. Interview with author, 5. 09. 03.
68. Stephen Levine and Nigel Roberts, 'Their Ways: A Comparative Assessment of New Zealand Prime Ministers and the News Media', *Muldoon After Gustafson*, Palmerston North, 2004.
69. Ibid.
70. Palmer, p. 151.
71. Ibid.
72. Interview with author, 5. 09. 03.
73. Bassett, p. 113.
74. Edmund Bohan, *Edward Stafford: New Zealand's First Statesman*, Christchurch, 1994, p. 159.
75. Barry Gustafson, *From the Cradle to the Grave*, Auckland, 1986, pp. 180-81.
76. Raewyn Dalziel, *Julius Vogel: Business Politician*, Auckland, 1986, p. 158.
77. Ibid.
78. Ibid, p. 159.
79. Michael Bassett, *Sir Joseph Ward*, Auckland, 1993, p. 106.
80. Keith Sinclair, *Walter Nash*, Auckland, 1976, p. 357.
81. John Henderson, 'Labour's Modern Prime Ministers and the Party: A Study of Contrasting Political Styles', *The Labour Party after 75 Years*, (ed. M Clark), Wellington, 1992, p. 99.
82. Henderson, 'The Prime Minister: Powers and Personality', p. 111.
83. Ibid, p. 112.
84. Ibid.
85. Ibid.
86. Ibid.
87. Ibid, 113.
88. Johansson.
89. Interview with author, 10. 09. 03.
90. Interview with author, 5. 09. 03.
91. Bassett, 'The Essentials of Successful Leadership', p.119.
92. Interview with author, 5. 09. 03.
93. Simon Sheppard, 'Ranking New Zealand Prime Ministers', *Political Science*, Vol. 50, July 1998.
94. Ibid, p. 82.
95. David Gee, 'Keith Jackson: analyst of NZ political leaders', *The Press*, July 21 1993, p. 13.
96. Barry Gustafson, *His Way*, Auckland, 2000, p. 16.
97. Levine and Roberts.
98. Barry Gustafson, *From the Cradle to the Grave*, p. 191.
99. Interview with author, 5. 08. 03.
100. Interview with author, 6. 06. 03.
101. Ian F Grant, *The Unauthorized Version: A Cartoon History of New Zealand*, Auckland, 1980, p. 4.
102. Nicholas Garland, "Political Cartooning', p.4-8 *Quiplash* (New Zealand Cartoon Archive newsletter), No. 7, 1998.
103. John Marshall, *Memoirs*, Vol. 1, 1912-1960, Auckland, 1983, p. 129.
104. Gordon Minhinnick, 'Introduction', *The Unauthorized Version*, Auckland, 1980, p. 2.
105. Quoted in Ollie Stone-Lee, 'Seriously Funny Work', BBC News Online, November 5 2001.
106. Gordon Minhinnick, 'Prime Min: The cartoons of Gordon Minhinnick', Auckland Museum, October 18 2002-January 18 2003.
107. R M Burdon, *The New Dominion*, Wellington, 1965, p. 35.
108. Michael Bassett, 'In Search of Sir Joseph Ward', *New Zealand Journal of History*, Vol. 21, April 1987, p. 121.
109. Marshall, p. 131.
110. Quoted in 'The Business of Being a Cartoonist', p.10, *Quiplash*, Vol. 9, 2002.
111. Quoted in 'Cartoonists Hung, Drawn and Quartered?', p. 4, *Quiplash*, Vol. 9, 2002.
112. Karl du Fresne, 'The Daily Smile' exhibition catalogue, 1994, p. 2.

1 HENRY SEWELL

1. David McIntyre (ed), *The Journal of Henry Sewell 1853-7*, Vol. 2, Christchurch, 1980, pp. 122-23.
2. Ibid, Vol. 1. p. 136.
3. Ibid, Vol. 1, p. 62.
4. Guy Scholefield (ed), 'Sewell, Henry', *A Dictionary of New Zealand Biography*, Vol. 2, Wellington, 1940, p. 290.
5. McIntyre (ed), Vol. 1. p. 37.
6. William Gisborne, *New Zealand Rulers and Statesmen*, London, 1897, pp. 88-89.
7. Scholefield, *Notable New Zealand Statesmen*, Christchurch, 1946, pp. 49-50.
8. W P Morrell, *The Provincial System in New Zealand*, Christchurch, 1964, pp. 94-95
9. McIntyre, 'Sewell, Henry', *Dictionary of New Zealand Biography*, Vol. 1 (1769-1869), Wellington, 1990, p. 393.

2 SIR WILLIAM FOX

1. Keith Sinclair, *A History of New Zealand*, London, 1980, p. 105.
2. Edmund Bohan, *Edward Stafford:New Zealand's First Statesman*, Christchurch, 1994, pp. 55-56.
3. David McIntyre, *The Journal of Henry Sewell 1853-7*, Vol. 2, Christchurch, 1980, p. 12.
4. Guy Scholefield, *Notable New Zealand Statesmen*, Christchurch, 1946, p. 59.
5. Bohan, p. 184.
6. Raewyn Dalziel, *JuliusVogel: Business Politician*, Auckland, 1986, p. 90.
7. Scholefield, p. 62.
8. Raewyn Dalziel, Keith Sinclair, 'Fox, William', *Dictionary of New Zealand Biography*, Vol. 1 (1769-1869), Wellington, 1990, p. 136.
9. Ibid, p. 137.
10. Jill Trevelyan, *Picturing Paradise*, Wellington, 2000, p. 2.
11. William Gisborne, *New Zealand Rulers and Statesmen*, London, 1897, pp. 125-27
12. W P Morrell, *The Provincial System in New Zealand*, Christchurch, 1964, p. 95.
13. Trevelyan, p. 8.
14. Dalziel, Sinclair, p. 138.

3 SIR EDWARD WILLIAM STAFFORD

1. Edmund Bohan, *Edward Stafford:New Zealand's First Statesman*, Christchurch, 1994, p. 72.
2. Alfred Saunders, *History of New Zealand*, Vol. 2, Christchurch, 1899, p.168.
3. Edmund Bohan, 'Stafford, Edward William', *Dictionary of New Zealand Biography*, Vol. 1 (1769-1869), Wellington, 1990, p.405.
4. Ibid.
5. Raewyn Dalziel, 'The Politics of Settlement', *The Oxford History of New Zealand*, Wellington, 1981, p.101.
6. Bohan, *Edward Stafford*, p.110.
7. Guy Scholefield, *Notable New Zealand Statesmen*, Christchurch, 1946, p. 75.
8. Bohan, p. 287.
9. Scholefield, p. 68.
10. Bohan, p. 367.
11. Ibid, p. 219.
12. William Gisborne, *New Zealand Rulers and Statesmen*, London, 1897, p. 88.
13. Bohan, p. 367.

4 ALFRED DOMETT

1. William Gisborne, *New Zealand Rulers and Statesmen*, London, 1897, pp. 110-11.
2. Ibid, p. 166.
3. Guy Scholefield, *Notable New Zealand Statesmen*, Christchurch, 1946, p. 84.
4. Jeanine Graham, 'Domett, Alfred', *Dictionary of New Zealand Biography*, Vol. 1 (1769-1869), Wellington, 1990, p. 110.
5. Guy Scholefield (ed.), *The Richmond-Atkinson Papers*, Vol. 2, p. 35.
6. Scholefield, *Notable New Zealand Statesmen*, p. 86.
7. Keith Sinclair, *A History of New Zealand*, London, 1980, pp. 141-42
8. Gisborne, p. 112.

9. Scholefield, p. 85.
10. Gisborne, p. 116.
11. Ibid, pp. 116-17.
12. Ibid, pp. 117-18.

5 SIR FREDERICK WHITAKER

1. William Gisborne, *New Zealand Rulers and Statesmen*, London, 1897, p. 72-3.
2. Ibid, p. 71.
3. Downie Stewart, *Sir Francis Bell*, Wellington, 1937, p. 290.
4. W J Gardner, 'A Colonial Economy', *The Oxford History of New Zealand*, Wellington, 1981, p. 65.
5. Gisborne, p. 72.
6. R C J Stone, 'Whitaker, Frederick', *Dictionary of New Zealand Biography*, Vol. 1 (1769-1869), Wellington, 1990, p. 587.
7. Judith Bassett, *Sir Harry Atkinson*, Auckland, 1975, p. 122.
8. Stone, p. 587.
9. Gisborne, p. 74.

6 SIR FREDERICK ALOYSIUS WELD

1. Jeanine Williams, 'Pastoralist and Maoris: Frederick Weld at Wharekaka', *New Zealand Journal of History*, Vol. 11, No. 1, April 1977, pp. 46-47.
2. Guy Scholefield (ed.), 'Weld, Sir Frederick Aloysius', *A Dictionary of New Zealand Biography*, Vol. 2, Wellington, 1940, p. 480.
3. Jeanine Graham, 'Weld, Frederick Aloysius', *Dictionary of New Zealand Biography*, Vol. 1 (1769-1869), Wellington, 1990, p. 579.
4. Williams, p. 52.
5. Guy Scholefield, *Notable New Zealand Statesmen*, Wellington, 1946, p. 99.
6. Ibid, p. 105.
7. Jeanine Graham, *Frederick Weld*, Auckland, 1983, p. 107.
8. William Gisborne, *New Zealand Rulers and Statesmen*, London, 1897, pp. 173-74.

7 GEORGE MARSDEN WATERHOUSE

1. R M Burdon, *The Life and Times of Sir Julius Vogel*, Christchurch, 1948, p. 89.
2. Guy Scholefield, *Notable New Zealand Statesmen*, Christchurch, 1946, p. 111.
3. William Gisborne, *New Zealand Rulers and Statesmen*, London, 1897, p. 259.
4. Scholefield, p. 112.
5. Burdon, p. 89.
6. Raewyn Dalziel, *Julius Vogel: Business Politician*, Auckland, 1986, p. 153.
7. Ibid, p. 156.
8. Guy Scholefield (ed.), 'Waterhouse, George Marsden', *A Dictionary of New Zealand Biography*, Vol. 2, Wellington, 1940, p. 470.
9. Ibid.
10. Burdon, p. 89.
11. Dalziel, p. 156.
12. Scholefield, *Notable New Zealand Statesmen*, p. 109.

8 SIR JULIUS VOGEL

1. Raewyn Dalziel, *Julius Vogel: Business Politician*, Auckland, 1986, p. 39.
2. Edmund Bohan, *Edward Stafford: New Zealand's First Statesman*, Christchurch, 1994, p. 184.
3. W J Gardner, 'A Colonial Economy', *The Oxford History of New Zealand*, Wellington, 1981, p. 71.
4. Judith Bassett, *Sir Harry Atkinson*, Auckland, 1975, p. 84.
5. R M Burdon, *The Life & Times of Sir Julius Vogel*, Christchurch, 1948, p. 58.
6. Raewyn Dalziel, 'Vogel, Julius', *Dictionary of New Zealand Biography*, Vol 1 (1769-1869),Wellington, 1990, p. 566.
7. William Gisborne, *New Zealand Rulers and Statesmen*, London, 1897, p. 186.
8. Bassett, p. 44.
9. Keith Sinclair, *A History of New Zealand*, London, 1980, p. 163.
10. Dalziel, *Julius Vogel*, p. 302.
11. David Hamer, *The New Zealand Liberals*, Auckland, 1988, pp. 21-22.

12. William Pember Reeves, *The Long White Cloud*, Auckland, 1950, p. 238.
13. Dalziel, p. 9.
14. Ibid, p. 9.

9 DANIEL POLLEN

1. Edmund Bohan, *Edward Stafford: New Zealand's First Statesman*, Christchurch, 1994, p. 237.
2. Ibid, p. 237.
3. Raewyn Dalziel, *Julius Vogel:Business Politician*, Auckland, 1986, p. 205.
4. Ibid, p. 209.
5. Guy Scholefield (ed.), 'Pollen, Daniel', *A Dictionary of New Zealand Biography*, Vol. 2, Wellington, 1940, p. 173.
6. William Gisborne, *New Zealand Rulers and Statesmen*, London 1897, pp. 263-64.
7. Scholefield, p. 173.
8. Gisborne, p. 264.

10 SIR HARRY ALBERT ATKINSON

1. Guy Scholefield (ed.), *The Richmond-Atkinson Papers,* Vol. 1, Wellington, 1960, p.157.
2. Ibid, Vol.2, Wellington, 1960, pp. 210-11.
3. William Gisborne, *New Zealand Rulers and Statesmen*, London, 1897, p. 224.
4. Judith Bassett, 'Atkinson, Harry Albert', *New Zealand Dictionary of Biography*, Vol. 1 (1769-1869), Wellington, 1990, p. 8.
5. Judith Bassett, *Sir Harry Atkinson*, Auckland, 1975, p. 113.
6. Bassett, 'Atkinson, Harry Albert', p. 9.
7. William Pember Reeves, *The Long White Cloud*, Christchurch, 1950, p. 253.
8. Bassett, *Sir Harry Atkinson*, p. 170.
9. Ibid, p. 171.
10. Ibid.

11 SIR GEORGE GREY

1. Edmund Bohan, *To Be a Hero*, Auckland, 1998, p. 14.
2. Bernard Cadogan, *New Zealand Journal of History*, Vol. 33, No. 1, April 1999, p. 117.
3. David Hamer, *The New Zealand Liberals*, Auckland, 1988, p. 18.
4. Keith Sinclair, *A History of New Zealand*, London, 1980, p. 81.
5. William Pember Reeves, *The Long White Cloud*, Christchurch, 1950, p. 171.
6. Raewyn Dalziel. 'The Politics of Settlement', *The Oxford History of New Zealand*, Wellington, 1981, p. 101.
7. Bohan, p. 209.
8. Reeves, p. 176.
9. Hamer, p. 16.
10. Ibid, p. 18.
11. William Gisborne, *New Zealand Rulers and Statesmen*, London, 1897, p. 202.

12 SIR JOHN HALL

1. W J Gardner, 'Hall, John', *Dictionary of New Zealand Biography*, Vol. 1 (1769-1869), Wellington, 1990, p. 173.
2. Jean Garner, *By His Own Merits*, Christchurch, 1995, p. 161.
3. Gardner, p. 174.
4. Ibid, p. 173.
5. William Gisborne, *New Zealand Rulers and Statesmen*, London, 1897, pp. 121-22.
6. Edmund Bohan, *New Zealand Journal of History*, Vol. 30, No. 2, October 1996, p. 187.
7. Guy Scholefield, ' Hall, John', *New Zealand Dictionary of Biography*, Wellington, 1940, p. 345.
8. Garner, p. 255.
9. Ibid, p. 232.
10. Bohan, page, 186.

13 SIR ROBERT STOUT

1. Judith Bassett, *Sir Harry Atkinson*, Auckland, 1975, p. 38.
2. William Pember Reeves, *The Long White Cloud*, Christchurch, 1998, p. 250.
3. Ibid.
4. Edmund Bohan, *To Be A Hero*, Auckland, 1998, p. 267.

5. Raewyn Dalziel, 'The Politics of Settlement', *The Oxford History of New Zealand*, Wellington, 1981, p. 106.
6. David Hamer, *The New Zealand Liberals*, Auckland, 1988, p. 22.
7. Raewyn Dalziel, *Julius Vogel: Business Politician*, Auckland, 1986, p. 272.
8. Keith Sinclair, *A History of New Zealand*, London, 1980, p. 218.
9. William Gisborne, *New Zealand Rulers and Statesmen*, London, 1897, p. 207.
10. R M Burdon, *King Dick*, Christchurch, 1955, p. 104.
11. Ibid, p. 128.
12. Ibid, p. 165.
13. David Hamer, 'Stout, Robert', *Dictionary of New Zealand Biography*, Vol. 2 (1870-1900), Wellington, 1993, p. 487.

14 JOHN BALLANCE

1. Edmund Bohan, *To Be A Hero*, Auckland, 1998, p. 263.
2. David Hamer, *The New Zealand Liberals*, Auckland, 1988, p. 23.
3. Ibid, p. 26.
4. Judith Bassett, *Sir Harry Atkinson*, Auckland, 1975, p. 159.
5. R M Burdon, *King Dick*, Christchurch, 1955, p. 97.
6. Michael Bassett, *Sir Joseph Ward; A Political Biography*, Auckland, 1993, p. 38.
7. Guy Scholefield, *Notable New Zealand Statesmen*, Wellington, 1946, p. 175.
8. William Pember Reeves, *The Long White Cloud*, Christchurch, 1950, p. 284.
9. Burdon, p. 98.
10. Tim McIvor, 'Ballance, John', *Dictionary of New Zealand Biography*, Vol. 2 (1870-1900), Wellington, 1993, p. 25.
11. Reeves, p. 284.
12. Keith Sinclair, *A History of New Zealand*, London, 1980, p. 176.
13. Hamer, p. 81.
14. Ibid, p. 79.

15 RICHARD JOHN SEDDON

1. David Hamer, 'Seddon, Richard John', *Dictionary of New Zealand Biography*, Vol. 2 (1870-1900), Wellington, 1993, p. 448.
2. R M Burdon, *King Dick*, Christchurch, 1955, p. 106.
3. Len Richardson, 'Parties and Political Change', *The Oxford History of New Zealand*, Wellington, 1981, p. 202.
4. Keith Sinclair, *A History of New Zealand*, London, 1980, p. 187.
5. Guy Scholefield, *Notable New Zealand Statesmen*, Wellington, 1946, p. 186.
6. Ibid, p. 185.
7. William Pember Reeves, *The Long White Cloud*, Christchurch, 1950, p. 298.
8. Burdon, p. 47.
9. Hamer, *The New Zealand Liberals*, Auckland, 1988, p. 198.
10. Ibid, p. 199.
11. Burdon p. 308.
12. Richardson, 205.
13. William Gisborne, *New Zealand Rulers and Statesmen*, London, 1897, p. 283.
14. Reeves, p. 301.
15. Sinclair, p. 190.
16. Hamer, p. 207.
17. W J Gardner, *Political Science*, Vol. 13, March 1961, p. 21.

16 SIR WILLIAM HALL-JONES

1. David Hamer, *The New Zealand Liberals*, Auckland, 1988, p. 127.
2. Ibid.
3. John Hall-Jones, 'Hall-Jones, William', *Dictionary of New Zealand Biography*, Vol. 2 (1870-1900), Wellington, 1993, p. 189.
4. Hamer, p. 240.
5. Hall-Jones, p. 189.
6. Hamer, pp. 127-28.
7. Michael Bassett, *Sir Joseph Ward: A Political Biography*, Auckland, 1993, p. 142.
8. F G Hall-Jones, *Sir William Hall-Jones*, Invercargill, 1969, p. 80.
9. Guy Scholefield, 'Hall-Jones, William', *A Dictionary of New Zealand Biography*, Vol. 1, Wellington, 1940, p. 347.

17: SIR JOSEPH GEORGE WARD

1. Michael Bassett, 'In Search of Sir Joseph Ward', *The New Zealand Journal of History*, Vol. 21, April 1987, p. 117.
2. Michael Bassett, 'Ward, Joseph George', *Dictionary of New Zealand Biography*, Vol. 2 (1870-1900), Wellington, 1993, p. 566.
3. Ibid, p. 567.
4. David Hamer, *The New Zealand Liberals*, Auckland, 1988, p. 257.
5. Ibid, p. 254.
6. Ibid, p. 255.
7. Ibid, p. 254.
8. Bassett, 'In Search of Sir Joseph Ward', *New Zealand Journal of History*, Vol. 21, April 1987, p. 121.
9. Hamer, p. 256.
10. W J Gardner, 'The Rise of W F Massey, *Political Science* Vol. 13, March 1961, p. 21.
11. Hamer, p. 315.
12. Matthew J Wright, 'Sir Joseph Ward and New Zealand's Naval Defence Policy, 1907-12', *Political Science*, Vol. 41, July 1989, p. 51.
13. Bassett, *Sir Joseph Ward: A Political Biography*, Auckland, 1993, p. 266.
14. Ibid, p. viii.
15. Ibid, p. viii.

18 SIR THOMAS MACKENZIE

1. Tom Brooking, 'Mackenzie, Thomas Nobel', *Dictionary of New Zealand Biography*, Vol. 3 (1901-20), Wellington, 1996, p. 303.
2. David Hamer, *The New Zealand Liberals*, Auckland, 1998, p. 313.
3. Ibid, p. 264.
4. Ibid, p. 351.
5. Michael Bassett, *Sir Joseph Ward: A Political Biography*, Auckland, 1993, p. 213.
6. Hamer, p. 352.
7. Brooking, p. 304.

19 WILLIAM FERGUSON MASSEY

1. W J Gardner, 'The Rise of W F Massey, 1891-1912', *Political Science*, Vol. 13, March 1961, p. 11.
2. Ibid, p. 14.
3. Ibid, p. 16.
4. Keith Sinclair, *A History of New Zealand*, London, 1980, p. 208.
5. Len Richardson, 'Parties and Political Change, *The Oxford History of New Zealand*, Wellington, 1981, p. 210.
6. Gardner, p. 26.
7. Richardson, p. 210.
8. Sinclair, p. 209.
9. Ibid, p. 240.
10. R M Burdon, *The New Dominion*, Wellington, 1965, p. 48.
11. W J Gardner, 'W F Massey in Power, 1912-1925', *Political Science*, Vol. 13, September 1961, p. 7.
12. Ibid, p. 8.
13. Richardson, p. 213.
14. Michael Bassett, *Sir Joseph Ward: A Political Biography*, Auckland, 1993, p. 224.
15. Gardner, p. 13.
16. Richardson, p. 216.
17. Tom Brooking, 'Economic Transformation', *The Oxford History of New Zealand*, Wellington, 1981, p. 240.
18. Burdon, pp. 58-59.
19. Ibid, p. 34.
20. Barry Gustafson, 'Massey, William Ferguson', *Dictionary Of New Zealand Biography*, Vol. 2 (1870-1900), Wellington, 1993, p. 319.
21. Sinclair, p. 239.

20 SIR FRANCIS HENRY DILLON BELL

1. W J Gardner, 'Bell, Francis Henry Dillion', *Dictionary of New Zealand Biography*, Vol. 2 (1870-1900), Wellington, 1993, p. 35.
2. Ibid.
3. W Downie Stewart, *Sir Francis Bell: His Life and Times*, Wellington, 1937, pp. 93-94.
4. Ibid, pp. 290-92.
5. Ibid p. 292.
6. W J Gardner, 'Bell, Francis Henry Dillon', *An Encyclopaedia of New Zealand*, Vol. 1, Wellington, 1966, p.193.
7. Stewart, p. 190.

8. Gardner, p.192.
9. Ibid.
10. Gardner, *Dictionary of New Zealand Biography*, p. 36.
11. Stewart, p. 295.
12. Ibid, p. 289.

21 JOSEPH GORDON COATES

1. Michael Bassett, *Coates of Kaipara*, Auckland, 1995, p. 22.
2. W B Sutch, 'Coates: the lonely New Zealander', *New Zealand's Heritage* 79, 1973, p.219.
3. Michael Bassett, 'Coates, Joseph Gordon', *Dictionary of New Zealand Biography*, Vol. 3 (1901-1920), Wellington 1996, p. 105.
4. Bassett, *Coates of Kaipara*, p. 122.
5. W. J. Gardner, *An Enclyclopaedia of New Zealand*, Vol. 1, Wellington, 1966, p. 366.
6. Sutch, p.220.
7. Gardner, p. 367.
8. Brian Easton, *The Nationbuilders*, Auckland, 2001, p.40.
9. Sutch, p.220.
10. Bassett, p. 5.
11. Easton, p. 41.

22 GEORGE WILLIAM FORBES

1. W J Gardner, 'Forbes, George William', *Dictionary of New Zealand Biography*, Vol. 3 (1901-1920), Wellington, 1996, p. 163.
2. W J Gardner, *An Enclyclopaedia of New Zealand*, Wellington, 1966, Vol.1, p. 718.
3. R M Burdon, *The New Dominion*, Wellington, 1965, pp.63-64.
4. Keith Sinclair, *A History of New Zealand*, Auckland, 1980, p. 247.
5. Gardner, *Dictionary of New Zealand Biography*, p. 162.
6. Ibid.
7. Ibid, p. 163.
8. Ibid.
9. R M Burdon, *The New Dominion*, Wellington, 1965, p. 132.
10. Ibid, p. 131.

23 MICHAEL JOSEPH SAVAGE

1. Keith Sinclair, *A History of New Zealand*, Auckland, 1980, p. 258.
2. Michael Bassett, *New Zealand Journal of History*, Vol. 21, No. 2, October 1987, p. 275.
3. Leslie Hobbs, *The Thirty-Year Wonders*, Christchurch, 1967, p. 35.
4. Barry Gustafson, 'Michael Joseph Savage', *NZ Heritage*, p.2361.
5. Leslie Hobbs, *The Thirty-Year Wonders*, Christchurch, 1967 p. 39.
6. Michael Bassett, *NZ Journal of History*, Vol. 21, No. 2, October 1987, p. 276.
7. Barry Gustafson, *From The Cradle To The Grave*, Auckland, 1986, p.135.
8. Keith Sinclair, 'The Lee-Sutch Syndrome', *New Zealand Journal of History*, Vol. 8, No. 2, 1974, p.114.
9. Barry Gustafson, 'Savage, Michael Joseph', *Dictionary of New Zealand Biography*, Vol. 4 (1921-1940), Wellington, 1998, p. 456.
10. Gustafson, *From The Cradle To The Grave*, p. 206.
11. Ibid, p. 267.
12. Bruce Brown, *An Encyclopaedia of New Zealand*, Wellington, 1966, Volume 3, p. 175.
13. Gustafson, 'Savage, Michael Joseph', *Dictionary of New Zealand Biography*, Vol. 4 (1921-1940), 1998, pp. 457-58.

24 PETER FRASER

1. Tim Beaglehole, 'Fraser, Peter', *Dictionary of New Zealand Biography*, Vol. 4 (1921-1940), 1998, p. 183.
2. Erik Olssen, 'Towards a New Society', *The Oxford History of New Zealand*, Wellington, 1981, p. 273.
3. Michael Bassett (with Michael King), *Tomorrow Comes The Song*, Auckland, 2000, p. 140.
4. Brian Easton, *The Nationbuilders*, Auckland, 2001, p. 67.
5. Keith Sinclair, *Walter Nash*, Auckland, 1976, p. 203.
6. Alister McIntosh, 'Working with Peter Fraser in Wartime', *New Zealand Journal of History*, Vol. 10, No 1, April 1976, p. 3.
7. Michael Bassett (with Michael King), p. 95.
8. Leslie Hobbs, *The Thirty-Year Wonders*, Christchurch, 1967, p. 42.
9. Sinclair, p. 204.
10. Hobbs, p. 59.
11. McIntosh, p. 3.

12. Ibid, p. 4.
13. Ibid p. 7.
14. Keith Eunson, *Mirrors On The Hill*, Palmerston North, 2001, p. 16.
15. Easton, p. 71.
16. Ibid, p. 68.
17. McIntosh, p. 19.
18. Bassett (with King), p. 357.

25 SIR SIDNEY GEORGE HOLLAND

1. Barry Gustafson, 'Holland, Sidney George', *Dictionary of New Zealand Biography*, Vol. 3 (1901-1920),Wellington, 1996, p. 229.
2. Barry Gustafson, *The First 50 Years: A History of the New Zealand National Party*, Auckland, 1986, pp. 14-15.
3. Gustafson, *Dictionary of New Zealand Biography*, p. 229.
4. Ibid, p. 230.
5. Gustafson, *The First 50 Years*, p. 60.
6. Brian Easton, *The Nationbuilders*, Auckland, 2001, p. 71.
7. John Marshall, *Memoirs:* Vol. 1 (1912-1960), Auckland, 1983, p. 140.
8. Keith Eunson, *Mirrors On The Hill*, Palmerston North, 2001, pp. 45-46.
9. Keith Sinclair, *A History of New Zealand*, London, 1980, p. 292.
10. Bill Oliver, 'Sir Sidney Holland', *Comment*, No. 9, 1961, p. 4.
11. Gustafson, *Dictionary of New Zealand Biography*, p. 231.

26 SIR KEITH JACKA HOLYOAKE

1. Ross Doughty, *The Holyoake Years*, Palmerston North, 1977, p. 15.
2. Robert Chapman, 'From Labour To National, *The Oxford History of New Zealand*, Wellington, 1981, p. 364.
3. Ian Templeton and Keith Eunson, *Election '69*, Wellington, 1969, p. 39.
4. Hugh Templeton, *All Honourable Men*, Auckland, 1995, p. 3.
5. Keith Sinclair, *A History of New Zealand*, London, 1980, p. 295.
6. G A Wood 'Holyoake, Keith Jacka', *Dictionary of New Zealand Biography*, Vol. 5 (1941-1960), Wellington, 2000, p. 234.
7. Anthony Wood, 'Holyoake and the Holyoake Years', *Sir Keith Holyoake: Towards a Political Biography*, Palmerston North, 1997, p. 45.
8. George Laking, 'Stranger in the House: A view of K J Holyoake', *Sir Keith Holyoake: Towards a Political Biography*, p. 154.
9. Templeton, p. 20.
10. Templeton and Eunson, p. 38.
11. Barry Gustafson, *The First 50 Years*, Auckland, 1986, pp. 75-76.
12. A Wood, p. 30
13. Keith Eunson, *Mirrors on the Hill*, Palmerston North, 2001, p. 90.
14. Gustafson, p. 76.
15. John Roberts, ' Who Won, Who Lost', *Right Out: Labour Victory '72*, (ed. B Edwards), Wellington, 1973, p. 250.
16. Gustafson, p. 106.
17. Doughty, p. 268.
18. Gustafson, p. 107.

27 SIR WALTER NASH

1. Barry Gustafson, 'Nash, Walter', *Dictionary of New Zealand Biography*, Vol. 3 (1901-1920), Wellington, 1996, pp. 371-72.
2. Keith Sinclair, *Walter Nash*, Auckland, 1976, p. 20.
3. Leslie Hobbs, *The Thirty-Year Wonders*, Christchurch, 1967, p. 63.
4. Brian Easton, 'Fraser and the Development of the Nation-Building State', *Peter Fraser: Master Politician*, Palmerston North, 1998, p. 124.
5. Ibid.
6. Keith Eunson, *Mirrors on the Hill*, Palmerston North, 2001, p. 50.
7. Sinclair, p. 260.
8. Ibid, p. 257.
9. H H Innes, 'The essential Walter Nash', *Journal of the NZ Federation of Historical Societies*, July 1978, p. 48.
10. Easton, p. 162.
11. Ibid, p. 125.
12. Bruce Brown, 'Review of *Walter Nash*', *New Zealand Journal of History*, Auckland, Vol. 11, No. 1, April 1977, p. 84.
13. Gustafson, p. 374.
14. Sinclair, p. 291.
15. Ibid, p. 259.
16. Eunson, p. 59.
17. Michael Bassett (and Michael King), *Tomorrow Comes the Song*, Auckland, 2000, p. 122.

28 SIR JOHN ROSS MARSHALL

1. Jim Eagles and Colin James, *The Making of a New Zealand Prime Minister*, Wellington, 1973, p. 116.
2. John Marshall, *Memoirs,* Vol. 1 (1912-1960), Auckland, 1983, p. 84.
3. Barry Gustafson, 'Marshall, John Ross', *Dictionary of New Zealand Biography*, Vol. 5 (1941-1960), Wellington, 2000, p. 337.
4. Marshall, p. 223.
5. Ian Templeton and Keith Eunson, *Election '69*, Wellington, 1969, p. 45.
6. Keith Eunson, *Mirrors on the Hill*, Palmerston North, 2001, p. 129.
7. Gustafson, p. 338.
8. Rita Ricketts, 'A Great Strategist', *New Zealand International Review*, Wellington, November/December 1988, p. 21.
9. Robert Chapman, 'From Labour to National', *The Oxford History of New Zealand*, Wellington, 1981, p. 367.
10. Eagles and James, p. 116.
11. Hugh Templeton, *All Honourable Men*, Auckland, 1995, p. 23.
12. Ibid, p. 30.
13. Barry Gustafson*, The First 50 Years*, Auckland, 1996, p. 114.
14. Templeton, p. 32.
15. Gustafson, *Dictionary of New Zealand Biography*, p. 339.

29 NORMAN ERIC KIRK

1. Margaret Hayward, *Diary of the Kirk Years*, Wellington, 1981, p. 21.
2. Ibid, p. 22.
3. John Dunmore, *Norman Kirk*, Palmerston North, 1972. p. 20.
4. Ibid, pp. 39-40.
5. Ibid, p. 42.
6. Ibid, pp. 63-64.
7. Michael Bassett, 'Kirk, Norman Eric', *Dictionary of New Zealand Biography*, Vol. 5 (1941-1960), 2000, p. 272.
8. Tony Garnier, Bruce Kohn, Pat Booth, *The Hunter and the Hill*, Auckland, 1978, p. 103.
9. Ian Templeton and Keith Eunson, *Election '69*, Wellington, 1969. P. 76.
10. Colin James, *The Making of a New Zealand Prime Minister*, Wellington, 1973, p. 81.
11. Ibid.
12. Garnier, et al, p. 62.
13. Ibid, p. 124.
14. Ibid p. 182.
15. Keith Eunson, *Mirrors on the Hill*, Palmerston North, 2001, p. 134.
16. Hugh Templeton, *All Honourable Men*, Auckland, 1995.
17. Frank Corner, 'Kirk Presents a New Zealand Face to the World', *Three Labour Leaders*, (ed. M Clark), Parlmerston North, 2001, p. 166.
18. Bassett, pp. 273-74.

30 SIR WALLACE EDWARD ROWLING

1. Russell Marshall, 'Rowling as Prime Minister and Leader of the Opposition 1974-83', *Three Labour Leaders*, (ed. M Clark), Palmerston North, 2001, pp. 189-90.
2 John Henderson, 'Bill Rowling: The Man and his Politics', *Three Labour Leaders*, (ed. M Clark), Palmerston North, 2001, p. 198.
3. Jim Eagles and Colin James, *The Making of a Prime Minister*, Wellington, 1973, pp. 93-94.
4. John Henderson, *Rowling: The Man and the Myth*, Auckland, 1981, p. 91.
5. Marshall, p. 189.
6. Jim Anderton, 'Kirk and Rowling: Recollections and Significance', *Three Labour Leaders*, (ed. M Clark), Palmerston North, 2001, p. 55.
7. Hugh Templeton, *All Honourable Men*, Auckland, 1995, p. 34.
8. Keith Eunson, *Mirrors on the Hill*, Palmerston Noth, 2001, p. 158.
9. Henderson, 'Bill Rowling: 'The Man and his Politics', p. 196.
10. Barry Gustafson, *His Way,* Auckland, 2000, p. 319.

31 SIR ROBERT DAVID MULDOON

1. Spiro Zavos, *The Real Muldoon*, Wellington, 1978, p. 76.
2. Colin James, *New Territory*, Wellington, 1992, p. 94.
3. Robert Muldoon, *Muldoon*, Wellington, 1977, p. 84.
4. Barry Gustafson, *The First 50 Years*, Auckland, 1986, p. 118.
5. Ibid, p. 122.
6. Ibid.
7. Hugh Templeton, *All Honourable Men*, Auckland, 1995, pp. 39-40.

8. Ibid, p. 224.
9. Barry Gustafson, *My Way*, Auckland, 2000, p. 4.
10. Zavos, p. 212.
11. Templeton, p. 113.
12. Brian Easton, *The Nationbuilders*, Auckland, 2001, p. 252.
13. James, p. 94.
14. Templeton, p. 65.
15. Gustafson, p. 7.
16. Easton, p. 249.
17. John Marshall, *Memoirs,* Vol. 2 (1960-1988), Auckland, 1989, p. 241.

32 DAVID LANGE

1. Vernon Wright, *David Lange Prime Minister*, Wellington, 1984, p. 122.
2. Ibid, p. 98.
3. Ibid, p. 103.
4. Hugh Templeton, *All Honourable Men*, Auckland, 1995, p. 88.
5. Roger Douglas (with Louise Callan), *Toward Prosperity*, Auckland, 1987, p. 19.
6. Wright, p. 126.
7. Ibid, p. 128.
8. Bruce Jesson, 'Gaining the World and Losing a Soul?', *Metro*, December 1987, p. 132.
9. Ibid, p. 133.
10. Jane Kelsey, *Rolling Back the State*, Wellington, 1993, p. 16.
11. Colin James, *The Quiet Revolution*, Wellington, 1986, p. 160.
12. Interview with author, 11. 08.03.
13. Kelsey, p. 31.
14. Keith Eunson, *Mirrors On The Hill*, Palmerston North, 2001, p. 196.
15. Ibid, p. 213.
16. Harvey McQueen, *The Ninth Floor*, Auckland, 1991, p. 26.
17. Brian Edwards, *Helen: Portrait of a Prime Minister,* Auckland, 2001, pp. 190-91.
18. Interview with author, 6.06.03.
19. Interview with author, 11.08.03.
20. Chris Laidlaw, *Rights of Passage*, Auckland, 1999, p. 108.

33 SIR GEOFFREY WINSTON PALMER

1. Geoffrey Palmer, unpublished autobiographical notes, 1992, p. 14.
2. Ibid, p. 55.
3. Hugh Templeton, *All Honourable Men*, Auckland, 1995, p. 205.
4. Palmer, *Unbridled Power* (second edition), Auckland, 1987, p. 69.
5. Bruce Jesson, 'Plastering Over The Cracks', *Metro*, November 1989, p. 215.
6. Palmer, unpublished notes, p. 7.
7. Ibid, p. 10.
8. Jesson, p. 216.
9. Palmer, unpublished notes, p. 2.
10. Keith Eunson, *Mirrors on the Hill*, Palmerston North, 2001 p. 215
11. Colin James, 'Palmer and Clark: Can They Manage', *Management*, September 1989, p. 34.
12. Ibid. p. 36
13. Geoff Skene, 'Parliamentary Reform', *The Fourth Labour Government* (ed. Boston and Holland), Auckland, 1987, p. 86.
14. Eunson, p. 218.
15. Tim Grafton, *The Dominion*, September 5 1990, p. 4.

34 MICHAEL KENNETH MOORE

1. Mike Moore, *Hard Labour*, Auckland, 1987, p. 16.
2. Ibid, p. 35.
3. Ibid, p. 192.
4. Ibid, p. 151.
5. Hugh Templeton, *All Honourable Men*, Auckland, 1995, p. 194.
6. Keith Eunson, *Mirrors On The Hill*, Palmerston North, 2001, p. 235.
7. Jim Bolger, *Bolger: A View From The Top*, Auckland, 1998, p. 27.
8. Bruce Jesson, 'The Worst Government in Living Memory', *Metro*, December 1990, p. 178.
9. Eunson, p. 238.
10. Bolger, p. 132.

11. Eunson, p. 247.
12. Dani Rodrick, 'Free Trade Optimism: Lessons From the Battle in Seattle', *Foreign Affairs*, May/June 2003.
13. Mike Moore, *A World Without Walls: Freedom, Development, Free Trade and Global Governance*, New York, 2003.
14. Colin James, 'Things To Do To Fix Up Globalisation', *Business Herald*, Auckland, February 19 2003.

35 JAMES BRENDAN BOLGER

1. Warwick Roger, 'Gentleman Jim', *North & South*, Auckland, July 1996, p. 63.
2. Hugh Templeton, *All Honourable Men*, Auckland, 1995, p. 64.
3. Ibid, p. 145.
4. Barry Gustafson, *His Way*, Auckland, 2000, p. 364.
5. Gustafson, *The First 50 Years*, Auckland, 1986, p. 150.
6. Ibid, p. 164.
7. John Campbell, 'Going Nowhere?', *NZ Political Review*, April/May 1996, p. 9.
8. Jim Bolger, *Bolger: A View From the Top*, Auckland, 1998, p. 175.
9. Keith Eunson, *Mirrors On the Hill*, Palmerston North, 2001, p. 266.
10. Bolger, p. 162.
11. Ibid, p. 120.
12. Ibid, p. 167.
13. Warwick Roger, 'Three Days In Another Town', *North & South*, July 1997, p. 54.
14. Eunson, p. 252.
15. Ibid, p. 268.
16. Roger, p. 48.

36 JENNIFER MARY SHIPLEY

1. Deborah Coddington, 'To The Manse Born', *North & South*, November 1992, p. 10.
2. Wendyl Nissen, 'Jenny Shipley', *Filling the Frame*, Auckland, 1992, p. 71.
3. Ibid, p. 72.
4. Jane Clifton, 'Jenny Shipley and the chamber of secrets', *Listener*, February 16 2002, p. 16.
5. Nissen, p. 74.
6. Jim Bolger, *Bolger: A View From the Top*, Auckland, 1998, p. 39.
7. Bronwen Reid, 'The Doubt of the Benefit', *Time*, July 5 1993.
8. Rosemary McLeod, 'Jenny & Ruth', *North & South*, August 1991, p. 49.
9. Nissen, p. 70.
10. Clifton, p. 17.
11. Bolger, p. 253.
12. Ruth Laugesen, 'New leader may face Mission Impossible', *Sunday Star-Times*, November 9 1997, p. C2.
13. Clifton, 'Ready when you are', *Listener*, November 15 1997, p. 19.
14. Laugesen, p. C2.
15. Colin James, 'Is it time for a change of woman at the top?', *NZ Herald*, November 24 1999, p. A19.
16. James, 'Politician of the Year', *NZ Herald*, December 22 1999.
17. Michael Laws, 'Bill won't lead Nats out of the wilderness – yet', *Sunday Star-Times*, October 14 2001.
18. Anthony Hubbard, 'Shipley's Golden Silence', *Sunday Star-Times*, November 9 1997, p. C3.

37 HELEN ELIZABETH CLARK

1. Virginia Myers, *Head and Shoulders*, Auckland, 1986, p. 151.
2. Brian Edwards, *Helen: Portrait of a Prime Minister*, Auckland, 2001, p. 89.
3. Ibid, p. 93-94.
4. Myers, p. 159.
5. Janet McCallum, *Women in the House*, Picton, 1993, p. 149.
6. Ruth Laugesen, 'Savage Honeymoon', *Sunday Star Times*, July 2 2000, p.C1.
7. Colin James. 'Is Clark in her Prime?', *Management*, August 2003, p. 36.
8. James, *The Independent*, December 4 2002.
9. Bruce Ansley, 'Prime Mover, *Listener*, July 27 2002, p. 21.

PREMIERS AND PRIME MINISTERS OF NEW ZEALAND AND THEIR TERMS IN OFFICE

Henry Sewell		7 May 1856 – 20 May 1856
William Fox		20 May 1856 – 2 June 1856
Edward William Stafford		2 June 1856 – 12 July 1861
William Fox		12 July 1861 – 6 August 1862
Alfred Domett (CMG)		6 August 1862 – 30 October 1863
Frederick Whitaker MLC		30 October 1863 – 24 November 1864
Frederick Aloysius Weld (CMG KCMG, GCMG)		24 November 1864 – 16 October 1865
Edward William Stafford		16 October 1865 – 28 June 1869
William Fox		28 June 1869 – 10 September 1872
Edward William Stafford (KCMG)		10 September 1872 – 11 October 1872
George Marsden Waterhouse MLC		11 October 1872 – 3 March 1873
William Fox (KCMG)		3 March 1873 – 8 April 1873
Julius Vogel		8 April 1873 – 6 July 1875
Daniel Pollen MLC		6 July 1875 – 15 February 1876
Sir Julius Vogel KCMG		15 February 1876 – 1 September 1876
Harry Albert Atkinson		1 September 1876 – 13 September 1876
Harry Albert Atkinson (Ministry reconstructed)		13 September 1876 – 13 October 1877
Sir George Grey KCB (PC)		13 October 1877 – 8 October 1879
John Hall (KCMG)		8 October 1879 – 21 April 1882
Frederick Whitaker MLC (KCMG)		21 April 1882 – 25 September 1883
Harry Albert Atkinson		25 September 1883 – 16 August 1884
Robert Stout		16 August 1884 – 28 August 1884
Harry Albert Atkinson		28 August 1884 – 3 September 1884
Sir Robert Stout KCMG		3 September 1884 – 8 October 1887
Sir Harry Albert Atkinson KCMG		8 October 1887 – 24 January 1891
John Ballance	Liberal	24 January 1891 – 27 April 1893 (died)
The Rt Hon Richard John Seddon	Liberal	1 May 1893 – 10 June 1906 (died)
William Hall-Jones (KCMG)	Liberal	21 June 1906 – 6 August 1906
The Rt Hon Sir Joseph George Ward Bt, KCMG	Liberal	6 August 1906 – 28 March 1912
Thomas Noble Mackenzie (KCMG, GCMG)	Liberal	28 March 1912 – 10 July 1912
The Rt Hon William Ferguson Massey	Reform	10 July 1912 – 12 August 1915
The Rt Hon William Ferguson Massey	National	12 August 1915 – 25 August 1919
The Rt Hon William Ferguson Massey	Reform	25 August 1919 – 10 May 1925 (died)
Sir Francis Henry Dillon Bell GCMG, KC, MLC,(PC)	Reform	14 May 1925 – 30 May 1925
The Rt Hon Joseph Gordon Coates MC	Reform	30 May 1925 – 10 December 1928
The Rt Hon Sir Joseph George Ward Bt KCMG, GCMG	United	10 December 1928 – 28 May 1930
The Rt Hon George William Forbes	United	28 May 1930 – 22 September 1931
The Rt Hon George William Forbes	Coalition	22 September 1931 – 6 December 1935
The Rt Hon Michael Joseph Savage	Labour	6 December 1935 – 27 March 1940 (died)
The Rt Hon Peter Fraser CH	Labour	1 April 1940 – 13 December 1949
The Rt Hon Sidney George Holland CH, (GCB)	National	13 December 1949 – 20 September 1957
The Rt Hon Keith Jacka Holyoake	National	20 September 1957 – 12 December 1957
The Rt Hon Walter Nash CH, (GCMG)	Labour	12 December 1957 – 12 December 1960

The Rt Hon Sir Keith Jacka Holyoake GCMG, CH (KG, QSO)	National	12 December 1960 – 7 February 1972
The Rt Hon John Ross Marshall CH, (GBE)	National	7 February 1972 – 8 December 1972
The Rt Hon Norman Eric Kirk	Labour	8 December 1972 – 31 August 1974 (died)
The Rt Hon Wallace Edward Rowling (KCMG)	Labour	6 September 1974 – 12 December 1975
The Rt Hon Sir Robert David Muldoon GCMG, CH	National	12 December 1975 – 26 July 1984
The Rt Hon David Russell Lange (ONZ, CH)	Labour	26 July 1984 – 8 August 1989
The Rt Hon Geoffrey Winston Palmer (KCMG, AC)	Labour	8 August 1989 – 4 September 1990
The Rt Hon Michael Moore (ONZ)	Labour	4 September 1990 – 2 November 1990
The Rt Hon James Brendan Bolger	National	2 November 1990 – 28 February 1996
The Rt Hon James Brendan Bolger	National/ United Coalition	28 February 1996 – 16 December 1996
The Rt Hon James Brendan Bolger (ONZ)	National/ NZ First Coalition	16 December 1996 – 8 December 1997
The Rt Hon Jennifer Mary Shipley	National/ NZ First Coalition	8 December 1997 - 26 August 1998
The Rt Hon Jennifer Mary Shipley (DCNZM)	National-led minority	28 August 1998 – 10 December 1999
The Rt Hon Helen Elizabeth Clark	Labour/ Alliance Coalition	10 December 1999 – 15 August 2002
The Rt Hon Helen Elizabeth Clark	Labour/ Progressive Coalition	15 August 2002 –

Note: Awards in brackets were received after the term(s) in office.

INDEX OF NAMES

Cartoonist entries are in italics.